HOLTBY on ART and POETRY:

"I think modern art, in England anyway, has fallen under the pernicious influence of Augustus John. The Slade School calls every charming picture "pretty-pretty" and flies to the other extreme, in mistaking the grotesque for the beautiful. The poets are just as bad; for those who have energy and freshness fear to become Sunday-magazinish and write their *Wheels* and *Rolls* and other atrocities under the impression that they are out-Henleying Henley, and discovering a new pathless world of *vers libre*, free from the trammels of such minor accessories of poetry such as rhyme or metre or even musical language . . ."

HOLTBY on WAR:

"But here, in this grey city, there is all the sorrow and dignity of a conquered people. Never believe anyone when they tell you that it is more dignified to win than to be defeated. It isn't true. Here in the streets, lit no more brightly than London during war-time, English Tommies march up and down, looking very gay, friendly and irresponsible. Their canteens are in the best hotels, and a lovely building down by the Rhine. Outside are great notices "No Germans allowed." The money for their food is all paid from the German taxes, and the German children crowd round their bright lit windows, watching them gobble up beefsteaks. It is one of the most vulgar things that I have seen . . ."

HOLTBY on PATRIOTISM:

"Patriotism — love of country. How excellent an emotion — not, I think, a virtue, except in so far as any strong feeling has more strength, more virtue in it than tepidity. When we speak of it as a proper and decorous sentiment towards the State, we wrong it, as a man wrongs a woman whom he loves merely because she is his wife. The love of country is a feeling for the countryside — its hills and villages and race of men. It is a thing wholly individual and un-moral, as the love for another person is individual. To confuse this love of country and race for an adulation of the State lies at the bottom of much pain and confusion — of sentimentality and positive danger, too, I think. To raise it into a civic virtue, to clothe it with pomp of armies and banners, to stain it with blood and to slay before it as before an unholy altar sacrifices of gold and men and men's liberty — this is not patriotism any more than the lust of a senator who lays before his mistress the spoils of a state and of his rivals in love . . ."

LETTERS TO A FRIEND

WALMER BELLES-LETTRES

inaugural volume

.

WINIFRED HOLTBY
1898 - 1935

LETTERS TO A FRIEND

by

WINIFRED HOLTBY

edited by

ALICE HOLTBY and JEAN McWILLIAM

with a preface by

JEAN McWILLIAM

ADELAIDE
MICHAEL WALMER
2014

Letters to a Friend first published 1937
This edition published 2014

by

Michael Walmer
49 Second Street
Gawler South
South Australia 5118

ISBN 978-0-9924220-2-8 paperback
ISBN 978-0-9924220-3-5 ebook

PREFACE

In September 1918 I was sent to take charge of the W.A.A.C. unit at Huchenneville, eight kilometres from Abbeville. It was a Signals unit carefully hidden in the orchard of the château of Huchenneville so that communications might not be destroyed. It had been moved there from Abbeville when Abbeville was badly bombed. The women were in tents and it rained every day, but in the gardener's cottage we had a mess room and a little kitchen and I had a tiny bedroom. There were about fifty of us, one hostel-fore-woman, twenty-eight telegraphists, eight telephonists, two stenographers, two typists, one forewoman waitress, three cooks and five or six general domestics. It was a difficult unit because it was isolated and no administrator had stayed there longer than eight weeks, but it had the advantage of being controlled by the colonel who had his headquarters at the château nearby.

He and his staff of four officers were responsible for arranging for the southern part of the line the trains which the British might run on the French railways.

On the other side of the orchard from our huts the men had their camp. They too were telegraphists and tele-phonists for the most part but there were engineers, chauffeurs and orderlies as well.

At W.A.A.C. headquarters in France there was a Somervillian called Haythorne who was second in command in France and an old friend of mine. She was anxious that I should stay longer than eight weeks at Huchenneville and rang me up one evening and asked if I was lonely. I told her I was rather and she said that there was a girl in the ranks who had been a year at Somerville but was too young to have a commission. She would have her brought out to be my hostel forewoman.

A few days later I had orders to go to Camp Three in Abbeville to fetch my new hostel-forewoman. The colonel lent me his car for he was always kind about giving the W.A.A.C. lifts. When I arrived at Camp Three I found a tall, pale, tired-looking girl waiting for me.

"Are you Holtby?"

She saluted smartly and answered, "Yes, ma'am."

"Then you are to come to my unit."

"Yes, ma'am."

"I hear you have been a year at Somerville, and I was there years ago."

"Oh! were you?" with relief.

"Yes, and now you are coming to a very uncomfortable unit. If you step off the duck-boards your shoe will be sucked off by the mud. The women are in tents. I have a small room in the gardener's cottage. There is a loft above it without doors or windows. You can have that as a habitation if you like. All the water we have is carted, and when one of the horses is ill it is limited. Baths are difficult. But I suppose Rosalind and Celia had difficulty in getting baths in the Forest of Arden."

Winifred chose the loft and was there until German prisoners had built us huts. She was a wonderful forewoman, but inclined too much to do things herself instead of making others do them. She used to come to my orderly room with the marks of sooty fingers on her cheek.

"What have you been doing?"

"Trying to light the fire in the boiler in the ablution hut."

"That is Silver's duty."

"Yes, ma'am." But with an unrepentant grin.

As ours was a signals unit it never slept, but had day and night shifts, and Winifred and I did not go to bed until the last shift came off duty at two in the morning, so in the mornings we had tea and toast in bed. The partition between our cubicles was so thin that we could hear each other crunching toast.

Australians came to rest in the village of Huchenneville after ten months in the line, and as soon as they arrived they found their way to our recreation hut. We were dancing one evening by the light of one candle to the music of the accordion played brilliantly by the colonel's batman. Suddenly an Australian officer said close by me, "Why have you only one candle?" I answered that our ration was short and the next day he sent me a bag of candles, the first of many kindnesses.

Winifred used to write stories by candlelight sitting at the kitchen table completely absorbed while cooks and general domestics and Australians and other W.A.A.C. moved in and out and about. They were stories of the unit and she imagined us all in the Forest of Arden, wistful but happy exiles like the duke and his followers. She called these stories *The Forest Unit*. And Huchenneville was Arcadian. A medlar tree grew by the gardener's cottage. In spring, after the Armistice, the trees in the orchard threw their fountains of snowy blossom into the tender air. There were daffodils, anemones, violets, periwinkles, primroses and oxlips in the woods around us and tawny squirrels. The beauty of Huchenneville in the sad world gave unreality to our lives. We had wandered into Arcady, but in all that beauty we had rough experiences.

After we were demobilised, Pugh, one of our cooks, and Newman, a general domestic, went to Australia. Dot Hastings, a stenographer, went to Canada and married there. Winifred returned to Somerville and the first letters were written while she was there.

Bridgewater, a forewoman waitress, came to South Africa with me when I came to Rhodes University College as a lecturer in English in January 1920. She trained as a nurse and was a very good one and now she is married and lives in Rhodesia. I became the headmistress of Pretoria

High School for girls in January 1924 and I am still in Pretoria.

The letters are haunted by an Arcadian atmosphere, and I have put the poem Winifred sent me in 1926 at the end instead of in its chronological place because my thoughts still have a secret trysting-place amongst the green and gracious trees of Huchenneville.

The first time I met Winifred in September 1918 she drew herself up and gave me the W.A.A.C. salute.

The last time I met Winifred in February 1935, she drew herself up, beautiful and glowing, and as my train moved, with a radiant smile she gave me the W.A.A.C. salute.

ROSALIND.

1920

9, Bevington Road,
Oxford,
Easter Term, 1920.

DEAREST ROSALIND,

I feel ashamed that you should have read my last letter. Please at once delete from your memory any unwonted pessimism. The true explanation lay in the quantities of cold college mutton of which I had rashly partaken at lunch.

This week I am feeling quite virtuous and lively. For one thing, this morning I walked nearly ten miles, with two other people, from Wood Eaton to Prattle Wood and back by Beckley and Marston Ferry. It was a gorgeous morning, clean, sharp air, with the green of grass very bright and cold under grey hedges and swinging catkins. The roads were fine and hard, made for walking, spreading themselves across the hills, and opening out at the crossways to tempt us on. We talked about burlesques and school discipline and Dostoievsky and porridge, and whether bread and cheese and beer are really better than stuffed olives and champagne, and neckties and dons and all the thousand and one silly things that one talks about on a long morning when the air is frosty and the roads are dry.

One very pleasant thing happened this week. O.U.D.S. acted *Antony and Cleopatra.* It was a most beautiful and dignified piece of work. Cathleen Nesbitt came from London to be Cleopatra, and though she's young and slim, and not at all like an experienced woman of fifty-two, who I suppose was really Cleopatra, she was a wild, passionate gypsy, fascinating and repulsive, hysterical and dignified. The scene where she heard of Antony's marriage to Octavia was a masterly performance, the most tempestuous and convincing thing I have seen for ages. Antony was a youth called R., whom I had occasionally heard at the Union, making very bad speeches in a very attractive voice. He is about six foot five and carries himself well. How much he really acts, I do not know; but by being dignified and restrained, with just the touch of weakness that was really Antony's, he never once jarred or spoiled a fine situation. Isn't it just absolutely right that those two fine people, who walked like gods in their triumphs, should have lacked the courage to die before their slaves showed them the way? The setting was excellent, especially the scene in Pompey's galley, where they caroused under a velvet-dark sky, lit by one swinging lantern, with the singer high in the poop, singing in a clear, perfect tenor voice, and below them the deck all russet red, and the drunken dancers tossing gold wine cups as they sang.

Another pleasant thing was a tea party we had on Wednesday. Did you know Mrs. K. in the W.A.A.C.? She has come up as a fresher this term to do history, and is one of the most amusing people I have ever met. She came at four on Wednesday and we started laughing almost as soon as she entered the room. When she left at six we were still laughing, sides aching, eyes running. A most indiscreet woman, with a heaven-born sense of humour and the touch of vulgarity that makes the whole world kin. (I believe that is an epigram of yours. I love it and make frequent use of it!)

The fourth nice thing that has happened is that my newest tutor, Mr. Stocks of St. John's, approved of a paper that I wrote upon "Hobbes' Theory of the Natural." Now I am convinced that any one who can write a paper with such an imposing title must be a very learned person; but to have it pronounced good is almost more than my moral equilibrium will stand. Alas, pride comes before a fall. My own tutor tells me that unless I learn to spell and to curb my unruly sentences, I shall never get through life with any credit. Alas!

This is a very egoistical letter. But I can't write about you when I'm not sure what you're doing. (This is *not* a hint for letters. I know you haven't time and I know you hate writing, and no news is good news, and anyway I've had as many letters as I deserve.)

Grace,[1] I think I told you last week, is in Shropshire, nursing babies. Mother is very well. I've actually had quite a number of letters from her this term—a most unprecedented occurrence. (Isn't "most unprecedented" redundant?)

Au revoir—dear Coz—Yours,

CELIA.

Somerville College,
June.

(I don't know what the date is, but it is a Sunday, all checkered light and ringing bells and clean streets full of shining people.)

MY DEAREST ROSALIND,

Thank you ever so much for your long letter which was a great joy and far longer and nicer than I deserved. So you are going to carve a new school out of the desert—a ripping job and should satisfy your pioneer spirit. I wish I could come and see you at it. Will you be wanting a history mistress a year next October? I should like to come, I think, if you would have me, for a year or two at least. I want to see you and Africa. I simply long to travel and see strange things and people in a far land. I am not so sorry that you are leaving R. as I thought. It is a pity for R. but the work certainly does not sound good enough. You can do so much more and there are others who could fill your place there. South African education sounds like a twentieth-century building—all straight lines and a fear of originality. It is a pity all these educational authorities can't come to Oxford for a time first and learn that examinations and orthodoxy don't really matter. Perhaps you with your wild school may teach them a little. I have an idea that it will. Something tremendously keen and alive,

[1] Winifred's elder sister.

13

with the girls riding "wild animals" and wild hobbies, and thinking almost more than they read, and fitting their work into their lives—not shutting it off between the covers of a text-book.

Grace is staying here. She has been here ever since half term and will stay till I go down. She has lodgings at the back of Walton St. and lives in my room. She lives on the river, in the garden and among the girls here, and makes herself invaluable by shopping, chaperoning river parties, and making dresses for the Going Down Play. Oxford is lovelier than ever this year. The blight of the war has gone. Magdalen is head of the river again and the cycles swarm through Carfax like bees in June. There have been some very good lectures in the schools—Belloc, Laurence Binyon and Masefield have been telling about poetry, play-writing and story-writing. Masefield's lecture on story-writing was about the best I have ever heard. He has such a charming personality and so glorious a sense of humour. The hall was crowded from end to end. Admission was by ticket, but more cheating went on there than in a card-sharpers' den.

I never saw so many wild roses by the Cher. We gathered armfuls the other day. There are buttercups, and blue dragonflies, and a flurry of bees and swallows and some very admirable and astute little water rats that bustle in and out among the flags and clean their comical whiskers with scrupulous care.

There goes the lunch bell—O.U.D.S. are acting *As You Like It* in Wadham Garden in Commem Week. We could show them how! When Rosalind shall ruffle in her khaki doublet and hose, and Celia shall drive little Waacs with a garlanded crook, and the medlar flowers shall bloom over a Forest of Arden in Picardy. Celia has not found her Oliver yet—strange to say, there is an Oliver, whose name *is* Oliver, but Celia has not burst into a wrath of love—rather the other way round—and angry notes have passed.

But all is well—and Celia's heart is not even fluttered.

I have written one short poem which is probably going

14

to appear in Oxford Poetry. It is gloriously miserable, the result of its author being most melancholy happy listening to a Brahms' symphony very well played on a violin.

THE DEAD MAN

I see men walk wild ways with love,
  Along the wind their laughter blown
Strikes up against the singing stars—
  But I lie all alone.
When love has stricken laughter dead
  And tears their silly hearts in twain,
They long for easeful death, but I
  Am hungry for their pain.

Here is another:

HARVEST AT ANLABY

The heavy wains slow moving go
Across the broad autumnal wold
To great brown-throated men below
Who gather in the glowing gold.

And thus it was they harvested,
They harvested at Anlaby
Before the Danes from Bessingly
Flooded the manor like a sea,
And left Earl Godwin's barley red—
      At Anlaby.

The lovers linger down the lane
When moths awake and small owls cry.
Their dresses fade, as pale moons wane,
And glimmer as they wander by.

And thus it was they made their vows
They made their vows at Anlaby,
When all the wolds were young as they
Among the dusky sheaves they lay,
And kissed beneath the darkened boughs
                At Anlaby.

        Much love always,

                                        CELIA.

                        Bainesse,
                            Cottingham,
                        Yorks, Sept. 26th, '20.
MY DEAREST ROSALIND,
    I am afraid it is long enough since I last wrote to you,
and make my apologies. It is not because I had forgotten
you or had never been thinking of you, but because, in
spite of whatever Arnold Bennett may say about it, we have
to live on twenty-four hours a day, and part of that time
we have to sleep. In those twenty-four hours I've been
trying to read for six, remodel my winter wardrobe,
entertain, or at least be present at the entertainment of the
innumerable guests that weekly bestow upon us the joy of
their company, eat, answer such letters as demand answers,
and amuse myself. There you are!
    I suppose you are back at R.—till—when? I wonder so
much what you are going to do and whether South Africa
is proving as barren and unprofitable as ever and whether
you still have the exile feeling. I would give much to see
you, tall and fine and trusty, with your boy's hair and your
face brown from African sun, come striding up our dapper
little garden here, instead of the card-playing ladies who
trip up with their reticules in their hands and society
smiles on their faces, every now and then.
    England's in a horrid mess, Mac o' my heart. We're all
running after the moon. Some of us want to get rich by

the unaided effort of others; others want to have their rights—only they don't know what they are, but they intend to have 'em. Others insist that the panacea for every evil is that the government should do it, and still more that the government should pay for it, as though Lloyd George had found a gold mine in the garden of No. 10 Downing St., and had only to put down his hand to supply us with our pensions, indemnities, two shillings a week rise in wages, cheap coal, electric massage, twopence a case divorce and railway transport. And at Oxford and other places where they still cherish ideals of Utopia, we weep because we can't make archangels out of men all in a hurry, forgetting it's taken a good many thousands of years to make a man out of a monkey, and when we think now and then we see his wings sprouting, we weep to find that the only superfluous excrescence on his person is a remnant of his monkey's tail! However, I suppose we shall shake down somewhere. The railway strike is postponed for another week, and I actually saw last week in one of the papers that a journalist had the courage to stand up before the British public and say that the only way to get more money was to make more goods, and the only way to get more goods was to work harder. I see that Belgium's got back to its 1913 coal output. We ought to be ashamed of ourselves, we ought.

Have you read *What Not*, by Rose Macaulay? Wasn't she up at Somerville somewhere round your time? I think she's delicious. I love it where she says:
"It's a damned silly world."
"Yes, but it would be a damned dull one if it wasn't."

Do you know Herbert Trench's *Oh dreamy, gloomy, friendly trees?* I'm sending it to you because it reminds me so of those tall trees on the way through the woods from Huchenneville to Limercourt.

I send a queer sonnet I wrote the other day. It happened when Grace was playing the refrain of an old song that I swear I had never heard before, yet every note, plaintive haunting, elusive, was familiar. It sounded like a call to nothingness, which so many of us seem to follow. (I was feeling melancholy after a large, undigested feast on Hume and Butler) so I wrote *Ignis Fatuis*—which leads from nothing to a dead world—and the moral is—don't read sceptic philosophy on an empty stomach—it's bad for the Muse!

I wonder how Bridgewater[1] is getting on? Oh, I must tell you, when I was in London at the Regent's Palace Hotel having dinner, I looked across and saw, at another table, Dicker,[2] very smart in a pink dress, dining with Corporal Gandy,[3] now Mr. Gandy, of some one or other's office in Derby. They are engaged, as I had suspected they might be, and he had been spending the holidays with her people. Both were beaming and happy looking—Dicker plumper than ever. She tells me that L's[4] engagement is broken off, and she seems very miserable. Hafford is back at home, looking after her father. It was so nice seeing them. Dicker says she often gets Huchenneville-sick.

I have been talking to various people who all say if I want a job anywhere after Somerville I must train, so next year I'm going somewhere—not Oxford—to train. I particularly want another atmosphere—too much Oxford would make me think the world was made for the benefit of historical research. What about Bedford College? I've got to write my novel too, so it will be a busy year!

Much love—ever yours,

CELIA.

O dreamy, gloomy, friendly trees
   I came along your narrow track
To bring my gifts unto your knees,
   And gifts did you give back.
For when I brought this heart that burns—
   These thoughts that bitterly repine—

[1]Hostel Forewoman at Huchenneville who came out to S. Africa with me.
[2]Very efficient forewoman stenographer at Huchenneville.
[3]A telegraphist at Huchenneville.
[4]Forewoman clerk at Huchenneville.

And laid them here among the ferns
  And the hum of the boughs divine,
Ye, vastest breathers of the air,
  Shook down with slow and mighty poise
Your coolness on the human care
  Your wonder on its joys—
Your greenness on the heart's despair,
  Your darkness on its noise.

Isn't it nice?

IGNIS FATUUS

I hear you singing through the summer rain
  Mournful and low, a half-forgotten air,
Of women wailing through their fallen hair,
  Or dead leaves drifting down a dreary plain.
And long ago when Babylon was fair
  Listening I lay within a marble hall
Watching the rainbow-dripping fountain fall,
  And rose to follow your soft singing there.
Lonely from star to star I follow still,
  Lured by an echo, while about me lie
The ghosts of spinning worlds that leap and die.
  Untouched by time, from starlit hill to hill
You lead me, till alone we traverse soon,
  Remote and dead, the mountains of the moon.

9, Bevington Road,
Oxford, Oct. 20th, 1920.

MY DEAREST ROSALIND,

I've been meaning to write before, but it has been
particularly beginning of termish. I am in digs here in
Bevington Road, but fortunately they are very pleasant ones
and I am thoroughly content. I have a little room with
cream-washed walls and a sloping roof. The window over-

19

looks many gardens, all full now of gold and russet trees. I went the other day to Tubney Woods and came back with great branches of spindleberries that I put in the brass shell-case I picked up on the road from Bray to Corbie and in the bowl that Brownie gave me before he left the camp.

You may have heard from Beatrice that we have been initiated into the mysteries of Degrees at last. I went to the first ceremony, which was most impressive. The Sheldonian was crowded with people—mostly women. The few men who first received their degrees were quite in a minority and looked almost like interlopers. The most dramatic moment came when the doors at the end of the Shel. were thrown open and the principals of the five colleges came in and processed slowly up the central aisle, to the rousing applause of the spectators. I'll try and get you a *Chronicle* which has a full account of the ceremony—meanwhile I send you on *Isis*, which may amuse you a little. Oxford journalism is as wild and youthful as ever. I'm trying my hand at bits of it and writing verses for the *Chronicle* and short stories for the *Outlook*—but they are unremunerative labour, I fear. (There were, when I wrote the last page, about five other people in my little room, so I finally had to abandon the attempt.)

It is now Sunday morning. We have not lit the fire yet, because of the coal strike. I don't know what to believe about the strike. It's the same as Ireland. Every paper yells defiantly at different people. Asquith is organising meetings all over the country and getting excellent speakers to tell the people what dastardly things the British government is permitting—or even authorising—in Belfast and Cork. The Lloyd Georgians inform us that this is merely a move on Asquith's part to enforce a general election and get back to parliament. All the people I know who have been in Ireland tell us that both the government and Sinn Fein are fools and liars, and if we'd only clear out of Ireland, and leave her to settle her own hash, the millennium would come quite quickly. Others—but they are Tories, so don't count.

Before I came back here I spent a delightful week with a family called R. in Dorset. H. was at Somerville, only, being very delicate, she went down without taking schools. Her father is a retired Indian judge, a beautiful, stately old man with a splendid white head, and fine blue eyes. He reads the *Morning Post* every morning at breakfast, and the lessons every Sunday at church, and damns democrats with delicious thoroughness on every possible occasion. I told him I was very glad these were democratic days, because if they weren't I shouldn't be staying with him. He looked very puzzled, poor lamb, because hitherto he had thought me a perfect lady! The house was charming, with long low rooms, the walls painted dull blue, with strange engravings in mellow, gilt frames, above long bookshelves. The garden was walled around and inside it were herbaceous borders and flagged walks with grass growing between the paving stones. Lady R. was very beautiful and gentle and clever, with a kind, gracious manner that was more terrible than an army with banners. Dinner was an imposing ceremony. We lived very simply; but at quarter to eight we assembled in the long, dim sitting-room, and Sir A., very beautiful in immaculate dinner jacket, came forward and gravely gave me his arm. H. and her mother took up the procession, and we slowly went across the hall, and sat down, each to a mutton chop, or a spoonful of cheese on toast! The family was very witty and clever, and well up on all burning questions of the day. They talked a certain amount of mild politics from a Tory standpoint, and have an exquisite taste for literature and pictures, loving particularly all products of the eighteenth century. I must have exercised remarkable self-control because H. tells me her mother's comment on me was that I was a "dear little thing"—but I enjoyed myself more than I have done for years.

Beatrice Hill showed me the Fugue and the poems. I had seen the poems before, of course. You told me *Prince Memnon*, sitting in the tawny-striped chair at Huchenneville, with your long white hands behind your head. I loved it.

21

The Fugue made me very happy and very sad—very happy because it is so charming—so full of the exquisite fairyland of Picardy—very sad because I wonder what's happening to Brownie[1]—and when shall I see you again? I want to go to South Africa. I'm going to write, you know, but to teach too, until I'm a bit older. I can't think I have anything particular to tell the world yet, when I hardly know what it's like to live, and know not at all what it's like to suffer.

We gave your work to a girl here called Huxley. Her father edits the *Cornhill*, one of her brothers edits the *Athenæum*, and another is on the staff of the *London Mercury*. She has sent them to her brother, who will send them to the paper he thinks will both pay best and be the best. I thought that was the best thing to do. If we just sent them to a paper we thought of, we might send them to the wrong one, and Margaret Huxley is a very useful person to have about, and awfully nice too.

Do excuse this scrawly writing. My hands are rather cold. It's a raw day, with the mist rolling up off the river, and the black twigs dripping from every tree.

Grace is coming up again this term to play round Oxford a little—and meanwhile I am working. But I *can't* work hard. I simply can't. My mind won't stick to the thing in hand. It runs off on to stories and things all the time. If they were any use, I should not grudge the time. But they aren't.

Good-bye for the present. I think about you often, and when the stars are bright and the moon is full, I'll stretch my arms out across the world and cry "Salute to adventurers"—and I greet you on your passing.

With love,

CELIA.

PS.—Pugh[2] wants to go to New Zealand with a family as cook. The other day I got this letter, which, of course, I answered, feeling a condescending fool, that I should write

[1] A chauffeur at Huchenneville whom we all liked.
[2] One of the cooks at Huchenneville.

and tell some one that Pugh is sober and honest—she who is older, and wiser, and stronger in almost any way than I am! Isn't it silly?

9, Bevington Road,
Oxford, Nov. 11th, 1920.

DEAREST ROSALIND,

This is not a real letter, because it's ten-past one and I ought to be in bed. It's just to say thank you for your long letter and the photographs. I like your bobbed hair—I do, I do. And I like the queer bare hills behind you and the sunlight on the swing.

I'm so glad Bridgewater[1] is going to train. Rosalind dear, don't kill yourself running behind the bicycle. I know what they are. And so the poor pupil is black and blue? Well, well, Kimberley will benefit by her bruises—or I hope so.

I'm glad you aren't in England now, in a way. It's not a very nice place for some things. I don't know if we're strangling Ireland. One hears such conflicting reports. *The Times* and the *Daily Herald* are at each other's throats—but if it's true—then I can't bear the processions to-day and the fireworks and noble sentiments about the Unknown Hero and the rest of it. It seems like an appeal to sentiment to carry England away from the realisation of a practical evil that is crying for redress—as though we could weep over Belgium and murder in Ireland—— But I don't know—the truth seems so hard to find and if we know— *cui bono?*

Meanwhile—the sun shines and the air is clear and frosty on the hills, while in the valleys the grey mist lies soft as an unborn dream. Every tree is aflame with vivid leaves and berries. In the Meadows, the river is high and flowing. There rarely was a fairer autumn. There are such lots of lovely things in the world, why must we go and spoil them

[1]Bridgewater trained as a maternity nurse at Kimberley.

by doing ugly deeds and thinking ugly thoughts? To-day has been the prettiest day—every colour was clearer—every air was fresher, than on ordinary days—as though the world was having a birthday. How can one help loving it?

I want to see the monkeys in your fairyland. I mean to come. But where will you be then?

Miss Lorimer and Mrs. Anderson have both asked after you. Miss Lorimer takes me to dinner at the High once a term to ask how you are!

Will you teach me to surf ride when I come?

Yours,

CELIA.

9, *Bevington Road,*
Oxford, Nov. 22nd, 1920.

MY DEAREST ROSALIND,

I am writing this in haste, my loins girded and my staff in my hand—because there is much work to do, and so little time in which to do it—also there are other things besides work, and they take time and thought.

Grace came here on Friday. I love having her. Her peaceful presence makes small things insignificant and big things more worth while. Also she does my shopping and makes my tea. This is not bathos!

Yesterday we went to see *The Only Way*. Martin Harvey was here. It is one of the plays that I used to dream of seeing when I was small—ever since I read Dickens first. I must confess that I was deliciously thrilled yesterday. Later, on thinking it over, I've decided that those sort of plays of the noble prodigal are really rather immoral. It is so much more interesting to be the sinner that repenteth, and so much harder and duller to be one of the ninety-nine just persons, that I can't help thinking it puts temptation in people's way to do the sinning and trust to luck for an opportunity for the redeeming heroism at the end. And that's such a gamble, because one might be knocked over by a motor-bus on the way to the Goat & Whiskers—and then where's your "only way" coming in? Really, you know, it was much more heroic of Charles Darnay to leave Lucie and a perfectly comfortable, happy life in England, to risk his life in France for an old servant for whom he had no sort of affection, than it was for Sidney to take Charles's place, knowing that "It is a far, far better thing that I do than I have ever done. It is a far, far better rest that I go to, than I have ever known." And yet in the play Sidney carries the hearts of the audience from the beginning, and Charles is stigmatised as a prig! Poor ninety-nine! I've a love for the sinners myself, though, and I suppose it's in human nature.

I had an amusing time on Wednesday. I think I told you in my last letter how Miss H., late of the Waacs, asked me to tea. She was a D.A. at Connaught Club and a U.A. at Catterick. A Miss X. was also there. I was very much overawed by two such lofty officials. Miss H. is charming—tall, and dark and gentle, with a quiet manner and kind eyes. Miss X. is killing—I've seen her type thousands of times at Folkstone—shortish and fair and bossing, with quantities of scandal about all the administrators you ever heard of. She'd never seen either of us before, but she started talking as soon as she got in and continued until we left at six-thirty—two and a half hours solid tongue-flow. I heard all about the intimate private history of Misses E., I., B., and all the rest of 'em. Mrs. B. came in for it hot. Bostall Heath was pulverised, Connaught Club turned inside out, Folkstone annihilated! Overseas was perfection—but then, X. had been there, and a grain of mustard seed works wonders, especially when it is so acutely spiced!

I'm going to tea with Miss H. on Monday. She hardly got a word in edgewise with the other lady. I walked to the bus with X. afterwards, and she told me her opinion of Miss H.—"A typical Connaught Club administrator." If so, I like Connaught Club. I held my peace. Then she turned and asked me, "Why was I a hostel forewoman?" I told her I preferred it. Also I considered myself too young to be an administrator, too untidy to be a clerk and too inefficient to be a cook. She did not like me much, I think!

There's rather a mangy set of papers—but some quite nice reviews. Louis Golding is an Oxford poet of sorts—you saw his things in *Oxford Poetry*. He's rather an interesting person though. I think we shall hear more of him.

Your

CELIA.

Bainesse,
Cottingham,
Sunday, 13th Dec., 1920.

MY DEAREST ROSALIND,

Here I am back at home, and all the family sends its love to you. I told Daddy I was going to write to you and he at once asked me to send his best wishes—love, too, I think, if he dare. "Miss M.," he said, "Yes, I think I could get on with her. She's a real good sort, isn't she?" That's the highest compliment he ever pays to any one. So you see, you have made a conquest. I hastened to reassure him that you were a real good sort and that I would convey his message.

Behold us in a Cottingham white with snow. Margaret,[1] when she goes out, is buttoned up to her little round nose in soft, white, woolly things. She has fluffy white gaiters and a short, bunchy coat and a round, bunchy bonnet and in these she staggers manfully out to her pram, calling out, "Moke, pretty moke," at the snow. Her idea of its likeness to smoke must have come from her love of the big, smoky bonfire Green has been making for the last few days at the bottom of the garden. In the frosty afternoons that preceded this storm of snow, the white smoke rose as softly as now the white snow falls and the small person found equal delight in both phenomena. She is very active now, and an awful handful, for the perils of back stairs and slippery

[1] The daughter of Winifred's adopted sister Edith, who lived with the family at Cottingham.

26

oilcloth, and doors that open suddenly and bang one's head, are becoming an hourly nightmare to poor Edith. However, the child seems to flourish in spite of everything.

We are giving a dance in the schoolroom here on the 18th—not an elaborate one this time, as we make all the refreshments ourselves and have a discharged soldier and his brother to fiddle and play the piano for us. But it should be fun—if only things did not take time. Time has become the most precious thing I have now, till June. Witness my love for you, that here I write pages of small paper while the clock hands tick away, seconds, minutes and hours! And here on my table lie Davis's *Norman Conquest* and Stubbs' *Select Charters*, and a long line of grizzly, hard-headed, close-fisted Norman kings to be encountered and dealt with— with their patient, laborious policy, and tenacious purpose, hammering the wilder genius of a decadent Teuton England into compact and orderly shape, to fit her for that great part she will later play with the Europe that once laughed at her as the "little island on the outmost fringe of the world." A queer world this, that has seen Assyria, and Egypt and China and Mexico and a wild procession of God knows how many other civilisations rise, and cry that they at least have come to stay—and vanish into a darkness and the shadow of a flame.

But we mean to make this the one that endures—though one wonders whether some day the men of Abyssinia will walk wondering over the moss-grown foundations of Piccadilly, and say, as they trudge back to their sandwiches and picture postcards—"What an interesting old town this must have been. Dear me, how long ago, Belinda? I have no head for dates!" Why Abyssinia?—Oh, I don't know— why England?

At least, the old civilisations never covered the whole world. They were at best a light that shined in the darkness, and the darkness comprehended it not. Now, though it may still be full of shadows, the darkness comprehends. I do not know what wild hordes of barbarians could beat upon the gates of our Rome. Germany may have been an empire of "Huns"—but there's a kind of heroism that is not entirely barbaric in the way in which they are facing the consequences of Versailles—capital levy and the rest of it, that our politicians dare not demand of England.

Here's a story mother brought back the other day from a bridge party.

A miser died and went to heaven. Peter stood at the pearly gates, jingling his keys and talking to Gabriel. "Please, I've come," said the miser. "Oh, you have, have you?" said Peter. "Well, what have you done? Hurry up and state your case, as this gentleman and I are busy." "I saw a blind beggar in the street and I gave him threepence," said the miser. "Oh, d'you think that'll do, Gabriel?" said Peter. "That's nothing," said Gabriel. "What else did you do?" "I saw a starving woman with her baby. She cried at my gate and I gave her threepence," said the miser. "Will that do?" asked Peter. Gabriel shook his head. "What more?" he asked. But the miser had no more to tell. "What are we to do with him?" asked Peter. "Tell him to take his tanner and go to hell!" said Gabriel. And they shut the gates in his face.

Here's another from the same source.

A farmer had engaged two girl landworkers the day before. He had sent them to market with the horse and trap and was anxiously awaiting their return. It was an hour later and raining fast. At last he went after them, and found them half-way from the town. The cart was drawn up under a hedge, and one girl was standing up in the cart, sheltering the hind quarters of the horse with an inadequate umbrella. "What the —— are you doing?" he asked. "Well," said the girls, "our book of instructions said that when we took a horse out, on no account were we to let the rein get under his tail."

Good-night, fair Rosalind, and much love.

Always your

CELIA.

28

Here's a little song I wrote the other day.

VAGABOND LOVE

Love is a vagabond
  Roving at will
All round the world, over
  Valley and hill.

Should he pass by your door
  Pretty maids, pray,
Call to him cunningly,
  Bid him to stay.

Snare him with loveliness,
  Coax him with Joy,
Blue beads, and gold, for a
  Fugitive boy.

Did you not hear but now
  Light footsteps fall—
Laughter along the road
  Clear as bird's call?

Little he's guessing that
  I'll have him soon—
I built a house for him
  Under the moon.

There, with dark moss below,
  Small stars above,
I'll hold him prisoner,
  Vagabond love.

1921

DEAREST ROSALIND,

It's after twelve, and I've been working fairly hard most of to-day, so am nearly dropping asleep, but must not miss the mail if I can help it; but you'll forgive a stupid and rather uninspired letter. I enclose a letter I had from Pugh the other day. I dare say she is right. I spoke to the two Aussie boys we had with us for Christmas and they said that a capable girl cook is just the kind of person who makes a lot of money there—£4 a week is the average wage in a country hotel, and the country is screaming for servants.

They were such charming boys—neither had been in the war, as they were then only in a military college, and were too young to be sent over, though they begged and prayed to be allowed to go. They have just finished their course in the Australian Sandhurst, and have been sent here for a year to see the English methods before they go back to take up their commissions in the regular Aussie army. They were clean, healthy, brown, shining people, with charming manners, and immaculate socks, and delicious, gurgly laughs. They were both sweet to Margaret, danced like angels, ate like young ostriches, and were most amusing company. There was nothing to choose between them, except that the hair of one was curly and the other straight!

We went one night to the pantomime in Hull. It was the silliest show, *Cinderella*, with the most hideous chorus you could ever dream of in your worst nightmare, but we all laughed uproariously. I thought mother would explode. There was one female in tights—six foot four if she was an inch, with a figure like this and false teeth three sizes too large, that clicked when she spoke! She was Philippe, the Prince Charming's equerry. Prince Charming himself, or rather herself, for she was a buxom damsel with a nicely-rounded figure, had a voice like a corncrake with a cold in its nose; but she warbled sweetly-sentimental ballads about keeping a little sunshine in your heart, and the applause was terrific. There was, however, a real pumpkin, and a real coach with two live ponies, so we got our money's worth— and Cinderella would have been almost pretty, except for her squint!

I am now trying to make up lost time and doing a little work; but, oh me, I have a muddled sort of a head, and things go in plain pig and come out such very fancy sausage that no examiner would recognise them. I'm not sure that I could myself!

I wished you a good New Year at twelve o'clock on Friday night, when the bells clashed out that 1921 had come. I hope you got the message.

Good-night—bel amie.

Your CELIA.

9, Bevington Road,
Oxford, Feb. 20th, 1921.

DEAREST ROSALIND,

First of all, to thank you for your letter of January 25th, 1921. I love writing the weekly epistle, so you are not in my debt, but rather I in yours, for the fair things one sees and hears become fairer when one gives them to a friend, and all "brave, gay, amusing things" lose their splendour on a lonely road. Don't you like the phrase I put in inverted commas? I met it in a review of one of the modern, dismal, psychological stories. The reviewer asked the author if the world was barren now of all gay things that once adorned it —and he laughed at the solemn "newly brutal and direct" touch, as, indeed, it needs to be laughed at. I think modern art, in England anyway, has fallen under the pernicious influence of Augustus John. The Slade School calls every charming picture "pretty-pretty" and flies to the other extreme, in mistaking the grotesque for the beautiful.

The poets are just as bad; for those who have energy and freshness fear to become Sunday-magazinish and write their *Wheels*[1] and *Rolls* and other atrocities under the impression that they are out-Henleying Henley, and discovering a new pathless world of *vers libre*, free from the trammels of such minor accessories of poetry such as rhyme or metre or even musical language.

The context of these didactics is—that Mr. Alfred Noyes came to lecture to Somerville last week. The entrance fee only being one shilling I went—one shilling isn't much to look at the one modern poet who tried to write an epic and succeeded in producing four good lyrics. Have you read *Drake*? I did once—all through. During influenza. The surprising part is that I rather enjoyed it. But that's a confession that Somerville, clever, modern, emancipated Somerville, reared on *Wheels* and the *London Mercury*, would blush to hear. He read his own poems, and not very well, more's the pity. At least, the difficulty with him is that, having spent so long in America, he has acquired an unfortunate hybrid accent which rings strangely through his most English verse. Also he did not read his best things—the songs from *Drake* or the *Robin Hood Ballads*. Instead, he recited *The Highwayman*—you remember that in the hut at Huchenneville? *The Lord of Misrule*, some of the Touchstone satires, which are really pleasant and most neatly versified; some Anglo-American things which I didn't like (they're from his new book, and attempting to be grandiloquent, ended in being merely pedestrian), *The May-Tree* which is delightful, and *The Barrel-Organ*. Do you know that? It has one charming song in it—"Kew in Lilac Time." I expect you know it, but in case you don't, I give it to you. I'm quoting from memory, so pardon if I make mistakes.

"Come down to Kew in lilac time, in lilac time, in lilac time,
Come down to Kew in lilac time. It isn't far from London.

[1] An Oxford publication edited by Edith Sitwell.

35

And you shall wander hand in hand, with love in
summer's wonderland.
Come down to Kew in lilac time. It isn't far from
London.

"The cherry trees are seas of bloom, and soft perfume,
and sweet perfume,
The cherry trees are seas of bloom—and oh, so near
to London.
And there, they say, when dawn is nigh, and all the
world's a blaze of sky,
The cuckoo, though he's very shy, will sing a song for
London.

"The nightingale is rather rare, and yet, they say,
you'll hear him there,
At Kew, at Kew in lilac time, and not so far from
London.
The linnet and the throstle too, and after dark the
long halloo,
The golden-eyed tewit-tewhoo, of owls that ogle
London.

"For Noah hardly knew a bird of any kind that isn't
heard
At Kew, at Kew in lilac time, and oh, so near to
London.
And where the rose begins to pout, and all the chestnut
spires are out,
You'll hear the rest without a doubt, all chorusing
for London.

"Come down to Kew in lilac time, in lilac time, in
lilac time,
Come down to Kew in lilac time, it isn't far from
London.

And you shall wander hand in hand with love in summer's wonderland,
Come down to Kew in lilac time—It isn't far from London."

It should be sung on a spring day by tall ladies dressed in green and garlanded with flowers.

Rosalind dear—how like you to live on two shillings for a fortnight. But what happy letters E. writes. And what a splendid thing to give her such a chance. I hope the third shilling has come in now. The world will be richer for E.'s nursing, even if our Rosalind goes poorer—and indeed that is how she should walk in the Forest of Arden, with her shepherd's script emptied; for she gave her jewels to a wandering wrestler.

The New Zealand post was a very long way away. Are you going to stay in South Africa? Perhaps one day I'll come and see you, but not next year, I fear, for I've to write *Anderby Wold* as soon as I go down, and lecture to the W.E.A., not about "old unhappy far-off things and battles long ago" that so many teachers of history re-create; but living, vital movements that hold each man to-day. We've got the present to make as the people of olden days had their centuries, and it's not a blind play of circumstance, but the power and grace and energy of men and women that made it. But it's no use just saying that. You've got to show them how it was done, and write it in the books they'll read, and sing it in their bath, if they won't take it dry. And even then they probably won't listen, but'll go on pitying themselves no end and running up and down the world calling to God Almighty to put them out of their misery—and all the while they hold the key to the door of their own escape—only they're so impatient and blind and blundering.

(Ed. The correspondence is here concluded.)

All the morning I've been gathering primroses in Tubney Woods—almost as lovely as our Huchenneville Woods. My hands smell all earthy, because I dug them up

37

with my fingers—such strong roots too. It's a better smell than ink.

I've been doing five-finger exercises lately with metres and moods from different poets, to make myself elastic. There isn't much time here for studying poetry. But here's an attempt at Swinburne which may entertain you. It's on the versification of the *Sea-Mew*.

> The dim brown woods are weeping
> Beneath an ashen sky;
> On barren branches swinging
> The last pale leaves are clinging,
> Before, with thrifty reaping
> The cold wind bears them by,
> Where dim brown woods are weeping
> Beneath an ashen sky.
>
> Their golden treasure squandered
> The trees are stark and bare.
> No promise born of May time
> Rings through the dreary day-time;
> Where once blithe breezes wandered;
> No, beggared by despair,
> Their golden treasure squandered,
> The trees are stark and bare.
>
> Of beauty followed blindly,
> Of beauty that must die
> Can we not store the treasure,
> Has losing them no measure,
> Or must we love so kindly
> And loving, pass it by?
> Of beauty followed blindly,
> Of beauty that must die.

If I'd been true to the Swinburnian sentiment, I'd have left it at that, but being in little mind for such doubtful comfort, I had to add another verse.

When yet my heart remembers
The glory that was May
Has life no gift of laughter
For what may follow after?
What care we for Decembers
That March winds waft away,
When yet my heart remembers
The glory that was May?

Now I must go and toast crumpets and get ready for a
Sunday afternoon treat—real tea and scandal. The latest
is that R., the Antony of O.U.D.S., stroke of the Pembroke
eight, staunch teetotaler (they say), paragon of all academic
virtues, has become engaged to Cleopatra, Miss Cathleen
Nesbitt, saucy little actress of thirty summers, with a big
future. Ah, well, next year perhaps they'll let women
students act in O.U.D.S. Then there'll be less danger to
susceptible Antonies.

Here comes tea——

Love,

CELIA.

9, Bevington Road,
Oxford,
Sunday, Easter Term, 1921.

DEAREST ROSALIND

I am burning with indignation, having just returned
from a walk with a miserable undergraduate who says he
can't bear *As You Like It.* He is an intelligent youth too,
whom I should have credited with nicer sense. He knows
Shakespeare far better than I do, and discourses learnedly
upon the new critical text of *The Tempest,* just issued by the
Cambridge Text Society, and has read more Elizabethan and
Restoration literature in twenty-two years that I could hope
to read in a lifetime, and yet he says he does not understand
how Shakespeare could have produced so ill-constructed a

39

play. I turned upon him more in sorrow than anger, and from Summertown to Wood Eton maligned his judgment. He took it all quite calmly, I must say, and conceded that "there might be something in it," but even so, thought that Celia and Rosalind were silly, and Jaques the only character worthy of the author. What is Oxford coming to? However, I console myself that only last summer O.U.D.S. gave an almost perfect performance of it in Wadham Gardens.

I've walked about seventeen miles to-day and having just eaten a large supper of toasted ham we cooked over the fire, feel pleasantly torpid.

Talking of Torpid[1]—the House of course are head of the river again after Toggers, New College second, and Worcester third. Good old Wuggins really made a gallant show. Rumour hath it that they had a cellar flooded in Beaumont St., and used to practice there before a row of mirrors. At any rate their efforts must have been rewarded last Monday when they bumped Magdalen—Magdalen, who swore to take everything that was going—Toggers, Eights, Soccer, Footer, the athletic championship and all. So far, they have only got the running cup. The whole university rejoiced in their defeat at Toggers and a cheer went up that seemed to mean, "Great Babylon is fallen, fallen!"

I've spent last week reading about Wycliffe and the Lollards—awfully interesting though scholastic theology needs a mind reared on syllogisms to comprehend it properly.

Have you read *Richard Furlong* by Temple Thurston? I read it in bed last week. I always read before I blow out the candle. It's gorgeously, astoundingly bad. And how that man sells his books too! To take the taste away I bought Shaw's *Man of Destiny*. The worst of Shaw is that though I like reading him, he depresses me first by his utter contempt for the intelligence of mankind; secondly, because I never really understand what he's driving at, and

[1]Torpids—otherwise known as "Toggers"—a boat race held at Oxford towards the end of the Easter term.

hate to confess my ignorance. Other people seem to know exactly how to take him. I wonder if I'm stupid, or if Shaw is not as easy as they make out. He's certainly got a bee in his bonnet about insularity.

Vera and I are writing the G.D.P.[1] It is a musical comedy of the *Chu Chin Chow* variety, called *Bolshevism in Baghdad: A Somerville Night's Entertainment*, and is all about a sultan, weary of the frivolities of his Hundred Wives, who sends to Somerville for three enlightened young dons who come to turn the harem into a women's college. It isn't very funny, but has infinite possibilities of caricature and topical allusions, which are the main thing.

Au revoir, take care of yourself.

Love from yours,

CELIA.

[1] The Somerville *Going Down Play*.

GOING DOWN PLAY, 1921.

A SOMERVILLE NIGHT'S ENTERTAINMENT

"BOLSHEVISM IN BAGHDAD"
A Psycho-Analytic Experiment

Committee
MISS KENNEDY
„ THOMAS
„ BRINTON
„ HOLTBY
„ DESMOND
„ E. ROBINSON
Accompanist: „ SALINGAR

IN BAGHDAD

SCENES

PROLOGUE—*The Harem of the Caliph's Palace*
THE PSYCHO-ANALYTIC REVELATION

SCENE I.—Bolshevist Baghdad		*The Harem*
SCENE II.—Salvation from Somerville		
(*An Associated Idea—A Vision of Italy*)		
SCENE III.—Institution of Anarch		*The Harem*
SCENE IV.—Eastern Eights		*A Barge on the Tigris*
SCENE V.—Vinolia of the Baths		*The Harem*
SCENE VI.—Cupid, Camels and Conspiracies		
		Bevington Road, Baghdad
SCENE VII.—Reception of Royalty		*The Harem*
SCENE VIII.—Compromise		*Convocation House, Baghdad*

EPILOGUE—*Harem of the Caliph's Palace*
(Three hours after the Prologue)

CAST

CALIPH OF BAGHDAD	*Holtby*
CHIEF QUEEN	*B. M. Bell*
ALIBABA (Vice Chancellor of Baghdad University)	*Liddell*
NOYESI VACHELLI	*Desmond*
MINISTER OF FINANCE	*Vaughan*
ANTONI RAMAGI PASHA (Grand Vizier)	*Brinton*
POLICEMAN	*Shelmerdene*
ALDOBORA	*Irons*
PROF. OF PETTY ARSON	*Abrahams*
PROF. OF FORGERY	*Brigman*
JUNIOR PROCTOR	*Fraser*
LOTUS	*Harvey*
VIOLET	*Moore*
WATERLILY	*H. Reid*
CYCLAMEN	*Simpson*
CRABAPPLE ⎫	*Gilchrist*
PINEAPPLE ⎬ Triplets	*Nicholson*
OAKAPPLE ⎭	*Redman*
VERONA	*Hepburn*
LADY RADCLYFFE	*Bruce Bell*
INNKEEPER	*Fraser*

Oxford Dons

MISS MAGENTA MCTAVISH	*Kennedy*
MISS CLEOPATRA O'NESBITT	*Brittain*
MISS CHECKMATE	*Glover*
MISS OCTAVIA DEWDROP	*Cobb*

Other Queens on the Harem

APPLEBLOSSOM (President of Anarch)	*Bruce Bell*
LAUREL	*Watson*
RAGGED ROBIN	*Dickey*
CELMOND	*Harris*
MAYFLOWER	*Abrahamson*

43

HOP FLOWER	*Huxley*
BLUSH ROSE	*Wadsworth*
DAISY	*Hutchins*
MARSHMALLOW	*Aldridge*
ANZORA	*Nuttall*
VINOLIA	*Grierson*
AURORA (Junior Proctor's sister)	*Powell*
MISS CONCRETE	*Lunam*
STAGE MANAGER	*Thomas*
BEGGAR	*Waite*
UNDERGRADUATES	{ *Wadsworth* *Hutchins*
BULLDOGS	{ *Davis* *Cannon*
CAMEL	{ *Vaughan* *Huxley*

MAGGIE   *E. Robinson*

MY DEAREST ROSALIND,

Thank you ever so much for your long letter. I loved hearing all about what you do, and Jane, and Mrs. W., and the kitten and Agnes and Sabina. It all sounds far more like a fairy tale than a real place.

When I said, "I don't know much about you," I did not mean a complaint. I think you are wonderful to write so often, and I love getting your letters; but I don't want you to bother when you are tired and busy. You know Mother and I have an agreement never to write, except when she has something to say. I often don't see her handwriting for weeks—but there never were two people closer together —and though I might not hear from you—provided you were all right—we should not be any further apart. But I like writing. It's easy every week, if you don't mind all the silly, unexciting little things.

I can match your kitten and chicken stories—in fact I can go one better. We have five Buff Orpingtons, four Rhode Island Reds and a large Red Mania, who occasionally forgets the dignity becoming to her age and family connections and careers wildly over the daisies on the strip of lawn at the back of the house. More wonderful yet, our best charlady, who lives in a long-gardened cottage across the way, has nine of the blackest, shiniest baby pigs the Lord ever made. Their mother Jenny is large and grey, with a genial, phlegmatic disposition and a weird complexion—the result of a misguided attempt to cross Berkshires and Tamworths. She chats in a conversational way to Mrs. P., whom she regards purely as groom of the chambers, when she enters her palace with the daily meal; but to strangers she is reticent and condescending, exhibiting her offspring with pride concealed by a faintly patronising manner. Mrs. P. is a little like Jenny. I think that propinquity engenders a certain mutual imitation among characters not naturally rigid. Both have the same maternal instincts, the same manner and—though I say it in no disparaging way, Mrs. P. being an excellent woman and the best drawer of fowls in Cottingham—no faint resemblance in their appearance.

I have practically fixed up now about the flat I am going to in London. I am sharing it with two other girls—Vera Brittain, the friend from Oxford with whom I stayed in Cornwall, who has got a job on *The Bookman*, reviewing academic books, etc., and who will also take half-time teaching jobs—Clare Leighton, granddaughter[1] of the artist, and daughter of Robert Leighton, ex-editor of the *Daily Mail*. Her brother was engaged to Vera, but was killed in the War, and she herself is a student at the Slade School and paints rather modern portraits, after the style of Augustus John—the usual Slade revulsion from the pretty-pretty, that ends generally in what I should call the ugly-ugly. Apart from her painting—and though I laugh at it, I can't help seeing she is clever—she is a charming person and I think we shall rub along quite well.

I have not said anything about the Strike, because it is the one topic of conversation in England just now; anyway it's sad thinking and writing.

Take care of yourself—and the hens—and don't go buying any more of your own eggs.
With much love,
CELIA.

Oxford.

MY DEAREST ROSALIND,

I really mean to write this week if I can get it done. I am in the middle of packing to go down and my room looks like nothing on earth—except a room when one is packing. It's all over—Schools and Going Down Play, and the last Saturday, and all that—and now we're clearing up

[1]Actually Clare Leighton is not granddaughter of Lord Leighton, though he was a family connection.

the orange peel and banana skins and striking camp. Schools weren't a great success. I don't have my viva till July 21st, and the results will not be out until August 1st, because there were 450 people taking history; but I know pretty nearly how well I've done—somewhere round the thirds, I think.

The Going Down Play was great fun to do. I'll send you a programme. It was chiefly successful as a spectacular show. Eastern clothes are very easy to make effectively out of bedspreads and half a yard of butter muslin, so the stage blazed with blue, jade, scarlet and orange. Unfortunately, the jokes did not go down frightfully well with the first year; but the dons loved it, and the Pen[1] said it was " most amusing, really most amusing"—so I suppose that is some compensation for hours of strenuous labour—and, as the Caliph, I did wear most heavenly orange trousers! If I had felt any temptation to become conceited, I should soon have been cured, for next evening I went to see *Fanny's First Play*. It is about the most amusing comedy I have ever seen. I loved every minute of it. Even the Shavist sermons. Have you seen it? Do you know the lovely tickly-inside feeling that a Shaw play gives when it's really well acted? The " Darling Dora" last night was splendid. She had a perfect cockney accent, a scarlet hat that would have knocked you down by sheer brilliance if you met it in the street, a fascinating giggle and more personality than any girl I have seen on the stage for months.

They are taking the Census to-night, and our landlady, Mrs. W., has decided to go and spend the night with her sister so that Miss F., the young don in residence here, shall not discover her age. She is a widow—moreover, a widow who for twenty years was cook to the Rector of Bursley Magna— " not a Vicar, you know, Miss 'Oltby; though I'm a Wesleyan myself and always does go to the Sunday School festival, I says it myself as shouldn't, 'e was a rector and a real nice gentleman. And if it 'adn't been for the War and butter that 'ard to get, me 'aving an 'elp in the kitchen, and

[1]Miss Emily Penrose, Principal of Somerville from 1907–1926.

you know what young girls is—the way they do eat, to be sure, and I always was one to go without that others might 'ave plenty—I never would have gone, for 'e says to me, 'e says, ' Mrs. W.,' 'e says ' must you leave me?' And I says, ' Far be it from me to do an ill turn to any one, though 'e be a rector and myself a Wesleyan and not 'olding with such; but live an' let live,' I says." However, acting, I suppose, upon her oft-reiterated principle of "live and let live," she would rather pay for lodgings with her sister for the night than divulge the date at which her living began.

I am going down on Tuesday and going almost straight away for a holiday to Bridlington. I'm going with Grace and Edith and Margaret and a girl called Kathleen Tennyson, whom you may have met at our dance. We are going to sit on the sands, read novels, ride donkeys, eat ice creams, listen to nigger-minstrels, bathe and do every other really seasidey thing. I am dying for an intrigue with a pierrot! I feel that after Schools, it would be the only adventure that would not prove an anti-climax! The difficulty will be that no donkey may be sufficiently powerful to sustain my buxom form—not that I am very buxom now. I have grown most elegantly thin. When you knew me I was like this: Now I am like this:

These lines are not intended for whiskers— they just Came!

(Academic dress is rather hard to draw.)

48

This is a very foolish letter but my mentality is suffering from slight exhaustion. After a change of air I may be more intelligent.

Much love, my dear—and more than many thanks for your letters.

CELIA.

Bainesse,
Cottingham,
E. Yorks, June 26th.

ROSALIND DEAR,

There has been yet another letter from you for which I say "thank you"—a note telling me that you are going to the Victoria Falls for three weeks. I hope you have a good holiday, and see lots of beautiful things, that the weather is kind, and the people kinder, the trains not too full of grit and coal dust, and the ox-wagons, if you go in any, not too slow and bumpy. What else can one wish a traveller in South Africa? Good company, good weather, and good luck?

I am, as you see, at home, and experiencing for the first time in my life a summer holiday without the thought of work for next term waiting upstairs to be done. That is —I have breakfast at nine-thirty, do a little vague house-work, such as washing breakfast things and tidying my room, drift down the village on an errand, or put on my second-best hat and meet the Hull train, bearing its load of Cottingham ladies back from a pre-lunch shopping. In the afternoons I play tennis; in the evenings, bridge. It's very delightful—for a week; but I have scores of things crying to be done.

(a) A curtain-raiser called *For Ninety-Nine Just Persons* —about the return of the prodigal son seen from the other brother's point of view. For a long time I've been convinced he had one. The "unto this last" idea appears to be well authenticated as consonant

with the best Christian standard of justice; but I
never could quite see it hit the balance.

(b) I want to go on with Anderby Wold.

(c) I suppose I ought to read for my viva. Though when
there is not a single paper which I imagine to be so
complete a production that a viva on it is unnecessary
it is rather difficult to know where to start.

Meanwhile there is Margaret, who is too adorable for
words. She has just been picking "ee-aws," i.e., sticks in
the garden. Her curls are on to her shoulders now, and are
brown near her head, but pale, delicate gold where they
twist into ringlets. She runs with a slightly unsteady
swagger all over the garden, in little blue frocks decorated
with birds, mauve and pink and primrose. She makes
quaintly inconsequential remarks in the middle of quite
sober conversations. Altogether, it is not surprising that
all Cottingham has lost its heart to her. When she goes
up the village in her pram, she greets every other passing
baby with "Hallo, Michael," or "Dere's Peter Saner," or
"I seen Tommy Jackson." On her birthday, suitors of
varying ages from six months to four years come and offer
gifts and good wishes to a lady beautifully impartial in her
favours. The little girl babies are less favourable. I think
their button noses are occasionally put out of joint.

It's a "Special Call to Prayer" to-day for the industrial
troubles, summoned by the Archbishop of York. Cottingham has gone to pray, in its rustling silk coats and prettiest
cotton frocks—to come home to curse the miners, grumble
about coal supplies, and sentimentalise over the out-of-work.
As far as one can see in this polite surface of society, everything is going on exactly the same as usual. We in the
East Riding are well away from any industrial centre, so
are spared any sights of suffering that might offend the
delicate susceptibilities of the upper middle classes. I don't
know what is going on in the manufacturing and mining
districts. The strike pay must have run out ages ago. It is a
mystery what they are living on—or existing on, rather.

50

I suppose it's plucky; but I am sure it is mistaken. Tax-payers cannot subsidise a perfectly healthy industry. I suppose compulsory training in economics for every potential striker would not really do any good; for the instinct to get as much and work as little as possible is deeper embedded in most men than any temporary conviction of right reason could uproot; but it might save us from a few absurdities.

This last page looks rather pessimistic. I'm not really. The more I read of past history, the more I believe in progress, whatever Mr. Bernard Shaw may say. To relieve the atmosphere of gloom, let me tell you a story I heard at a tennis party yesterday, hardly proper but rather nice.

The archdeacon's wife was engaging a maid.

"Do you go regularly to church?"

"Oh yes'm."

"Do you read your Bible?"

"Yes'm. Sometimes'm."

"Have you ever been confirmed?"

"Only one 'm and it died."

Here's another from the same source:

A boy in a Scots village wanted to get married. He went to his father.

"Father, I want to marry Janet McTavish."

"Dinna do that, laddie. You canna. She's your sister."

Undaunted, he waited a few months and then returned to his father.

"Father, I want to marry Mary Findlay."

"You canna, laddie. She's your sister."

The process was repeated once or twice, the boy always receiving the same answer. At last he went to his mother. "Mither," he said, "I canna get wed, for father says every lass in the village is my sister."

"Nay, laddie, dinna fash yoursen. He's not your father."

After that, I had better say farewell for this week, and good luck for your holiday-making, which will be over when you get this, I fear.

Much love, my Rosalind,

CELIA.

10 Oakwood Court,[1]
Kensington, W.14, July 25th.

ROSALIND DEAR,

Thank you for your last letter and the enclosures, which I return in case you like to keep them. I am going to meet Pugh on Tuesday. She is coming out to lunch with me and we are going to "sit in a gallery somewhere, and suck a stick of chocolate" and look at pictures or a melodrama and talk.

Your Miss A. sounds like Aunt Hester in *A Bill of Divorcement*. Have you read it? It's a new play by Clemence Dane, and wonderfully fine. I went last night with Vera. Aunt Hester is one of those people who put conventions before human needs, and read the prayer book aloud while some one is undergoing mental torment. They carry the Almighty in their pockets as an additional means of discomforting their enemies.

I'll send you *Perilous Seas* again. I believe as it stands it is rather too long to answer any requirements of the periodicals just now. The Fugue was even too long for the *Athenæum*, though the editor liked it. Very few people take things as long as the Cornhill. If you could make two or three short things out of it, I might get them placed, as I have made the acquaintance of a very good literary agent, a man called Somerville, a friend of Mr. St. John Adcock, the editor of *The Bookman*. About 3000 words seems to be a popular length for a sketch like that. I love the things you write. I want other people to love them, too. I'm just getting to know literary people now. Yesterday

[1]Then the home of Vera Brittain and her parents.

Vera took me to tea at the Leightons'. Robert Leighton, the ex-editor of the *Daily Mail*, and his wife Marie Connor Leighton, writer of amazing novels of crime and convicts and blue-eyed heroines, that sell by the thousand. They live in a queer little jumbled house, hanging on the side of its twin in St. John's Wood. Mrs. Leighton is the most wonderfully alive thing I ever met. The dimples come and go in her cheeks; her eyes are blazing with vitality and humour and interest; her hands are white and plump, and graceful in their quick gestures. Mr. Leighton is like a deaf sea-lion, in a morning coat and soft collar; but he has dear, winkly blue eyes, and the kindest manner in the world. And how they talk! Hall Caine to Hardy, George Meredith to O. Henry, Andrew Lang to George Moore— they know them all, just intimately and surely and as a matter of course. Mr. Leighton's talk is a monologue as he is stone deaf; but the monologue is like a chapter of the most interesting literary memoirs you ever read. And they say they'll help me. It's all Vera. She was engaged to Roland Leighton, who was killed in the war. They love her, and she has told them that I write, and they are interested in any of her friends. But they are splendid people, and I'll make them see your work, too, when I know them better. You *shall* go on writing, Rosalind dear, you *shall*.

I went for my viva on Thursday. At the time I loved it. Only when it was all over I realised what had happened. I had been viva'd for forty minutes—for a First, they say, though I don't believe it—and I made a perfect fool of myself. I never thought the viva would matter much, and I suppose I lost my head, only in a funny sort of way. I enjoyed myself and laughed, and made the examiners laugh sometimes; but I never gave them a single piece of useful information, though they gave me chance after chance to do so, and I knew most of the things, really. So I shan't get a First; but I had a good run for my money.

I'm staying here till next Thursday—going to theatres,

meeting interesting people, interviewing Cook's, etc., about our Italian tour, and buying winter clothes at the sales. I'm getting a black fur coat for £15. It has to do for a long coat, coat and skirt, and furs for the winter, so is not really very extravagant, as I could never have got all those things and an evening cloak for the money. I've also got for £6 a black lace evening frock turned up with blue. All these things are good—but oh, Mac o' my heart, how I'm longing to get my teeth into some *work*. Not just playing about, but really doing something that will be of some use, however small. I'm tired of being educated. I want to start justifying my existence somehow. Don't you know the feeling?

Send me another story. I'll send you my play when it's done.

My love to you

CELIA.

PS.—This house has two of the nicest cuckoo clocks you ever met. In the hall is a big clock, with a fat cuckoo, who has a large, important bass voice. In Vera's room, where I'm writing, is a little clock, crouching upon the wall, swinging its naughty leg (it only has one, and two weights like pine cones). Its cuckoo is little and blue, with a soft, rather kind little voice. I turned it all the way from 2 to 12.30 the other morning, and made it sing at all the half-hours. You would love it.

Bainesse,
Cottingham,
E. Yorks, August 28th, 1921.

MY DEAREST ROSALIND,

I have such a lovely long letter to thank you for, that I feel ashamed of my recent scraps of correspondence. Of course you are right that, in a sense, letters tell one nothing. You write and you write, and in the end there is nothing said; but I was able to wander a little way with you, in

African trains over strange country. The very names—
Kimberley, Bulawayo, the Matoppos—all have a far-away
charm like the names of a fairy tale. Well, next time I
write I shall be able to tell you of fairy tale names. Next
week, if all goes well, I shall be in Milan, having arrived
the day before from Paris.

I have started my novel, and it gives me unbelievable
joy and pain. The writing is great fun; but ye gods, the
sorrow of wrestling with a style like mine! I can't think
why I was cursed with this inordinate desire to write, if
the high gods weren't going to give me some more adequate
means of expressing myself than that which my present
pedestrian prose affords. I know what I want my characters
to do, I know what pictures I want my readers to see; but
there's all the difference in the world between knowing
and writing, though I suppose the knowing is the first
step in the game, and the realisation of one's defects the
second, so I may get going some day.

> "If thy faith be entire
> Press onward, for thine eye
> Shall see thy heart's desire——"

At least, Vera is always reminding me of that, and I suppose
she may be right. Only, when one's sentences trundle
clumsily across the stage, and the scenes one meant to write
with such dramatic constraint become merely rather
tiresome melodrama, it's a little difficult to keep one's faith
entire. I told you what it's all about, I think: A girl of
eighteen, who married a Yorkshire farmer, twenty years
older than herself. The story begins when she is twenty-
eight, and has no children. For the sake of a farm that
has been in the family for five hundred years, she married
an older man whom she did not love and threw in her lot
with a passing generation, and the fate and ideals of the
Old Farmers. It is in the days just before the War when
agricultural conditions were beginning to change. She
realises the coming change, realises, too, that her marriage

placed her on the losing side. Then when it is too late she rebels against her circumstances. The new things, that rightfully belong to her youth and vitality, become embodied in the person of a young Socialist, David Rossiter, a younger son of a wealthy Midland squire, whose father has refused to pay for his last year at New College, because of David's inflammatory speeches at the Union. He has gone to the North, and joined the staff of a second-rate Radical newspaper, and meets my farmer's wife while on a campaign, speaking in the villages against the very system which she and her husband represent. They learn to love one another, and the woman finds in him the youth she sacrificed to serve the land. Then trouble comes. A labourer's strike, not organised by David, but traceable to his speeches, followed by a stack fire, ruins the Robsons, who had crippled their resources buying off the mortgage from the farm. David is shot by a drunken Irish harvester, and Mary turns to find her place in the world in her husband's need of her comfort, when all the old things are falling in ruin about them.

It sounds rather silly in a synopsis, but I think it may do better in the long story, and anyway, no one can say I don't get my knowledge of farming conditions first hand. One hears so much of the courage of the pioneer, that it seems not out of place to talk for a little of the courage of those who, seeing the things they have given their lives to, passing, raise no hand to prevent the coming of the new, that may mean for the world salvation, but for themselves, and all that they stand for, certain destruction; of those who, leaving their work perforce unfinished, pass by with no self-commiseration, no vain bewailing of a glory that is gone; but with the wave of a hand in the darkness, and a salute to the adventurers who have found a better road to perfection.

Does this all sound very sentimental? I should hate it if it were, but it's so hard nowadays to draw the line between "cleverness" and sentimentality.

This is as usual a very dull exchange for yours, and all about myself, too, although I don't seem to have said much. Next week, though, I shall have many adventures to recount if the gods be good, though I shan't make such delightful telling of them as you.

I've got to stop now. Lots of writing to do before I go away. Among other things, I'm coaching a girl by correspondence for the Somerville History Scholarship.

Au revoir, and much love.

Ever yours,

CELIA.

Pension Visentini, Campo Santa Barbara,
Nobienigo, Venice, September 8th.

ROSALIND DEAR,

I'm giving you my address at the top of this queer little note-book letter, not because you will ever be able to write to me here, but because the name of the place conveys something of its charm, and also, perhaps, you may some day have the fortune to visit Venice, and if so, you may stay at this charming pension. It is a stone building with square, low-ceilinged rooms. To reach it we climb up two flights of steps, smelling of darkness, and sea water, and incense. By day, they are gloomy; by night, two candles in snake-shaped holders illuminate the corners. Our room is at the top. It has a mosaic stone floor, mosquito nets over the beds and two flat windows that look down on to the small stone square that is Campo Santa Barbara. The Campo boasts a café with outdoor seats at one end, a pump in the middle, and at one end a flight of steps leading down to the Grand Canal. If we crane our necks we can see the Canal from our bedroom window, and all day and night we can hear the motor-boats and steamers humming up and down. We cannot hear the gondolas, for they are perfectly silent, except when, negotiating a corner, the gondolier gives one warning cry, or when a particularly artistic gondolier sings a barcarolle as he goes up the canal. The singing, though, is usually put on, I imagine, to catch the ear of a sentimental tourist, as are certainly the white drill blouses with sailor collars, such as our gondolier donned this morning when approaching the railway station.

Venice is far more like its tradition than any other place I have seen. From the moment one steps out of the station, on to a stone pier, crowded with men in blue blouses, waving boathooks, and all shouting at once, till the moment that the pension door shuts out the last view of the boat poles, sticking like the masts of ships out of the Grand Canal, there is no doubt that this is Venice. Vera says that parts of it are like Valetta—but not even Valetta has these winding canals, these unexpected little Campos, mostly built round a church or palace, and certainly neither Valetta nor any other place in the world has the Piazza San Marco. I was prepared for the Campanile, the Doge's Palace and the Cathedral, but not for the vastness of the piazza, its arcades flanking the most fascinating shops built under old palaces—shops brimming with glass work and beads and rare silks from the East in gorgeous colours. Outside the arcades are rows of tables and chairs, where the people, generally in the smartest of clothes, sit and drink wine and coffee.

At night a band plays Wagner, and every one walks about listening, and Vera has bought me a black Venetian shawl, so I walk about listening, too, and the postcard sellers and little bare-legged boys look at my yellow head and say, " Please, Mees. Good-morning"—a comprehensive phrase which in Italy seems to mean anything.

Yesterday Vera and I started out early and took the train to Bassano, a little hill town at the foot of the Tyrol, where there is a wonderful view of Mt. Grappa—the chief Italian defence during the war. We hired a car at Bassano from a dear little fat hotel-keeper, who took a fatherly interest in two such youthful and unsophisticated looking Inglese and insisted on accompanying us to interpret in

French from the chauffeur, who could only speak Italian. We went on a zigzag road of hairpin curves, right up through the mountains on to the Asiago Plateau, where the English fought. It is one of the highest battlefields in Europe, all among pine woods and barren slopes strewn with white rocks. There are shell holes and trenches, but these do not seem untidy like those in France, for the hills themselves are full of jagged points and holes, and the little white cemeteries are hardly distinguishable from the stone-covered hillside.

It was an amazing drive. From every turn of the road the mountainside dropped sheer down to the plain below, where the Piave and Brenta—though they are really fine rivers—glittered like tiny silver threads. It was like being in an aeroplane. We had a Fiat car with a wonderful engine and it flew up and down the hillside, and round those curves like a living thing. Brownie, a little the worse for wear, swooping down the Rouen road, was nothing to our beautiful Italian driver, with his fierce moustaches—yet one never felt nervous. He was so wonderfully skilful. The reason why we went to such expense was because Vera's brother was killed and buried there in 1918 and we took some roses to his grave. The Italians were full of charming tact and sympathy and helped in every possible way to make our journey easy. When we had got back to Bassano, the hotel-keeper insisted on driving us down to the station in his car and getting our tickets for us, and refused to take any money even for the car.

On Monday we go to Florence. We have to take a train at 6.10 in the morning, and as it takes about an hour to reach the station (gondolas are not rapid), we shall have to start early.

I must go and write home and then have tea with Vera on the Piazza San Marco, and then ride right out to the Lagoons in a boat.

Au revoir and much love,

CELIA.

59

ROSALIND DEAR,

In this place where there is so great an *embarras de richesse*, I hardly know what to tell you first, or which of my recent pleasures to pass on to some extent, in return for your delightful pilgrimage through Africa. For Milan is orderly and prosperous, containing two or three unique but isolated treasures—the "Last Supper" of Leonardo da Vinci, the Cathedral, the courtyard of the Sforza Palace. And Venice is brilliant and beautiful, but its brilliance is the brilliance of decay, its gaiety superimposed by strangers; its beauty a mausoleum. But Florence is exquisitely alive, with the same vitality and freshness that made the Renaissance here the wonderful flowering time it was. The people are gay and dark and polite. In the shops they gain by courtesy all that they lose by unbusinesslike methods and a tendency to reply "Domani" (to-morrow) to all one's inquiries. I went the other day into a chemist's to buy glycerine for Vera, whose throat was sore, and only remembered when in the shop, which was some distance from our pension, that I neither knew the Italian for "glycerine," nor had my dictionary in my pocket. The fat little spectacled chemist knew neither French nor English. I gesticulated, experimented with every kind of pronunciation and facial expression. The chemist gesticulated and poured out upon me a rapid stream of perfectly sound but unintelligible advice. Finally a little Frenchman entered the shop, come to buy something for his wife, who had toothache, and he fortunately knew French, but no Italian. However, I knew enough French to explain my case to him. He produced a French-Italian dictionary from his pocket, and together we explained our requirements to the chemist, and I returned triumphant with my glycerine. All through the chemist was as amused and polite as the shoemaker who, on another day, opened every box in his store to find shoes large enough for me, and when his quest proved hopeless, congratulated me upon the admirable growth of my figure. But no wonder these people are polite, for they work in shops that have hardly altered since the fourteenth century—mosaic workers, squatting on sunlit loggias—jewellers, on benches of blackened oak hundreds of years old; carvers, breaking off their work to eat long rolls of brownish bread, with ham and salad trailing out at the corners. And in the evening they all, labourers and shopkeepers, and respectable notaries in black coats, and little gay girls in organdie muslin frocks, and old beggar ladies, go to the Piazza Signoria, where a band plays, and there are little tables outside the cafés, where one drinks sirops and "birra," or eats delicious water ices, using a fourpenny drink as a pretext for occupying a seat throughout two hours' unrivalled entertainment. For, even apart from the band, which plays Verdi and Wagner with real enthusiasm, and the crowd, which is delightfully naïve and appreciative, and therefore thoroughly entertaining, the Palazza Vecchia and the Loggia Lorenzo, which rise from the Piazza into the dark blue sky, are the loveliest things in Florence. Then, too, there are pageants to keep them amused. We waited three hours yesterday in the upper window of a florist's shop to see a procession, dressed as in Dante's day, of two thousand youths and maidens, on foot, strewing garlands, or on horseback wearing armour, just as they once returned from the Battle of Campeldino. The Florentines wore their costumes with charming grace and lack of self-consciousness. The streets were a solid block of enthusiastic crowd. And King Victor Emmanuel himself, whom I saw in the morning at the Palazza, came to see the show. They even turned him into a pageant, announcing his arrival by cannons, and an aeroplane flying over the town, dropping rose, green, and gold-coloured leaflets, like roseleaves, over the crowds. A bizarre contrast to the fourteenth century herald, dressed in white embroidered with the scarlet lily of Florence, who announced his presence from a balcony high up on the Palazza wall. Meanwhile when Florentines are tired of the world and its excitements, among the cypresses of Fiesole, two miles away, and hundreds of feet above Florence, is a Franciscan convent, built on the site of a Roman fortress—the most restful and beautiful of places where little dark-eyed monks flit about the shadowed cloisters and gardens, blazing with autumn flowers, and where in the church there is a charming altar by Mino da Fiesole and a Giotto fresco and pots of fresh flowers before the images.

Also, here one eats figs and peaches and rolls and salads and ices and coffee and lovely little cream cakes, and I *never* want to see cold beef again.

Much love,

CELIA.

Hotel Giotto,
Assisi, October, 2nd, 1921.

ROSALIND DEAR,

I've just come back from a steep and stony walk up the hillside to St. Francis's hermitage monastery of the Carceri. It is only about three miles from Assisi, but the road goes in hairpin turns up the side of a hill, with holm oaks above and olive groves below, and a wide panorama of the Umbrian plain—at least I suppose it's the Umbrian plain, but one is never sure of things like that, any more than one is sure of Wessex or the Hill Towns of Italy. I have been in both without knowing it. To keep us company on the way there, were occasional peasant women, in blue petticoats rolled round their hips, and portly baskets of washing cleverly balanced on their heads. Or sometimes a farmer—very fat, on a thin brown donkey—came ambling by, and once, a curly-headed baby with two great dogs. But mostly there are only little creatures—green and brown lizards and scarlet and blue grasshoppers, and butterflies of every colour. After walking up and up for about an hour, we suddenly turned a corner of the road and came upon a deep ravine, very dark and green and quiet, wooded thickly with holm oaks and spanned at the narrow end with an arched stone bridge where St. Francis stood to bless the birds. The monastery itself consists of a series of cells of irregular shape and size, cut out of the solid rock; but St. Francis was a sensible man, besides being a good one, for he chose his hermitage at a place just where the head of the ravine opens out, and each window looks down a long vista of oaks to the plain below, and across the plain to the Appenines.

We were shown round by a charming little friar. Incidentally, all Franciscan friars seem to be small. I do not know whether the humility of their founder has imbued them with a delicate kind of physical shrinkage, or whether the Franciscan life does not appeal to men of large stature. He talked to us all the time in slow, simple Italian, and was easy enough to understand. We saw the chapels and oratories, and descended some steps to an underground passage that emerged in the forest on the hillside, near a grotto where Francis is supposed to have wrestled with the devil. Not a bad place to wrestle in either, for there are trees all round and moss on the rocks and little mauve cyclamen growing out of the crevices. In the spring, our friar told us, the place is a mass of orchids, crocuses, snow-drops and primroses. They all seem to grow together here. In fact, in a cottage garden yesterday, Vera found chrysan-themums and crocuses growing together in defiance of all seasons.

Assisi is just now crowded with pilgrims for the Feast of St. Francis. Our hotel is so full that we are feeding in the reading-room and other guests in the entrance hall, as the dining-room is completely occupied by priests and friars, who talk at a tremendous rate and seem to enjoy their holiday immensely.

To-morrow we go on to Rome, but our great difficulty is to extract any information about trains, etc., from these citizens of Assisi, who are completely obsessed with their festa and have little time to waste on eccentric young

Inglese. They all seem to think us very young and inexperienced. The Italians are charming and fatherly. The tourists, English and American, very patronising, but we have discovered a lovely way of keeping off tiresome and well-intentioned old ladies, who will insist upon giving us volumes of gratuitous information. We wait till one has told us how "interesting" a certain place is and what we ought to see, and why, and inquired whether we have friends waiting for us, and whether we have had any difficulty with our digestions over Italian food. Then we turn to one another, and start talking quietly and impressively about my forthcoming lectures on Medieval Personalities—and with startling suddenness, the ladies "fold up their tents like the Arabs and silently steal away."

Much love,

CELIA.

Bainesse,
Cottingham,
E. Yorks, October 23rd., 1921.

ROSALIND DEAR,

It's so cold in England! I had no idea what winter was like. Why is it that where the sun shines and the rivers are warm and the grass is as cosy as a feather bed, one forgets entirely the meaning of an English October? There was I, basking among the roses and lizards of the Forum, with the marble ladies in the garden so warm one might watch for their breathing, and another day—two days or three pass, and here am I in Cottingham, with a nose as red as the pomegranates in Signora Friscio's basket—she who sits at the corner of the Via Victor Emmanuel II.—and my hands are purple as the border of a Cæsar's toga.

Well, well, there are always fires and hot-water bottles and my fur coat to gladden the heart of man!

I'm off again to-morrow though. On my way through London I spent two mornings making inquiries about

64

South Russia at the War Office and the Foreign Office, which have led to the receipt of a letter on my arrival here, asking me to take George's brother—the one who is Russian professor at Newcastle University—for an interview with a secret service agent, who is going to Constantinople, and from there can make further investigations about George[1]. It's a wild-goose chase, of course. But wilder chases have found geese, and, as our goose is rather precious, it is worth the chasing. At least it takes away that horribly impotent feeling that comes of sitting still and doing nothing, and it would be so much better to learn that he had been shot in the first instance, than for Edith to sit waiting, apprehensive of every shadow that crosses the doorway, of every voice that echoes from the road. I believe, even if we did get George home, he would be a nervous wreck. I fear that to learn he was dead would be the least of her sorrow. Men don't go through two years of hell and return unscathed. But even if it leads to greater suffering for her, we must do something. His brothers seem willing to sit down and wait. I can't. She has suffered enough. I want her to learn he is dead, have one good weep, and then be at peace. Because you can be at peace when a man is dead, as you never can when he is captive, or still more, when he is on your hands a daily and hourly anxiety and sorrow. But I have a queer feeling that he is alive, and that we shall find him.

Well, well, this is dismal writing. Probably because my nose is red, my thoughts are depressing. In another half-hour I shall be in front of the drawing-room fire, thawing my bones back to liveliness and my thoughts to humour. By the time you get this letter, I shall be in some crazy seventh heaven of delight over some trivial pleasure. I always am bounding up and down, but the ups have it by a long way, because the grass is so green, and the sun so kind and the people of the world so infinitely dear—among

[1]Husband of Winifred's adopted sister. "Missing" in Russia after the post-war campaign.

whom you are one of the dearest, Sweet Coz, although I do tease you with my long and gloomy letters.

Do you know a Mrs. Green who was in charge of one department of the Y.W.C.A. in France? I have rashly undertaken to introduce her to a Cottingham audience at a public meeting next week. My speaking never was exactly fluent, but as I have promised to lecture next time, I daren't refuse any opportunity to get into practice.

I've just got hold of *The Anchor*, by Michael Sadler. *Privilege* was good. Have you read *The Romantic*, by May Sinclair? Not very pleasant, but distinctly clever—a study of cowardice. She spoilt it by introducing an exceptional physical explanation. An explanation of cowardice is needed, that has no structural, but only a nervous significance.

Much love, dearest Coz,

Yours,

CELIA.

Bainesse,
Cottingham,
E. Yorks, November 6th, 1921.

ROSALIND DEAR,

Thank you so much for your letter this week dated October 11th, 1921. I give you the dates in this business-like manner, because it is as well to know which I have received last. I was so glad to have it, and glad beyond everything that in H. you have found at last a congenial companion in Africa. I have feared so often from the tone of your letters that you have been very lonely there. Every one seemed either so old or so young—too old to enjoy the things which you enjoy, and to have any enthusiasm or vitality left, or too young for real companionship. I may be maligning them, of course, but that is what it sounded like. And she sounds splendid and will be so glad to have you too. I know what it is like to go to a strange place thinking that I should find no one at the end of it for companionship at

66

all—and, at the end of my journey, to meet you. So I can sympathise with E. and congratulate her on her wise choice of a stopping place in South Africa. To think that my letters have been any sort of comfort or joy to you is a great pride. I only wish they had been more adequate.

Vera has just sent me the review of an undergraduate's novel about Oxford life. The review is written by Rose Macaulay, and when I read it I almost hope that I never shall publish a novel for fear it should deserve criticism like that. I pass it on to you. I fear that one may be the unfortunate possessor of "the artless unpointed style of those under twenty-five years of age." Also I may lack cynical detachment. My one hope for salvation is that the story is not about myself, and that, if my heroine is my ideal for myself, then heaven help me! Although she is really a much nicer person than I am, she is so very far from an ideal of any kind, and only on the very last page do I say good-bye to her with a sort of hope that she may have learnt a little sense from her tribulations, and if not common sense, then perhaps a little of that most uncommon sense—a sense of humour. But I can't help being a little worried by style, for when I read an ill-written book by some one else, its tediousness infuriates me, while a crisp, invigorating or delicate and musical style gives me even more satisfaction than a good story. Have you read *Quiet Interior*, by E. B. C. Jones? The story, like to-night's pancakes, is naught, but the mustard—in other words, the style—is good. The word-pictures are pricked out as clearly and finely as the illuminated borders of a fifteenth century missal.

Isn't this a deplorable pen? But the tragedy at present overshadowing my life is that I have broken my fountain pen, and crossed my one relief nib, and life without a pen is almost unlivable to me. That's why I curse the Fates so heartily for not endowing me with prettier writing—or even more moral writing for, according to all experts, mine denotes a most slack and self-indulgent character!

On Friday I went to a dance in Cottingham, and there

67

met a little dark man with a moustache called Barnes, who danced most particularly well. After a foxtrot, we sat talking, and for want of something better to say, he remarked, "I don't see why men should be so handicapped in dancing, having to wear these stiff leather shoes. Now girls can get beautifully soft things of satin and brocade. No wonder they dance easily." I said, "Oh, but you know it's quite possible for girls to dance in laced leather shoes." "Have you ever tried it?" "Yes, I used to when I was in the Waacs, and after the Armistice we had lots of dances and I used to wear the ordinary brown shoes belonging to my uniform." "Where were you in the Waacs? Were you in France?" "Yes, I was near Abbeville." "What, you never were out in a little camp somewhere along the Rouen road, where a Waac administrator used to ask our men out to dance in a hut?" "Do you mean Huchenneville?" "Yes, an administrator with a Scots name, and very jolly dances— the spring of 1919." And then the next dance struck up and my partner bore me away before he told me his regiment or anything. I don't even know if he was English or an Aussie. Do you remember him? Small, dark, moustached, beautiful dancer, name Barnes? I don't, and he did not know me, but there's no other camp about eight kilos out of Abbeville along the Rouen road that gave dances in a hut in the spring of 1919, and had an administrator with a Scots name, is there? I must meet that man again and elucidate the mystery.

It's time I got to work. I have a lecture to prepare about St. Francis of Assisi.

Au revoir, my dearest Rosalind, and much love,

From

CELIA.

ROSALIND DEAR,

They say it is bad manners to type one's letters, but I want to get this new wheel into running order, so perhaps you will excuse this temporary lapse of good behaviour. Personally, if any of my correspondents wrote as badly as I do, I should be only too pleased for them to adopt some method of communication which did not necessitate my struggles with their calligraphy. Did you know—but of course you would—that you can spell calligraphy with one L or two? I didn't until I looked it up this minute. I have adopted the family dictionary, because I considered that my need of guidance was greater than that of my parents who continually say they can't think why I spell so badly.

The great event of this week has been a sort of drawing-room meeting, given in the village schoolroom, but called drawing-room as far as I can gather because one has tea at it, in aid of the Y.W.C.A. When you were in the W.A.A.C.'s did you ever come across a Mrs. Green? She was for a time U.A. at Calais, and after that in command of 500 girls on the east coast. A really charming person, she is now finance secretary for the Y.W. and goes about speaking in favour of it and asking for subscriptions. I had to speak first, and say something about the work of the Y.W.C.A. during the war, and then she spoke about its work to-day. Evidently it is in great financial straits. Then we gave tea to sixty odd ladies. (I don't mean that the ladies were particularly odd. The "odd" refers to the number.) We made all the buns and cakes ourselves for the tea, so it was quite like a Huchenneville dance again.

I'm still at the same work, preparing my lectures, and writing the novel. The latter is a very slow job. For days I get stuck and can't get on at all, then I have a real rush and write a whole chapter at a sitting, and the next day it all comes out and I have to start all over again. Which takes time. However, I suppose it will get done some day.

Mrs. Green asked me if I would lecture to the girls' clubs connected with the Y.W. when I get to London. I'd like to if I have time, but I must do some paid work, and with my teaching and writing I shall be pretty busy. But I should like to do something with a more immediate justification than writing. I'm always terrified of being no good in the end, or else of being knocked down at a street crossing before I have made any justification of my existence. I suppose that it is terribly egoistical cowardice, but life has been so kind to me I should be too unutterably mean if I never did anything in return, and sitting at a table writing stories is so pleasant—although I find it jolly hard work, not having been gifted with a natural, flowing style— that I sometimes wonder whether it isn't just a form of shirking.

I heard rather a pretty story the other day:

TEACHER: Now, children, I want you to understand the different uses of our members. The eyes were given to see with, the nose to smell with, the feet to walk with.

TOMMY: Boo-hoo, I guess I was made all wrong then, 'cause my nose runs, and my feet smell.

With which refined and fragrant anecdote, dear Rosalind, I will say au revoir.

With much love from

CELIA.

Bainesse,
Cottingham,
E. Yorks, Nov. 20th.

MY DEAREST ROSALIND,

I've just been seeing again the old mare I used to ride at Rudstone. A retired lawyer living in Cottingham has bought her, and rides her sedately for about six miles a day, with a groom following at a discreet distance. The doctor has

70

ordered a little equestrian exercise for his health, and he seems quite to enjoy it. It's a splendid home for my old girl, though she is degraded in her rank. I called her "Good Queen Bess," but he only calls her "Pretty Peggy"! Talking about Good Queen Bess, Clemence Dane has just produced a new play called *Will Shakespeare*, in which the queen figures rather largely, and, I gather, finely; but the critics are very much down on the author for playing havoc with history, and making her "Will" kill Marlow in a tavern brawl, be tricked into marrying Ann Hathaway while loving another woman, and write *As You Like It* at Queen Elizabeth's command, shut up in a chamber till he has completed a play. I gather there are yet other inventions which are possibly not convincing but must at least be interesting. What a strange personality that woman must have—artist, actress, schoolteacher, novelist and finally playwright. Well, she has got her success at last, for, even if the critics damn her play, the public will flock to see the damned, especially since it follows such a brilliant success as *The Bill of Divorcement*. That, by the way, is still running.

This week has been quite peaceful. Most days I have been working. I am reading for a lecture on Leonardo da Vinci, and find the reading so attractive I cannot bring myself to abandon it, and try to reduce so many delightful days of study into the narrow compass of a fifty-minutes' lecture to rather unintelligent children. I don't know if I'm right, but I'm treating the children, or rather shall treat them, as though they were of a higher rather than a lower average of intelligence. When I was at school, I loathed being talked down to, and it strikes me that a child of fourteen is as capable of understanding any idea as the same person of forty, provided only that unfamiliar words and figures are not used. Is that true? I know how irritated I used to be with the forced simplicity of some of the lessons in school, when I knew that, by exacting from us a little more attention and thought, the teachers could have presented a far more interesting and useful lesson. Do you know

Merejkowski's *Forerunner*? It is a most fascinating picture of fifteenth century Italy, with Leonardo as the chief figure, but Savonarola, Ludovico Sforza, Beatrice d'Este, Machiavelli, Cæsar Borgia, Mona Lisa Gioconda, Andrea Soljano, and all the others coming in. What always amuses me in a historical novel is the way in which all famous people of the day meet one another so conveniently. Have you ever read Beerbohm's *Savonarola*? It's the funniest skit on that sort of thing that I have ever come across.

I'm going up to Oxford for my Degree on the thirtieth, and mother and father are motoring up too. It will be rather fun, I think, though the actual degree giving is dull enough. When you come to England, you'll have to take yours. It will be nice seeing Miss Penrose and Miss Clarke and every one, though.

Mother is very well, but is having one of the occasional days in bed that really do her so much good. She went out with daddy to a dinner party last night—a very rare thing for her. She works so hard these days, she has little time or energy left for social amusements, though occasionally when she comes in from Bridlington she plays a little bridge. Last night she actually won three halfpennies at nap!

How are you, and what are you doing? I like to think of you and Miss H. scampering about on "wild horses." I expect you are a splendid cavalier now. I have almost forgotten how to ride, but it's just as well, for I see no immediate prospect of being able to do any. In England it is so fearfully costly now, and the horses are all such bags of bones, or bumping chargers. All the best ones, like the men, seem to have gone to the wars and not returned, or have come back crocks, or emigrated on their return.

Well, my dear, au revoir. Take care of yourself, sweet Rosalind, and receive this letter with much love.

From

CELIA.

10, Oakwood Court,
Kensington, W.14, Dec., 3rd, 1921.

My Dearest Rosalind,

I am staying here, after having been at Oxford to get my Degree, and am now seeking posts for next term and a flat in which to live. So far, only one post has materialised—the Italian lectures at St. Monica's. I am to receive the noble sum of £15 15s. for six lectures. I call that good. Now I am seeking odd classes and private pupils to pay my board and lodgings.

Talking of board and lodgings, we have been consistently told that the latter are almost impossible to acquire, especially in the Bloomsbury neighbourhood, where we must be in order to read at the Museum. Yesterday morning I started off at ten-thirty to look for a flat, rooms, anything at all, where Vera and I could live and move and have our being when neither teaching nor reading. I went to an agent, who seemed unaware of the existence of anything less magnificent than an eight-guinea "mansion"; and offered me one dirty, horrid address in Lamb's Conduit Street, at which, when I arrived, there was no one to open the door. Then, in despair, I remembered that once, when we had been house hunting, we saw a very nice landlady in a house called either Hesperides or Olympus or something equally highfalutin', and that the house was set behind a garden wall, with two trees and three King Charles puppies, and that it was somewhere near the British Museum. Of course, in anything less than a fairy tale, my three puppies and two trees and vague recollection of a name would have been a somewhat scanty direction; but I found a familiar street, and followed my nose, which is always crooked, until I came to a house set behind a garden wall, with two trees, and on the door was written "Elysium." So I knew I was all right. Then I rang the bell, and the kind landlady came, and though I could not remember her name, and she had forgotten mine, she remembered my face and how much I had liked the dogs, and we resumed our friendship. Of course, her own house, which

73

is the unique kind of perfect lodgings, was, as ever, full, but she sent me to "a Mrs. Langley, who has a cousin, who has a house, which is sometimes let to students," and I went and saw Mrs. Langley, and the cousin, and the house, and got home in time for tea, with a beautiful little flatlette, made out of a large studio, partitioned in dark-brown wood, with creamish walls, practically in my pocket. It opens out of a house, let off in bedsitting-rooms to students, and costs us £2 12s. a week with light and hot water, and a nice, blue-eyed housekeeper, all thrown in. And I'm boring you with all these details because it is a fairy story, and these things do not happen in London. They are just magic. Only when you see a house with a name like Hesperides or Olympus, you know it is all right; even if you have no idea where it is, and the name is really Elysium.

Next week is a sale for the Somerville Endowment Fund, in the house of Lady Norman. We are selling books and Christmas presents, and various celebrities are coming. Hugh Walpole is going to open it; Rose Macaulay is selling books, Cathleen Nesbitt is helping at the fancy stall, and H. A. L. Fisher's daughter of ten years old, Mary, has a bran tub. Vera is helping Rose Macaulay, and I am helping with the bran tub. All the S.C.R. who can leave Somerville are coming, and every one who is any one will be there. I wish you could come, though I expect you have seen enough bazaars.

Have you been riding? I saw a woman to-day, going down to the park, on a charming bay mare, dressed in a khaki habit. (The lady, not the mare.) She was really riding rather beautifully, and that is a rare sight in town.

Au revoir and much love.

CELIA.

Bainesse,
Cottingham,
E. Yorks, December 11th, 1921.

MY DEAREST ROSALIND,

Pugh and Newman have got their passages booked for April some time ago, so they will be all right. I am going to see them both when I go to London on the twenty-ninth. I'm glad Dickson will keep an eye on them. It is a daring enterprise, but so is life of any kind, don't you think? Personally, I believe it is far more perilous to stay at home than to go abroad and try new fields. I hope your tawny beads and *The Lee Shore* arrive. I am sending a few more magazines. I see that Walter de la Mare has published a new volume of poems. I'll try and get the cutting for you from the *Observer*, when my family have finished with it. Father reads the sport sheets and advertisements, Grace, the court news, Edith the politics and drama, mother everything in turn and I the reviews. So it gets well handled. I try to read the politics too, because, what with Ireland and the Washington Conference, life is rather exciting just now. But I wish papers would publish a plain list of facts, and leave the arguments to people who have an inclination for them. One grows so weary of polemics. I think Garvin is as impartial as any one; but that may be because I like his daughter. It is terribly difficult not to be personal, and Viola Garvin has dark, wistful eyes with purple shadows below, and a white, wedge-shaped face, with a very scarlet mouth splashed on to it, and black, bobbed hair that waves round her like a dark angel's halo. And she walks with a limp, and has a sweet, ironical voice, and overworks herself passionately over everything she does; so that when I read Garvin's articles, I see Viola's heavy eyes and soft, curling smile across the pages, and think that a man with such a daughter must be rather nice. Probably he's very ordinary really.

I spent last Wednesday in most distinguished society. Somerville gave a bazaar at the Corner House, Cowley

Street, Westminster, lent by Lady Norman. It is a most fascinating house. The drawing-room, where we had most of the stalls, is all fifteenth century Italian. The walls are lined with exquisite leather, gilded and stamped with a pattern of leaves and flowers, in gold and dark, dim reds and browns. The furniture is all dusky carving and leather-work; and there are high, narrow windows with small panes.

I spent the day before helping Vera and Rose Macaulay to arrange the book-stall. Weren't you at college with Rose Macaulay? She is charming to work with. The kind of person who refuses to be a figurehead, and suddenly bursts out with, "I say, why aren't you sitting down? You'll be dead tired standing." Most Olympians don't think. . . . Then, at the bazaar itself were Hugh Walpole and J. D. Beresford and Mrs. H. A. L. Fisher, complete with husband and daughter, and Lady Rhondda and a few others. Hugh Walpole is large and fair and jolly, not at all like the person who wrote *The Dark Forest* and *Fortitude*. I talked to him, and tried to sell him calendars and window wedges, and he was very clumsy and knocked things off the stall, so he had to make friends, and laughed a good deal, and said that Oxford women weren't half as alarming as he had been led to believe.

You ask about my writing—— Well, it goes on slowly and it's very bad. I don't suppose I shall try to publish it. But it is sometimes great fun to do. Last night my hero and heroine met for the first time. They meet on a country road, when the heroine's pony gets a stone in its shoe, and the hero, for various reasons, is sick on the road. I think, at least, that this is original. In parts, it is almost amusing.

Much love, my Rosalind.

CELIA.

76

Bainesse,
Cottingham,
E. Yorks, December 18th, 1921.

ROSALIND DEAR,

I've got your letter now dated November 22nd, 1921 (How business-like that sounds—"Dear Madam—yours of the 22nd inst. to hand.") and am so glad you like the beads. They came from a small, crowded shop, opening on to the Piazza San Marco, where a bent, Jewish man sold all day strings of coral and amethyst, ivory images, wrought caskets of silver filigree, and mosaics of gold and blue and vermilion—a fascinating shop where the walls were hung with swaying chains of glass and china beads that tinkled in the wind. They will have come from strange places, and gone to yet stranger lands, when they journey with you perhaps to Hermanus (what a name!) up in the wilds of Africa.

You sounded very strenuous in November, with 220 three-hour papers; but now I imagine you are on your journey, or luxuriating at your £5 5s. hotel. I'm afraid the prices are about like that at home. The little country hotel at Boars Hill, where we went to for a week-end sometimes from Oxford, was fifteen shillings a day, and with a good many extras. All living is rather dear, though here clothes and things are cheaper than they were.

I am glad about H. She sounds so comforting and stable. I'm glad you have some one to drink morning tea with and to accompany you when you canter on the hard roads. There were hounds here on Friday. Uncle Tom rode with them on a beautiful bay horse, very powerful and uncomfortable it looked. They had a great run and killed in the dining-room of Raywell Sanatorium for tubercular discharged soldiers. There never was such excitement in the sanatorium.

May you really come home next November? Oh, I do hope I'm in England then. I may have gone to Vienna but I think not. It would be so nice to see you. I have my little flat in London, and you must come here.

Here we are in a whirl for Christmas—so many parcels to go away, so much to get ready. Two homeless Australians are coming for Christmas. Last year we had Australians too—very civilised ones. One of these is funny. He writes funny letters. I hope he won't be too funny when he comes. I fear egg-coloured hair and a taste for puns.

I am reading *International Relations* before I do my book, and writing *Anderby Wold*. Bits of *Anderby Wold* are very bad; but I read some of it aloud last night to Vera, who is staying here, and she said bits are beautiful. She's a very critical person, and doesn't usually like novels about places, so that's a lot for her to say. There's a description of a Christmas tree being slowly dressed up—and a morning on the wolds after a storm that are rather nice. I'm much better with the places than the people. As soon as I do soliloquies I run fearfully to seed—and Yorkshire people never talk much. It's trying.

Yesterday Father took us for a motor run. It was such a lovely afternoon we just had to hire a car and go. There was a flood in Hull in the evening—not bad, but the tide rose over the dockside and swept, knee-deep, up several of the busy, dockside streets. It caused a sensation among the Saturday evening crowd.

I'm reading all about the evolution of diplomacy, and treaties, and international law. It is very engrossing. It makes the war a much more comprehensive thing. You can't get away from it here at all—so much unemployment —so many placards: "This we did for our country. Thus is it repaying us," and such memories to heal. Well, I dare say we'll get over it. And Ireland, after this stressful time, seems to be finding settlement, but with much bitterness on both sides. One wonders if it could have been prevented— perhaps not. We are not yet so very tolerant or civilised.

Au revoir, dearest Rosalind. Always much love.

CELIA.

It's no use wishing you a happy Christmas, my dearest Rosalind, for by the time that this letter reaches you, the decorations will be pulled down, the berries fallen from the mistletoe, and the bones of the turkey will have long ago vanished from the stockpot. Still, this is Christmas Day, and whatever nuisance it may be, and however the promptitudes of "grown-up-ness" and twentieth century anti-sentimentalism may lead us to declare our boredom with the whole darned affair, we did dance round a Christmas tree last night and had a pudding ablaze, and parcels in a fishpond for us all, and there are to be sausages for breakfast. Also we have two "lonely Aussies" staying here. Their names are Bladon and Wilson. Bladon is tall and clean shaven and talkative, with lots of gold in his teeth that makes his smile more twinkly than it is by nature. Wilson is shorter, with a moustache and beautiful eyes. He plays the violin—very out of tune, bless 'im—and mother loves him dearly.

Later: My optimism was unjustified. There were no sausages for breakfast! But still I've had lots of lovely presents. Mother has given me some lovely old blue china plates and a Wedgwood dish, with the most perfectly carved flowers on it and little Greek men and maidens dancing—a most delicate and elegant thing—a real joy. Last night we had a wild party and played "nap" with nuts for counters. And to-day we are going to have round games. The maids had a party too, last night, and I don't know who made the most noise. At twelve o'clock we started to wash up—just like Huchenneville days. We had the house decorated too, with holly and mistletoe and Margaret's toys which, as usual, make the whole place like a menagerie. But she is blissfully happy to-day, absorbed in the contemplation of her new dolls' house, which ought really to be spelled with capital letters, and is certainly one of the world's wonders. It has four rooms, each with a curtained window and appropriate furniture, and lots of exciting little deedaws (dolls, in other words. Margaret has her own vocabulary). At present both the Australians have been commandeered to admire its beauties, and Grace and I have a few moments respite for letters. But such a lot of letters, Rosalind, and so little time. And treaties and *Anderby* calling me vainly to read and write and get about the day's business.

The new Hugh Walpole is out, *The Young Enchanted*, continuing the story of Peter Westcott from *Fortitude*, and Henry and Millicent Trenchard from *The Green Mirror*. A most charming book—very fresh and romantic, with occasional serious passages full of rather fine stuff. I do like that man. I am sure he must be as nice as his books. Surely no one could write books nicer than themselves. It's all very well to say an author may put his best into books, and leave his personality rotten. But a man is what his best is. There's no means of putting it here or there, or dividing it between Sundays and weekdays, work or play.

Where are you among your hills? I'm always meaning to look Hermanus out on the map. I will this afternoon, and send you a greeting there. I expect you are weary after so many papers and things to correct. It will be a holiday well earned and, I hope, very pleasant.

The garden is full of sunlight, and there's a sort of spring feeling in the air, quite wrong for Christmas. I must go out, and see what the day is like, and possibly listen to the Salvation Army band up the village. It is a cheerful band— very full of blow and go. And well patronised by Cottingham, which has few excitements.

Au revoir, my Rosalind. There's a wee hanky to blow your nose on off our Christmas tree.

From

CELIA—with love.

1922

ROSALIND DEAR,

As you see, this is from my new address. It is a queer little place. Do you know Doughty Street? It must have been near where you sometimes were when you worked at the university. It is a broad road, with houses behind iron railings down each side; a road that rises towards each end, to a square and trees, and open spaces. The houses all look very grave and sedate. It is difficult to imagine frivolous people running up the steps in silk stockings, or limousines with actresses standing outside the door. Sometimes, I believe, there are silk stockings, and quite a considerable amount of frivolity, because the place is chiefly inhabited by London University students, who are, I believe and you know, on occasions, most frivolous. There are some living here at 52 Doughty Street. I have not seen them yet, because Vera and I let ourselves in and out of the front door with our latch keys and walk straight along the passage to our own little front door, that has a green curtain hanging across it. Inside, it all really looks charming now. We have a hall mantelpiece with some blue Spode plates which mother gave me, and an old brass candlestick, and my polished shell-case, and four blue pots from Malta, that Vera brought, and my blue mug from the Huchenneville estaminet. I think it looks beautiful; but I dare say people could criticise it.

Does all this bore you? You've had a little flat too, and probably feel very blasé over the delights of our first house-keeping. You know quite well the triumph of entering the ironware department of Shoolbred's and ordering an enamel basin for the kitchen sink, with the air of a housewife of fifty—and of keeping your glove on so that the shopwalker shall not notice the absence of a wedding ring. And perhaps you know Theobald's Road, where one has lunch, and where there are restaurants to suit every taste, from the Stewed Eels and Tripe shop at the corner, to Tibbald's Restaurant, with placards by "Fish" and art-blue tablecloths, and an earl's great niece at the cash-desk. There are also several pawnshops, and a second-hand furniture dealer's where one can hunt for genuine antique fire-screens and pewter pint mugs (made in Manchester, 1921). Still, it is a very nice street, though a lady whom I met at a tea party yesterday called it a "hole." That was an awful lie. It is raised rather than sunk, from its vicinity, and is more like a ridge than a hole; besides which, it has many very "un-holish" fascinations.

I suppose you are back now from your holidays—or not yet? New Year's Day was queer. We forgot New Year's Eve until twelve o'clock, when the sirens woke us, sounding the "All Clear" through London. Rather a charming idea, that. The "All Clear" for 1922—1921 gone. Peace to its ashes! It was quite a pleasant year. A little turbulent, what with Ireland and India, and the squabbles about the Pacific, and Studdart Kennedy saying that the world's no better for the war, and England is no place for heroes to live in, and Lloyd George saying that England is the land of the free, and therefore we must do something quickly about Ireland to prevent people thinking us a little tyrannical, and the out-of-work men tramping about the street under banners, and the R.38 smashing up in the Humber, and people dreaming again for a moment of German spies. Still, that's over. And Mr. Bottomley has resigned from the editorship of *John Bull*, and Dail Eirean is going to meet again after the New Year, and the Prince is spreading smiles (we hope) over India, and Prebendary Gough declares that morning's at seven, and all's well with the world—so I suppose it is.

Anyway, here's good luck to you and a speedy holiday to England, where I can once more see you.

Au revoir, and a happy New Year—With love from
CELIA.

84

ROSALIND DEAR,

My brain and tongue both feel rather exhausted, as I have spent the morning cleaning our kitchen—the stimulus to this unwonted energy being a whole new tin of Vim—and simultaneously conducting with Vera a most heated discussion upon "What is individualism?" She has to coach a candidate for an entrance examination at L.M.H. and, having set her an essay on "The Age of Elizabeth was the age of Individualism," proceeded to thrash out her coaching first, as usual, over the O-Cedar mop and dusters. But, also as usual, we drifted from political systems and revolts against authority into the social sense of primitive man and, having ransacked the ages for examples of individualism, we wound up, just before lunch time, having achieved nothing except the remarkable conclusion that we both started our arguments from the standpoints of entirely different definitions, and had better leave the subject alone for the present! However, intellectual conflict is a wonderful galvaniser of physical activity, and the flat shines like a new pin. (By the way, why a new pin? Why not an old one? Sometimes they shine like anything. You should see them on the pavements in Theobald's Road, when I want to pick them up for luck, and refrain from a sense of social dignity!)

The novel is nearly finished—the first draft, I mean. I am on the last chapter. Afterwards there must be polishing, and repolishing, and dividing of chapters—mine always straggle out too long—and lots of other business. The end is rather sad; but then, it has to be. And my heroine, being a quite good but very limited woman, is very irritating. But then again, having had her upbringing, she would be. I only hope my readers—if ever I have any—won't think she is meant to be perfect. I rather dislike her myself, but like *Yellow Dog Dingo*, she turned out like what she was—"She had to." Don't you love the *Just So Stories?* About the elephant's trunk, and the cat that walked in the wet, wild woods, waving his wet, wild tail, and the kangaroo that wanted to be quite different from every one else and tremendously run after by four o'clock in the afternoon? We have a cat that walks here, who is very wild, though not wet, being a person of most fastidious habits. She walks along the partitions of our cubicles at night, and glares down upon us with amber eyes as large as millwheels, like the dog in *The Tinder Box*. She is black but comely, and very temperamental, with an embittered attitude towards life in general, and an inveterate antipathy to shoe-strings.

I am living quite peacefully, no more jobs yet. I fear this term will have to pass, but next term I shall be able to say I have "experience," and that may help. Otherwise I write and learn German, mornings and evenings, and in the afternoons walk, or sit in Clare Leighton's studio and watch my portrait growing. Clare is a large, lovely person, with heavy masses of straight brown hair that falls each side of her round, dimpled face, and is gathered into an untidy bun at the back of her neck. On the rare occasions when she is not carrying a paint brush between her teeth, she has a most ingratiating smile that sets all her dimples twinkling. She generally has a smudge of paint across her face, and her overall is always buttonless; but she is most orderly and thorough about her work, and has a friendly and tolerant disposition, a gift of making charming and ingenuous generalisations, and a most comfortable and refreshing personality. When I sit to be painted, she quotes yards of W. H. Davis and other modern poets of the countryside, and whistles like a blackbird.

I am sending you some *Time and Tides*. The annotations in the most modern copy are mother's. She sent it on to me.

I hope that all is peaceful with you, and that you are feeling better for your holiday, after all those hundreds of examination papers.

Au revoir, and much love,

CELIA.

86

ROSALIND DEAR,

Your letter sounds so cheerfully warm. Christmas beetles humming, and quivering air, and shower baths in the corridor, while here I sit, in an arm-chair over the gas stove, toasting my toes and drinking hot milk, while I wait for the kettle to boil for our hot-water bottle. Still, it's warmer than it has been; and yesterday evening Vera and I went for a walk after tea across Cannon Street Bridge and passed four flower shops golden with daffodils and jonquils, and heard all St. Paul's singing with starlings. I've never heard so many starlings as there are down in the city on a Saturday evening. We passed one quite little tree, with every branch thick laden, as though it had suddenly sprung into singing leaves—but the leaves chattered, and flew away, and flew backwards and forwards before they alighted again on the branches. One man was standing watching it as we went; when we came back he was still there, standing on the pavement with his hat on the back of his head, watching the starlings.

I'm sorry Africa's so unsettled. It must be uncomfortable for any loyalists living there. All the same, if the majority in the country want to separate from the British Empire, I think they ought to go. The day of imperialism is passed. I heard its curfew sound when the guns startled the pigeons in Huchenneville orchard on Armistice day. Imperialism is really nothing more than dynamic and aggressive nationality. Nationality, patriotism—these were good things and noble things. I'm not sure that at one time they weren't two of the finest things in the world. But, like many other good things, they were only a stage in the development of man's social consciousness. Man may be, as Aristotle says, a political animal, but he is also endowed with sufficient self-love to make his duty to his neighbour the subject of a divine commandment, not a natural instinct. In order to acquire a trained social instinct—which you can call altruism or public spirit or whatever you like—he had to be educated in co-operation. And this education began, like all other branches, in a narrow way, by attachments first to an intimately connected body of people in the family, then from the family to the tribe, from them to the punitive tribal king, and so through the state, in all its varying forms from city to empire, till at last it embraced all people of the same race, living under the same rule: in other words, nationality. But directly the evolution of nationality was accomplished, the nations suffered from swelled heads—imperialism—and imperialism went to Germany's head worst of all, and the result was the war. What we want now is the transition to a still wider sphere of international co-operation, where empires don't matter, and patriotism becomes parochial, and the service of mankind at large is the only consideration.

Well, after this long dissertation (it's all right, I'm not going to begin again) I'll tell you some news, if I have any. By the way, I don't suppose you'll be able to read the last two pages. They were written in bed last night, much to the detriment of my calligraphy.

Sir Ernest Shackleton, the Pope and Lord Bryce are dead. Three fine men in very diverse ways. Peace to their souls. The Pope seems to have struggled hard in a very difficult position. Amazing, isn't it, that in spite of so-called modern enlightenment we are still capable of being priest-ridden? What dark shadows of the primeval forests still hang about our minds! Mithras, Balder, Apollo—gods of light and beauty, at war with gods of darkness and horror—Satans—and the priest, the medicine man, with his charms and incantations to keep the dread thing from us. Neither Shelley, nor Darwin, nor H. G. Wells can quite whistle away the phantoms.

I went to a real dinner party on Saturday night, in a wonderful flat over Harrods. We had many amazing courses, and dessert off gold and crystal plates. And I wore a lovely evening frock—black lace with a steel-blue sash—and caught a stiff neck—and last night cooked and ate eggs and bacon, rejoicing. It's lovely to live in the lap of luxury—for three hours.

I must go, it's ten to ten, and I must try to be at the British Museum by ten. I read there every morning now from ten to one. I like it, in spite of the stuffiness and gloom. There's a concentrated atmosphere that is rather attractive.

Grace has knitted me a sweet, blue woollen jumper and skirt. It cost eleven and ninepence and looks £10! It is the very softest blue, sort of grey, sea colour, with crochet edgings and little tassels at the waist. I feel such a dog.

Au revoir and much love,

CELIA.

The Studio,
52, Doughty Street, W.C.1,
February 5th, 1922.

ROSALIND DEAR,

Your letters are like windows opening into a strange continent, where white heifers strain against the yokes of ox-wagons, and perilous bays are alive with sharks, and savages with bare feet play bridge in wooden huts. They are beautifully warm and sunny windows, and pleasant to open on these cold days, when the streets are full of fog and mud, and the newspaper boys blow on their purple fingers; and we discuss whether the trouble of cleaning the studio after a coal fire isn't worth the warmth and comfort of sitting round it. I'd like to see your short hair. I'm not sure that it would not be rather beautiful in spite of all you say. What a pity you did not cut it earlier, when you were in the Waacs, and save yourself all those tangles at night. I remember how it used to fly out with electric sparks on frosty mornings. Mine is more mangy than ever, but I daren't cut it, because it looks so horrid when it's short, and it might never grow again.

I like your story. Why is it that women who do things for which they may be ostracised by society are nearly always so much finer than the perfectly decorous matrons? I don't believe that marriage in the ordinary, middle-class, comfortable way is really good for women. It seems to make them so complacent and dependant. Bernard Shaw says that marriage is all very well, but that it absolutely puts an end to the adventurous outlook on life. If one has a household and children, it's not easy to be anything but a housekeeper. I think it's better not to marry.

I haven't done anything very much since I saw you last. I read in the British Museum in the morning. After lunch I go out a-walking. After tea I correct my novel, and after supper I learn German—and that's all. This is occasionally varied by seeing people, by going in the afternoon to Clare Leighton's studio and having my portrait painted, or by visiting other friends. It's very quiet, but not at all dull— and then once a week I go to lecture at St. Monica's about Italian people in the Middle Ages.

All my family is coming to town for Princess Mary's wedding. They are quite excited about her engagement to a Yorkshire man. We know the Lascelles' agent at Harewood House very well, and I suppose they all feel a proprietary sentiment about their future neighbour.

Mrs. Brittain has given us a wonderful pink azalea for the flat. It stands on the side table in our sitting-room, and makes the whole place look lovely. We have put it in a pink and white and green bowl. All the streets are very full of women selling flowers—violets, jonquils, snowdrops and daffodils. They look so gay and spring-like.

My hands are better, but they hate the cold. One day I'm going to be rich enough to spend my winters in a warmer country—perhaps. I can't see myself ever being a financial success at anything very much though. I wish I were. There are such heaps of things one wants money for. A girl is coming to tea to-day who has just passed her Somerville Entrance Exam. She is thirty-three, and has been teaching ever since she left her convent school in Belgium. She has no degree and is a Roman Catholic. She became a Roman Catholic at the convent, where her parents sent her; but because, as the result of their plans for her education, she was converted, they have been horrid to her ever since. Dot went to earn her own living—working at very inferior schools because she was not specially qualified. Then when her father lost his money and her mother developed diabetes, she went home to nurse them. They were still horrid to her, so she went back to teach, and practically starved herself to pay an attendant to look after them. Now at last she has saved a little money, and passed her entrance exam for Somerville, and is hoping to realise the dream of her life by going to read history there. And she does not think she can afford to go to College. I wish I were a millionaire.

I am going to lunch with the Brittains to-day. They are very sweet to me, and treat me as if I belonged to their family. It's like having two families. They are having their Christmas turkey for lunch, because it never turned up on Christmas Day! So I must go and curl my hair in its honour.

Au revoir, Sweet Coz, and a good term to you.
                    With much love,
                              Ever your
                                        CELIA.

                              The Studio,
                    52, Doughty Street, W.C.1,
                              Feb. 10th, 1922.

ROSALIND DEAR,

I suppose you are back now in the middle of the term, and I hope you're having a pleasant one. The decorum of college donism must be rather strange after the savagery of bathing among the sharks. I do hope one of them didn't bite your toe or your nose off! You must come home whole in November. Will you come back for your holiday then? It would be lovely. I shall be back from Vienna then and in London again, if all goes well. It's so nice to be in London—the one place where one can see almost every one. It's so much nearer South Africa than Cottingham.

I've begun my lectures, too, and so far like them very much. It's a very well-behaved school, so the classes are easy to manage. All the girls have dark blue overalls, and neat pigtails. I take the top form for a class just after the lecture. There was one girl who struck me as being rather particularly intelligent, so I asked her a good many questions, and only after the class was over discovered it was the History mistress! She was very young, and had on a dark blue dress which just matched the overalls, and had attended my class as a kind of politeness—also, I suppose, to see how I managed it, and whether I was worth my two and a half guineas!

Later.—I've just come back from having lunch and tea at the Brittains, and while I was there I picked up a book by E. V. Lucas, *Verena in the Midst*, which you may or may not have read. The point about it is that I found in it a poem which entertained me so much that I learnt it by heart to repeat to you. I must say it now, before I forget my lesson. Please imagine me standing before you, my hands behind my back, quite a good and decorous little girl.

> "I recollect a nurse called Anne
>   Who carried me about the grass,
> Until one day a fair young man
>   Came up and kissed the pretty lass.
> She did not make the least objection,
>   Said I, ' Ha, hah!
> When I can talk, I'll tell Mamma.'
>   That is my earliest recollection."

There! Isn't that nice? Haven't you frequently seen that triumphant "I've seen you at it" look about a baby's face?

I have. And then people say, "The pretty little innocent!" Not they. The only comfort is that by the time they can talk they have forgotten all about it, and so don't tell Mamma.

I went to tea on Monday with a young married couple. The girl was at Queen Margaret's when I was there. The man invents gramophone improvements, and composes music. He has set that verse of mine, *The Dead Man*, that you saw in the Oxford Poetry Book, to music. It is very modern music, with exciting chords, that suddenly change from major to minor—or is it minor to major? I wish I was musical! He kept on asking me whether I thought the harmonisation effective, or whether I thought the inverted tenths too reminiscent of César Franck, and for the life of me I could only say, "Oh, very nice," like a hen when she hatches a duck's egg. So trying never to know whether a thing is arpeggio or staccato or what! I know lots and lots of musical terms, but never can fit them properly on to the things I hear.

Miss F. ought to be in G. by now. I told her you were the nicest person there, and that she was to go and call upon you. I expect she will. She was at L.M.H., but I believe she really likes Somerville best, which, of course, shows her good taste.

I have some more papers for you next week. I'm hoping to find one with a description of the late row at Oxford. Do you know Maude Royden has been forbidden to lecture there by the Vice-Chancellor? He has also refused to admit the Grand Guignol company to the theatre, and has sent down two undergraduates for running a Communist paper called *The Free Oxford*. Then a strange story appeared in the paper, and lots of photographs, because some one had sent the dear man a box of poisoned chocolates. People said it was the outraged Communists, and made an awful song and dance about it, until the other day another notice appeared in the paper to the effect that the chocolates were stuffed with tooth-paste, and it was all a hoax. Anyway, he has made himself notorious, which I suppose is something. Vice-Chancellors generally lead such quiet lives, unless they are heretics, or Wycliffites, or harbour disreputable characters. Dr. Farnell is getting nearly as famous as Lady Diana Manners or H. G. Wells.

I've been asked to give a lecture on Gothic Architecture to a school at Forest Gate. Knowing nothing about it, I have gaily consented. Fortunately it's with slides, and they fill in a good deal of time.

Au revoir, and much love, my dear,

CELIA.

52, *Doughty Street, W.C.1,*
Feb. 19th, 1922.

MY DEAREST ROSALIND,

Thank you so much for your little note, which was more charming than many letters. I am glad you are back at work in a peaceful term, glad you are happy, glad that there is work for you to do. There always would be for you, though. Some people would never be wasted anywhere, and I suppose nobody need be. I will tell Mother, though I am sure she has never thought of you as a failure. She likes and admires you more, I think, than any of the friends I have brought home, though I think she is always a little astonished that a college don, and a great and dignified person like yourself, could ever find any reason, except that of propinquity, for companionship with my general immaturity. However, I don't think she bothers her head much about that—but she will be glad to know that South Africa is satisfying.

I had Pugh and Newman to tea on Wednesday. Pugh has had 'flu—like most people here—but was otherwise very well. Newman is much, much thinner. One would hardly recognise her. She does not seem to have cleared the rheumatism yet from her system; but I wrote to the hospital where she works a few months ago, and they said that the voyage to Australia will do her good. They have to go for a medical examination, anyway, before they sail. Pugh is writing to the Salvation Army matron, who goes out with every boat of this kind, and is going to deliver herself and Newman into her hands—a very good idea, I think. They both seem to be fairly well equipped—both have rugs, greatcoats, and a good supply of underclothing. Pugh's father expects to be discharged soon from the Arsenal, so she is very anxious to be getting away and earning money. The demand for domestic workers seems very great in Australia—far larger than the demand for nurses or clerks. I hope they will be all right.

At St. Monica's on Friday I was given a great armful of catkins and palm. I've put them in my shell case on the mantelpiece. They look perfectly charming. Pugh and Newman—the naughty things—brought me a bunch of pinky-white tulips, and Vera and I had already bought some jonquils, so the whole place looks like a flowering garden. It is a joy to me every time I go out and come in again to see it.

Yesterday was unkind. When I looked out in the morning there were bright little fluffy clouds, and respectable patches of blue sky, and the sun shining. When we walked out in the afternoon, dressed to suit the weather, a cold wind blew, and frost nipped our noses, and the red wings on Vera's new hat were blustered round most cruelly—an unkind day. So we did not go to St. James's Park to look at the bulbs, but crept home and made ourselves an early tea over the fire. I had a German lesson in the evening, and was very stupid over it. I can't make my tongue twist round all those guttural words. I quite like reading German, but I hate to talk it. It makes me want to spit continuously —a most impolite language.

I am so much looking forward to your letters about the veldt, and trekking, and leading savage lives in the wilds. Your letters are full of new and exciting things. I'm afraid mine are very dull. The pleasant things that happen—like

95

going out to dinner, or meeting a man at the corner of the street with a barrel load of hyacinths—don't make very good telling, and for the rest, I read history and German, and lecture to my children. They are nice girls. The head one squints.

Much love,
Ever your
CELIA.

52, Doughty Street, W.C.1,
Feb. 26th, 1922.

MY DEAREST ROSALIND,

I do hope that when you receive this your rheumatism will have vanished. Ox wagons sound most perilous conveyances. I don't like the idea of your poor back being so refractory. I had an idea that water jugs were always rather tedious things to manipulate. I have every sympathy with the people who are always too tired to handle them. Personally I hate washing poisonously, and if I didn't have a daily bath—which I love—I'm sure I should grow slowly grey—but not with age!

Your letters are more than a joy. Through them one can live two lives—quite respectably—a rare thing in these days. Why is it if one leads a double life that every one tacitly assumes that one of them is disreputable? Talking about being disreputable, Mother, who is up for the week-end, and Vera and I went to a really charming play last night called *The Faithful Heart*. It was about a young sailor boy, who goes to Cowes with an innkeeper's daughter at Southampton in 1899. In 1919 he is a very important person—joined the army during the War, and is now a lieutenant-colonel. He is engaged to a rich and charming girl. He has been offered a lucrative permanent staff job. He is thoroughly in love with life, when Blacky II., the daughter of the innkeeper's daughter at Southampton, and of the sailor boy, turns up with a letter from her mother.

The mother had died when the child was born. There is a delightful scene between Blacky II. and her father. The girl was brought up in a convent, and speaks in a precise, old-fashioned manner. "You see," she says, "you are not like other girls' father." "Why not?" he asks, quite hurt. "Well, you see, you are not a real father. You are only illegitimate." We all loved it. In the end, the father goes off back to sea, taking his daughter with him. It is an unusual play. Vera said, "It's so rare to see a man fulfilling his obligations on the stage."

I think I might like Bridge at Bushman's River better than at Cottingham. My Bridge is very wild. I trump my partner's tricks, finesse too violently with my knaves, and never can remember whether one is supposed to lead out of strength into weakness or out of weakness into strength. These things seem to me quite arbitrary. I can see no logic in the game, though I know there is one. I am the despair of my partners and the irritation of my opponents, should they care about a decent game. So there it is. I generally find an excuse not to play.

Grace and Edith are coming to Town to-morrow for Princess Mary's wedding. We shall all stand in the crowd on Tuesday, while people trample on our corns (I have three) and run their umbrellas into our ears, and ruin our hats. I always swear I'll never go in another crowd. But I always go again—and get trampled on, and knocked about, and ruin my hat, and swear I'll never do it again—and do. Alack for life—and my hats!

I must stop. It is tea time.

Au revoir, and as always with much love,

CELIA.

52, *Doughty Street, W.C.1,*
March 5th, 1922.

MY DEAREST ROSALIND,

Dissipation is harmful to the soul, tiring to the body, and exasperating to the temper. I have had an orgy of dissipation. Last Monday I joined my Mother and Aunt for lunch, I shopped and tea'd with Grace and Edith, I dined at the Regent Palace and I went to *The Truth About Blayds* at night. *The Truth About Blayds* is excellent. Norman McKinnell is a Victorian poet of great celebrity, who tells tales of Ruskin and Whistler, Tennyson and Carlyle. Of Whistler he says that no man ever said so many spiteful things to you, but you endured them in the hope that next moment he would turn and attack one of your friends. He lives with his daughter and her husband, his grandson and granddaughter. Another younger unmarried daughter, Isobel (Irene Vanbrugh) has given up her love and her life to nursing him. His granddaughter has given up her painting because of him. His grandson has abandoned his electrical engineering to become a politician, because he is the grandson of Blayds. His son-in-law (Dion Boucicault) has sacrified any other literary ambitions he may have had to become the Secretary of Oliver Blayds, and when Oliver Blayds is ninety he confesses on his birthday that he never wrote his poems at all, but stole them seventy years ago from a consumptive young genius who died in obscurity. The next two acts of the play are concerned with how the family of Blayds behaves when it finds it has been cheated. Of course, the old man dies conveniently and gets out of all the fuss. For the rest, you get a delightful comedy, witty and cynical, heart-breaking at times—acted with unusual finish and brilliance. A most refreshing play.

Next day I stood in a crowd—as I knew I should stand—and people trod on my corn, and stabbed me with umbrellas, and buffeted me with elbows. At intervals I heard cheering, or saw in the distance the bobbing feather on the helmet of a mounted guard. Otherwise I had an excellent view of the shoulders—rather greasy—of the man in front of me, and an excellent taste—rather flavoursome—of the feather in the hat of the woman by my side. And at intervals I heard my aunt say that if we had set off earlier we should have had a good view, and the woman at my side say she was accustomed to any sort of rudeness in crowds, but that this was insufferable.

That is what one called watching the procession of the Royal Wedding. I saw in the papers afterwards that the bride was very shy and charming; that her "I will" was softly murmured, and that she stopped the procession to lay her bouquet at the foot of the Cenotaph amid many moist eyes.

After the wedding procession, I had lunch at the Carlton. Then I walked down Oxford Street, and returned to have tea at Callards. Then I changed and had dinner at the Regent Palace. Then I went to a rather poor revue called *The Fun of the Fayre* at the Pavilion. Then I went to supper at the Piccadilly. Then I came home in the sma' wee hours, having eaten four ices, three courses of hors d'œuvres, oysters, chicken, snipe, petits fours, sole, turbot, jambon à la espagnole, and many other things, to be greeted by Vera asking me if I would like some hot milk! I woke next day with a bad temper and a pimple on the side of my mouth, and have decided I will attend no more Royal Weddings. One eats too much.

I have spent the rest of the week recovering my mental and digestive equilibrium—humiliating to realise how closely the two are interdependent—and yesterday went to the movies by way of a gin and bitters after a night out. I think I am now cured. But it will be a long time, please Providence, before I dissipate again. If the Prince of Wales marries, he can do it without any assistance from me!

Au revoir, my dear, and much love. I send you some more papers.

CELIA.

ROSALIND DEAR,

You won't get much of a letter this week, I fear, for I have been wrestling in spirit and body all day revising and typing two stories, and I still—in spite of considerable but erratic practice—find a typewriter exhausting. How and where are you, and what doing? Is the hot weather with you, and are you sitting on a doorstep in the sun arguing heated African politics? It sounds a pleasant occupation—given a comfortable doorstep and considerate sun.

London is beginning to put on its summertime appearance. All eyes on Genoa and French obstinacy, Carpentier and French heavy-weight, the shops and French fashions. We are Francophiles, in our interest, at any rate. There are three Galsworthy plays on—a Bernard Shaw and an English Opera season—if I don't sell some stories soon so as to have some theatre money I'll have to sell my jewels. (Jewels. Item: one gold brooch. There was a turquoise in it, but that has come out; one pendant, size of a half-penny, presented to me by a loving cousin when I was nine, because Grace had measles, so I couldn't be a bridesmaid. Item: several strings of beads—mostly strung with my own fair hands, or acquired in strange lands—I fear of little value.)

What nonsense this is. Seriously, though, I am back here—very glad to be working again. Holidays are all very well, and I found plenty of dressmaking and relatives to occupy mine, but one feels as though one's stays were off all the time. Do you wear any now, I wonder? You used to say you wouldn't. . . .

My grey cloak is quite pretty. The collar turned back and lined with blue, and very wide hanging sleeves. I made it all except some of the stitching, and Nursie helped me with that.

This is no sort of a letter, but I am rubbing my eyes to

keep them open. I will write later on when greater energy inspires me, and I may have more to say. So I'll keep this open. The mail doesn't go till Thursday.

Till then au revoir, and much love.

Yours as ever,

CELIA.

Bainesse,
Cottingham,
E. Yorks, Sunday, April 23rd.

ROSALIND DEAR,

All eyes on Genoa this week. We are all diplomatists nowadays, and far cleverer than Lloyd George at dealing with these complicated East European affairs. So far it seems as though he will manage to avoid wreckage of the conference. But if France pulls away, there will be desperate trouble. The worst thing about it is that we who have had no enemy on our soil, whose Churches—with a few minor exceptions—have not been destroyed, whose villages have not been desolated, nor our fields turned into scrap heaps, have no right to say to France: "Dear little boy, forgive and forget. Lloyd George is at Genoa, the League of Nations at Geneva, King Karl is (possibly) in Heaven, all's right with the world," and so obtain the cancellation of indemnities, the reinstatement of Russia, the solvency of Central Europe and the Golden Age, all by shaking hands politely across a table. If only one could conduct politics by ignoring human sentiments, the millenium would have come years ago.

Meanwhile we read the *Observer* and love Lloyd George, and read *The Times* and sneer at him, and read *John Bull* and hate every one—and here we are.

I left London and came North here on an April day of daffodils and snowstorms seasonably combined. I love still that detached, fluent sort of feeling a train journey gives —one life over, another to come—in between a pleasant

101

book, the rocking and clamour of the train and the flash of green fields past the window. I've just been reading the *Life and Confessions of Oscar Wilde*, by Frank Harris—a most arresting and memorable book. If I wanted to teach clean living and thinking to some one old enough to think and intelligent enough to realise, I think I would give them not the Bible, but Frank Harris on Oscar Wilde. It is a sane book, just, reasoned, pitying. Frank Harris has a bee in his bonnet about the British Press. He is ungenerous to British Society and British Law; but to his hero he is neither sentimental nor bitter. He deals with that sordid tragedy of wasted genius and fatal amiability with a reverence and sincerity that is far more effective because so much of the book is necessarily unsavoury.

How are you? I'm holiday-making. Reading, walking, playing tennis between the storms and making summer clothes. This pen is Daddy's. The language I use while using it is mine exclusively—a cosmopolitan anthology collected during my travels through this estimable planet. Can you read it? The writing, I mean, not the language.

Were the pen better I would write more.

Au revoir, and much love as ever.

Yours,

CELIA.

52, Doughty Street, W.C.1,
April 28th.

ROSALIND DEAR,

An instinct made me postpone writing your weekly letter, which I nearly always do on Sunday, and I'm so glad I did. For to-day comes your long and most interesting letter of March 27th all about the Johannesburg strike and the South African underworld. Rosalind, you must write a series of little articles—short ones, about two columns long—that's about six typewritten pages, or seven or eight of your handwriting. I'll get them typed and send them to *Time and Tide*. The others were rather long to place. I've heard at last from the Cornhill. They do seem to have forgotten your sketch. I'm so sorry. But I have another copy, and I'll try elsewhere. But it's long for most papers. But sketches of South African life, of the underworld of "low whites," of the Dutch women with their hair down, nursing their babies in the stations, of Stellenbosch University, if that's allowable—these I am sure I could place. Probably in *Time and Tide*. I'm getting to know the staff of that. Lady Rhondda really runs it, and she has written asking Vera for an interview apropos of an article she wrote for the paper. Once we get in touch with that we can get things in, I think. And your letters are wonderfully interesting. I keep them all. One day we may edit them together and let the world see them. But now *do* write some sketches in odd moments, if you have any. Short ones, and non-party. It's difficult to place party stuff. We can write about politics, but from the non-committal point of view of a historian or literary observer. And I'll try and talk to the *Time and Tide* people about them. Your letters are too good to be lost. I feel greedy having them all to myself.

Anderby Wold is still with Cassells, and they utter no sound. I'm sure nothing will come of it there. I can't get my novel published, and I can't get a paid job; but I'm very happy and very busy, and wouldn't alter my mode of life for £9000 a year! I lecture and interview and address meetings and write articles on child assault and unmarried mothers, and visit my Waacs and bohemians and am much too busy to make money!

I went to Plumstead last Wednesday and had tea with the Pughs. They live in a neat little two-storied house with a strip of garden in front and a strip of garden behind. They keep twelve fowls, a Pomeranian dog, a canary and two cats. The house is polished and scrubbed and dusted from top to toe. Mrs. Pugh is a neat, quiet, humorous person, with a spice of sharpness about her manner that makes it interesting. We had tea in the kitchen—salmon and tinned pineapple and bread and butter and home-made buns and strong, strong tea. They were very nice to me. I am to go again and visit Mrs. Pugh when her daughter has sailed. Mr. Pugh works at the Arsenal; he is a large man with a white moustache and quiet manner. The brother is a conductor on Number 53 bus.

I saw Pugh's outfit. It seemed very sensible. She has a large stock of underclothes, all very plain and strong that she can wash herself. She says Newman has the same. I am giving Newman a strong purse bag to keep her tickets and things in, and a hot water bottle, and Pugh a dispatch case and a brandy flask. One needs a brandy flask when travelling. I've often been glad of mine. I liked their house so much, and Mrs. Pugh. They are thoroughly nice people.

Here we are very quiet. Most of the newspapers are full of the Genoa Conference, the Armstrong murder and many other murders, and the Irish business, which seems as bloody and hopeless as ever. One wonders if they will ever find peace in that sorrowful island. Sometimes the only remedy would seem to be a sudden submersion under the Atlantic.

I'm writing stories about the nursing home I used to work in. I don't suppose they'll ever get published. But there it is.

I envy you your warm weather. Here spring plays with us cruelly. Good Friday was wonderful. I went out in a thinnish dress without a coat and saw the lilac bushes growing green in Gray's Inn Gardens, and the chestnuts bursting into fat little buds. Yesterday a cold wind blew all day and rain in gusty showers, and to-day is cold still.

We have a crimson azalea in our flat—a wonderful thing, all ablaze with blossoms. When its petals fall off the long pistil I put them on again, and they look as good as new!

Any other news? Well, Mother sent us a roast chicken

for Easter, and we have been gorging. I must go. This is a poor return for yours, but a placid sort of life makes dull reading.

Don't forget the articles. If you want material, I'll send back some of your letters.

Much love as ever,

CELIA.

52, Doughty Street, W.C.1,
Monday, May 15th.

ROSALIND DEAR,

I have been in luck's way—far more than I deserve after the wretched little scraps of a letter I sent you last week. I have had three communications from you, all in one week, and each one as nice as the last. First came your delightful letter about your summer—or is it winter?—clothes. I like the sound of the green dress very much—and the black evening one. I'm having a black dress made, too—a very soft crêpe de Chine, most of it plain, but with a soft pattern of greens and blues and mauves on the sleeves, and in a panel down the skirt, and one large blue tassel at the side. I'm so glad you liked the crick lights, and that they were what you wanted. It was fun buying them.

Did you go for your walk to the Kowie along the hot sand? Thirty-eight miles is a long way. I hope the one you overtire won't be Rosalind.

I'm so glad H. is such a nice person. It warms the cockles of one's heart to hear about nice people. Talking of the same agreeable subject, Vera had tea with Rose Macaulay the other day. R. M. is helping Vera to publish her novel. It's a very good book. I want to send you a copy when it comes out. Vera and I had often talked over Rose Macaulay's books, and I had told her what you said about cynical detachment, so Vera asked R. M.: "Miss Macaulay, why do you pretend to have such an air of cynical detachment about things? I'm sure you haven't

105

really." And Rose laughed and said, "Oh, I'm trying not to sound as if I had, but you know I get so excited about my characters that if I didn't do something to keep them in order, they'd get out of my control altogether." She really is a nice person. She spends hours of her time gratuitously helping people who want to get on—a foolishness with which I know you will have much sympathy. They were talking about Somerville and Vera asked her if she remembered you. She said, "Yes, of course I do."

Pugh and Newman are sailing at the end of this month. They had a terrible fright at first, poor dears, for Pugh's papers ordered her to sail in June, and Newman to go in May. However, we managed to get them transferred, and they go together.

On Saturday Vera and I went to a matinee of Galsworthy's new play, *Windows*. One of the girls acting in it used to live at the next village to Rudstone, and I know her well. We went up afterwards and had tea in her dressingroom. A queer room—all clothes and rouge and lookingglasses—bare and crowded at the same time, but interesting.

I do hope you come over in July next year. It would be lovely to see you again. Is the fare a frightful lot? I wish I could help to bring you over, but I'm sending £100 to a girl to help her to go to Somerville, and am rather low. Only to-night I'm feeling rich because I've just got the offer of a job to go and lecture Kiplingesque jingoism to a young ladies' finishing school on Empire Day for £2 2s.! When I earn one pound I always feel a millionaire, though the money comes in slowly. I am sending out whole fleets of short stories now, that return with beautiful promptitude. One day I suppose a miracle will happen, and one will not come back—and then I shall be able to reimburse myself for all the stamps wasted on futile expeditions.

The Forest Unit[1] is bad. Apart from a certain affection I have for it because those were pleasant days in Huchen-

---

[1]These sketches are still in existence, but she never thought them good enough to publish.

neville, I should hate it. It is slovenly and sentimental, and those are two deadly sins.

I must go, my dear Coz. It is late, and this must be sent off to-morrow, or it will miss the mail.

Take care of yourself.

Much love,

Yours,

CELIA.

52, Doughty Street, W.C.1,
May 30th, 1922.

ROSALIND DEAR,

The mails are speeding up. Here am I answering your letter of May 2nd, and it is still May. How strange that Lady Rhondda should be a friend of H.'s—yet not so strange, I suppose; most of our friends seem to know each other. I saw Miss Tuke last night at Lady Rhondda's, but was not introduced. I also met Miss Kempson. Were you at Bedford with her? I did not get a chance to ask. She was very gay and spirited. I am sorry H. hates Grahamstown. I hope she does not go.

You asked me about X. Certainly she reaps little material reward for her exertions. Her work is voluntary at present, and rather laborious, I imagine. She seems very badly off. She was wearing a pretty but rather old-fashioned evening dress last night, in which she looked exceedingly nice, but she said she bought it for 15/6 from a friend of H.'s. I don't know how she lives, earning nothing. She wants to go up to Oxford, and can't afford it. Also she is kind to people who can give nothing in return. She took quite a lot of trouble to get a job for Vera and me. It is to write one of a series of historical biographies for M. O. Davis, the principal of Bangor University College—probably we are to do "C 19 Women." It will be fun, but all depends on the approval of the Clarendon Press. Also she has been very good trying to help us to meet interesting people, and

107

do the kind of work we want to do—and we can do nothing to advance her interests. One does not help insignificant people for one's own profit, and if she does cultivate the influential, so do I if I have a chance, because the more influence I can acquire, the wider my sphere of work can be, and the more I can do the things I want to do. I dare say she feels the same.

I am so glad you won the race with your Income Tax. It must have been a near thing. It would have been terrible to be arrested for refusing to pay. Income Taxes may be an economic necessity, but they are a human catastrophe.

£8 a month isn't much to live on here. It costs me about £12. But I think you could do it. For one thing, you will please come and stay with us in Yorkshire during the summer holidays. The family all love you and would be so delighted to have you. Father continually asks me how you are. And I would most love to have you there. Then there always is an extra sofa (3 ft. long!) in our flat, if you should run out of board-lodging before your holiday is up. The beds are too small to share. Vera and I tried once during a thunderstorm, when the rain went through on to her bed, but never again! The sofa is preferable! The one comfort in these days is that absolutely every one seems hard up, so no one feels out of it if they are short of money.

You ask where I get my lectures. Everywhere. Last term I gave a course at a school where Vera used to be. They particularly wanted medieval Italian history for the girls. I had just returned from Italy, and was rather keen on medieval history, so that counteracted my lack of experience. I got the architecture lectures through the history mistress of a school in Forest Gate. She told me of three schools that wanted lectures on architecture, and asked · me if I had heard of any one when I was at Oxford who would give them. I wrote back recommending myself. I also hear of odd ones through the agent Truman & Knightley's. Also I speak for the Six Point Group once or twice a week. It is not paid, except my expenses, but it is good experience. One gets such varied audiences. Also I love it. The Six Point Group was badly off for speakers. People need to know about it. I am going to Wansford to speak this afternoon. Lastly, I lecture for the League of Nations Union. That only pays rarely, but it is a very good advertisement, as they only take trained people as speakers. I love lecturing. Always before people have told me, " Little girls should be seen and not heard," when I wanted to air my views. Now I can be both seen and heard, and people sit and listen. My views aren't worth much, but it only seems fair that the people who have had the chance of education and have been trained to grasp intelligently and explain intelligibly the various things people hear about but don't quite understand should do it—or what's education for?

I went to spend last week-end at St. Monica's—a glorious country, all May and lilac sweet scents, and a thin slip of a moon at night, and the faintest twitter of a nightingale. Do you remember the one at Huchenneville?

I must go.

Much love,

Yours ever,

CELIA.

Vera sends her love. She is looking forward to seeing you.

52, Doughty Street, W.C.1,
June 14th, 1922.

MY DEAR ROSALIND,

Suddenly from blazing sunshine and dazzling pavements are we plunged back into winter—the wind tearing all the nice clean leaves from the trees, and the rain sweeping up Doughty Street like all the municipal watercarts at work together.

Yesterday was a beastly day. I got up late. By the first post came a letter to say I had not got the nice teaching job at Streatham. By the second, my novel back from

Cassells after 10 weeks' waiting. I got caught in the rain at lunch time; went off to interview Hodder & Stoughton, and was told their list was closed on autumn bookings; couldn't find a new stick to fit our old O-Cedar Mop, and was involved in a host of minor misfortunes. Don't you know the sort of day? The one drain of comfort lay in a very nice letter from Newman Flower from Cassells, to say that their reason for refusing my book lay entirely in their belief that its tragic ending would militate against its popularity, but that they were very interested in my work, and asked for the first offer of any further books I might write. I don't know whether that was just sugar for the pill. Every one says that a book with a sad ending has no chance of a sale these post-war days. People are too much concerned with living down their own tragedies to take much interest in other people's, I suppose.

Well, well—I've written off to Methuen, and meanwhile am beginning three new books at once—Historical biographies, a joint farcical thing with Vera called *That Last Infirmity*[1] about the adventures of two youthful aspirants to fame in London, and a social study of a northern provincial town.[2]

Did I tell you last week how much I was loving, gloating over, revelling in *Lord Jim*? There are golden sentences there—rich and glowing—and bright, crystalline ones—and others as soft and dark as twilit water. It is lovely to read something so good. I don't know why I never loved Conrad before so much.

The Bill to Amend Criminal Law goes before the House to-night. Since I wrote last I have been talking about it in Hyde Park. We had a big crowd—over 500, they said. I did speak, as one of the others had fallen out. It wasn't nearly as frightening as I thought. The crowd was delightful—so courteous and orderly and attentive. I stood on a platform as big as a dinner plate. It wobbled all the time.

[1] This never went beyond a preparatory scheme.
[2] Later her second novel, *The Crowded Street*.

On Friday I held an open-air meeting outside Hampstead Tube Station for the League of Nations. That was killing, because I had to collect my own crowd. I stood on the pavement at the street corner and shouted to the empty air, two workmen, a motor-van, the policeman at the cross-roads, and a dog catching fleas on the curb. The policeman wanted me to move on, but after the two ladies supporting me declared the nobility of our intentions, he let us stay! He said the League of Nations was "interesting."

I got a nice crowd in the end, and we had 10-minute lectures—from me, and a W. E. H. Woking, Oxford-voiced, ex-officer-suited young man with two volumes of Yeats under his arm, and a girl just back from nursing typhus in Russia. The two last just came out of the audience, and we asked them to address the meeting. We had a debate, too, on Communist Internationalism *v.* the League of Nations. Altogether very interesting. Hampstead crowds are full of unexpected elements. Bohemians in sandals, Church- and State-y gentlemen in frock coats, who declare that one is "undermining the prestige of the British Empire," workmen in overalls, small children in ditto, fierce Socialists in red ties, and fiercer journalists in no ties at all. The policeman is conscientious but polite. It is all very funny. Incidentally highly instructive—to the lecturers, if not to the lectured.

Much love—always,

CELIA.

52, Doughty Street, W.C.1,
June 20th, 1922.

ROSALIND DEAR,

I like your puppy. He sounds a lovely beast. I hope his eczema is better. It is a horrid complaint and trying to the temper. I like puppies. I do not like our landlady's black cat—lean and yellow-eyed and malevolent. It sits on the partition between our sitting-room and kitchen, glowering down at us with eyes like saucers. It spits when we approach it. When I go to the front door it stands like a lion in the path. Once when Mrs. Brittain gave Vera some cold chicken for our supper, the cat crept in and ate it all. It makes noises at night like lost devils. It hates me fearfully, and most cats like me quite a lot.

I agree with you that it's a gift to have convictions. Some people have them about everything from hygienic corsets to God. Some people have none. Others have just one or two—definite but firm. I think I'm like that. I believe that legislation must alter with changing circumstances. I believe that a co-operative institution like the League of Nations, although imperfect, is better than armed neutralities, or quadruple alliances or balances of power. I could not speak about most things—certainly not about religion or mathematics or any of the really important things. But I believe that when you want something quite definite—like the alteration of four clauses in the Criminal Law—it is rather a relief to get up on a stand at Hyde Park and tell other people that you want it. If you can tell five hundred people, that is better than four hundred. It is possible that five out of the five hundred may decide that they want it, too. And they tell their next-door neighbour, and the next-door neighbour tells the clerk at the end of the street, and he tells Mr. Thompson, who tells the clergyman, who writes to *John Bull* or a Member of Parliament, and that makes Public Opinion. I think there is a great deal to be said about making Public Opinion. On the other hand, of course, it mayn't. No one may take any notice at all. There is always a risk about most things.

I don't know that eloquence ever altered the world, but I am quite sure that knowledge sometimes does. Eloquence and information have often little connection, but there are occasions when information can only be imparted wrapped up between a paradox and a peroration.

I am not eloquent. Sometimes I talk like a bored child repeating a lesson. Unfortunately one can't fix meetings when one feels like talking. I don't think it matters drifting so long as one doesn't stand still. Every one drifts. The people who think they are quite sure where they are going to and why, drift as much as the others, only they call it by a different name. It's the moving that matters, surely.

I wonder if you'll get your headmistress-ship. It must be interesting to be a headmistress, but very lonely. I'll wish it for you if you wish it.

I ought to be writing a story. Did I tell you I had begun a new novel? It's called *The World Is So Full*[1], and is about a girl who sets off in life at a small country town thinking that the world is full of interesting things, and then the small country town tells her that because she is a girl, there's only one thing in the world—love—sex—what you will—and when she has played for that and lost it, she thinks the world is empty, until the end of the book, when another woman, who has tried many kinds of life, takes her away from the town and gives her people to look after and things to do, and she has no time to consider whether the world is empty or not, and so she finds it full. It sounds silly, put in that bald way, but it will be more sensible, I think, when it's done.

I took *Anderby Wold* to Methuen's the other day. Marched in bold as brass and asked to see the literary director. I waited for ages in a little room with the manuscript under my arm. Then I was shown into the office. I said at once, "It's no use you looking at this if you don't want a book that hasn't a happy ending."

He was a tall, spare man of about 60, with a kind, clever face and white moustache. He made me sit down and asked me a few questions about the book. Then we started to talk about happy endings. He said that the general public read books to be amused and did not want to be left depressed. They had enough sorrow in their own lives, etc., etc. I said that a sorry person reading a book with a conventional happy ending comes to the last paragraph,

[1]Published as *The Crowded Street*.

and finds the inconvenient husband killed, the lost will found, and the lovers in each other's arms doomed to live happily ever after. Their natural comment will be—at least would be if they were at all like me, and that's all any of us have to go on—"Yes, that's all very fine for these people. Their husbands (if not nice) die, or (if nice) are rescued from the Arabs or lions or something; their fortunes (if declining) are revived, and they find their way to a lover's arms. But what about me? My husband won't die (or has died), I haven't sixpence-halfpenny, and see no likelihood of ever having a lover. What hope is there in life?" Now, my idea of a happy ending is where circumstances go right and wrong higgledy-piggledy, as they do in life, and at the end the hero or heroine is still undaunted, with plenty of hope and enjoyment of such fine things as are left, and a kind of promise of better luck next time—perhaps. Not very gay, but more cheering really to people needing cheer. Perhaps I'm wrong. He said I was. We argued for half an hour or more, and when the telephone rang twice and people asked to see him, he told them to wait. I got frightened in the end that I was boring him, and went, but he came downstairs with me, still arguing. Then, at the bottom of the stairs he suddenly turned and shook my hand and smiled. "Remember that I have been talking quite commercially," he said. "Don't take it all too seriously, but don't forget all I said."

Afterwards I heard he was E. V. Lucas.

Wasn't it sweet of him to let a nonentity like me argue with him for half an hour in the middle of his busy morning? They won't take my book, of course, but they have my thanks for charming manners.

After I'd got away I thought of hundreds of clever things to say to him—I always do *after* an interview.

They have begun to put little metal rabbits on the buses that go into the country here. Isn't it nice of them? The Underground Company have the nicest advertisements that ever were. Because of those rabbits, Vera and I are going to High Beach on Thursday if fine—on a rabbit bus. The rabbits sit on top of the bonnet of the motor, with their paws raised.

Good-night.

Always love from,

CELIA.

52, *Doughty Street*, *W.C.1*,
June 28th.

ROSALIND DEAR,

Your letter from the desert (7/6/'22) has arrived even now, so soon. Letters from the desert travel quickly. My desert is filled this week with the sound of muffled drums and Chopin's *Marche Funèbre*. I stood on the rise of Fleet Street on Monday morning and watched Sir Henry Wilson's funeral procession pass up Ludgate Hill. It was one of the most impressive sights I have ever seen. Even the fat man who kept knocking me into the road could not really spoil the solemnity of the ceremony. English people may not be picturesque in their everyday emotions, but when they are roused to indignation, and express it by the awe-inspiring silence of vast multitudes, it is a thing worth witnessing. Goodness knows the rights and wrongs of that horrible tangle. I know very little about Irish politics, I regret to say, and the more one learns the more puzzling and complicated they seem, but anyway Sir Henry Wilson was a distinguished and widely respected personality, and it was a shameful thing to murder him.

On Saturday I went to Hyde Park and heard the unfortunate supporters of the League of Nations speak to a tossing forest of umbrellas in the pouring rain. There was a procession, and a bevy of limp, bedraggled banners, chiefly inscribed with the insignia of the Lithuanian Mission which intends to make its new-born presence as a nation felt. There was a brass band—with the rain pouring into the trumpets. There were the Archbishop of York, and Lady

Astor and Mrs. Philip Snowden and Baron de Bunsen and a score or more of other celebrities all gallantly defying the weather. Vera and I stood about for half an hour and then retired—more easily daunted, I regret to say, than the speakers.

I wonder if you'll get the Johannesburg job, and if you'll like it when you do. Don't give away all your salary if you get it. You deserve a little money to spend on riotous living for yourself. It is a mistake not to riot sometimes. I, for instance, had two taxis to-night, to go to dinner at Artillery Mansions Hotel in a new frock. It was only to meet a Sister-Tutor of University Hospital, but she is a nice woman and appreciates nice clothes. By all means send the £5, and I'll try and find you dresses. Have you any idea at all where I can get the sort you want? And will you send me measurements? How silly of me to ask now—you'll have sent the money long ago, I expect. Anyway, I'll do my best. I love shopping, so it will be a good excuse.

I am trying to write a novel that won't write itself. It nearly drives me crazy. I can't get the words, although I know what I want to say. I ought to let it alone a bit and can't. That is very wrong, and will lead nowhere.

Good-night, my Rosalind. Good luck to you, and brave journeying.

Ever with love,

CELIA.

52, Doughty Street, W.C.1,
July 5th, 1922.

ROSALIND DEAR,

How have you spent your week? Mine has been mostly dodging raindrops. People call this summer! Do you know, I bought one charming cotton dress of blue and green and mauve, and I made another grey voile with soft grey ribbons—and have I worn them? Not a bit of it! I've been going about in a mackintosh and a temper, cursing my extravagance for buying the things.

Yesterday I started going to teach at Hayes Court School. It is an amusing place. The house is lovely—an old private house among the woods on Hayes Common, with delightful gardens all round, long herbaceous borders and rose-covered arches. The headmistress is taller even than I, with pleasant manners. My children wear green jumpers to their knees—or considerably above them in most cases—and have bare legs. A little cold in this weather, but they seem tough young creatures. They are very polite, and seem quite easily amused. They keep rabbits in hutches they make themselves during their carpentry class. Sometimes the hutches are not very well made and the rabbits escape. Then in the middle of a class some one sees her beloved Black Prince or Suzanne Lenglen or Evangeline bobbing across the lawn, and there is a wild stampede to retrieve the truant. I have lunch at a round table, beautifully polished, with nice old crystal goblets to drink from and a silver bowl of roses. The headmistress and the music master —a round-faced, placid youth who studies bus routes for the duration of the meal—have it with me. The girls act as waitresses. I am told that the school is being run on Canadian lines. Does every Colony have lines of its own? What are South African ones? I wonder if you have heard any more about Johannesburg. The Grahamstown people will be sorry if you go, I am sure, but it is horrid to be poor.

I still have no job for next term, and don't know if I shall find one. I fear that I too recklessly reject the ones I don't want, but some of the things sent by the agency are very entertaining. For instance, yesterday I was asked to go and be daily governess to two little boys of 9 and $11\frac{1}{2}$ at Barnet!

To-morrow I am going to the offices of the Six Point Group to hear Lady Rhondda speak on the Sex Disqualification Removal Act. The Lords are very rude to her to-day, I see in *The Times*, so I expect she will be rather worked up, and the meeting should be exciting.

I was in a real bus accident to-day. Nobody hurt, but some glorious screams. I had just got up to leave the bus at the top of my street and was elbowing my way along (of course the bus was full inside, because it was raining—it always is), when suddenly I found myself embracing an old lady in front of me. A young woman behind me had been thrown violently down on to the knees of a young man, and sat there screaming—whether from the shock of the collision or from dismay at her compromising position, I cannot say. Then every one, with the characteristic suddenness of a British crowd after any sort of emergency, began to give each other advice, all very fast. After feeling ourselves over to see that none of us were killed (after all, the question of whether one is still alive is the most important after an accident), we began to inquire what actually had happened. Then we found we had run into a dray, having skidded right across the road. The step of the bus was smashed, and the dray a little damaged, but otherwise we were all right. The fourth thing that everybody did—the first three were screaming, advising and feeling—was to try to get out of the bus, every one having a vague idea that they were now safer on the pavement. I really did want to get out, as I had come to the end of my journey, but when I presented myself at the door, the much-tried conductor said, "Just a minute, miss. It's all right. You keep inside. No damage done," and pushed me back again. I said, "But I want to get down here." Said he, "Now, don't you be anxious, miss, it's all right." Winifred: "But this is my road." Bus Conductor (soothingly): "Now, then, you sit down again. It's *quite* all right." Winifred (desperately): "But I want to get out. My home's up that street, and I'm late for tea." Every one in the bus all at once: "That's right. Let the young lady out. That's her home." Bus Conductor (disappointed): "Of, if *that's* all!" (Lets me out.)

Much love,

WINIFRED.

Only twenty days since you wrote your letter, my Rosalind, telling me about your cottage. You say your letters are dull—why, they're delightful. Vera makes me read aloud to her all the bits describing Africa. You must write those articles. I couldn't—but you can make us warm with the hot sun and the blue gums and the cathedral tower through the trees. I like your cottage. I'm glad you have had an orgy of entertaining. That sounds such a nice hospitable thing to do.

We, too, have been having an orgy. I will send you the result. I bought the new books that I most wanted to read and trusted that they would meet the needs of your friend. I'll tell you what there is:

1.—*If Winter Comes.* You said you wanted that, and certainly it is worth reading, if only to know what has so much enraptured the British public. Besides, it is an interesting book "to hold children from their play and old men from the chimney corner," and that, I suppose, is the true vocation of all books, however high we may talk about psychological masterpieces and the rest of it.

2.—*The Garden Party*, by Katherine Mansfield. Short stories because they are nice for chance guests—easy to pick up and less tantalising for one's bedside than a novel that can never be finished unless we put undue strain on our host's fund of hospitality. They are new, too, and strong and modern, and much talked about. Also a little less unpleasant than *Bliss*, though that's not saying much. But interesting, anyway, and vivid enough, even though one finds that afterwards the tales elude one's memory strangely—perhaps just because they are not tales.

3.—*The Forsyte Saga.* Galsworthy to counterbalance the excessive modernity of Miss Mansfield. Much Galsworthy, too—three novels and two short tales under one cover, so that you may have your money's worth. A good book for a remote farmhouse where books are rare.

4.—*The Altar Steps*, Compton Mackenzie's latest, and, they say, his best. I haven't read it, though I mean to have a look at it before it goes. But they—that terrible, impersonal, irrefutable They—say that this is good, and at least the subject promises interest.

5.—*The Memoirs of a Midget*, by Walter de la Mare. I hope she has not got it. I love it—but, then, I may be prejudiced, because Walter de la Mare can make a garden stir and sway beneath the moon like no other living writer. I never knew so cool and delicate a book—fiery, too, in parts, and fierce and bitter, with a shrill, piercing bitterness towards the end, but abounding in exquisite descriptions and clear, marvellous pictures etched exquisitely as with a diamond-pointed pen.

That's all. I wish there were more, but books are a tyrannous price now. It is a weighty matter choosing books for a stranger, but these are all so different that surely one may please.

I have been lecturing, teaching and writing—sitting up, too, till all hours. On Friday, Saturday and Sunday I spoke to open-air meetings. On Friday I was moved on by a policeman at Hampstead. I made all my own crowd that time. The man who was supposed to give me a start forgot the date, and I had to stand on a pavement with just two little League of Nations Union ladies as audience and yell across the empty street. It took me twenty minutes to raise that crowd, but I got such a big one in the end that we had to move off the cross-roads, and I went like the Pied Piper with my crowd at my heels and a genial policeman by my side. I spoke from eight till after ten—not all at once, but answering questions, and being heckled by socialists and communists, and all the other strange "ists" that hang round Hampstead. And at the end men in dinner jackets and women in evening cloaks on their way home from parties hang on the outskirts of the crowd and look supercilious, and old men come and weep over me and ask me why I spend my time in this vain talk, and do not try to lead men to God.

It's a sorry, funny, exciting, wearying, interesting business—and goodness knows if any good comes of it. I don't. Probably I'm the only gainer, since I can write when applying for a remunerative job—"Have lectured to many audiences in London and Yorkshire on historical and social subjects" (save the mark), and unsuspecting headmistresses take me to their bosoms, entirely unaware of the disreputable tubthumper they are admitting to their most select academies for the daughters of gentlefolk.

I am here all this week. Three more times to speak in Hyde Park. My ideas on morality are drying up. I had a controversy at one meeting with a prostitute, and I must admit she was the better man of the two. A rotten life— and this was an intelligent girl with a charming voice and and any amount of spirit. The exam papers to correct. My infants did their exams to-day. Heaven send they made head fra' tail of my papers! Also that their principal sends my cheque before I go abroad.

To-morrow I go to the House of Lords to sit as meekly as possible taking notes for the Six Point Group while the Equal Guardianship of Infants is discussed by a learned committee.

This is a disjointed letter. I hope you can read it. Vera says she never thanks me for my letters if she is tired. They take too much deciphering. Read this when you are feeling strong and vigorous.

My love to you,

CELIA.

MY DEAREST ROSALIND,

Holidays are brief, rushing things, spent chiefly packing and unpacking. I shall be quite glad to return to-morrow to the more restful process of work. Vera and I are soon going to move into a new flat—a proper flat, not a studio with cubicles, but a truly wonderful place, with real walls and a real front door, and a little hall, and a sitting-room with a window overlooking Doughty Street, and a gas fire, and a kitchen sink, and lots of cupboards. It will be a truly lovely place. Also we are going to have a servant—or at least a woman to come for an hour or two every morning.

I have applied for three jobs next term, and shall probably get none of them—for one is practically promised already to some one else, one prefers a R. Catholic, and one requires a diploma in economics. There is always a curious fatality about the jobs I pursue—for some reason or another I just fail to fit. On the other hand, if I do not pursue, they sometimes fall into my hands without any trouble. Exactly the same happens with my flats and hats and friends!

I have just accomplished a great triumph with the kind help of my family, and made for myself a grey woollen stockinette dress, with flowing sleeves and panels of astrakhan. Really very pretty. I had to speak at a meeting at Bridlington yesterday, had no new clothes, and dared not face my audience in the same frock I wore last time—hence the feverish activity of Mother, myself and three visitors, and a dress that went to be pressed in the kitchen exactly half an hour before my train started. The best of a London audience is that it varies every time, and the same dress will do. A Bridlington audience is unvariable, and one's dress must change.

I am just rereading *The Old Wives' Tale.* What a tragedy it is that Arnold Bennett must now write of his *Pretty Lady* and *Judith,* and all other demi-mondaine atrocities, when he is capable—or was capable—of producing an exquisite piece of realism like *The Old Wives' Tale.*

I enclose a letter from Pugh that came yesterday. They do not seem to be finding Australia a bed of roses, poor dears, but I hope Pugh will find some work to suit her soon. She really is a nice girl, and her mother a thoroughly nice woman.

It has rained most of the time I have been at home. The English climate is enough to make one weep—the one comfort is the delicious smell of it. Even as I write there comes from the garden outside my window a scent of stocks and roses, wet grass and acacia that is perfectly entrancing, and makes me regret London. If only London smelt as nice as the country, it would have hardly any disadvantages.

An old charwoman from Rudstone has come to spend two or three nights with us, and we are having such a talk over old neighbours and the village. The woman herself is a dear—a little neat lady with iron-grey hair parted down the middle and wrinkled hands that she folds decorously over the black-and-white spotted apron. She talks in a gentle, self-depreciating little voice, but her sense of humour is shrewd and observant, and she retails us all the latest scandals with almost alarming lucidity!

How and where are you, and how goes the house? I have just been looking at your charming photograph again. I like that sunny-looking verandah. I hope you get the sun to suit it.

Au revoir. I must continue my packing.

Much love,

Ever yours,

CELIA.

MY DEAREST ROSALIND,

I have to thank you for the long letter about your interview. By now you will know whether you have or have not received the appointment, and comments long after the event are as stale as last week's bread. I wonder very much, though, and wonder, too, how you will like it, and whether the sinister town will prove less sinister upon further acquaintance.

I hate to think of you running such narrow races with the bailiffs. How strange a thing it must be to be a person so full of riches one never has to take thought for the morrow. All the nice people of the world seem poor. Clare Leighton, the artist girl who painted my portrait, spent yesterday with us. She was chopped out of her job by the Geddes axe, and is now hunting for work in every part of London. D. G., a charming singer, with pale-gold bobbed hair and a face like a wood nymph, can't find work, and spends her time wondering whether she'll travel by bus to save her shoes or walk to save the bus fare. I, who am really more lucky than the rest because I have a small income and a home to go to, having just taken on a new flat and bought a charming array of new clothes, cannot now find any paying work, and am told by the L.C.C. that they have 500 teachers on their waiting list, and by various other august bodies that nobody wants part-time teachers. Meanwhile, I can get plenty of unpaid lecturing, and have got a book published—or at least about to be—but I get no money for that till June, 1923. And you, racing with the duns. What an impecunious world we live in! And all manage to look so smart on it. You with your 19/6d. gloves, I with me new (unpaid for) hat. Our complaints form a kind of beggar's opera full of rag-tags and bobtails of amusement.

I have just written a story about Yorkshire. It's really about Ravenscar, the place where I was staying with Mother. Parts of it are true and parts wild fantasy. I'm going to take it to the Cornhill and see if I can make them have it. Then, if they are nice, I want to take your sketches again.

I hope you got your articles into the paper about the teaching of English. They would be so pleasant to read, and I hope that they were pleasantly paid for!

To-day Vera and I walked in St. James's Park. It was rather nice and not too full of people, though the grass on Sundays always is a little untidy, littered with recumbent figures. People asleep in a park aren't beautiful at all. The sparrows are, though. There is one patch of new sown grass, railed off, and the sparrows have a lovely time there. The grass is rather long, and simply alive with birds. They have a sort of lilac bloom on their breasts at this time of year, and are most friendly, having grown out of their springtime scaredness, nor yet being too sophisticated to enjoy human society. Two very large and majestic pigeons stalked among them in portly fashion. We tried to touch one, but it was not condescending enough to let us approach. There is nothing quite so condescending as a large park pigeon.

Our new little flat is going to be adorable. We move there on Tuesday. It has blue and mauve and fuchsia covers and shot blue and mauve silk cushions. And I have blue delft plates to put on the dark oak dresser, and a blue lustre bowl filled with dried and shredded lavender. And we have lots of books, and Vera has a vase of blue pottery from Malta that we will fill with purply flowers. One has to climb lots of stairs, but that does not matter, for our windows get the afternoon sun, and intending visitors won't care to call.

I am going to try and write an essay about Wycliff and intellectual doubt for the *English Review* or something. I have a lot of stuff about him that I got at Oxford, and it seems a pity not to use it. It won't get taken, though, I fear. That's the worst of wasting much time on being erudite. It *is* such a waste.

Have you read *The Clash*, by Storm Jameson? A curious

book, in some places showing real genius. Her descriptions are exquisite, wonderful. Her people are queer, sinister puppets, with the strange life of puppets. They move in a sharp, uncanny light like the light under the sea. They talk with disturbingly clever talk, such as one never really hears, and it's all shockingly, disquietingly alive.

As a counter-irritant, I've been reading Lytton Strachey's latest book, *Books and Characters*, which is so singularly pleasing. I believe I mentioned it in my last letter. I'm still reading it—parts for the second or third time.

They are going to produce another Drinkwater play, *Mary Stuart*. I want to see it badly.

Such a thing is fame! Passing a car shop to-day, I saw in the window a new Ford coupé, and below it a placard thus:

> "If Winter Comes
> This Freedom
> From Chills and Ills
> May be obtained by Ford coupés."

What must Hutchinson think? And in nearly every hat shop, velours and furs are marked "If winter comes," while some one else has stuck it on a cough lotion!

Au revoir, my Rosalind, and my love to you,

CELIA.

58, Doughty Street, W.C.1,
Sept. 27th, 1922.

MY DEAREST ROSALIND,

I don't know whether to be glad or sorry that they have appointed Miss T. instead of you. Although it would have been an honour, and all that sort of thing, I cannot help thinking that to a heaven-born teacher of English like yourself a headmistress-ship would involve a certain amount of wing-clipping. One has so many plumbers and accountants to interview, so few opportunities of showing South

African Jans that their thumbs may pluck plums from a printer's pie as nimbly as those of English Jacks. Your charming article on the teaching of English seems to me a protest against your relegation to a headmistress's office. I hope that your un-Goblin wares found sale in the Cape market. If not thoroughly goblin, they are at least touched by Faery, and that is a great thing in these terribly materialistic days.

I hope that you enjoy your house. It sounds nice, also the stoep and the Kaffirboom on the lawn. Your letters are full of strange colours and perfumes that I cannot read— far more bewildering than alien names.

We thought our new flat Paradise, so knew that there must be a serpent in it. To-night we have found the serpent— mice. I don't mind them so much, though I hate to find our rosy apples nibbled, and our candles bitten to the wick, but Vera loathes and fears them, having once had influenza in a room where a mouse was caught in a trap and squealed and dragged it about the floor all night, and she was too terrified to cross to the door and escape. So to-night we have been having a great game, covering all available food with pie-dishes and putting all else into a tin suitcase, and stuffing up all holes in the wall with newspaper. I have pushed nearly a whole *Times* under the floor with the help of our mop handle.

I've been writing little sketches of life on the Yorkshire Wolds for the Country Page of the *Morning Post*, and have offered to do them popular histories of such alluring subjects as the Rotation of Crops, Copy Holders Ancient and Modern, and Turnip Townshend. But I don't suppose anything much will come of it.

I am going to Liverpool—your Liverpool—to lecture for the League of Nations Union on December 1st. My subject is to be "Historical Attempts at World Unity," and it should be interesting. My host, Mr. Macdonald, sent his girls to your school, and they knew and love you.

I had a letter from Miss Fowler last week, asking me

to go to Queen Margaret's, but I cannot yet, for the journey is too expensive, and I cannot spare the time.

I have been reading an interesting book called *Mainspring*, by V. H. Friedlaender—a new writer. She sometimes sends poems to the *London Mercury*. It is a good novel—not so distinguished as either *Search* or *The Clash*, but having a good story well told. The theme is to some extent similar to that of *This Freedom,* but differently worked out. The heroine is an artist who eventually renounces the man she loves for the sake of her art. It is a hard thing to do well, but the author somehow has made it convincing both that the girl would act so and that her pictures would be worth it.

I went to spend the week-end with our landlady. She has a cottage in Hampshire not far from Hindhead. To get there is complicated. You walk to Chancery Lane Tube, you change at Oxford Circus; you take another tube to Waterloo, you catch a train to Guildford; you change at Guildford and go to Haslemere; you get out at Haslemere Station into a bus. You go four miles by bus, then get out, carrying your luggage, and walk two miles along the road and moor. When it gets dark, her friend takes a lantern and walks in front, swinging it above the heather. When you arrive at the cottage, you have to make the beds, cook the supper, open up the house, draw the water from a well, and then clear it all up. Then you go to bed. This is on Friday night. On Sunday afternoon you start it all over again to come home! And yet they do it every week.

Vera and I certainly enjoyed it, because Hampshire smells nice, but we have vowed with a great and mighty vow never to do it again.

I must go to the post, or this won't catch the mail.

With love, my Rosalind,

Yours as ever,

CELIA.

ROSALIND DEAR,

I ought to be writing at my book, but I can't. I'm sleepy and my brain is woolly, and ideas won't come. It's a poor sort of compliment to you to use such a time for answering your letter, but I wanted to write, and to-day's Wednesday, which means that the mail goes to-morrow. So I will. I have just got your letter with the "Spring Song" in it. It's delicious, piercingly sweet and clear as a bird's song.

I am glad that you, too, believe in the League of Nations. It is a sorrowful thing when one's friends despise one's most loved aspirations. I do not think you could have a better way of teaching charitableness to the English than by teaching the Dutch our literature. Our actions are not always dignified, and our politics not always disinterested, but our poetry is finer than our politics. I was speaking out at Ilford last night, and came home on the top of a bus through West Ham, Stepney and Bow Road. I wish I were an artist. I wish an artist would paint Bow Road at half-past ten on an October evening. The sky between the houses is very quiet and clear and starflecked. The houses are reared black and solid, pierced here and there by shining wounds of light from the uncurtained windows. They stand on shining feet, their lowest storey is full of gaiety. There are cafés and fruiterers and chemists, and grocers and fried fish shops, with golden slabs of fish on the white marble. The pavements are full of people. They talk of the gay life of the rich; it's absolutely deadly compared to the gay life of the poor—that hilarious street society—the cinemas, music halls, billiard saloons, dances, whist drives, sermons, political meetings—and at intervals are coffee stalls and eel stalls and fruit stalls in the street, and a glass at the Public House to crown it all. There are naphtha lamps that flare with a cheery smell one never knows from electric light. Coffee stalls are surrounded by a wittier throng than the tables of the Ritz or the lounge of Claridge's. There's so much passing backwards and forwards, such an interchange of personal humour that from the top of the bus I felt horribly bourgeois and isolated and wanted to go at once and eat fried fish and chips out of a newspaper. I once did, in the garden at Rudstone. I gave the gardener's daughter threepence to go and buy them for me from a man who came to the village with a cart on Fridays. They tasted more delectable than anything I had known before, and I got well scolded for them—as you can imagine. I believe my hair smelt of frying-fat for days!

I have at last got a job. It is to go twice a week to a rich young woman in Mount Street. Her mother is American, and she has been for three years in America at school. She is tall and slim, with golden hair and dark eyebrows, charmingly arched. Her nails are manicured and she wears a double string of pearls, and her manner is that of a sophisticated woman of the world. But she is very intelligent. She has read an immense amount of scattered, desultory stuff, and she thinks she would like to go to college. So I am to read with her, and criticise her essays and try and put some political economy and history into her pretty head. She is nineteen, and makes me feel fifteen! However, it is interesting work, and I hope she pays me well.

The flower women in the street are selling chrysanthemums and we are wearing furs. We light our fire o' nights and begin to order hot lunches. I envy your blue skies.

Vera is making an immense success of her speaking. Everywhere she goes they ask for her again. She has letters from M.P.s and paragraphs in the paper, and all the time she just laughs a little and takes it quite as a matter of course. One day she will write.

I have not heard from my family for days, so presume they are all right. I met a cousin on Monday, and she said she heard that Mother has been ill, but is well again. I hadn't. They try so much to spare me any anxiety about anything that sometimes it is a little trying.

I must go and learn Assyrian history to teach my pupil. She has an alarmingly inquiring mind.

My love to you,

CELIA.

58, *Doughty Street, W.C.1,*
Oct. 14th, 1922.

ROSALIND DEAR,

Your letters come full of heat and sunshine. The birds do not crouch for shade under the telegraph poles here, but on Friday I went with Vera into Epping Forest on top of a bus, and we walked among falling leaves and half-clothed trees and heard a hundred birds about the berry bushes. I have never seen such berries. The bushes flare with crimson. Their branches are so heavy-laden that they hang sideways. The birds are clamorous round them. We kicked yellow leaves lying underfoot, and saw the sun beat flame from the bramble-bushes. There were a few brambles, but Epping Forest gives them little hope of maturity. There are too many week-ends and picnickers with eager, searching fingers. But the sun was keenly bright and the air clear, no scent of smuts and petrol. We walked through lanes and common, and had tea upstairs in a large dining-room over a public house called "The Castle" in Woodford. There were stuffed penguins on the sideboard, and aspidistra plants in hanging baskets, and on every table were chrysanthemums, small, garden, pale-hued chrysanthemums with many leaves, thrust anyhow into large plant pots. We ate bread and butter and damson jam and large slabs of currant cake, and had tea from a large brown teapot. The waitress was large, too, and very cheerful, with a harsh, pleasant Essex voice, that is so nearly cockney and yet not quite. We came back on the top of a bus through streets gay with naphtha.

I hope you will be able to arrange your Greek papers. It will be a long time to wait for the exam. otherwise; but

131

how nice it is to feel that you are really coming. If you want a bed for part of the time, we really can give you one, for Vera has a large double bed, and I can go into it, and you can have my room. Is it really possible that you may come back to London? Of course I want that. It will be so fine to have you in London. Would you like inspecting? Here everything is so strange in the teaching world. I'm glad I'm not really in it. The Government pledges itself to educate children properly, then pleads economy, and 500 history teachers in London are out of work. Perhaps inspectors could do something—urge the necessity for larger staffs of teachers. The children are herded together, fifty or sixty in a class. How can they learn? They can only be flung facts, here and there, higgledy-piggledy, like the Staff flung bacon and bread pudding at us at Connaught Club—not even giving forks to eat it with. You talk of an intellectual activity. I do not know. Some people here are normally and sanely active; others are active with the hysterical urgency of neurasthenia. I talked yesterday to a girl who has just returned from travelling on the Continent. She is rich; she is intelligent; her mind is blazingly clear and active, with the fierce clarity of flame. She has no occupation, but spends her life inventing for herself interests and calling them services. Only she sees too clearly for her peace of mind, and when she has assisted a struggling artist, played at a charity show, danced at a club, and been brilliantly entertaining at a dinner-party, she returns to her room and says: "My aunt took an overdose of veronal last week. My friend is slowly poisoning herself with drugs. The world is full of people inventing interests for themselves to keep their thoughts from death and their wits from madness. Society is a convention to screen the loneliness of men's lives, civilisation a cloak to hide the nakedness of their barbarity, and through it all the theologians chant endless psalms of empty words, and they are blindest of us all. Why should I invent interests to keep myself alive? Why should I, too, not be brave enough to take my life into my hands and go with it into nothingness?" And then she goes sane again and finds that it is not the world that is out of joint, but herself and her friends. She is a nice girl, and very finely intelligent. I think that she is coming to work for the League of Nations. One can work there for no money and no reward of fame—or perhaps that very little and very remotely. But at least the demand to work comes from without, from a need for things done, and not from within oneself from a need to do things. And that, I suppose, is what makes it worth while to live—that there shall be a claim from without upon one's life.

Austria is a dead country, stinking in its own corruption, full of clever neurotic people who once conformed to a standard of discipline through the influence of the Court. The Court has gone, and they are left without a motive for control or for activity. They find their bodies clamorous with the urgency of animals and have no motive for denying them. Their minds are bitingly clear and destructively critical. They see their own corruption, hating it, yet have no strength left to leave it, but only laugh above the ruins of their world, then drug themselves with veronal to find sleep. Their souls died long ago. What is one to do? Is that what happened to Babylon, to Greece, to Rome before the barbarian beat down the gate? My friend said, "I am sick of clever people. I want to marry a kindly, stupid man and rear large families. I will be a brood-mare, for I am weary of being a product of the twentieth century, barren and destructive." I told her that her children would be neurotic and her husband driven to despair, and that she had much better find some hard work to do and stick to it. Besides, there is the husband to be found—one can find the work oneself.

You are not a ghost. In every word you write you are a thousand times more alive than many people here. I hope you will come to London and see whether you prefer it to Africa. But I wonder? Will the place let you go? Supposing the blue gums are really more full of poetry than the Thorn, Ash and Oak, and the Watsonias more seductive than Lady's Fingers. Will you stay? I wonder.

I may be going to help Mr. Percy Harris of the L.C.C. to try and get into Parliament as Member for Bethnal Green. He is a keen supporter of the League of Nations, in politics vaguely liberal, as a man very human. Bethnal Green is about the roughest district to canvass in London. Vera went there to speak about the League to some of his poorer women. They were keen and intelligent. Her fine intelligence gripped them. She is small and dark and pretty, and speaks with clear simplicity. Her appeal is unsentimental, reasoned and finely serious. Then she goes down all shy friendliness and talks to the women. They loved her at once. All crowds love her. I have seen her in Hyde Park, speaking in her grave, clear scholar's voice, calm, unimpassioned words, and holding crowds by the restrained vitality of her presence. Mr. Harris wanted her to work for him. She can't spare all the time, so I am perhaps to help. It will be interesting.

I don't know of a single girl who teaches mathematics and botany, but if I hear of one, I'll tell her about the Church School, St. Winifred's.

I keep your letters.

My love to you,

CELIA.

58, *Doughty Street, W.C.1,*
Oct. 23rd.

MY DEAREST ROSALIND,

Not a letter but a little note to send you my love and to say I will write properly after the General Election. I have been appointed Political Secretary to Mr. Percy Harris of Bethnal Green. He is an Oxford man—read History—an Independent Liberal, and his main object in life is to promote the League of Nations. His wife is an artist and a dear. Meanwhile, the table is spread with notes on speeches, etc., and I am writing this while I drink my tea, having just returned from a meeting at Hampstead on the League.

It is fun to be busy. One hardly has time even to miss the plays one doesn't see. There's *The Immortal Hour* at the Regent, and Drinkwater's *Mary Stuart* at Everyman, and the Swedish Ballet and Lopokova—and new books coming out every day. And even at the end I doubt whether my activities will make any one a whit the wiser or happier. But at least it keeps me out of harm's way, and Mr. Harris is a fine man, and I do believe in the future of the League —so that's that.

It grows colder every day—the fires are all on and the skies are angry red at night.

I look forward to your return.

My love,

CELIA.

58, Doughty Street, W.C.1,
Oct. 29th.

ROSALIND DEAR,

Your letter about the English notes set me, too, in a fever of indignation. I do hope that you publish your notes and that the whole business gets cleared up. It was a miserable trick to play. The one comfort is that you hear quite unbiased tributes to the merit of your *own* work. But it is all a trying and a tearing business.

I'm glad you have your lovely garden. The festoons of wisteria and roses sound most attractive.

I am still electioneering. The real happiness of the business is Bethnal Green. It's saddening, too, for the poverty is dreadful, but the spirit of the people and their friendliness is so much better than I had dared to hope. I work in a little room at the top of an old house in Bethnal Green Road. It is thick with the dust of ages, wax flowers, aspidistras, and portraits of all the agent's family. The agent is an old man over seventy, with a cigarette always

135

hanging from his lip, *very* dirty, very shrewd, a teetotaler, with an immense sense of brotherhood towards all the world. I have been over the schools, and the children are sharp as needles—or hopelessly stupid. The buildings are a crime—huge class-rooms, no hall in some cases, dark corridors, and primitive sanitary arrangements. But the work is alive and most of the teachers devoted. A few dugouts, of course.

Percy Harris is a dear, but absent-minded. I went with him to inspect a school last week. He's on the L.C.C. He arrived at the right day and the right time, but the wrong school! We had to *run* all across Bethnal Green in the rain to reach the right one! There are no taxis there. A fine sight— Percy leaping ahead, and I sprinting behind, my fur coat trailing after me, and a dispatch case fluttering in the breeze. Such was our dignified arrival to inspect and present prizes. Every one there calls me "Mrs. Harris" and Percy lets it pass, as the real Mrs. Harris does not mind, and it saves time. I want to know what will happen when the real Mrs. Harris turns up just before the election. I'm afraid that they will think she's "the other woman"!

My rich American shows signs of nerve strain already in working for her exam. She has beef tea in the middle of the coaching, can't finish her essays, and has to take special exercise. Viva the Middle Classes!

My book's not coming out till January. The really awful thing has happened. I took Vera's to John Lane and made them interested in it and her, but they won't publish it. They returned it yesterday. I've got the MS. She doesn't know yet. It's a horrid thing, for her book's miles away better than mine, only Yorkshire stories just happen to be in fashion and college ones aren't. She has given me introductions to her friends and all and helped me to get on— and now *I'm* getting on and her book *won't* get itself taken. She is so generous, she says she's pleased with my success, but when that is due so much to her, and she is so keen to publish too, I feel—— And now I've got her political job which she longed to take but couldn't break her teaching contract. I was able to take it because I had not been able to get a job.

Yet if I don't take the opportunities that come my way, nobody would benefit. I can't make other people's luck, though I seem to take it all myself. It's the case of the "haves" and "have nots" again. At present I'm a "have," I suppose. And it's a rotten situation. I seem unable to give my friends any of my having, though I'd so infinitely rather they had it. I need so little to make me amused with life, and luck makes me come and take everything without wanting to. I suppose I shall suffer for it one day. Meanwhile, the only thing to do seems to be to use the opportunities as best I can. Never be a "have," Rosalind. If you're a "have not," all that is yours is your own. If you're a "have," all that you get seems to be somebody else's and the joy of having them goes or goes at intervals. Most of the time one is riotously happy just enjoying the things. Always is the desire to share them at the back of one's mind, and the ache of impotence, and the anger of knowing that other people could use your chances better.

This is a grouse. Don't take it too seriously. Never take my letters too seriously. But it is a relief to write to you, who will understand, and perhaps laugh a little at me—as I need laughing at.

You must let me know in good time when and where you arrive in June, dear Ghost. At least you will find one welcome, but I guess a many more.

My love,

CELIA.

Rosalind Dear,

It is a shame about your house. I do hope that you find another. It was very evil of the man to deceive you so. Grahamstown morality seems strangely subtle for a comparatively young civilisation, but deceit seems to be the natural attribute of a house agent, and I have no doubt that one said to a neolithic holiday-maker, "Here, sir, is a nice dry cave. Those trickles on the wall, sir? Mere exhalations from the natural heat. Those bones at the back? The fragments of past feasts. The shadow of yon dynosaurus? Merely a drawing on the wall. And singularly cheap—the carcass of one wild dog." Then, when the unfortunate lessee turns up, he says, "Excuse me, sir, but this cave is let. Your inquiries? Oh, I thought you only came to look at the view from the opening. I let it to the present tenants two moons ago," etc.

I am still electioneering. I expect that in many cases it is a sordid game, but Vera has a wonderful knack of picking up genuine people, and Percy Harris is really sincere. He is only forty-seven and has gone quite white—largely with the troubles of Bethnal Green. His artist wife is charming. She carries a copy of Milton's poems about with her to the committee rooms, and reads *Lycidas* in between interviewing constituents, and a fear of "growing grovelling" while Percy reads *Little Plays of St. Francis*. All the children in all the schools know him and they all talk about him as "Percy." It is a splendid thing to work for a man like that.

I went to a meeting at the Central Hall, Westminster, the other day and heard Rebecca West speak. She is about thirty, slim and dark, with straight black hair swept off from her forehead and falling in straight bobbed curtains each side of her pointed face. She is rather beautiful and speaks very charmingly. I did not know she was like that. Did you read *The Judge*?

My love,

Celia.

138

Rosalind Dear,

Your notes on the teaching of verse composition have come and have fascinated me. From your opening paragraph until the end I think it an enchanting revelation of the poetry that lives in the child's brain and of the lovely mind of their teacher. I want every one to read it. I want to send it to Oxford. May I? So many girls leave Somerville to teach English and will, I am sure, have to teach verse composition and do not know how. Even though this is written for use in Africa, it is strangely suggestive for teachers in England. I want at once to go and teach verse composition—perhaps in Bethnal Green.

I must not stop and write. It is nearly twelve, and I have been selling all day at the bazaar for the four Oxford colleges. We have made nearly £2,000 in two days. We had at our stall over 1,000 books to sell. It was fun.

So good-night. But thank you, my Rosalind, for your charming mind.

With much love from

CELIA.

58, *Doughty Street, W.C.1,*
Nov. 27th.

Dear Rosalind,

May I have some more notes on the teaching of verse composition? I have sent the copy you gave me to Miss Young, the English tutor at Somerville, and asked for orders. They are so charming that I feel sure several girls who are doing English now and are going down to teach will be glad of them. And if Somerville takes them on, I will send copies round to the other colleges and get orders in the same way. I feel sure that they ought to be better known.

Do you know Fiona Macleod's poetry? I wish that *The Immortal Hour* could still be running when you come to town in June. It is the most beautiful and lovely thing. The music is by Rutland Boughton. It is full of strange rhythms from Celtic folk-songs—weird and strange. I went with Grace and Vera on Thursday night. You can go in the gallery for one shilling. We liked it so much that we went again yesterday afternoon. It is in the Regent Theatre, King's Cross, so near here. Every time I have one shilling, and an evening, I am going until it comes off.

We made nearly £2,000 with the bazaar. It was full of celebrities, but mostly dull, social ones—minor duchesses and so on. We had Rose Macaulay and John Buchan at our stall. She was, as usual, tall and swift spoken. He is smallish and modest and clean shaven and twinkly eyed, and not at all precious. Do you remember *Salute to Adventurers*? A nice book.

Next week I am really going to settle down and write again. This week I have been gadding. I am speaking to-morrow in the Royal Pavilion at Brighton. It should be amusing—the experience, not my speech, which is on the White Slave Traffic, which is never amusing.

I must go. I have to call on my relatives.

Much love, my Rosalind,

CELIA.

58, Doughty Street, W.C.1,
Nov. 29th.

ROSALIND DEAR,

It seems so strange at this time of year to be writing a Christmas letter that I can hardly bring myself to do it, and so have been postponing and postponing till now I fear I may be too late. I am sending you a few little trifles with my love—a fan to keep you cool when the lizards sing and the air quivers with heat, and a little soft travelling cigarette-case for your pocket, and a pair of silk stockings for your nice straight legs. I always liked your legs. They look so nice in gaiters. What an indecorous and unfeminine statement! But why shouldn't one like legs? They are so much more than things to walk on—fat legs, thin legs, bandy legs, squat legs, straight, slender, elegant legs— unusual indications of the personality supported by them!

I am so glad your book is going to be reviewed in the S. A. Quarterly. It certainly deserves it. I have sent a copy to Oxford and am awaiting orders. It must get well known. Couldn't you publish an English edition too?

I was speaking at Brighton last Monday—the first time that I have ever been there. But I only saw the inside of the station, and of the car that took me to the Royal Pavilion. But I did travel up in the train with two little chorus girls who interested me very much. They had been sent to play in a show—some revue, I fancy—at Brighton, and were so disgusted because they had been asked to provide their own make-up and shoes that they were flying back hot-foot to London to give the agent a piece of their mind. They were rehearsing the pieces all the way back in the train!

This is, after all, not a Christmas letter. But it comes with my love and my very best wishes for your happiness, *and* many hopes to see you in June. Don't forget there is a room here awaiting you.

CELIA.

58, Doughty Street, W.C.1,
December 6th.

ROSALIND DEAR,

To-day is a day of wind and sun and blown leaves about the street. I have lessons and a lecture to prepare and books to change at Mudie's, and Clare's new studio to inspect. To-morrow I go adventuring to Liverpool. I shall stay with Mr. M., your admirer—the little wiry Labour chairman who quarrels on principle with every one who wears diamond earrings, and who swears by the Belvedere School. He is going to show me Liverpool and his daughters and the inside of a democrat's house. This is as it should be. I am very excited and amused at the prospect. It is a lovely thing to go touring England with a League of Nations Union to pay the expenses. I pray that it may not be too cold so that my nose is blue. I hate blue noses—also upon principle.

My pupil for the Cambridge Scholarship exam is delightful to teach. She is full of enthusiasms. She has a new one every week. Once it was Fabianism, another time stage decoration, another time Nietsche, another time Proportional Representation. Last time it was lecturing to the American workman upon the true spirit of co-operation. I encourage them all. I think it is very nice that she should want to do all these things, don't you? But I always tell her, after each enthusiasm, "The only way that you can really do anything is by having a mind trained as only university education can train it." And she believes me. Then we sit down and discuss the Constitutional Issues of the Revolution of the C. 17. And in the middle she has a new enthusiasm. And we track down Agrarian Capitalism, or the Pauperisation of the Proletariat by Poor Laws to its dastardly origin until she grows calm again. Isn't it fun? I do hope she gets through.

I spent the week-end in the country at St. Monica's. On Sunday afternoon I went for a walk on the Surrey Downs. There were woods all bronze with bracken underfoot, and oak trees not quite bare. And I heard a blackbird sing, and the wet grass whisper, and I saw racing clouds and clear, bright water. And we had chicken and cream for supper.

On Monday when I came home I found a ticket for a matinee of the *Cenci*. Sybil Thorndike is playing in it at the New Theatre. A half-Italian amateur is Count Cenci. The scenery is simple, dark and wonderful. The dresses are vivid and very lovely. But the play—— Should such things be acted? Were the Greeks not wiser who subdued their horrors, who tortured off the stage? This is most terrible. Nothing is spared us. And Sybil Thorndike has a golden voice that breaks your heart with those exquisite verses. But nothing of the horror is hidden. I do not know. A wonderful play, marvellously acted, perfectly staged—but why was it produced at all? Perhaps I am inartistically squeamish. I prefer *The Immortal Hour*, though I know it nowhere touches the greatness of the other. At least it is a pleasanter afternoon's entertainment. I suppose I might say the same of *Charley's Aunt*. What is the drama? Why do we go to theatres? Isn't it queer that the most beautiful things are frequently the most unpleasant?

Has your rain stopped? Indeed, I hope it has by now, or you will be flooded indeed. It is long enough since you told me that you had to walk a mile round to Rhodes.

Have your holidays started? Are you well? Are you having a pleasant time?

Au revoir, my Rosalind, and much love,

From

CELIA.

58, Doughty Street, W.C.1,
Dec. 17th.

ROSALIND DEAR,

I have slept, eaten, lectured, coached, looked for the last pit-seat of *The Laughing Lady*, missed it, caught a cold, cured it, read *Main Street*, supped with my aunt, shopped for my Christmas presents, and bought Adolphus since last I wrote to you. By far the most important event was the buying of Adolphus. He is a tortoise. He is small, urbane, phlegmatic and herbivorous. I only discovered this morning that he was herbivorous. It was nearly too late. I bought him at an ex-officers' arts and crafts last Friday. Whether he ranked as an art or a craft, and in what way his existence was attributable to an ex-officer, I do not know. But there

143

he was, the one desirable thing in the exhibition, looking immensely bored, and surrounded by Polish dolls, gilded oyster tubs, embroidered baskets, home-made chocolates in painted boxes and bamboo tables. I bought him, took him home in the bus, tucked him up with moss and shavings in a boot box by the fireplace, and fed him on raw fish. He sulked. I put him on a newspaper and made him walk the length of it three times. He still sulked. I bought a cod steak on purpose, and gave him a juicy, raw piece, and cooked the rest for our supper. He still sulked. To-day I got out the encyclopædia and looked up "Tortoise," and behold, he is not a fish-eater at all, but is herbiferous! I went to lunch at the Brittains, and their maid gave me two Brussels sprouts. I have given them to Adolphus. He is so lively that he frisked all over the sitting-room. Vera had to dig him out from under the couch. He is eating his sprouts now, in the boot box by the fire, and is behaving beautifully. I am going to take him to Yorkshire to-morrow to give to Margaret. I would like to keep him here, but it is not kind when we have no garden.

I have been to call on the Pughs. They are such nice people. They have a brown Pom, and a lovely Persian cat, and a canary. They also keep fowls in a nice little back garden. They give me tea and are full of advice about colds and buses and Adolphus. I am lecturing at Woolwich after Christmas and shall go again.

My bath is overflowing. Excuse the smudges. This is horrid blotting paper.

Much love,

CELIA.

ROSALIND DEAR,

By the time you get this, Christmas will be a thing of the past, but my thoughts are with you now, and my love. Curiously enough, I have just had news of a sort about you—a long letter from Miss F., who tells me how she met and liked you, and how you came to the house where she was staying and how you and she and two men sat up till 1 a.m. talking and reading poetry.

I am home and having Christmas. We do it properly here—plum puddings and Christmas tree and small boys at the door every few minutes singing

"I wish you a Merry Christmas and a Happy New Year,
And please will you give me a Christmas box?"

Yesterday father and Grace and I walked up to the Hull Sanatorium on the hill to see the Christmas decorations. The sanatorium is arranged like a camp—rows and rows of huts, opening onto verandas, standing among the gardens of what used to be Cottingham Castle. It was a lovely moonlit evening, very still and full of stars. All the huts were lit with coloured lights and lanterns. Every ward was festooned with holly and coloured flowers and great bowls of imitation almond blossom made from beech branches and pink paper. There were lanterns among the trees and at the doors of the huts. You never say anything so gay and pretty. I do love Christmas in an institution. It seems so much gayer and realler than in a house—even if the people are incurable consumptives.

We have an Australian student staying here for Christmas. He is researching at Cambridge on Genetics and Heredity, and is most interesting. He knows Julian Huxley and nearly all the modern biologists and talks about his work in the most simple and natural way. During the war he was a major in the veterinary department of the 1st division, but I have not gathered that he knew any of our friends.

I return to town on Friday to start work again. I shall be glad. I don't really like holidays very much. One feels so lazy, and yet I can't work here. It's too cold and too full of people—but chiefly too cold.

I hope that your houseparty is going off well. I'd love to transplant myself to it for half an hour and see you all.

Au revoir, my dear, and much love as ever,

Yours,

CELIA.

1923

ROSALIND DEAR,

The calabash has arrived and is a joy. It came just the morning after I returned here. It lives by the side of the fire and is full of cigarette boxes, matches, sweets, string, chestnuts, and all the hundred and one things one wants down by the fire, yet never has because there is nowhere to put them without being untidy. And we won't be untidy because we both hate sham Bohemianism which, having none of the splendours of art, imitates its follies. So when our visitors come, I say, "Will you help yourself to cigarettes, matches, chocolates, chestnuts, and whatever else you like?" and hand them the calabash. Surprise and pleasure all round. You shall see when you come here in the summer. I do love its tightness and firmness, and the way its lid fits on so solidly.

Your letter has also come about Miss B. You will have been weary at the end of it all. I hope that you are having a good holiday with people who are sane and peaceful and not tiring. I suppose that it is worth it though, if you have saved her sanity.

It is a strange thing how one turns to people who have been either in the corps or the V.A.D. at times of crisis. Sometimes one wonders if all that queer war period was only a wild and stupid interruption, but I do know that one seems to rely more and more upon the people who shared its waste and follies.

Huchenneville, though, for all the wildness of its hares, seems to have been less wild and foolish than most places. I still long sometimes for those woods, and the acres of cowslips beneath the trees, and the daffodils and catkins and kindly green of the roadsides. It was a lovely country place.

149

I have a new dress. It is only a grey and blue knitted one, but I bought it yesterday at a sale. I've never got up early and gone to the first hour of a sale before, but Vera and I saw fascinating woollen dresses in Harvey Nicholls's catalogue for £2 2s., and in outsizes, so thought the chance too good to miss. I hadn't meant to buy one, but I've decided to sell all my last winter's clothes, and a tennis coat, and should be able to raise the £2 2s. and get my dress for nothing! To say nothing of a cheque I got from the *Morning Post* last night for 31s. 6d. for a wretched little scrappy article. If you feel inclined to write anything about farms or animals or country life for the Saturday morning Country Page of the *Morning Post*, they do pay you quite well. Mine was only about 400 words.

Adolphus is dead. He died on Saturday. He tried to get out of his box in the night and fell on his back and died next morning. Alas, alas!

The Times to-day quoted such a nice little poem by William Kean Seymour. It has so few poems now, that one must be content with small mercies. This is only part of the poem, but it swings with a hard, marching rhythm that I like:

CÆSAR REMEMBERS

Cæsar, that proud man
    Sat in his tent,
Weary with victory,
    With striving spent.

Where the grey Chilterns
    Coiled and slept
That hard-lipped Emperor
    Vigil kept.

But Cæsar cared not
>> For dyke or wall,
Faint and remote
>> Came the bugle's call;

Soft in the shadows
>> He saw, and heard
A Roman garden,
>> A Roman bird.

Walter de la Mare might have done it, but more mistily. That man is running too much to ghosts—a pity, for he has such magic to command.

I am reading *The Judge* by Rebecca West. How packed with detail and as full of pictures as the National Gallery. But, like a gallery, a little satiating. One feels, "What a clever girl, to write like this, to know so much, to understand chemistry and politics and typewriting, and poinsettias in a Spanish garden and debauchery and seafaring life and a man's view of sex and suffrage." And one is so busy thinking all this that the story gets lost, and then one skips. Yet she fills me with depressed humility. I may gibe at her, but I could not do a quarter as well as this.

There is an amusing play on, called *Bluebeard's Eighth Wife*—an adaptation of a French farce, light and witty. It contains the first bedroom scene that I have seen that has been really funny and not at all vulgar. And it also has a man who is drunk and yet a perfect gentleman—an unusual double achievement for one farce.

It is growing cold. I must stop and get into bed. I am in my dressing gown.

Good-night—and a happy New Year to you, my dear,
>> CELIA.

My Dearest Rosalind,

I am vexed with myself to think that I missed last week's mail. I had left it to write on Wednesday evening and then was ordered off to lecture for the League at Tufnell Park, and a fearful fog came on and I did not get in till too late, and the mail goes Thursdays. I can catch it by the evening post, but not the midnight one. I was sorry. I love your letters so, it seems discourtesy to miss a mail.

Your story has come. Of course I like it better in this form, but it's a sad story for all its delicate charm of phantasy. Shall I try to place it? It's difficult, though. I wish I knew how to get short stories into the world. When one reads the trash in magazines, one is filled with amazement. I do not know why *Two Primroses and Three Violets* did not see the light of day. It was more charming than a hundred that present their parents with handsome cheques.

I am writing a book[1] about a girl who never found romance. She sought for it always in the arms of a knight, according to the best traditional tales. But she found no knight, no kisses, nothing but respectable spinsterhood. So when her friend's lover was killed, and every one said, "Poor Delia, poor Delia," Muriel was only torn by jealousy. For Delia at least had her memories, and romance had never failed her. It isn't until the end of the book that Delia herself takes heart o' grace and starts to laugh at fortune again, and picks up Muriel with her and gives her a new romance, that she finds happiness—and even then it's not a particularly exciting sort of happiness, but a kind of coming to terms with life and a foregathering with beauty and pleasure and usefulness and the thousand funny, queer, exasperating things of life. So I wondered of your Nicolette and of my Muriel which would owe the least to life— Nicolette, who found romance and lost it, Muriel, who sought and never found.

[1] *The Crowded Street*, her second novel.

It's not a good book, more's the pity—but I will try to make it so.

What will happen next week, goodness knows. Here are the French mobilising, and the German Ruhr magnates defiant, the newspapers broiling, and people actually becoming excited for once about foreign politics instead of the Ilford murder or the Russell divorce. This at least is refreshing, but possibly rather expensive if we have to pay for common sense in our press topics by another war.

Surely somebody will persuade France of the futility of trying to pursue two contradictory policies at once. She wants reparations, for which Germany must be financially solvent. And she wants security, for which, in her opinion, Germany must be crushed. In the present policy she pursues the second object at the expense of the first. However——

To-day we saw snowdrops and violets sold in the streets for the first time. Coming out of Shepherd's Bush Tube Station I almost fell into an old woman with a great basket piled with little bunches, so darkly blue and so perfectly white. The whole road seemed filled with them. It was a glorious sight.

There was such a nice party at Bedford College a week ago. It was given by the Somerville Association in the hall— the one with the gallery. Miss Penrose and Miss Bruce and Miss Pope and Miss Darbishire and Miss Farnell were there in full force, and Rose Macaulay and Miss Kemp. Did you know Miss Kemp? She'd be ages before your time, but she's a wonderful woman. She has travelled all through China and Turkestan and forded rivers and climbed high mountains and been entertained by robber chiefs—but even more, she has recorded these intriguing experiences in the most delicious sketches—Chinese temples, pagodas of gold and jade, amber and ivory carvings, terrapins of jasper, magnolia trees blossoming in temple courtyards, Buddhist monks, swinging bridges, holy mountains hidden behind the mists, donkeys, coolies, Imperial palaces, lotus flowers,

153

joss-sticks and prayer mats, war gods, Confucians, Dorvists, herself in Thibetan dress, and so on. She gave us tickets to a lecture she was giving at the Royal Asiatic Society—that's how I know what her travels were like. She is nearing sixty, plain, amused, with white kid gloves, a butterfly in her hair, and boots with no nonsense about them. She talks in a deep, chuckly voice. I believe that for many women sixty is about the jolliest age. They have overcome their illusions and their physical disabilities, and have not yet lost their sense of humour or ability to eat three square meals a day.

The Royal Asiatic Society has At Homes in a big library, where you stand round a table in company with scholars and missionaries, and nice, brainless-looking peers who have been to India, and their wives and daughters and sisters. And nobody knows anybody else very well, and everybody seems to cherish a secret suspicion that somebody else is going to eat all the tea first, which would make them inclined to be rude and snatch seed cake from their neighbours, if they weren't at the same time aware that their neighbour might be a celebrity. As an audience, it is sticky. As a tea-fight, it is greedy, unsociable, and a little more undecorative than usual.

In our room we have small narcissi among dark laurel leaves. They look like syringa.

I have corrected the proofs of *Anderby Wold*. It looks rather meagre in print.

My very dear love—

CELIA.

58, *Doughty Street, W.C.1,*
Jan. 28th.

ROSALIND DEAR,

I left you in my mind going off in an ox wagon, with Bridgewater, stores, kaffirs, bedding, visitors and goodness knows what! I do hope that you arrived in safety at your

154

destination, with neither rheumatism nor breakage casualties nor any of those sad sort of things, and that Bushman's was worth the trek.

They are asking us here whether it was true that aeroplanes were used to bomb the natives after the Bondleswart Rebellion. I don't know. I wondered if you had heard anything of it. It sounds pretty beastly, but people say such unfounded things, one does not know.

My aunt who used to have a typewriting office in Trafalgar Square is leaving town. She gave me a lot of old office equipment that she had no further use for, and among letter files and paper weights was the MSS. of my Orchard Unit stories. Poor darlings, they were bad, weren't they? I am overwhelmingly thankful now that nobody would publish them, though at the time it seemed quite devastating. I wonder if after another four years, *Anderby Wold* will seem as puerile. I expect so, as it seems rather small fish now. And yet if I live and grow I will and must do something good before I quit. *Quien sabe?*

Another article returned by the *Morning Post* yesterday. Those sanguine prophets who depict the young writer entering a rosy path of bowing editors and importunate publishers after the acceptance of her first book are a little beside the mark.

I am so sorry that this letter smudges. It is an extraordinary thing why I never can find blotting paper that blots. Whether I buy it or steal it—generally the latter—it always develops immediately the strange quality of blotting with smudges every paper I touch.

I've discovered a new cure for a cold. Wash all your handkerchiefs. I went to coach my American on Monday, and found her in bed with what my uncles term delicately "a roarer." She made it even more ubiquitous than it might have been by her habit of blowing her nose on ten handkerchiefs and scattering them when used upon the floor for the maid to pick up! The consequence was that next day I also had a "roarer" and used all my handkerchiefs.

Then on Friday, which is a busy day anyway, I set to work and washed those handkerchiefs one by one, and dried and ironed them. It seemed to take hours. That night, my cold went.

Have you ever seen the blue beads in the Egyptian room in the new wing upstairs at the British Museum? Never, never have I seen such glorious, soul-stirring blue. There are beads and scarabs and fragments of broken porcelain and shards and enamels, but all are the same perfect and heavenly blue. Greener than lapis lazuli, greener than the Mediterranean on a sunny day, and yet bluer than anything one can imagine that is blue.

They are selling little Cape plums on the stalls now. I give you a recipe for a pretty sight. Buy an earthenware bowl. You can get them at sevenpence-halfpenny in Judd Street here. Paint it blue—a rich, bright-royal sort of blue. Buy half a dozen Cape plums as red and rich as you can find, some tangerines and some green, green apples and a bunch of dark-blue grapes. Put them in the bowl and set it on your table. There will be joy in the house.

My very dear love—

CELIA.

58, Doughty Street, W.C.1,
Friday.

ROSALIND DEAR,

I fear that I have missed this week's mail. I'm so sorry. Thursday leapt upon me out of the void, and I could not realise that another whole week had come and gone. I have lived in a whirl of semi-utilitarian gaiety—the most amusing kind, of course. One can be as frivolous as one pleases if there is a semblance of altruism in frivolity. I have glutted myself with an orgy of meetings. I have heard Lady Astor at the Westminster Central Hall; I have heard Sir Frederick Maurice at London University; I have heard Percy Harris at Bethnal Green, and myself at H. The H.

meeting was for the League of Nations Union in a Women's Conservative Club. The club held its meetings in an army hut, hidden carefully behind some trees in the grounds of Mrs. X's handsome detached residence. Doesn't that convey a lot? I had a violent argument with her about whether one should treat maids with a haughty reserve or a free and easy camaraderie. I, of course, plunged for the latter. We were drinking tea and eating our club buns in a corner of the hut after the meeting.

She: My dear, I am an older woman, with considerably more experience, and I know.

W: Well, I don't know that that makes such a lot of difference. I've lived among young people, I am one, and know what they feel like.

She: Well, you can't afford to let them get disrespectful. Servants are so hard to get nowadays, you've got to stick to the ones you have, and you've got to prevent their becoming familiar.

W: If you don't think they treat you with due respect, why don't you try some others?

She: But you simply can't get maids nowadays.

W: Doesn't that rather give your case away? There are young girls to be had.

She: I believe you think I'm a horrid old woman.

W: I think you're rather a dear—but I don't agree with you a bit.

Then we quarrelled amicably about the League.

She: A perfect idea, perfect. But, between you and me, *quite* unfeasible.

W: Every reform always has been unfeasible until it has proved itself to be practical.

She: Of course, I dare say I should support it in public. My husband does. But, of course, he's such an idealist.

W: Idealists are the only really practical people (didactically).

She: (amused) My dear child, you haven't lived with one for thirty years like I have.

And so on. We parted the best of friends, with mutual amusement.

I really started to tell you about the garden. It is lovely. The day was dull, with a wet, cloudy sky—the sort of day when the lawns are so vividly green they almost cry aloud—each blade of grass a shrill, metallic cry of bitter green. The borders lay below bare black trees. They were choked with rockeries and dripped over by sodden shrubs, but the crocuses grew between the stones—all purple and white—no gold. Everything there cold, wet colours—grey paths, grey house, grey rockery, and purple flowers. But it was nice to be there after London.

Did I tell you that Vera and Clare and I are going to Whipsnade for a fortnight after Easter? We are going to stay at the post office there, 800 feet up on the Chilterns. Clare will draw cows and sheep, and other beasts in which her soul delights; Vera and I will write and write and write. And in the afternoons we will walk, and come home and eat enormous teas, and then read novels over the fire and smoke or talk and laze until bedtime. It sounds too good to happen. I hardly dare think of it in case it does not happen. I haven't been in the real country (Cottingham isn't country) except for that week-end at Ravenscar with mother, ever since I left Oxford. Like the man in the psalms, my bowels yearn towards it. And we fit in well as a trio—Vera, wiry and fiery, full of sudden laughter and tears and petulance and affection; Clare, large, calm, rocklike, naïve as a child, firm as an elder, soothing as Mother Siegel's syrup, and withal most delightfully intelligent—and myself, I—oh, well, I love them both and they endure me—so there we are.

Ah! a mouse—my deadly enemy—has just poked its head from under a crack in the wainscot. I go to prepare its nightly supper of bread and poison!

158

With these murderous thoughts I will conclude. But to you goes my love, and come soon to England, and
Yours ever,
CELIA.

58, Doughty Street, W.C. 1.
Feb. 12th.

ROSALIND DEAR,

Behold me, a little jaded after a night more or less sleepless with the effort to rise at five-thirty, endeavouring to master Kant's *Critique of Pure Reason* as criticised by Hegel over a tea of bread and treacle in the kitchen, while the soup boils over, my handkerchiefs dry on the line, and a half-annotated speech on "Women in the Civil Service," lies at my elbow, being flouted for the sake of a note-book containing a half-finished lay of a Cosmopolitan Cock! What an immense sentence, and how truly unliterary! The truth is that I believe I am trying to do too many things at once, but it's all such fun it would be impossible to know where to begin pruning. My present novel is causing me difficulties. Some fiend, not incarnate, led me to choose a heroine with a vague and inefficiently philosophico-mathematic mind. Thank heaven it *is* vague and inefficient. To reproduce efficient mathematics would task my powers beyond breaking point. Then the girl who has done the cover for my book—Clare Leighton—went with me to John Lane the other day, and we asked him to publish a animal book. It is to be called *Temperamental Tails, Being a Versatile Volume of Astonishing Animals, depicted by Clare Leighton and described by Winifred Holtby*. She does woodcuts —most charming and humorous. I write verses—solemn absurdities, about the Cantankerous Cuckoo, the Pertinacious Pig, the Bilious Bull, the Sabbatarian Sheep, and so on. I think that they are going to do it. Clare is a charming, a plucky child. She was never educated. She had a nurse till she was sixteen, and was never allowed even to post a letter

159

without a maid. Suddenly she insisted on learning drawing. She was allowed, after great difficulties, to attend the Brighton Art School twice a week. She practised all day. She drew at night and at odd moments and on the kitchen table. They came to London. She went at intervals to the Slade. She took all her certificates on about quarter the proper training. She exhibited two pictures in the New English and one in the London Group. When her family went to the country she insisted upon staying in town to study. She taught at an elementary school three days a week to gain money for her classes. She went to stay with an uncle. She slept on a sofa in his flat. She paid ten shillings a week for the run of a studio. She painted like a fury. One day her headmistress told her that she was Geddes-axed from her school. She had no job—no money—nowhere to live. If she went home it meant typing and doing housework and good-bye to her work. Then Vera stepped in, and took her to her agent, Truman & Knightley's. She took her to St. Monica's and introduced her to the headmistress. She promised to look after her whatever happened. The St. Monica's people liked Clare so much that they had her to teach one day a week. The agent found her two more jobs. Clare is earning £6 a week. I got her to do the cover of my book and introduced her to John Lane. The directors fell in love with her—her candour, her childish naïveté, her decided talent. They want her work. She has taken two unfurnished rooms. She has furnished them with painted barrels, a camp bed, an old deal table, two chairs and her painting things. Everything in the room she has painted blue and black against the cream-washed walls. She has crimson coconut matting on the floor, and blue curtains. She has filled a blue bowl with crimson apples and set it on her black tablecloth. She is happier than almost any one I know. One day she will be great.

Here the door-bell rang and behold, your letter. You are bathing by the river. Oh, take care of the sharks! There is white, warm, clean, wonderful sand. And you have warm, wonderful bathing. How warm it sounds. Here we have daffodils sold in the streets, and in the parks are crocuses. A man to-day had a primrose in his buttonhole.

My dear love,

CELIA.

58, Doughty Street, W.C. 1,
Feb. 18th.

MY DEAREST ROSALIND,

I will begin this letter now while the bath is running, and may be then it won't get finished until after the mail has come in with yours. I hope, by the way, that when it comes it will be to bring me word from you, for if you remember the tenor of your last letter, it has left me wondering whether by this time you are in Grahamstown or in a shark! It is a tantalising thing—to put it at its mildest—to leave yourself on the shores of a shark-infested stream, while your friends, several hundreds of miles away, have no possible chance of pulling you out!

Yesterday morning was so full of sun and wind and racing clouds that we took the bit between our teeth, left our work, and walked to Hyde Park, and from there to Kensington Gardens, and on, and on, among the crocuses fresh pricking through the grass, and lilacs, budding with tight dots of green, and gay, fresh grass.

Have you read *Hidden Lives*, by Leonora Eyles? A splendid book, fearless, terrible, sane and never hopeless—touched with the solemn beauty of triumphant fortitude. I would like to meet that woman. She has a pleasant touch of humour, too, and such excellent sanity. A very different book, more tragic even because only more literally true, is *Peaceless Europe*, by Signor Nitti, the ex-premier of Italy. It gives one furiously to think—if one has not thought already. What a mad world we live in, with poverty, dirt, ignorance and all the seventeen thousand deadly sins of apathy and indolence and superstition and the seventeen thousand still more deadly virtues of respectability and its kindred—and yet men seem content to talk about "our English honour" and such rot. If only they would stop this idiotic spending of millions on entirely unnecessary armaments and spend a little on education or housing.

I really must stop these tirades. You, poor dear, you must get tired of my Jeremiads. Do you often laugh to yourself and say, "Poor thing, she's very young. I hope she's not worrying unfortunate humanity to death with her ingenuous solicitude." You wouldn't say it like that, of course, but I often wonder how I would chuckle if I had my letters to read over again—and blush too, to think how silly and violent they often are.

D——! Excuse the blotches on the other side of this sheet. It doesn't much matter if you can't read what's written there. I was only laughing a little at myself, and you can do that for me. Thank you.

The reason for the blots and my explosion is Mr. —— my excellent dyer and cleaner, who presented me with his compliments and an elegant blotter—after charging nine shillings for cleaning my grey stockinette frock, which I call exorbitant. I suppose he thought that the blotter would soften my heart. Instead of that, it entirely destroys the beauty of my correspondence, and I love him not a whit the more.

For more frivolous preoccupations this week, I have ordered a darling hat—a huge black one of straw and marocain, turned up at one side of the back, with slim, drooping gold feathers. I tremble to think of the price, especially as I have just lost a job. A Mrs. Q wanted me to coach her daughter for seven and sixpence an hour. I will not go anywhere for under ten shillings. Considering the preparation necessary to give anything like an adequate coaching, even that is little enough. I get fifteen shillings from the American, but she, alas, comes to an end in March. Then I am going to send round my syllabus and testimonials and make a bid for lecturing in schools. I must and will go to Heidelberg. Having persuaded the Union to hold a school there, it would never do not to go. And the bookbinders are still striking, so *Anderby* mayn't be out for months. I agree with the bookbinders, personally. The publishers want to reduce their wages because prices are going down. But they aren't reducing the prices of the books. Very soon they'll be reducing the remuneration of the unfortunate authors.

Desmond of the *Daily News* called here on Thursday. I knew his daughter at Somerville and he came to give us advice about free lance journalism. A dear, vague, friendly person, with brown eyes full of humour, and a charming, kindly voice. He has drifted all round the world and out again, and talks with an indolent but pleasant charm of German prison camps and Russian hospitals. He seems to live in a world of kindly people and singing birds and leisurely sunlit picnics. Even when he was a prisoner of war, people seem to have been kind to him, and German women gave him new-laid eggs, and sentries let him buy books and walk in the fields, and what he remembers most are the pointed red roofs of the little homely town.

My bath is ready. Au revoir.

My love as ever,

CELIA.

58, *Doughty Street, W.C. 1,*
27.2.'23.

ROSALIND DEAR,

Your last letter which came yesterday tells me of you about to leave by ox-wagon on the twelfth of February. That doesn't seem so far away. On the twelfth you were packing up your caravan, and I was buying a wonderful pair of patent leather shoes in Shadwell for 17s. 11d. I went there to lecture. I remained to buy shoes in the rain. There are dozens of little shoe-shops there kept by greasy

163

women who are Jews, or if not Jews, so like them that you wouldn't know the difference. But the shoes are lovely— and they actually keep seven and a half without blinking! A characteristic immensely endearing to one of my gargantuan stature.

My dear, you say your spirits are at zero. What am I to say that can raise them, even by one degree? I, who am hundreds of miles away, and who am also one of the so-called fortunate of this earth, and so am barren of comfort? What I could say would, I suppose, only deserve the fate that usually attends attempted consolation from such as I—"academic platitudes—all very well for you." Rosalind dear. I spend part of my life in Bloomsbury, part in Bethnal Green. In Bethnal Green there are neither prickly pears nor mimosa, though a few faded daffodils languish on a street booth, and one narrow window is cold with white funeral flowers. It says much for a people among whom beauty is associated solely with mortality, and roses and lilies only bloom for funeral wreaths. Some of the children at the school where I was working yesterday are continually being absent. They are absent because they are ill. They are ill because they are sleeping regularly in the same room as three brothers, the new baby, their mother and father and the cat. One of the babies has ringworm. The mother is suspected of tuberculosis. The father is out of work. He is out of work because his cabinet-making master has failed. And the master has failed because trade is bad, because our markets are curtailed, because in Poland and Russia and Germany thousands and millions of people are starving instead of fulfilling their destined economic function as purchasers of British and Indian goods. Oh, Lord, what a world! If you know of any remedy, do come home and help us find one. Sometimes it would seem as though there were no time for dreams or friendships or romances because the world is sick to death, and some one has to put it right.

Yet what's to be done?

164

I went last night to a conference of the Eighty Club, and heard twenty or thirty earnest gentlemen, all well-meaning, all intelligent, make speeches about the present economic situation. And we drank coffee and smoked expensive cigarettes, and sat under portraits of Gladstone and Mr. Asquith and talked pleasant philanthropic sentiments—and all the time were feeling fierce and hot inside, because that afternoon at Bethnal Green I had seen jolly boys of fourteen and fifteen, bright and keen, doomed within a year, many of them, to be hanging round street corners, reading the betting news, and half hoping to avoid the job that doesn't come.

This evening Vera has been reading up for a League of Nations speech, and we've got hold of the information about the bombing in Iraq. We really have been using aeroplanes to bomb recalcitrant villages into submission—some because they harbour thieves, some because their chief men will not fulfil their administrative obligations, some because of "anti-British propaganda." Then we warn them, it's true—give them time for repentance and submission—and after that, drop bombs, by way of pro-British propaganda, I suppose. What a world!

Have you read *Hidden Lives* yet? It is very good. I've also just finished *Follow My Leader*, by Mary Agnes Hamilton—quite interesting, but not so good. A bit too propagandist.

I had a long letter yesterday from Mr. Macdonald of Liverpool. I thought he had forgotten me, and here he's coming up to town, possibly to see me after his business. I like him so much.

On Sunday I walked through the Park and saw the people riding in the Row and thought of our rides. Never, never shall I forget your wild career on Windy. Something of it has gone into the book I'm writing now, and of Ken's gallant rush to the rescue. But my Connie is round and bouncing, very different from you. And she rides for sheer bravado, because Godfrey only notices Clare. And she falls off too, right at the end, and comes home covered with mud and glory.

Mother has just been made a member of the Yorkshire County Council. I got a wire on Saturday night, but no letter yet to tell me how it went. It is a very conservative locality, and she is the first woman to get elected.

I send you a *Time and Tide* containing an article of Vera's, with which I think you will agree. It is founded upon much experience. I originally tried to write it. It was I who was reading Charlotte Brontë, but I couldn't get it down well enough. I haven't the article gift. It's a very different thing from writing novels. My style is either too pedantic or too entirely colloquial. Hence my elegant collection of editorial regrets. I also send you a little sonnet of my own I made the other day—not very good, and, Vera says, too much like Christina Rossetti—but I hadn't read Christina's song till mine was made.

My dear love,

CELIA.

NO MOURNING—BY REQUEST

Come not to mourn for me, with solemn tread,
Clad in dull weeds of sad and sable hue,
Nor weep because my tale of life's told through,
Casting light dust on my untroubled head.
Nor linger near me while the sexton fills
My grave with earth—but go gay-garlanded,
And in your halls a shining banquet spread
And gild your chamber o'er with daffodils.
Fill your tall goblets with white wine and red,
And sing brave songs of gallant love and true,
Wearing soft robes of emerald and blue,
And dance, as I your dances oft have led,
And laugh, as I have often laughed with you—
And be most merry—after I am dead.

ROSALIND DEAR,

Aye me, this pitiful world where money matters so
much. Money just now has made my room look pretty.
For the enormous sum of 1/8 I have tall tulips, purple and
crimson, in my shell case, purple and crimson anemones on
the table, and a tiny bunch of primroses in a rough blue
pottery bowl. I have not been in to the real country since
last year at Ravenscar, and I have not been out of London
at all since Christmas, except last Wednesday for one day
at Dover, where I went to lecture—longing for a fine day
and sea breezes. I got the breezes all right, but so lusty
were they that I turned into a café and spent all the time
I was not lecturing crouched over a radiator, wishing that
I had brought my fur coat!

I have been reading *Desolate Splendour*, by Michael
Sadler. I think it is a clever and amusing book. Fine,
full-blooded melodrama, a wicked earl with painted cheeks
and giant negro servants living in the Boulevard St. Ger-
main; an equally wicked old villainess plotting over her
playing cards—a very questionable collection—in a Tower
called "The Devil's Candle"; a hero who has been a rake,
and who is reformed by the innocent devotion of the
beautiful and luckless heroine. What better ingredients for
a really good story? And the style is dignified and musical,
the setting picturesque, the detail generous, and the whole
delightfully readable. Get it if you haven't.

Quite a different sort of thing is Masterman's *England
after War*—a most tragic and pitiful indictment of our
shallow optimism, full of splendidly eloquent passages
and descriptions which, if sometimes over coloured, are
always interesting.

My work for this term is over, and both my ewe-lambs
doing their examinations. What a heartrending task is
that of the invigilator, watching her beloved pupil groan
with agony over a perfectly fiendish paper! I wonder that

examiners are not rent by remorse for the agonies that they inflict. If neither of them get in I shall lament most bitterly, for they are both clever and pleasant children.

I want a new Spring hat. I want to colour-wash the walls of our sitting-room plain cream; I want to buy a great battalion of mauve and crimson tulips; I want to have a day in the country; I want to hear *The Immortal Hour* again; I want to see Drinkwater's *Oliver Cromwell*; and I want to hear Daisy Kennedy play the violin. Heigh ho! What a selfish list of wants. Never mind, I shan't get any of 'em yet, so I might as well "stay wantin'." I tell you, though, that the streets of London are alive with lovely things. Yesterday I saw a fat white puppy, so fat he could not run properly, but rolled over and over, getting tangled up with his lead, and finally, completely fatigued, sat down and proceeded to eat it with sad deliberation.

I saw a market woman in a white apron, holding a flat basket full of primroses. She had three feathers in her hat, and the sunlight slanted down on to her basket from above the tall grey houses.

I saw Piccadilly Circus like a real circus, with the policemen playing circus policemen, and the clowns and ladies, and the motor-buses red and blue and orange, and in the middle a great clump of flowers round about the market women who wore round straw hats.

I saw Brixton all lit up for Saturday night, with the shops glaring and laughing to each other, and holding out pots and cauliflowers and crêpe de Chine and iced cakes and bicycles and fried fish and toy engines and gramophones and dusters and newspapers and cheese. "... 'I saw a little girl crying,' said the Moon." ...

My love to you,

CELIA.

MY DEAREST ROSALIND,

Thank you, my dear, for your last letter. I have just come home and told them that you don't think you can get a holiday this year. Everybody is most disappointed. They had all looked forward so much to seeing you, and had hoped that you might be able to spare a little while to come up here.

I have come home till the 11th, and then am going to take Vera into the country if I can. The strain of her own work, coming on top of a series of overwhelming blows during the war, is almost too much for anybody, tough though she is. I can do so little except take her temporarily away from it.

This country is not as warm as London. A few daffodils are out, but the trees are hardly in bud, and there are berries still upon the holly bushes. We were to have gone for a picnic to-day, but it is too cold. I have a cold as well, which does not tend to make picnics very pleasant. I am going to stay at home and make myself a pair of cami-knickers instead—blue birds on mauve, and mauve birds on pale blue. They should be pretty! Then we are going to celebrate Bank Holiday by all going in to the theatre to-night to see *Paddy the Next Best Thing*. The last play that I saw was a matinee of *Everyman*, done most impressively at the Old Vic. I had not been to the Old Vic before. The audience was rather too respectable and West-Endish for my liking, but the play was done well and very simply, and I liked it. How far more true to life is the conventional formality of fifteenth century rhymed couplets than the so-called realism of the modern drama. I am intensely interested in the decorative ornateness of the modern German theatre, where stage effects, both of drama and of spectacle, have beautiful designs and patterns instead of every nail as it

169

would have been in the *real* express train, as advertised at Drury Lane!

I have just finished Sheila Kaye-Smith's *A Challenge to Sirius*. It is a great book, full of true and expressive passages. Do you know it? Here is one:

"He saw his life as a good thing, and he saw happiness, towards which that life had always consciously or unconsciously struggled, as merely a relative good. The real stuff of life was experience, in which sorrow and fear and disaster had as important a part to play as beauty and joy. The idea that happiness is the object and crown of a man's life was just a primitive illusion, and he had passed beyond it now. He saw his life as good because it had been full and rich, though its chief spoils were anguish and sorrow. Life justified itself. It might be cruel, treacherous, ironic, but it was life, and pain was as much a part of it as joy."

Here is another—when Frank has knelt in the barbaric primitiveness of a Roman Catholic Church in Utacan:

"For now he knew the secret of the mystical union which he had felt existing between the Church and the forest. When he knelt in the Church and looked up at the crude and hideous effigy of the Crucified, the Indian boy all dabbled with blood, tortured and naked and heartbroken, he saw the other side of the mystery which he had pondered over in the forest by the broken altar of forgotten priests. He saw a God who did not merely absorb experience through him, but shared it with him. There was not one pang of his lonely wandering life, no throb or ache or groan of his up to that moment when the light of his eyes and the desire of his heart were taken from him at a stroke, that had not been shared by God. For if man has known the stars, so God has known the dust."

Much love to you,

CELIA.

170

Bainesse,
Cottingham,
E. Yorks, April 8th, 1923.

DEAREST ROSALIND,

I sent you a copy of *Anderby Wold*, and hope that it arrives in safety, though the lady at the post office lashed it about most cruelly with her scissors to see whether I was true in saying that the book contained no letter. I hate to think of my first-born coming undressed half-way across the sea and arriving naked in a foreign land, but if he will, he will, and Mercury, God of Travellers, aid him. I have had several reviews already. Some are amusing, some aren't. The best of all was from the *Sunday Express.* It wound up: "I found nothing remarkable in *Anderby Wold.* The picture wrapper of a hay-cart by C. Leighton is excellent; the novel not so." The local press, of course, is gushing—because Mother is very popular. Everything else is non-committal except one gentleman on the *Sheffield Independent* who, for some reason or other, was very kind. I have also had nice letters from "J. E. Buckrose" and Aldous Huxley. John Lane sent the latter a copy, thinking that he still reviewed for *The Nation and Athenæum.* He wrote to me to tell me that he no longer did any reviewing, but was going to write to me to tell me what he thought of the book directly he had time—a very pleasant sort of letter—not at all patronising.

On Wednesday I go to Whipsnade in the Chilterns, for a fortnight or possibly three weeks. It rather depends how things turn out and whether I have to get back for any jobs. I am going to try my lecturing. I have typed out most impressive circulars, but don't know if I shall get anything out of them. The journalistic stunt does not seem to have leaped into success in spite of *Anderby*; though I keep on sending out stories, articles and poems they are but homing pigeons.

We are very excited, as we believe that Grace is really going to get engaged to a particularly nice doctor—a Scot.

171

He is intelligent, ambitious, dogged and kindly, with just a taste o' the de'il in his temper to give him a bit of zip; but a thoroughly nice man, I think, and though both are of the slow-coming-on temperament, I really think that they care for one another—and I should so like him as a brother-in-law! However, it is on the knees of the gods.

The other day I stole from Mother a copy of *The Shropshire Lad*. For some reason or other I had never got hold of it before, and only read one or two of the poems in anthologies. I have been nearly wild with delight over my belated discovery—isn't the *Cherry Tree* fine? And that poem to Terence on why songs—and, of course, I think also books—may be sad and yet please? And the two-verse fragment about the "light-foot lads"?

I've read nothing except poems this week to please me. Arnold Bennett's *Mr. Prohack* is quite interesting in parts. E. F. Benson's *Relentless City* is quite pleasant, but much like a thousand other books. *Original Companions*, by Isobel Wylie Hutchinson may be good, but it is quite beyond me. The beginning bored me, and the end I could not understand. Worst of all, the damned book I am writing is like the drivelling of a weak-kneed sea calf. If I were sufficiently strong minded, I should tear it up and start again. But I don't. Perhaps because there are only two chapters to write, and I want to see it finished, however bitter that sight may be. But I doubt if I dare show it to John Lane. I am thoroughly dissatisfied with it, and hate myself for being so.

Well, well. If we haven't a grouch against Fortune, we seem unable to avoid one against ourselves.

Au revoir, and much love.

Ever your,

CELIA.

The Post Office,
Whipsnade, Nr. Dunstable,
Beds, April 14th, 1923.

ROSALIND DEAR,

This must be one of the loveliest places in England. It is a small village, 800 ft. up in the Chilterns. There is a village green, shut in by gates north, south, east and west. You may let your cattle feed on the green, or geese or sheep or horses, but not goats or pigs—I don't know why. All the same, there are goats and pigs, a mother goat and a little one. And as for pigs—the funniest thing happened yesterday. Vera looked out of the window and called me to see a black sow and seven baby black pigs, darlings. Then we went back to work. Then a little while later, down came a sharp shower and Vera went to shut the window—and behold! the black sow had been washed white, and all the little pigs were pinkish grey! We were so disturbed by this phenomenon that we called Mrs. Andrews, the post mistress and our hostess, and she told us that they were not one family, but two families. (That sounds somehow like the Athanasian Creed, doesn't it?)

Vera and Clare and I are staying here. We have a double room where Vera and I sleep and a tiny room where Clare sleeps and a sitting-room where we feed and where Vera and I write in the morning while Clare paints. The sitting-room is all white and clean, and the window looks on to a lawn and an apple tree, and three wallflowers and the village green. Also on to some wooden buildings. Now one of those wooden buildings is the lavatory, and to reach it you have to go through the post office, which is also a shop. And every time the shop door opens a little bell rings, and the post mistress comes into the shop to see if any one has come to buy. It is the most self-advertising place I ever encountered! Next door to the lavatory is another hut, and going out the first night in the dark, Clare opened a door, and as soon as she opened it she heard " Mai-ai-ai! Mai-ai-ai!" and felt something butt against her legs. It was the wrong door, and she was in the goat-house.

The country here is just the sort that people call typically English. There are downs and meadows and little copses full of violets and wood anemones and primroses. On the downs there are cowslips, and in the hedgerows are hawthorn and wild cherry and blue-eyed ground ivy. The villages have real thatched cottages. The post office where we are staying is not thatched. It has a grey-tiled roof and a little ivy growing up one side, and a shop and a telephone, and the post office and our charming sitting-room.

My stories still come home to roost. I only hope my novel sells, but the reviews aren't very encouraging, and personally the more I read the book the more I agree with the reviewers.

Here comes tea. Hurrah! And our nice, smiling, pink-cheeked post mistress. She feeds us on cream and butter and new-laid eggs and all sorts of nice things. I would like to send you some.

Much love as ever,

CELIA

The Post Office,
Whipsnade, Dunstable,
Beds, April 2nd?—Oh, I've forgotten.

ROSALIND DEAR,

It is you who are leading the strenuous life now and I who am lazy. Every day down here passes like another. We wake to the sound of birds, and the sight of the pear blossom outside our window. We breakfast leisurely and very late. We write in the morning, Vera upstairs in the bedroom, I in the sitting-room. We lunch like lords and then wander in the country between deeply-hedged lanes or on the downs. Our adventures are rare and pleasantly bucolic. To-day we had a small one. We were passing a yard where a mother sow lay with five little pigs. I did not notice that the gate was open, but chirruped to the

174

pigs in a friendly way, as one man to another, so to speak.
Then we walked on down the road, forgetting the pigs,
absorbed in conversation. As a matter of fact, I was telling
Vera about the really rather tragic crisis of my book. Then
we passed a lover and his lass—they grow thick here about
the lanes o' Sunday. We did notice that they sniggered at
us, but thought it was only country manners. A little
farther we passed an old man, and he stared, too. Then as
we got into the village street of Dagnall, a troup of small
boys started to laugh outright and point. We turned our
heads. Behind us, trotting patiently to heel, were the five
little pigs following like dogs! Eventually the small boys
chased them away—a good half-mile back to their home
in the yard.

The other day we had an even more striking adventure.
Have you ever met a Prophet, Rosalind? I have. Clare,
Vera and I were walking along the lanes to Studham, when
outside the Checkers Inn we met a respectable man, the
older side of middle age, carrying an umbrella. He called
to Clare: "You—the young lady on this side of me—surely
I have met you before?" "No, I don't think so," said Clare.
But, like all artists, she is of a friendly disposition. "Oh,
yes, but I have. Now, have you been in Richmond, or at
Hull in Yorkshire, say?" Clare hadn't. They considered
for some time where he might have met her, then at last
he said, "I'll tell you why I stopped you. Have you ever
met a prophet?" We all disclaimed that honour. "Then I
tell you that to-day you have met a prophet. I'm a good
man, even if I do sometimes take a glass of beer. And I
have a message from the Lord—I don't tell it to every one.
Now, you listen. If you have any genius in you—all you
three—let it come out. Have courage. The Lord means
you to speak. People have genius more often than we
know. But they lack Courage. If you have genius, the
Lord means you to let it out. Now I am a prophet—like
St. Paul. Neither better nor worse than St. Paul. But I
have a message from the Lord. I can see Jesus Christ

175

continually. When I am in bed at night I can hear the angels singing, and hundreds and thousands of the trumpets blowing. And the day will come when I shall stand upon the steps of St. Paul's Cathedral, and the people will be before me. There will be great crowds, and those who have mocked at me in the streets, the children of Dagnall and Whipsnade and Studham, they will come in awe to hear me, and the Day will be fixed. Then I shall lift up my arms to heaven and cry: ' Peace, be still.' And then you will see the Lord coming with glory and power. Even so, Amen. I tell you so that you may remember." Clare asked: "Do you know when that Day will be?" He shook his head. "Nay, nay. The Lord knows. He will tell me." Then, more briskly, he said, "Don't forget what I said about genius. And I spoke to you that you may say, ' Once I met a prophet.' Good-day to you." And he went up the road.

Have we met a prophet? And who goes about country lanes telling three untidy-looking young women that genius needs Courage? What do you make of it, Rosalind ?

My love to you,

CELIA.

58, Doughty Street, W.C.1,
May 8th.

DEAREST ROSALIND,

I am half drunk with sleep, or I would write you a more decent letter. As it is, this is just to avoid letting you have the possibility of an empty English mail, but I will write better later. Since I came back on Saturday night I have never stopped going once, and am sleepy, but it is only making up arrears, and I will be freer later. I have two lectures to give to-morrow that I still have to get up. Both are in different parts of Ilford—a democratic district of which I am becoming increasingly fond.

I can't remember if I told you that Vera's book has been taken by Grant Richards. I do like him so much. He is

176

the man who publishes for Alec Waugh, Eden Philpotts, S. P. B. Mais and Thomas Burke—also *The Shropshire Lad* and the Sitwells and lots of poets. So that is nice. Rose Macaulay has written her a very nice letter about it.

I have had to take my fountain-pen to the hospital, and am simply lost without it.

To show you irony. I wrote an article called "The Crime of Chivalry" for *Time and Tide*. I spent hours over it, and really it wasn't half bad. It was refused. When I was at home one night I scribbled the silliest of 500 words called "Happy Endings," and sent it for a joke to the *Daily Mail*, badly written, badly typed, absurd. The other day came a cheque for £3 3s. for it! It was worth perhaps the 3/-!

I was at a speakers' conference at the League of Nations Union to-day—Gilbert Murray was in the chair. He is the best chairman I know, I think. His quiet, conciliatory manner is a gift of the gods. He impresses me more than almost any personality I have encountered.

Have you ever been to the Geffrye Furniture Museum in the Old Almshouses, Shoreditch? I had half an hour between two meetings in Bethnal Green this morning, and went there. It is the most charming place—a quadrangle of Queen Anne Almshouses, with a lovely grass square like an Oxford College. Inside are rooms panelled with the spoils of old London houses, Adam fireplaces, C.17 ceilings, tapestries, cottage interiors with rushlights and spinning wheels, chairs and tables of all periods—really beautifully set out, and the smallness and quietness of the place is so delicious in that loud and dirty part of London.

Do excuse this writing. Next week my pen will be back, and I may be more wide awake.

Much love—ever yours,

CELIA.

ROSALIND DEAR,

A ring at my bell this morning called me downstairs
to welcome home my truant pen, his washer renewed and
his nib mended, so you shall have a letter. Whether the
letter will be amusing or not depends rather on the weather.
I am going out to dinner. Yes, actually I! It is an event
that happens once in a month o' Sundays. Greater miracle
yet, I am going with a Young Man. Not much of a young
man, I admit. He comes to my shoulder or thereabouts,
but he has a pleasant smile, a nice tenor voice and a decent
sense of humour. I am going to dine with him at Soho
and accompany him afterwards to a concert. He is not
really interested in me, but since I published *Anderby* and
am also known to be a member of the Eighty Club, he
cultivates me, thinking that one day I may be worth knowing. Poor misguided youth. However, the weather comes
in this way. If it rains, as it has been doing periodically
ever since I came back to Town, I shall have a taxi. My
one and only pair of tinsel slippers must not be tarnished.
If it is fine, I shall walk. In the former case, you shall
have a longer letter.

I have spent a thoroughly frivolous day. This morning
I wrote, certainly, but this afternoon was dedicated to the
manufacture of a table-cloth, a charming table-cloth, blue
sundour, the sort that never fades, like the joys of New
Jerusalem. There is one thing that I hate about making
table-cloths, and that is the ironing business afterwards.
I find it tyrannously difficult, and my cloth still has some
unlovely creases in it—but oh the joy of blue after my dusty
black. And a blue bowl on it full of star-like narcissus.
And I have two bowls of pansies, and one of lilies of the
valley, and an earthenware pot of wallflowers, and a great
basin full of bluebells and beech leaves, and my shell case
full of beech leaves and yellow daisies. What about that
for a room?

I have done little this week except make up for lost time. Two Managers' meetings in Bethnal Green, organising a Social at the Women's Club there, speaking, writing articles and working a little at my book—oh, and shopping. I had a *heavenly* shopping on Thursday morning. Vera and I went to Marshalls. I had £10 saved for summer clothes and the £3 3s. for my *Daily Mail* article. I bought a black marocain and georgette dress—readymade, with only a few inches to let down in the skirt. Then I found a pair of charming black suede shoes for 25/-, and some pale gold stockings to match the gold feathers in my black hat. Then I bought another hat of painted straw—a very large shape turned up behind, with a tiny strip of beautiful embroidery across the front, all different blues, and lots of little blue ribbons of different shades tied round and falling down one side. It is an angel. Then in Shaftesbury Avenue I found a shop where they sell pretty summer vests in pink and blue at 1/11 each. And two pork cutlets for lunch still kept me within my margin. I'm also renovating my blue and silver evening dress and turning it into a day one, and making a grey crepe dress which is costing me 12/6. So really I shall feel set up. What hideous frivolity! But I'm not going to Heidelberg or Vienna this year. Funds won't allow it. So I feel that I must wear some clothes in England.

I wonder if you'll get home in November. And if you'll stay if you do come. And if you'll be happy if you stay. I'd love to see you again. Sometimes I wonder whether you are really you—if you have the same long, white, slim hands, and the same wild, lovely hair.

I wish one could insure one's friends against bad luck. Wouldn't it be nice? A premium of six happy hours paid in advance, the capital to be withdrawn on three weeks' notice at any specified time.

Reviews are funny things. I wonder that people ever take any notice of them. I've had some curious ones—lots of them good, bad and indifferent. They nearly all go in couples. The *Yorkshire Post* tells me I have a socialist axe to grind. The *Daily Herald* tells me I don't do justice to socialism, and kill the only worth while person in the book. The *Oxford Magazine* tells me that I've no axe to grind at all, and deal impartially with both sides of the question. The *Dublin Independent* says that I have written a very remarkable book, and prophesies a future of glorious prospects for me. The *Irish Independent* asks blandly if I am one of the Village Idiots, and says that the numerous printers' errors are undoubtedly due to the fact that the compositor yawned so much over putting up the print that he could not see what was what! And so *ad infinitum*. The only thing to do is to decide that nothing really means anything.

Great ructions in this part of the world about the ridiculous Saar Decree. It is a little more than ridiculous, I fear, and will be very awkward to explain away at meetings.

No spring. Cold rain day after day. We have bought our summer hats, yet perforce we wear them with our fur coats—a dismal prospect for which I have no liking—especially as my fur coat is very much out at elbows. Vera and I are going up to Oxford on the 31st—our first visit except a night for our Degrees since we went down. If it still freezes, there'll be no river, no nothing.

I must go now and write to Mother. She is away in Newcastle with an aged relative who is ill.

Very much love, my dear, as ever,

Yours,

CELIA.

58, Doughty Street, W.C.1,
May 27th.

ROSALIND DEAR,

I had a wire last night to say that Grace has got engaged to our Scotch doctor, and I am very pleased. He is clever, ambitious, honest, with a real love for science and his profession, quite unostentatious, considerate and fairly strong willed. I think he is the sort of person with whom one could be great friends. I only met him when I went home at Christmas, and I did like him immensely. I do hope that they will soon marry and make me an aunt. It is a position I have always desired.

Last night Vera and I sold programmes at a performance of the *Antigone* given by the Woking W.E.A. tutorial class at the Old Vic for the Four Oxford Women's Colleges Appeal Fund. For a performance by working men and women, it was amazing; as a performance by any one at all it was beautiful and dignified. They sang the choruses to Mendelssohn's music. The chorus was entirely of women, dressed in yellow and orange. The leader, a really lovely girl in a flame-coloured tunic, moved with such dignity that I thought was only found among the women of the East. Antigone herself was tall and stately, the tutor of the class, but every person spoke with a conviction and appreciation of the beauty of the tragedy that entirely made one forget Cockney accents—a wonderful achievement. We had the Old Vic packed, and I took about 50/- in programmes alone—not a bad evening's work.

On Friday I went to speak about the League of Nations to the most intolerant and intolerable set of women it has been my misfortune to meet for a long time. Would you believe that in these days people still solemnly used this kind of argument: The League of Nations can be no good because:

1. President Wilson was a Baptist.

2. Lord Robert Cecil and the whole Cecil family are "simply crawling over with Jews." (What an expression!)

3. It is just a stab in the back to the British Empire to induce it to disarm and then let the International Semitics get a hold on the world.

4. It is against God's will, because God through His Son speaks of "When the strong man armed keepeth the house."

5. It is run by Little Englanders and Little Navyites who would have laid the honour of Britain in the dust.

6. It lays the honour of Britain in the dust because it leaves her not the sole judge of all her actions, and if God had not meant Britain to be the greatest nation in the world, she would not have been it.

7. If we don't punish wicked nations with the sword we deserve the curse of God.

8. That the League is an association of pacifist Jews, and therefore no Christian ought to support it. (When I pointed out that the League was neither pacifist nor Jewish but that Christ was both, they said nothing, but looked scandalised!)

And so on. For *three hours*. And in the end they, having invited me to come and speak, went down to tea, and would have left me entirely alone if one of the ladies (?) who was merely somebody else's friend, hadn't asked me if I would not like some tea, too, and shown me the way downstairs. At tea, except for my lady, they nearly all turned their backs on me, and only at the end the hostess came and asked me whether I should like a glass of wine! It was a house with two footmen and a butler, and nearly all the ladies were the wives of judges or diplomatists. What price our blinkin' haristocracy? It makes me feel snobbishly democratic. But what fun! If it wasn't so pitiable an example of the mentality of our erstwhile ruling classes, 1 should have loved it. As it was, I felt a little sad. But the slum women and co-operative guilds, and even the lusty Young Communists, have better manners.

On Thursday I went to four meetings—all very different. In the morning I spoke about Empire Day and the League to 300 little girls at an elementary school in Highgate. At three o'clock I heard Lord Robert Cecil give the Essex Hall Lecture—amazingly good. I'm so delighted that at last we have an idealist in the Cabinet. The man is great, with the humour, the dignity and the imagination of real greatness. At five I went to a select, smart and chatty meeting of the Six Point Group, after which I had my first interview with the Press—Mrs. Gossip of the *Daily Sketch*. Of course I lost all my opportunities, gave all the wrong details, and did not half use my chance to advertise —a chance I was longing for! I was so much amused at the idea of being interviewed that I never thought of what to say at the interview.

At night I went to speak at Barking to Town Councillors and Trade Unionists and Unemployed—a nice audience, and considerably intelligent.

I do think that our board school education is wonderfully good. Heaven send England an abolition of expensive private schools.

I am having the de'il of a time with my book. First it was too short; now it's miles too long, and back and back I have to go, wasting time over the beastly thing that will probably be no good in the end. The minor characters simply refuse to stay minor. The major ones insist upon telling me everything about their perfectly ordinary pasts as well as their somewhat amorphous and uninteresting presents. I'm calling it *The Crowded Street*, and, indeed, the title is somewhat apposite, for I feel overcrowded, smothered in a bewildering crowd of people and things. Some day, I suppose, I may get them straightened out, but now I am engulfed in the crowd. What fools we are to write—and I can't stop!

Still cold as March, windy as February, and sunless as November. What a climate! I think of lizards in the Forum and red roses up the statues in the Capitol. I think of Venice on an August day, and the Piazza Michael Angelo at Florence on an afternoon of quivering heat. And then I light the gas fire and warm my chilblains. I wear my fur coat out of doors and my jersey in the house. And this is May!

My stories still come back—a batch of 'em, three at a time, greet me at breakfast. It is a good thing that my appetite is naturally hearty! Meanwhile I go to Oxford on Wednesday for three days. Have you read *The Riddle*, by Walter de la Mare? Very eerie and lovely.

Au revoir, my dearest Rosalind.

With love,

CELIA.

58, Doughty Street, W.C.1,
June 5th, 1923

DEAREST ROSALIND,

I was so glad to have your last letter, though I'm sorry you don't like A. E. Housman. I can understand people disagreeing with his pessimism, but I don't know how you manage to dislike his colour, which is rich and true and full of the scent of earth. (Can colour be full of scent?) *Summertime on Bredon* is spacious as the downs, musical with the sound of bells across wide spaces—and few people since Shakespeare could have written a song so exquisite as:

> "With rue my heart is laden
>   For golden friends I had,
> For many a rose-lipped maiden,
>   And many a light-foot lad.
>
> "By brooks too broad for leaping
>   The light-foot lads are laid;
> The rose-lipped maids are sleeping
>   In fields where roses fade."

And the *Epitaph on the Army of Mercenaries*—magnificent in its scornful economy of words:

> "These, in the day when Heaven was falling,
>   The hour when earth's foundations fled,
> Followed their mercenary calling,
>   And took their wages, and are dead.

184

"Their shoulders held the sky suspended,
They stood, and earth's foundations stay.
What God abandoned, these defended,
And saved the sum of things, for pay."

Mind you, I don't agree with all his sentiments. I think
that much harmful rubbish has been talked about the
propping up of earth's foundations by the opposition of the
Allies to German Imperialism and the consequent destruction of a promising generation. I'm not sure that Mon-
tague's *Disenchantment* is not a truer picture of the defensive
armies; but if one should happen to have felt like Mr.
Housman, I wonder whether it would have been possible
to have expressed one's feelings with equal loveliness and
nobility. And as for colour—oh, Rosalind, Rosalind, what
trees are those that wear white for Whitsuntide? What
green gnomes like the cheerful companion that danced
before the wanderer through the wood? what furrows so
brown as that down which the ploughman walked, who
heard and killed the singing blackbird? Of course, you
aren't a Philistine, and are entitled to your own opinion,
but I can't suppress entirely my own—possibly quite false
—admiration.

I'm glad you're a philosopher these days. It is an eleva-
tion to which I am longing to attain. I may do one day,
but at the moment I am very much apt to be overwhelmed
by the pomps and vanities of this wicked world. Rosalind,
I just adore pomps and vanities. What is one to do about
it? Last night I stood in a crowd in Hyde Park listening
to an obviously sincere but scarcely eloquent lady of
immense municipal reputation and a most creditable record
of social work address a little group of about twenty bored
bystanders, too inert to go across the path to sing with the
Salvation Army. She was speaking for the London Council
for Promotion of Public Morality—Bacchus, what a name!
Her oration was a sort of Jeremiad in an awed undertone
(inaudible four yards away from her) about the terrible

and enormous wickedness of post-war England. The things that this poor lady had seen! The burglaries, the gambling, the assaulted children, the desecration of the Sabbath, the barefaced breach of each one of the Ten Commandments! (She went through each of these in turn, and at some length.) The horrible indecencies in public places! And so forth. And at first I wanted to laugh, and then I wanted to scream, and then I wanted to cry, because it's all so wasteful and pathetic; and we don't want public morality campaigns nor anything like that, but we want a girl with a violin and a man with a voice who'll stand where the Salvation Army stand, and strike up "Summer is a comen in," and "It was a Lover and his Lass," and "Drink to Me Only," if somebody will sing the alto. And we want drill instructors and folk dancers, and basket ball and broadcast loud-voice machines telling stories and singing songs to the aged and invalids and the lazy and retiring who object to disporting themselves in public. We don't want women police; we want women ballet-dancers and singing masters, who'll not be afraid of holding classes at a street corner· if necessary.

Our public houses are a perfect disgrace to civilisation, not because they're so full, but because they're so ugly. If people must drink to drown their sorrows and bad housing and unemployment, or whatever else they drink to drown, why must they do it on a sawdust floor standing up against a hideous bar, with not a scrap of colour about the place? Oh, damn, damn, damn this ugly country!

Pardon this ridiculous and unrestrained outburst. Maybe it's the result of attending two interviews for jobs, lecturing at one college and speaking in Hyde Park and writing letters till a quarter to one this morning, when the sky will rain, and I've got to be bridesmaid to Grace (I love her getting married, but I *loathe* being bridesmaid and looking like a stuffed Amazon), and I probably won't be able to go to the Assembly, and it's rained for weeks and weeks and Vera's father continues to be ill and——

Still, I don't think it is. I do want to start a campaign for the Prevention of Public Boredom. One day, when (?) I am *very* rich, famous and influential, I will.

Meanwhile I am yours as ever with much love,

CELIA.

ROSALIND DEAR,

No letter from you this week. I hope that means that you are well and happy and all right. Do you know I cannot remember if I told you about Oxford. My mind is a complete blank about what I wrote last week, or whether I told you anything I meant to. In the first place, the first night I got there, Miss Clarke, the history tutor, took me up to the High, where I sat between her and Miss Lorimer. Miss Lorimer as usual, asked after you at once, and so I took the opportunity to ask her about your exam. papers. She only told me what you have told me already, that the authorities are ridiculously, red-tapeishly adamant and that all attempts to induce them to send their papers out are useless. But if you could stay at home long enough to take Responsions in December and the Greek of your Intermediate in the spring, you could get your degree. Couldn't you? Or do you find it does not really count? I don't know, because when I've been asking for work here, people never ask me if I hold any degree, but only sometimes what class I got. I think it fearfully inconsiderate of Oxford. Just like its usual attitude of magnificent inconsiderateness to anything that does not come immediately within its own exalted sphere. Sometimes I hate Oxford. It must be so pleasant to recline gracefully upon the centuries like a lady on a sofa, and let the charwomen scrub about on their knees.

For the rest, since I wrote last I have done nothing very much. On Thursday—oh, yes, I did on Thursday; on Thursday I mingled with the gallant and fair, the titled and rich among the marbled terraces, rhododendrons and colonnades (two L's or one?) of Lord Leverhulme's palatial mansion (vide the *Daily Sketch*) at Hampstead. I went "to help" at a garden fête for the Six-Point Group and the National Women Citizen's Association. By the way, there are advantages in belonging to a lot of societies, one gets so many parties free by promising to "help"—in other words, one gets a free pass to all the shows, free tea, free tickets, prominent place among the great, introductions to big-wigs in white kid gloves, smiles, and the limelight, intro-ductions to little-wigs in flusters, muslin dresses and a hurry, rides in other people's cars and all the fun of the fair. In return I walked about in my grey dress (I made it myself last summer, but you'd never have known), a blue hat with a long, grey veil, and occasionally approached any one whom I thought looked really amusing and murmured plaintively, "Won't you buy a ticket for the fashion parade?" They hardly ever did, of course, but that did not seem to matter. I watched Aubrey Smith, the actor, playing clock-golf. He looks like a retired general—a part that he is fond of playing. His friends call him Aubrey, and his manner more nearly approaches that termed "The Oxford" than any I have met in the High. Ellaline Terriss—Mrs. Seymour Hicks was selling programmes—more or less. I tried to sell tickets to Marie Tempest, who, by the way, looks nicer off the stage than on it, has a distinguished nose and very nice manners. She couldn't come to my parade, for she was running a Thé Dansant in the Long Gallery, but she was very nice and affable. Lady Rhondda, large, in black, out-spoken and capable, like a cabinet minister (which she ought to be) and a successful managing director (which she is), presided at the opening. Lady R. is desperately shy when *tête-à-tête*, has none of the small social graces of the marchioness. Her lawsuit and plea for the right of peeresses to sit in the Lords is considered to be the ostentatious aggressiveness of a "nouveau aristot" by the very people who would have been only too pleased to profit by the result of her brains and her

188

guineas had they met with their just reward (or possibly unjust reward—*quien sabe?*). To the people who are neither great nor toadying, she is informally charming. Always, for instance, she is nice both to Vera and to me (a) because we are old Somervillians (b) because we work for her societies (c) because we write (d) because we never speak to her (e) because we're not a bit afraid of her. A nice woman, but rather a lonely one, I think. Possibly she wants to be nothing else.

After this orgy of magnificence, I arrived home to find poor Vera just returned from a lecture at Bedford College for the League of Nations Union, very sick, very ill-looking and with a temperature. The poor child had caught cold speaking in the rain in Hyde Park the night before. But now she is all right again, and we have just come back from a lecture and counter-lecture at the London School of Economics by Sheila Kaye-Smith and Rebecca West— J. C. Squire in the chair. Rebecca West was exquisitely dressed in smoke-grey silk and ninon, a huge hat with a dripping plume, and perfect sable coat; completely at home on a platform; really witty, sophisticated and mistress of the situation. A more amusing discourse I have rarely heard, her chief plea being that any subject is right if one can only pull it off, and that the real fault of the modern novelist lies in his readers. She was exquisitely funny, brilliant and often wise. I liked Sheila. J. C. Squire was amusing, as one might have expected—untidy, lean face, dark hair going grey, glasses and a stammar (or stammer?) Even then some one could not refrain from calling him a "squire of dames." I think it was Lord Knutsford—the chairman of the Hospitals Appeal for whom the lecture was given.

What a letter! Wouldn't you think that I were a real swell, moving among the high society, to read this twaddle? To tell the truth, I only run up and down, grinning like a dog, and come back in between to wash dishes, teach the Lower VI, write rejected articles, and make myself a new summer dress for eleven shillings. (I have made a lamb-grey crêpe with a pleated cape-collar and a silver buckle on a low hip belt. Finished it before breakfast this morning.)

I made lovely omelettes for supper to-night—the first since I left France.

I am going to a real ball on Thursday—the first ever—begins at nine-thirty, in the Cloth-Worker's Hall. Mr. Harris is taking me with his wife's ticket as she could not come.

Oh, dear, oh, dear—I am doing no work. My days seem to slide by, and I *cannot* get on with *The Crowded Street*. It's like a jelly that won't "jell"—cold, flabby, formless. Yet I know that the idea is there—somewhere—only I don't seem to have got it on to the paper. Oh, I write like a cook, a jellyfish or a porpoise would write. I deserve to make omelettes and dresses all my natural life—and occasionally teach the Lower VI. I can at least not make a complete fool of myself there. Oh, Rosalind, Rosalind, if I could put away ambition I might not fall with the angels—but I swear I'd rather fall with the angels than sit still in the oak pews of the congregation of the righteous. Wouldn't you? I'm talking rot now. I must go and have my bath. It's late and I'm teaching first period to-morrow.

I hope you are well. I hope you are happy. I wish you a hundred and a thousand good things and I love you.

Yours, foolishly but lovingly,

CELIA.

58, Doughty Street, W.C.1,
Sunday, June 17th.

ROSALIND DEAR,

I have just finished reading a somewhat depressing but very funny satire called *Futility*, by Gerhardi, about the Russian Revolution. I wonder if you have come across it? It's the sort of book that if you read in the train, people stop and turn round to see what's making you chuckle, and yet, in the end, when you have closed it, it leaves you with a feeling as empty, waste and melancholy as the vast Siberian plains which it describes.

I had a letter this week from a great friend of mine—the Scotch socialist from Liverpool, scolding me most fiercely for *Anderby Wold*. He says that there is no constructive psychology in it; no careful character study except Mary and that she is left ambiguous (who isn't?), that the book is a mere chronicle of people and events—most of the people being but sorry things who make us wonder sadly at our civilisation—and that it contains not the ghost of a message of hope or anything else for even the small section of the public who may read and understand it! What is one to do? My own beloved book, bad though I know it (he says it isn't bad—calls it competent and well-constructed but entirely without significance!), into which I meant to sound such a clarion call to courage and to action, and yet to plead for sympathy for those to whom action must mean suffering. What is one to do? And he one of the most intelligent of my readers to whom I have talked and talked and talked until the sma' wee hours.

Comes another letter from Kenneth Leys of Oxford, telling me "now that you are famous and very fine, you must not get puffed up. Yet when you go about instructing people, may you find great pleasure in it, though you will find yourself wishing to teach them all so much that they can never know, yet hesitate to give them anything but some simple and final expression of wisdom like the Gospels." *Me* "famous and very fine"—and to-day I let the milk boil over twice and the kidneys went bad!

Yesterday I went to a Musical At Home in Kensington—an affair not much in my line though I enjoyed wearing my best black frock. We did not even have strawberries and cream (Vera had bet me we should have), but I talked to a enchanting Japanese viscountess—can't tell you her name, for anything over eight syllables eludes me in a casual introduction. We talked about progress, and the attitude of Plato to women's suffrage, and bicycles and Egyptian civilisation and central heating, and whether the Japanese and English were more alike than the English and Americans because of the psychological effect of islands, and day-school education and America during the war and the Dutch school of painters. She has two children, a heavenly figure, and the prettiest broken English in the world—an unusual personality to encounter in a Kensington drawing-room, sandwiched between a doctor's widow in a feather boa and myself on a chair too small for me. People sang at the At Home. A girl in a grey dress was prettily childish over moons and boats and babies; a bright young baritone was unconquerably jolly over being the master of his fate and captain of his soul; and a stout Jewess in black marocain and a hat with pink roses did a kind of action song with a fan and much display of eyebrows and diamonds. Well, well!

I went to my ball on Thursday, but we did not stay late, and I wore my blue and silver with the top cut right off and only straps over my shoulders for a change. It was rash of me, though it looked quite smart, for what I'll do when I want to wear it for a garden party again, I don't know. It was a fine ball in the Cloth-Workers' Hall, and we had a fine orchestra and azaleas and quails in aspic and strawberries and champagne and little dangly programmes with gold monograms, and I danced with Percy whenever I had not another partner, so it was very nice. To-morrow I am being taken to the theatre and to dinner. On Thursday I am dining at Hampstead with John Williams, a friend of the Brittains. On Wednesday I am dining at the House of Commons with Percy before I go to speak for him on The Liberal Foreign Policy in Bethnal Green (from a van, I believe, like a hallelujah lassie in the Salvation Army), and I think that is all for the moment. I have never had such dissipation for years all on my own like this. I feel quite fluttered. However, I've finished my school job, though I'm sorry, for the girls were dears, so keen and intelligent, and I'm really going to write like a dragon this week, and going to get up early and finish my work—so I say. Alas, that good resolutions should vanish with the morn! And I don't suppose I shall have another such burst for months again.

On the ninth I'm going to Weymouth for three days to speak for the League, and in the autumn I've got a job to speak in Kendal for the University Extension people. I like travelling for nothing, though it seems mean to leave Vera alone in the flat, but I seem physically incapable of earning money *in* London.

My best beloved Yorkshire farm short story returned from the *Westminster Gazette* yesterday, though chaperoned there with the best wishes of the editor, and not so bad, I'll swear. I've never got a story off yet.

This letter is all "I" "I" "I", but as I haven't heard from you, you, you, how can I answer your letter? Oh, Rosalind dear, when are you coming home? The summer is cold, but there are delphiniums and roses, and the parks are full of birds and larkspur and little tip-tilted daisies.

I did a fearful thing on Thursday—was so busy cutting off the top of my dress for the ball that I forgot to go to a committee meeting. Wasn't it dreadful? And had to write and say, "unavoidably detained."

Do you know, in our care-committee on Tuesday it transpired that one little boy of thirteen, the child of a coster in Bethnal Green, is in the habit of bringing to his schoolmaster sums from £200 to £250, asking him to take care of them during school hours. When asked how he got them, he said that they were two days' takings at the fruit stalls. His father gives each of his brothers a fruit stall when they marry, and now between them they must be getting over £2,000 a year—and yet the child is one of the raggedest in the school and his ambition in life is to be a fishmonger What do you think of that?

Always with love,

CELIA.

ROSALIND DEAR,

I have your last letter—about clothes. The coat sounds so nice and the Condor hat—but you don't enclose the silk —only a piece of paper which I presume is not silk even in Africa! 25*s.* is an awful price. Wouldn't it be easier for me to send you materials from here some time. If you send indications of the colour, etc., you want. One doesn't pay duty to the colonies, does one? Or is silk prohibited?

I met Beatrice Harraden at Lady Rhondda's on Monday night. She is such a charming person. Her little alert head is all rumpled, grey, bobbed hair. She wears pince-nez and is evidently short-sighted, for she thrusts her head forward with a quick, bird-like movement when she wants to see things. She was wearing a strange, flowing cloak of green velvet and ninon, and some lovely carved beads, but her general effect was one of kind and human untidiness. She is gentle, unassuming, humorous and wonderfully considerate and sympathetic with the young idea. She treated me as though I were a reasonable and grown-up human creature instead of either a naughty child at a party (as some of my more distinguished acquaintances do), or as an intellectual and psychological phenomenon (as some of my less distinguished acquaintances do). In short, I suppose that she flattered me, and so I loved her, but indeed she is far more delightful than her books, though I always have thought *Interplay* exceedingly interesting and far too little known. Anyway, I sat on a cushion by her and we talked about *The Memoirs of a Midget*, which we both love, and publishers, whom we both fear, and rejected manuscripts, from which we had both suffered.

Then she promised to put *Anderby Wold* on the reading list for the Femina Vie Heureuse Literary Competition, which was a kind encouragement to a first novelist rather than a compliment to a first novel.

The *Spectator* tells me that I have a "strong sense of

situation" and should write a play. It and you are the only people who have said this. The *Nation* told me that I had "not seen it dramatically at all." What is one to believe? While the *Isis* remarks, "nor does the handling of the really dramatic situation at the end of the book compensate for the misshaped dullness of the first half"!

All men are liars.

Otherwise what would be the use of truth?

I am reading a naughty, delicious, ironic, exquisite book called *Jurgen*, by James Branch Cabell. The English is intoxicating. It goes to my head. Also I have a borrowed volume of the limited edition, wonderfully illustrated by delicate drawings of knights and devils, gnomes and witches and bats and cobwebs and fair, frail ladies. Cabell calls it a "comedy of justice." It concerns a paunchy and disillusioned pawnbroker of forty, whose wife is carried off by the devil, poor soul (a little act of courtesy rendered by the devil to Jurgen, who once spoke a good word for him to a Carthusian monk). Jurgen, determined on the manly thing, marches off to look for Lisa, but finds instead a centaur, the shirt of Nessus—a glittering trifle—and his lost youth. He thereupon sets forth, not finding Lisa, to seek Justice. He finds instead many fair, frail ladies, from Guinevere to Helen of Troy, and these he treats after his own conception of the fair and just thing.

> "But gat not his desire
> In any countrie nay condicion."

So at last he returns to his snug home, thinking "all these things may be right. Far be it from me to think that they are wrong. But still . . . Thus it was in the old days."

Last night I went to see Eva Spicer, a Somerville girl, dedicated to service in the Chinese Mission Field. She is really going to be a don at a girls' college in China. The service was in the Westminster Congregational Church—a large building. From 800 to 1,000 people were there. They sang hymns and prayed and then Eva addressed them. She spoke very simply and with great dignity, having common sense, also a knowledge of dramatic effect, combined with a forceful sincerity. I wish that people would lay aside the idea that a dramatic instinct is incompatible with sincerity. Consequently her address was most moving and impressive. It must be nice to decide to dedicate one's self to one particular form of service as she did when she was about twelve, and then train, prepare, and go, and do it. And on your going, have 800 people to pray over you and say that you do right. There is a satisfactory definiteness and conviction there about things.

The difficulty is to what can one dedicate one's self. I am blown about by a wandering wind of great pity and sorrow and desire, while my weakness and self-indulgence and timidity (to say nothing of my intellectual limitations) keep me tied to earth. (I do not feel a call to preach the Gospel in China. I sometimes do preach the only gospel that I know of in Croydon or Hoxton or Hyde Park, then people think that I am making a joke!) Really, one often wonders, with so many excellent people full of good intentions and aching to reform it, why the world remains such a wicked place. I live in these days in an atmosphere of good intentions about other people's welfare, that is elevating but rather depressing until one compromises by taking the will for the deed! To-day I am going to tell the good people of Darenth that they must organise for peace instead of war, while all that they really care about is whether the price of butter is going down, and will it rain on their best hat, and did Mrs. Thompson really cut them?

On Monday I went to the County Council to hear the representative managers try to raise the coming generation into a purposeful and instructed sanity of outlook. Instead I found a pack of men and women all quarrelling because Mr. W. took so long over his motion about the smoke nuisance that Mrs. R. hadn't time to make her carefully-prepared speech about education and evolution compared

196

with ignorance and revolution (Cheers and Hear! Hear!), apropos of the dilution of the London teaching staff with unqualified persons.

And down at Bethnal Green there is much excellent intent to abolish slums and educate the proletariat and what not. But really, it is frightfully important that Mr. X shan't be asked to present the prizes at the athletic display.

Oh, dear, oh, dear, oh, dear! Is this your modern pessimism, which is a peg? I'm not a pessimist. I'm a blind, blinking, staring optimist. If I wasn't I should go and commit suicide gloriously and ungracefully by a surfeit of marrons glacé. I had them at Lady Rhondda's t'other night, and am still sighing with delicious reminiscence.

I must go. This is a wild and wandering letter. All my letters are wild and wandering, but none so much as the ones I write to you. Wherefore it is proved that you have much generosity and patience, which all helps to add to one's hope of optimism. Patience is a very great virtue and a very great beauty. (Incidentally, it assures me that my letters will be read, which is always satisfactory.)

I love you very much.

WINIFRED.

58, Doughty Street, W.C.1,
July 3rd, 1923.

ROSALIND DEAR,

Your letter of the thirteenth has come. I love your letters. I love their spiritual quality. That seems a curious thing to say when you write to me of money, pimples and locust swarms. But you will know what I mean. The jumpers are not just medieval shapes of soft green satin. They are temples of your living spirit (which is not nearly as silly as it sounds). That is a lovely green. It should suit your charming hair.

Query? Shall I pay my rent, my milk and laundry bill, or shall I buy new shoes and stockings? Very difficult to

197

answer. A dividend for £6. 15s. 6d. came in this morning, but as I was overdrawn, it's not much use. Here am I living on the fruits of capitalism when I should be earning my living by the sweat of my brow. The trouble is that when my brow sweats, I get no money for the drops. I don't think that *Anderby* is selling well at all. I didn't expect it. You are too kind to say that it is "too good" to be a best-seller. I think it is too dull. Also the love scenes are too scrappy. I can't write love scenes. Molly B., who used to be secretary to Galsworthy, says that I shall never write till I have been in love at least five times. I protest. First, how does she know that I haven't been in love five times? I certainly was once, when I was seventeen, with a kind of gentle sentimental retrospect till I was twenty-two. Won't that do? Since then I have never found anybody who excites me in the least. I love oldish men like Percy Harris and Mr. Desmond and Gilbert Murray. I have a warm, respectful, half-humorous affection for them, and I feel pleasantly disposed towards Gerald F. and Grace's Peter. But I can't get excited. They are all too human, too much like myself, only better—solider, less sentimental, more unselfish. Alas! I fear that I criticise too much. And I take too much mental and physical exercise for the physical part to have much pull over me. So I shall have to go on writing my love scenes from observation and imagination. It's a pity, I suppose, but one can't fall in love merely as an artistic exercise.

I do so much know what you mean about the "escape." One can't describe it. Suddenly something happens and the earth falls away. The medieval mystics had one good explanation, but it's not quite that. There's a sort of clarity and serenity about the atmosphere.

I had two splendidly vigorous days this week-end. Suddenly summer came. On Saturday Vera and I played tennis all the afternoon at a hotel near Hendon with two youths from the League of Nations Union. On Sunday, Percy took Vera and Hilda Reid and me on to the river.

We punted from Datchet to Windsor and ate our lunch in a backwater near Eton. The fields were very darkly green and the water green and hard as jade. There are few swallows this year. I wonder why. Percy came with his pockets stuffed with little books—*Goblin Market*, Chesterton's *Wine and Water* poems, and *Shropshire Lad*. We lay under the willows among the daisy flowers and read aloud in turns, while the swallows almost touched our toes in brushing past.

Mr. Desmond turned up on Wednesday and took me to a labour demonstration at the Queen's Hall. It was to celebrate Bob Smillie's victory at the Morpeth election. After forty years of struggle, of privation, of hard, embittering fighting, this tall, grave old miner was chaired shoulder high across Queen's Hall and passed over the footlights on to the platform. The hall was full of brave, eager youth—school-teachers and clerks and students mostly. They wore cracker caps and held scarlet and blue balloons, and waved paper streamers. And instead of making many hot and bitter speeches about the tyranny of capitalism, they sang songs, about 2,000 of them, like the "Bonny, bonny banks of Loch Lomond." A little Scot from Glasgow conducted. And they danced and sang. Clifford Allen, the secretary of the "non-subscribers," who was nearly killed twice during the war with forcible feeding in prison as a conscientious objector, was in the chair. He is a very beautiful person with a face like the conventional pictures of Christ, only clean-shaven. He has a quiet, cultured voice and a simple manner. George Lansbury was there—a rough, strange mystic, with the training of a labourer and the mind of an Early Father. But Smillie has the most beautiful voice of all—and that Scotch intonation which I love. It was a strange meeting. But most unlike all political meetings that I have yet heard. Their economics may not always be sound, but their spirit is amazing and very beautiful. There was no bitterness, no hatred, but simple friendship and a talk of "my ain folk." "If socialism could come to-morrow in England," said George Lansbury, "I would not have it. It must come when all the people want it, no sooner and no later. We will have no bitterness, no war of classes. There has been a long night, when progress seemed to come through hatred. To-day we have seen the dawn. You may see the daylight." Oh, well—all very fine. We may.

Oswald Mosley and the Duke of Northumberland had a debate the other day on "Will the Ape and the Tiger ever die?" The pessimists won.

I must go. I have much to do.

My love is for you.

CELIA.

58, Doughty Street, W.C.1,
July 19th.

DEAREST ROSALIND,

I've sent off by this mail Vera's book. I do hope that you'll like it as much as I do. We've just had a rather exciting time over it. The *Daily Express* started a campaign against it as soon as it was out.· Called it "impossible," "an insult to women's colleges," and all sorts of horrible things. Poor Vera was fearfully upset, as she loves Oxford. To-day, when a huge article arrived headed "University Kisses" and containing the most ridiculous and yet venomous nonsense, we were thoroughly perturbed. However, agitation at the offices of the Oxford Women's College Appeal, *Time and Tide* offices and the publishers have secured the resolution that nothing suggested in the press shall be allowed to hurt Vera nor the colleges, and, to help us, the *Times Literary Supplement* has given it first place in a leading article on new novels this week and has been most just and interested. But it has been an agitating time! We had hideous visions of libel actions and all sorts of perilous adventures.

Meanwhile, the heat has passed and the rain rains, and we are busy winding up our business before we both go

200

home on Monday. I have another meeting to-night at nine and one on Saturday, but after that I go home—to more meetings. However, I'm going to have three weeks in Surrey to write—if all goes well.

I hope you are all right and well and prospering. No letter this week, but I don't deserve one anyway. Last week's effort on my part was feeble, and by the look of the clock, this will be sketchy, as I got my blue dress soaked on Sunday and have to renovate a black one instead before to-night's meeting. I wish sometimes that I grew feathers! I *won't* grow dowdy, though, like a hurried woman. I've bought some pretty blue stockinette and a sort of woollen tussore, to make myself a travelling suit to go to Geneva in. It should be pretty.

They are going to act *Hassan* at His Majesty's this autumn. I am longing to see it—the loveliness of Flecker is so refreshing. We have so much violence and ugliness in this semi-political life, we must have lovely things. I want it frightfully. Why am I grumbling? I saw yesterday the loveliest of Hampshire woods and gardens at Fleet, where I went to speak. I am most pampered by the gods. There were bell-heather in blossom and roses and a sweet chestnut tree in flower—and woods smelling of pines, and one tall white lily against the dark green.

What an incoherent letter. I'm not really suffering from softening of the brain—only from the lack of forty-eight hours a day.

My love to you—

CELIA.

Bainesse,
Cottingham,
E. Yorks, July 25th.

DEAREST ROSALIND,

I was most interested in your letter from the native college. One knows so very little about the colour question

201

here, and what one does hear is generally so horribly tainted by the self-complacency of the white race. Why are we so durnedly proud of ourselves? Is this civilisation good enough for any one? This civilisation of machines and chemicals that we erect so laboriously with such an infinite expenditure of care and patience. We are so hard-working and careful and exact and pitiably clever, and we do such wonderful things with our hands and brains—And yet the man and the woman—Has any better thing yet come than that which came from Galilee? And yet, I can't believe that Christ was the only revelation. There must be unplumbed possibilities in human nature. We are so busy with our patient erections of scientific invention. We build our aeroplanes and our wireless stations. And we don't seem able to pull our spiritual standard up to the level of our material civilisation. Yet I don't believe in "back to nature" and the primitive life. We've got to go on—our souls as well as our bodies. Only how? One feels so weak, so stupid, so bound down by a thousand weaknesses and limitations and bonds of self-interest or pity. What right, for instance, have I to preach? I, who have never made a sacrifice nor faced a grave problem, nor known sorrow nor pain nor any of the harder things of life? I can't even love as we usually speak of love. Here I am, pretending to be a writer and a teacher, one who would lead people's thoughts. I am only fit to give comfort to their bodies. And I can't even do that efficiently. I play with care committees and school boards and journalism and novel-writing. I write pretty, rather quiet and sombre short stories which nobody takes; and I do nothing, nothing to pay off the debt we owe—all of us who are happy—to the life that set us free from the usual cares of existence.

I always seem to be grumbling in my letters to you. I'm so sorry. It's only myself that I grumble at and possibly the stupidity of the people in authority. Though the Lord alone knows that the people not in authority are even more stupid. Do you see that we are going to spend £10,000,000 on a naval base at Singapore and £500,000 on an increase in the Air Force, and that they've turned down an expenditure of £12,000 on women police, to protect women and girls in London? Aren't we mad?

I want to go to America in the spring, to talk about the League of Nations. I don't suppose I shall go. I shall find the difficulties too great in the end—as usual—or I shan't be able to leave England, or I shan't find the money, or nobody will want to hear me. I shall find some grand excuse, never fear. I always do, to justify my own lack of grit.

Now, I won't grumble any more.

I am going back to Rudstone to-day for a garden fête. I can hardly believe it. They say that the village is changed. I'm selfishly glad. The more changed it is, the less I shall regret that we live there no longer.

I came home on Monday night. On Tuesday I went to Hull to see Grace in her wedding things. She looks lovely, tall and graceful and sweet. Since she became engaged she has found animation and beauty and a merry laugh—all the things that she lacked before. I am so glad. I only hope he's good enough. She'll give way to him in everything, with a sort of obstinate submission. He will be kind enough, and not too exacting. But it is a great responsibility for a man so to hold complete possession of a girl, as he holds her. But she is happy.

I wish that I could send you English flowers—tall delphiniums, star-faced daisies, beds of purple pansies, great dripping crimson roses, silver-spiked carnations—the garden is full of them.

A little red spider keeps running over my paper. If it weren't cruel, I would send him.

I must go and have lunch.

Au revoir, my Rosalind.

CELIA.

DEAREST ROSALIND,

I was reading your wonderful letter of July 7th, the letter where you describe your travels, the colour question, native education, Mr. Yergan, your eighty hours in the train, and as I read I thought, "What a wonderful life—a big, spacious life, full of romance and interest and useful work—the education of natives, the bringing of culture and ancient civilisation into a new, crude country, unique contacts, broad horizons, people and problems stripped of superficialities." And I felt small and ashamed of my own fretful, grumbling, egotistic letters. Then I turned the page and saw "What poor stuff I send you in return for your wonderful letters!" That is odd, for I never thought that my letters were much, but yours come with a breath from a far country. Always I love your letters. They are so *steadying.* I feel that I dare not do cheap or mean or selfish things when every week I feel myself before the tribunal of your lovely mind. Your judgments are so right. You are so wise—perhaps just because you "are most at your ease with simple people," as you say. I do understand why you like the natives and why they like you. But it is the beautiful part of you that strikes the high note for too sophisticated people—to your own disadvantage perhaps sometimes, never to theirs. For it is a beautiful and cleansing thing and civilisation has surely need of it.

I don't want you to go to Australia. It's such a very long way away—and you're settling and have friends and are finding work to your hand. But you know best. Maybe you weren't born to settle. You will do as the spirit moves you, but I hope that it moves you to England some time not too far away.

Clement de la Harpe, who is staying with us, comes from Rhodesia. He was for some time at Rhodes University, before he came to Edinburgh to take his M.B. He is a nice boy, earnest and keen about his work, and liberal-minded. He is going back to South Africa in the autumn to see his mother and may stay out there to be a doctor, but he rather wants to come back to Britain.

To-morrow mother and I got to Ravenscar on the moors as we did last year. It is very lovely there, wild and windy and rugged. Then on the eighth I go to Surrey, where the headmistress of St. Monica's has lent one of the school-houses to Vera and me. It is good of her.

At present I am dancing and playing tennis and going to Bridlington and doing a hundred other things, but my mind is in *The Crowded Street*, and I can't get it out. Not that the book's much use, and maybe I was a fool to re-write it. But it interests me vastly. My Muriel is not such a fine person as Mary. She is small in mind as well as body, only too often she lacks initiative and she can only show courage when she is driven into a corner. But there is good stuff in her if only she learns not to blame other people and things always for her own failures. Standing alone doesn't seem to mean refusing help or leadership. It means taking the full responsibility for one's own actions—and that's what she won't do—not yet. At the end of the book she's just begin-ning to see. And she thinks that adventure is a circum-stantial thing that happens to people, instead of being a vision of the mind and a gallant response of the heart to the curious or tragic or interesting things that life may offer. It's no good. That sounds silly here. I can put it into a story better than I can say it straight down.

I have to go and pack and get ready, and prepare notes for a lecture at Hull this afternoon.

Always my love, dear Rosalind,

CELIA.

Doric House,
Burgh Heath, Tadworth,
Surrey, August 9th.

Rosalind Dear,

Vera and I came here last night to this charming, sunlit place on the Surrey hills. Her aunt has lent us the house, together with Mr. and Mrs. Willett, the caretaker and his wife, to do the housekeeping. It is a strange, flat-fronted house, with a long Greek corridor in front, and a wide verandah supported by Doric pillars up which the ramblers climb—an ideal place for working. Everywhere in the house are rambler roses in great vases, and every room is sunlit and colour-washed buff and white, and spotlessly clean. I have come to try and finish my book. Goodness knows if I will or what it will be like. I get fearfully depressed with its stupidity—I can't design as I should like to. The whole life of my people comes to me—dull days, grey days, days of trivial things. I could write endlessly of the things that they do and say, just as endlessly as I could live them myself. But to choose the significant and dramatic moments—there's the problem. I wrote scenes and scenes, all during the past year, which I have destroyed, for they are valueless. It isn't the words and gestures of people that matter. It's their souls, and beyond that the universal soul. Is there a universal soul? Am I talking nonsense? Is there somewhere, pulsating through the stupidities and futilities of commonplace lives, that spark of divinity which some men call God? And is it the business of those who write to sweep away exterior things, or rather so to select and arrange them that the soul, the inmost movement, the divinity, is seen? But how, how, how? And why should I, who see so little, who am so full of distractions and self-indulgence, try to do it? Often I can see nothing but the trimmings. It's infuriating. And then the finished production is so maddeningly inadequate I sometimes wonder whether I am not just a presumptuous fool to waste my time. Here am I, in the most heavenly of sunlit hills, where long shadows climb across the sloping fields and where the roses on the pergola fling their faces up to a blue, Italian sky, and I am overcome with an entirely unnecessary emotion because I cannot adequately portray the inner significance of a non-existent person! What greater folly? I had far better go and organise summer outings for Bethnal Greeners or train myself as a nurse, or a welfare worker, or a sanitary inspector or even an elementary school-teacher, and do something satisfactory and tangible, and not be a parasite upon the community.

But I shan't, of course. I shall probably go on writing bad books for the public and cross-grained letters to you until I die!

I have come across a book of thirty-one short stories. In it is one by Ernest Bramah, who writes of exquisite, meticulous Chinese. I also read by him *The Golden Hours of Kai Lung*. What a style that man has—beaten, metallic, immaculate, finished as a piece of copper-work by Verrocchio, polished and hard as a carving of jade. It's as stimulating to read such magnificent workmanship as it is to plunge into a cold bath on a hot day.

Oh, Rosalind! An adventure—I had my first cold shower-bath last night! Such joy, after a hot and dusty journey—merely a flea-bite of a journey to you, of course, who think nothing of twenty-eight hours in a train.

For the last week I have been up to Ravenscar with mother, between the heather and the sea, where wild ringing winds blow and sea-birds cry all day. I lay on the heather and played so-called golf upon a distinctly rough and mountainous course. Mother is very wonderful and very dear. I have a tremendous debt to pay back to fate for her alone. She is happy over Grace's engagement, and as for Grace, she is a creature transformed. She is almost animated in Peter's presence. She'll let him walk over her, and she talks Scotch already and says, "Och, aye," and "Uh—huh?" But what does it matter when he'll be kind and considerate and adequate to her? Some people are made like that.

There are aeroplanes buzzing over here like mosquitoes, and a field gold with buttercups below my window. It's an August day to dream of. Why aren't you here to see it too? Always my love to you, dear Rosalind—

Your CELIA.

Doric House,
Burgh Heath, Tadworth,
Surrey, August 17th.

ROSALIND DEAR,

I do envy you your meercat. She sounds a lovely thing Indeed, I haven't forgotten Miss Hamilton's marmoset. When I was at home this time I came across the letter in which I described the day that Miss Hamilton invited me to tea. When I reached her house I found her standing in the rain outside the front door gibbering with rage. She had locked her key indoors. Her friend had gone motoring with the other. And you and a young officer and Miss Gurney of Somerville and I were coming to tea. We went and borrowed a ladder from a freshman along the street and climbed in through the bedroom window, just in time to make up the fire and toast the bread before you and the others arrived. I had forgotten. I had forgotten so many things. But what bad letters I write—slangy and flippant and without any form or comeliness. I wonder you stand them, or that I dare pretend to be interested in writing. Indeed, I have just been reading through such as there is of *The Crowded Street.* It is unbelievably bad. It has all the vices of *Anderby* and none of its virtues. But I shall have to finish it, for once before when I had got to just this point I tore it up, disgusted, and now it would be pure melodrama to tear it up again. I wish that I didn't so much despise the things I write, and yet be compelled by some inner lunacy to go on writing.

As an antidote, I'm reading international relations. It's stiff and good and hard. I pore over statistics of government bonds, and preferential tariffs and economic protectorates. I'm revelling in imports of foodstuffs compared with manufactured goods, and I'm trying to grasp the inner significance of pictures such as this, which outfuturise the best things Wyndham Lewis ever drew! However, no doubt I shall become very wise if I regard them patiently for long enough. Apropos of international finance, do send your orders here and let me shop for you if you think that it would be cheaper. Only let me have explicit directions. It would be so terrible if I bought you things that you disliked and you were compelled to wear them till the next mail came.

Vera and I are plotting how to come out to South Africa to see you. How and when? Two large obstacles at the moment—time and money. Time. Both of us earn our living during term time. Can one get out and back in a summer holidays? Money. How much does it take to travel? Oh, wouldn't it be lovely? If you don't come home soon, I'll have to go and see you, and Vera wants to meet you. She says that if she comes it will be like the trio in *Punch*: "Gee! there ain't much ham in that sandwich!"

S. Africa.

I heard from Miss Fowler this morning. She wants me to go and lecture at Q.M.S.[1] next term. I don't see that I can do it. I shall be in London all term time, and my last lecture is on the day that they break up. Bother terms—except in their money-earning capacity!

[1]Queen Margaret's School, Scarborough—her old school.

The field outside my bedroom window is a delight. In the morning it is speckled with buttercups round and bright as sovereigns. In the evening it is an entirely green stretch of grass. I suppose that the buttercups close up. The field looks as if they vanished. Not one stays to be seen. There are stars here at night far more wonderful than stars in London. I wonder how? They shoot and fly and spread long tails across the heavens. And sometimes the searchlights from Croydon fling out a noose of light (that's Fitzgerald, I know) and catch them—great hauls of them, and sweep them across the sky—to Croydon, I suppose—Query? What do they do with the stars at Croydon?

I have come to the surprising conclusion that I like routine. I like Mrs. Willett to bring me my cup of tea at the same time every morning. I like to meet the same round-faced fried egg smiling up from my breakfast bacon. I like to walk three times round the garden while she is tidying my room, and then to come straight to my window-table and write till one o'clock. And in the afternoons I like to walk through sunlit Surrey fields. There must be routine in the weather too—sunlight after lunch, stars after dinner, and a good sunset in between. After tea I like to write again, and after supper to drink tea and smoke a cigarette on the verandah before I read *International Finance* until ten-thirty and bedtime. Don't you think that that sounds an attractive time table? Alas, three weeks is the longest that will stretch for it, and then I must pack up my bag and go. It sounds luxurious, doesn't it? But remember that during term time we do our own cooking and washing and dish scrubbing, so Mrs. Willett is a joy and treat. Aren't we lucky to have been lent her and the house?

Vera is getting to look quite well on it. She has gone up about four lbs. already. As for me, I always live in terror of a double chin!

An English cow called Dunninald Daphne has yielded 3,000 gallons of milk in 291 days. Can you beat this in

South Africa? She has also had six calves in less than six years. I saw this in the *Yorkshire Post.*

Au revoir, my very dear Rosalind,

I love you.

CELIA.

Doric House,
Burgh Heath, Tadworth,
Surrey, August 21st.

ROSALIND DEAR,

Your letter came to-night telling me that I shall kill myself by overwork, and here am I not having struck stroke for two days. True, I did a little reading, a little typing and a little letter writing to-day, but that is all. I have been gathering showers of rambler roses, nodding sprays of mauve, pale-scented scabious, and wild, jagged flames of antirrhinum. I have been walking up and down a dark lane burrowed like a cavern between the heavily-branching elms. I have been watching the moon rise over the Epsom Downs, and the wind tear to ribbons an astounding sunset through my bedroom window. I am living on eggs and fruit and the fat of the land, and I am more spoiled and more lazy than a hedgehog. You've never seen such ragwort as there is here—acres of blazing gold on the slope of the downs, gold to ransom a kingdom if you would, and the magenta pink of willow-herb below—pink splashed lavishly on knap-weed and ragged robin, on self-heal and thistles, and the hedgerows frothing over with old man's beard. I'm as lazy as a bumble bee when the sun's full, and his furry body is sucked against the trumpet of convolvulus. I'm as fat as the toad that crawled across my path last night, when the owls were crooning and the road was a paler ribbon between the shadows of the grass. The toad moved delicately, with a painful laboriousness as though he had sadly over-eaten himself. I am sure that the hedgerows were

211

full of snails and slugs, rich and delectable, more rare to him than the luscious syrups and dark glowing fruits piled in that chill, moonlit Chamber on St. Agnes's Eve. Perhaps he had been carousing in the hedge bottom when some domestic instinct drew him home, reluctant but conscientious, to his wife. Anyway, I only just avoided putting an end to both his shameful past and his good intentions for the future, by stepping on him. Merciful providence looks after drunkards. My toad was crawling with the meticulous sobriety of the slightly intoxicated.

Absolutely nothing has happened this week. I have been up to London for a day's shopping and found that they have painted our flat afresh—cream walls and white paint. It looks so nice. I have written a little, read a little, thought a little, talked and eaten much.

I have come to one conclusion—that I must try one day to write a non-realistic novel. I'm not sure that much of modern complacency is not caused by the "realism" of modern fiction. We become so much uplifted by the gratifying contrast between our own lives and those depicted in our library books that we are apt to lose sight of any possible room left for improvement. Oh, for a man with the brain (composite or individual, what does it matter? The more the better) that went to the making of the Iliad. Oh, for a Dante to return, or a Euripides, to show men in tragedy not merely the unpleasant consequences of some line of action, but also to "purify their emotions by showing them fear of such things as should be feared, horror for such things as are truly horrible, pity for such things as should be pitiful." Nowadays when we aim at being heroic, we merely succeed in becoming romantic. Perhaps on the whole we had better stick to realism. Still . . .

I enclose a syllabus that may amuse you. The lectures have still to be prepared. I always hesitate to lecture until I have read more than I feel my audience will know—and as I always suspect it of having read most available books upon a subject, this harasses me considerably. Only when

I arrive at the lecture, the needlessness of some of my activity depresses me. However, I certainly do feel a little impressed by seeing printed so inevitably a course of lectures for which I am at present totally unprepared and which must be given in October—and in between my book's to finish, there's the Assembly, Grace's wedding and goodness knows what else! I don't work nearly hard enough, and there's the truth.

I'll get your hat, and anything else you like.

I love you—always.

CELIA.

Doric House,
Burgh Heath, Tadworth,
Surrey, August 28th.

ROSALIND DEAR,

Your letter this morning saying that you have got Vera's book. I hope, I hope that you like it; in spite of some crudenesses it is fine and sincere, like herself. She is a person whom life has battered, and who has been given by circumstance and heredity such a temperament that every blow and every snub, even every casual coldness makes a wound and a scar, where many people would hardly know that they had been touched. The War has left her with a real sickness of apprehension that makes a life of publicity and action extraordinarily tiring; but never for a moment does she give way, nor lose her sweetness, nor her tenderness for suffering, nor an imagination which is constantly trying to devise ways for protecting other people from the sorrow that she has known. Many, many things about her remind me of you, especially her faculty of imagination about other people's feelings. I want you to like her, for when you come home we will go together to theatres and big shops and good concerts, and we'll buy materials and make clothes if you like. And we'll look at the newest books and Vera shall play the piano (we'll have

213

one by that time) and we'll talk and talk and talk. It will be lovely.

We are aiming at moving next year into an unfurnished flat of our own, with a maid. We'll have a spare room where you can stretch your long legs (in our present one you'd have to curl up like a caterpillar!), and we'll welcome you, oh! how we'll welcome you. But you shan't send money for theatre tickets, for by that time we must have made our fortunes! *Anderby's* only so far brought me £23, but on Sunday I finished *The Crowded Street*. I'll try and get it out next spring. It isn't good, but I did mean it to be good. I think that there are one or two fairly good things in it, though—a description of young officers having a mock tournament with oranges on a lawn in the moonlight, and the feelings of a small child at a party, and a wild run down a dark farm at night, and a half-mad, half-wise crippled farmer, with a sort of religious mania in a wild, lonely farm upon the moors, and a girl in a stiff, red gown of dark brocade gleaming in the firelight like old, rich wine, as she sings with her head uplifted, and her proud, triumphant youth conquering the hearts and imaginations of people in a middle-class, unromantic drawing-room. There's a tennis game too, that is a little funny perhaps, and the sham adventure of a false alarm of invasion, and the real adventure of a girl trying, through fear and disillusion, to find herself. These things are in my mind, and in my mind I see them good, beautiful or heroic, or only pitiful. I doubt whether you or any one else will find them in the book, though, which reads like something of a dull, trivial story. But I tell you of them now so that when you read the story you shan't think, "What nonsense is this for Celia, who chronicles the petty trivialities, so artificial and unlovely, of mean, small people in a provincial town?" You must say instead, "Well, it's a poor book, and the pictures in Celia's mind I know were lovely, sudden jewels of colour, rapturous breaths of beauty, visions of nobleness and dignity in human nature—pity that creatures who could be so high are—herself most of all—so very contemptible too often."

But probably it won't get published. *Anderby* was not such a success that Lanes may want another. Jonathan Cape, though, wrote to me, saying that he liked my work, and Mr. Newman Flower says that he'd like to see another book of mine. He found *Anderby* "ended on too grey a note," but he said that he was interested in the author. So if Lanes fail me, I may still get my Muriel Hammond before the public.

I've just made myself a three-piece suit to wear this autumn, blue stockinette lined with grey silk, and fastened with a silvery buckle. It's rather charming and only cost £2 2s. 0d. Vera paid £8 18s. 6d. for hers to be made in Hanover Square, and I'll swear mine is nearly as pretty!

I must go and read *International Law*. It is fascinating, and a relief from novels too.

The downs here are wonderful. We walked the other day to the Derby grandstand. Racing may be wrong and a bit uncivilised, but that sweep of a course so historic, so packed with human significance, grips the imagination. Vera, who sees far clearer than most, through to the logical conclusion of things, says that it is wicked to spend so much money and time and trouble on horses, when children are growing up everywhere without a chance in life. It is true, quite true. And yet, on Epsom Downs, I, who have never seen a race, can feel the wild pulsation of the crowd, the noble movement of swift, perfect creatures, the response of imagination to such a contest. Oh, me! I suppose that one day I shall have to oppose racing and hunting and all other less civilised pursuits, but it's in my heart that I'd like to see the Derby run. The old Adam dies but slowly.

Your motor runs sound so sunlit. Here we have biting winds, even in August. We'll have to go to Africa soon.

I love you—

CELIA.

215

Hotel des Familles,
Rue de Lausanne,
Geneva, Sept. 4th, 1922.

DEAREST ROSALIND,

I'm watching history being made, and it's curiously efficient as a sedative! It's only about nine o'clock and I'm consumed with sleep. We arrived here on Saturday, and since then the Greco-Italian crisis has fairly swept us along. On Saturday afternoon we hung outside windows and balconies, watching the Council of the League discussing the action of Italy for bombarding Corfu. On Monday we saw the Assembly meet and elect a little, spare, dark, harsh-voiced man from Cuba as their President. I've seen Paderewski, and Nansen, who is adored as no hero of the olden days was ever surely adored—a great Viking of a man, in a wide-brimmed sombrero. He has long Viking moustaches, piercing blue eyes, an air detached yet kindly; he cares no whit for public opinion, but the world for public suffering. His manner disregards all conventions and formalities. He grips the hands of his friends with bone-splitting energy, and talks—or should I say shouts?—with what one journalist calls "the sleigh-dog voice." But not one man, woman or journalist of any nationality I've come across has words good enough for him; he's the twentieth century hero of romance, the warrior who has fought for instead of against civilisation, the adventurer whose adventures have won him the gratitude of millions. Then there's Lord Robert Cecil, his shoulders hunched round his ears, his coat too short, his long black legs that twist round one another when he gets excited—which is often here. There's Branting of Sweden, the man who dared to raise the Reparations question in the Council—a man of colossal girth, moustache and geniality, in an untidy, badly-fitting brownish suit, with a black band round his arm. There's Viscount Ishii of Japan, President of the Council, small, neat and non-committal, with a charming smile, and a white moustache most neatly clipped.

216

Oh, and Hanataux, the French delegate, small, foxy faced, with a clipped pepper-and-salt beard, restless eyes, unceasing activity. He always seems to be counting his chances, eyeing other delegates, shifting, weighing, balancing. There's no denying that the tension is great. France will back up Italy in trying to keep the dispute from the League. England will back up the small countries who have threatened to leave the League if the Council does not act for Greece. Who will win, goodness knows, but the voting for Vice-Presidents this afternoon gave Lord Robert 42 votes out of a possible 45, and Hanataux only 35. That's significant. But if the Council fails now, the League will be in danger of smashing. Every one here is hanging round with their tongues out waiting to hear and see. The new method of open diplomacy is certainly more exciting for outsiders than the old Talleyrand-Metternich way.

Forgive more. I will write you a proper letter later. I've been taking notes all day, and my hand is stiff.

Always my love,

CELIA.

Hotel des Familles,
Geneva, Sept. 8th.

ROSALIND DEAR,

In half an hour George's brother and sister, Nicolas and Sophie de Coundouroff, are coming to dinner. I have just returned from the Palais des Nations, after listening to the Finance Commission discuss League expenditure, and am taking this opportunity to send you a note of love instead of a letter. To-morrow Vera and I go to tea with Fräulein Mundt, the head of the German delegation at the International Labour organisation, and, whether you like Germans or no, a very charming woman. "Charming? Of course," say the Germanophobes, "all Germans are charming to English people nowadays. They have something to get out of them." But I don't believe that she is

217

that sort; she has a most cultured and solid mind—solid in the true sense of being rooted and based upon strong, deep, fine things. We take the night train to Paris, cross on Monday morning if we catch the boat train, which is doubtful—spend Monday night in London, and go on Tuesday to Cottingham for Grace's wedding on Wednesday. It's cutting things a bit fine, but I just had to stay. I can't find myself interested in weddings or Cottingham or aunts, or receptions, or anything at the moment. The Greco-Italian business is still hanging by a hair. By the time you get this letter it will probably be ancient history one way or the other; but I write from an office and a town tense with anxiety, when every moment messages are arriving from delegations, telegrams from voluntary societies, and notes from the Conference of Ambassadors at Paris, enveloping more and more in a web of verbiage the simple straight issue—that Italy by the bombardment of Corfu has broken the Covenant of the League and that the Council has still decided to hesitate and does nothing. Only Lord Robert Cecil, in the Council meeting of last week, stirred the place suddenly by his striking straight home to reality by the reading of the Covenant at the public session. He has made no speeches; he only makes suggestions; but if Providence is kind, his suggestions will make history.

People talk and talk on points of order, on points of honour, on points of anything but *the* point—but meanwhile the solid work of social reconstruction goes on. I heard to-day China, Rumania, Norway and Great Britain urge the Social Commission to instruct the Council to instruct the Governments of States Members (we go round in this way at Geneva) to employ women police, either uniformed or ununiformed, for the protection of women and children. I have heard China denounce and France and Greece support the practice of regulated houses of ill fame. I have heard Count Mensdorff on the reconstruction of Austria, and Poland congratulating Ireland on its entry to the League. I have seen the Abyssinian delegate, glorious in white satin

218

tunic and black and purple cloak. There is a real Redskin
Chief of the Iroquois Indians staying at this hotel, as well
as the delegate for Haiti and his five fat black-eyed daughters.
The latter are really rather charming. Charming, too, is
the Japanese Count Adatchi, and more than charming the
self-controlled dignity of all the Japanese here, who,
during this ghastly time,[1] never have shown the slightest
sign of bitterness or of hysteria. Many of them do
not know yet what has happened to their families. All
are cut off from their Government. Some have lost
most of their property. A fund has been opened here for
their help.

Charming, too, is Signor Salandra, the Italian delegate
here, officially the villain of the piece, but the villain of
no piece from his appearance—fat, genial, with a wise,
round, fine head resting practically on his shoulders, grey
moustache, twinkly humorous eyes, with fine wrinkles
round them, and a delightful dimple. His manner, even
during the most critical moments of the Council, is genial
and suave. But there'll be the devil to pay if we don't do
something about Corfu.

7.25. *Il faut partir* to my Russians. They went away
last time when I was a minute late.

Much love, my dear,

CELIA.

58, Doughty Street, W.C.1,
October 2nd, 1923.

MY DEAREST ROSALIND,

The money and picture of the dress has just come.
will try to get it on Thursday morning. It looks charming,
and I shall love to buy it for you. Shopping intoxicates me.
To-day I went down to St. Monica's for some classes.
To-morrow I probably go to Wiltshire to lecture for the
League of Nations Union. On Thursday I will buy your

[1] The period following the great Japanese earthquake.

dress. It shall be long and big. I will try it on—and lots of others! I *adore* dresses!

I don't know when I've enjoyed anything intellectually so much as preparing my first lecture for the University Extension. It is such fun reading new things. I knew nothing about early civilisations—Crete and Babylon, Cnossos and Thebes—names that fairly ring in one's ears. Did you know that at Babylon was a co-operative guild for women in industry, with high powers and imposing organisation, in which women might rise to positions of high authority provided that they did not marry? Did you know that they hunted hippos, antelopes, and ostriches on the banks of the Nile? I didn't. Preparing lectures is a recreation after the grind and toil of making up stories. There is labour in a novel that you can never find in study and reproduction. I suppose that real *teaching* is labour, too, creative, constructive labour. But lecturing is just fun. I only wish that it were as much fun for the hearers.

My story has come back from the Adelphi, and they cut down my article in the *Willesden Chronicle*. Ah me! Still, I don't mind. It does not seem to matter. I can't feel sad when my stories come back—I am only sad when I write them, because they are so unlike the ones I meant to write. (I believe that I have said that before—several times!)

I believe that I shall wander next year. I must see Europe before I'm much older. I hate talking rather violently on second-hand knowledge. You'll soon be a specialist on Imperial problems. There are people who say that the position of Europe is hopeless, and that the salvation of the white race must come from outside Europe—from the Colonies and America. Is that so? I heard a man talking about a tour that he had taken in Eastern Europe. He found in Poland the land one vast devastated area, passed over in turn by Germans, Bolshevists, Lithuanians, Bolshevists again and finally revolting peasants. In Lithuania, people are still living in dugouts—fourteen, for instance, in one dark, lice-covered hole. Near Danzig live a family of

Poles in a great, broken house. The furniture is all smashed futilely, wantonly. The peasants cut out the eyes of the portraits hanging on the walls. The grand piano will not play, because German soldiers strained it to death in four years, when the house was the German headquarters. Round the house are shattered forests, untilled fields and villages razed to the ground. There is a grave where the son of the house lies buried. He disappeared when he was twenty-two. Two years later the wolves disturbed a grave in the forest. The daughters of the house, two delicately-bred girls under twenty, went into the forest, identified the body by a ring and some scraps of paper, and brought back their brother to bury. When Mr. Whelan went to the house to stay, he found them living among the broken furniture with their old father. He said, "Won't you sing to me?" for they had all been musical. They said, "We have a piano, but it is broken." They stood up in the ruined drawing-room—a huge, shadowy space. The light had gone. Their father held up the single candlestick, and they sang together the Polish National Anthem, while the servants, peering in at the door, burst into tears.

That's Poland. There are children growing up all over Eastern Europe to-day without education or proper nourishment or any ideas of decency or civilisation. It's pure barbarism, lit by sparks of courage or pride or sacrifice. But what ghastly gloom all round. We seem to be rushing straight to another relapse into barbarism. Perhaps it doesn't matter. You can't crush civilisation utterly. The cycle returns, and each time it swings a little wider; each time the light burns more clearly. Even if we live to see Europe lose herself in the shadows of another dark age, our great-grandchildren will see the Renaissance—and for them we must keep the torch burning. We must work out our experiments as perfectly as possible while we have time, so that they need not waste theirs upon abortive schemes. Success is nothing, provided that we can advance sufficiently far to show the way—education, social justice, international security, intellectual emancipation and culture. We've got to keep those alive in the old countries as long as we can until perhaps the new countries are developed sufficiently to restore with their egoism the next civilisation, and to equip the new ones for their task.

What talk! But it's all in my head. I can think of little else for long.

I found a garden on Sunday, five minutes' walk from here—St. George's, St. Pancras. A lovely, walled-in, quiet place, of green grass and tall trees, and beds of dahlias—and old tombs, dripping over with crimson creeper, and quiet white stones, and red leaves everywhere. It was a joyful thing to find on the last evening in September—a golden evening.

Babel, by Cournos, is a wonderful book. *The End of the House of Alard* is intensely interesting. It makes one wonder about Sheila Kaye-Smith. She seems to have gone off on to quite a different tack. I have got *Jacob's Room*, by Virginia Wolff, from the library.

Well, are you going to train our new civilisation in Beauty? I don't think it sounds like failure if your students want to help you. I don't think it sounds like failure, the friendship with which they regard you! What a fool the philology enthusiast must be! To know words for the sake of knowing them is like saving money for the sake of having it. Money is only good for what it will buy.

My dear love,

CELIA.

On a rock by the sea at
Grange-on-Sands, Oct. 9th.

ROSALIND DEAR,

I am in the middle of a railway journey, between hills and lakes and sea. Here we wait for half an hour. The station comes right up to a rocky beach, and is practically washed by the sea. It's a glorious day, windy and sunny, with seagulls blowing about the air, so down I came to a rock, with my toes nearly in the water and my fur coat buttoned up all round me, and you shall have your letter. I have not bought your dress yet, because suddenly we found ourselves in the midst of a removal. One thing after another has gone wrong in 58 Doughty Street. Then our charlady decided that young women who dressed themselves up and went out at five o'clock at night and only came in at ten and eleven and twelve could not possibly be respectable, and in a storm of moral indignation shook the dust of our flat from her feet—owing to her ministrations, there was plenty to shake. So I went out and acquired a flat. (At the enormity of this statement my letter decided that it would stand no more, and blew off into the Atlantic! I have just retrieved it, only a little the worse for wear, as this is a rocky coast!) We are moving next month to 117 Wymering Mansions, Wymering Road, Elgin Avenue, Maida Vale, W.9. And Mrs. Willett is coming to housekeep. Once we have paid a premium to move in and the furniture, it will cost us far less than our present place, even with Mrs. Willett. So when I get back I will buy your dress.

I am now on my way to lecture at Seascale. I am drunk with happiness at the lakes and the sea and the hills.

Have you read *The Conquered*, by Naomi Mitchison? It is a wonderful book—a great work of imagination, full of tragic beauty.

The sea in front of me is molten steel. The sky is a faint, steelish blue, and there are sea birds crying. I wish that my paper could smell of salt for you. I stayed last night at Kendal, and this morning my hostess motored me across to Windermere and Troutbeck—a grey, stormy morning, with sudden gleams of sun against great, windblown clouds. People are singularly kind. This is an enchanting way of earning one's living. It makes me feel quite mean, thinking how much pleasanter it is for me than for most people. Of course, all lectures aren't in

223

the Lakes. It's just luck. To-morrow I go back to Windermere.

I feel that I should like to get up and run and dance and sing, because of the sea, and the hills, and the wind-blown gulls. There's a gull now, running along a smooth slope of steel-grey sand, close to my feet. If I am very still, wild as he is, he may come near. There is a lady gull, delicately silver, running to meet him, and the sea runs up to meet the birds.

I see my train coming round the corner. I must climb back to the station.

Au revoir.

My love to you,

CELIA.

DEAREST ROSALIND,

I have had your mauve dress sent off from Debenham's. I do hope that you'll like it. It's outsize, large for me. It may even be a little too broad. If it is, it takes in quite easily at the waist, and the hem will let either up or down as you want it. I hope that you like the colour. It lights up beautifully. There is a jade green, too, lovely, but a little cruder; so, as you said mauve first, I got the mauve. I wanted it myself.

I have just to-day been talking on the telephone to your nice Mrs. Lewis. I wrote directly she got here, I believe, and had a letter this morning from the Campden Hill Hotel. We are going to meet on Thursday or Friday afternoon and have tea together somewhere. She says that you are one of the most fascinating people in temperament and appearance whom she has ever met. I hope that she finds fortune in England. It is a depressing business, this walking round publishers—"but joy cometh in the morning"—for a few days. Then, what with the reviews of critics, the sarcasms of one's friends, the reproaches of one's own taste, there's precious little peace after publishing a book, and the first result of progress is to make one hate one's work. Truly, it's a dog's life, and I wonder that any of us are fools enough to start it. Eh, well!

So you are going to Australia—without even the prospect of a job. I dare say that it's wise. Your Africa does not sound the place to settle down in, as you say, and Australia needs the graciousness of all fine rare culture that one can bring it. I only hope that you find a post that will give scope to your personality. All adventuring is rash, and all innovations dangerous. But not nearly so dangerous as stagnation and dry rot. From grooves, cliques, clichés and resignation—Good Lord deliver us! He certainly has delivered you hitherto. I don't think that His deliverance will fail. I rather wish that I could think that you had some job in view before you sailed. My chief fear is that you should, for stupid financial reasons, have to seek a second-rate job. Are you going to be very short? Have you any money to go on with? Would £100 make it possible for you to get a better job? I was going to leave it to you in my Will, but there's always the chance that you might die first! Especially as I am younger. And I'm not going to have any children—Grace's will be well provided for. It wouldn't affect my income. I'm selling out some stock to pay the premium for our flat and furnish. Also a friend is having a little for college. So I could without inconveniencing myself in the least, and it would be a real joy. I don't mind the thought of you adventuring. I only dislike it when reckless waste of ability is the fruit of adventure. I believe that you could do splendid things in Australia. But you mustn't throw away the chance of splendour for the sake of bread and butter.

I do agree with you about unpleasant letters. They give you such a feeling that for days you cannot open your letters without a horrid feeling in your throat, even though you know that the person who wrote the original letter was mentally deranged. It must be a terrible thing to lose control of one's mind. I cannot help thinking of the mental agony that must be endured before the limit is reached, though I dare say that it is not greater than the mental agony of those who do not give way. I met an extraordinarily tragic little incident up in the Lakes, less than an hour after I had written you that letter in the sun.

We are moving into a new flat, and buying cheap furniture at Wallis' and heavenly cretonnes at Heals'. We have been spending too much time washing dishes, when we should be writing. We are settling down, while you are rousing up to take the road again. There are, after all, more sorts of adventure than one, and Keats saw a new ocean of wonder as surely as stout Cortez and his men "silent, upon a peak in Darien."

You keep my letters. I doubt whether I shall ever want to write my own diary. The things that happen to my friends are the only things worth recording. I was made to be a somewhat doubting Thomas, never a Messiah, not even a Peter. By the way, have you ever wondered what half-humorous despair of irony went to that declaration: "Thou art Peter. Upon this rock I will build my Church?"

Mr. Macdonald said that when he was young he believed that he might conquer and convert hundreds. Now he thought himself lucky if he could hold seven faces besides his own towards the light. I told him that he was ambitious. Christ only managed twelve, and they were rather wobbly. What do you think?

I wish that I could show you my mother's letters. She is a brave, generous and noble woman. But for two reasons they are not for exhibit: They are too personal, and they are written in a kind of curious cipher which only long experience can make intelligible. I used to be most puzzled by them.

I love you,

CELIA.

But by the time that you get this, I shall probably be at 117, Wymering Mansions, Wymering Road, Maida Vale, W.9, which is the new flat.

Vera forwarded a sheaf of letters on to-night, one from London, one from China, and yours from South Africa. I was glad of yours. I always am. You say, "Don't lose interest in aunts and weddings." I don't. I've got my eye on two weddings now, both immensely important. One is Grace's and Peter's. I went home for Sunday and they came to supper. They are living in a furnished house in Hull until they know whether he has got his Government appointment. They are like an old married couple. They take each other, and everybody else, most beautifully for granted. Grace is far more at home in the married state than ever she was in the single one. Now I know why she never could quite find her place as a girl. She was a matron out of her proper environment. Now she's in it. I hope that she has lots of clever, jolly, nice children. Especially sons, who'll flatter and spoil and tease her. She would like it so much.

To-day I have seen a rainbow, a moonrise, a sunset, a hail shower of unparalleled violence, and a thunderstorm. Is not that luxury?

The people with whom I am staying are practically millionaires. It is gorgeously luxurious. I do love luxury —for a night. If you are rich, you have lovely cars, and jars full of flowers, and books in rows, and a wireless, and the best sort of gramophone and meringues for supper. I agree with Bernard Shaw that poverty is a crime, not a misfortune, and that what's wrong with the world is not that there are rich capitalists, but that every one isn't sensible enough to be a capitalist. To-morrow I am going to stay with Viscountess Carlisle at Haworth Castle, where there are not only cars, but a real ghost—and footmen. How does one tip? I do wish that I understood country house etiquette. I feel like the Young Visiters, only there is no Mr. Salteena to tell me when I have lit upon the right "ideer."

A maid unpacks for me here—and I've been travelling for a week with one handbag—a different place each night, and I feel that my nightie could be cleaner! But there are roses on my dressing table, and my curtains are of soft sea-green velvet, and beyond the curtain I know, though I cannot see it, is the moon above Lake Windermere. Can one heart endure such felicity? (If only it weren't for worrying about tips!)

I love you—and I am going to say good-night and go and have a bath in a simply stupendous bathroom.

This morning I walked in the wind and the sun between the Atlantic and the great grey hills.

Au revoir, and my love to you.

Did I tell you that I had met and love your Mrs. Lewis?[1] She is sweet, and gentle, and her mind has a rare beauty. Vera and I went to tea with her in Kensington and talked publishers for hours.

WINIFRED.

Windermere,
Nov. 21st, 1923.

ROSALIND DEAR,

Another month, and you will be leaving Africa.[2] Well, my dear, luck go with you. It's a great adventure. If, as you say, you feel glad to be going, then you are probably right to go.

---

[1]Mrs. Lewis (Etheldreda) had gone to England to find a publisher for her first novel—The Harp. Her best known book is Trader Horn.
    When she sailed for S. Africa I sent her an introduction to Winifred knowing that she would give her help and advice about publishers.   J. F. M.

[2]I resigned my lectureship at Rhodes University College in October, 1923, because I was afraid I might settle in Grahamstown for life.   I decided to go to Australia and reserved a berth in a boat going there, but at the end of October Miss Hayworth, Warden of the Women Students at Rhodes University College, saw an advertisement in the Cape Times for a headmistress for the Pretoria High School for Girls. She urged me to apply. I did, and have been in Pretoria since January, 1924.   J. F. M.

I heard from a woman whose daughters are in Australia and who herself has lived in Africa, Malay, and U.S.A. that Australia is a good place for English people—far better than Africa. I hope that you may find it so. I hope that you are not forgetting what I wrote about that £100.

I am up here again, among mountains now covered with snow and lakes stilled to silver quietness. The days are calm, full of cold, silver sunlight, and the white hills almost lose themselves in a colourless sky. It is infinitely beautiful and restful. I feel that I do not deserve it. Moments come upon me when I hardly dare raise my head to look upon loveliness, feeling that I get so much and give so little. Here is beauty. Here is peace. No poverty, no bitterness, nor mean, perpetual strife mars the tranquillity of this wide country. What can we do but bless it and pass by?

> Look thy last on all things lovely,
> Every hour . . . till to delight
> Thou have paid thy utmost blessing;
> Since that all things thou wouldst praise
> Beauty took from those who loved them
>   In other days.

I found in a book by Hamilton Fyffe the other day this phrase, that struck me strangely: "I went and sowed corn in my enemy's field that God might exist." I can't remember who it is by.

When I get back to-morrow night I have one lecture for the League of Nations Union, then hey for the battle for free trade. It's a sordid game at most—yet somehow I believe there to be some beauty, some courage, some stirring after a worthier mode of life.

Let's hope we don't get so sentimental over it, though, that we forget all the import and export figures!

My love to you,

CELIA.

229

Rosalind Dear,

I am sending a little Christmas present with my love. The vest washes easily, needs no ironing or anything. I hope that it is big enough. I bought it because it was what an aunt gave me one year, and I was so pleased with it that I thought you might like one, too.

Your nice Mrs. Lewis is coming to tea, to bring the MS. of *The Harp*. She is staying with Hilda Reid, at a boarding house in Earl's Court. She asked me for advice where to stay, and I gave her the nicest person I know to stay with. They are both coming here this afternoon. Mrs. Lewis has written to say that Hilda has put new life into her. Hilda is one of the gentlest and most charming of people.

I have not seen much of them last week, for I was at first speaking in the North, and since I came back on Thursday have given four speeches in four quite different parts of the world. Yesterday night I was rattling round Hampshire in a terrible little Ford car, with the fog outside so thick that one could see nothing through the windows but rolling clouds of woolly mist. I thought that every moment we should crash into a wall, a cow, or a car—even a conservative! To-day I rub my limbs over and congratulate myself that I am still alive.

On Friday I was speaking for Mrs. Corbett Ashley at Richmond. She is standing as a Liberal, a free trader and a supporter of the League of Nations. She's a charming person with a wide knowledge and a quick, trained mind. I like to think of women like that in Parliament. While she was speaking, an old Scotchman from the back called out, "Why don't ye gang the whole gait and cry fer Labour?" She said, "There are many things in the Labour programme with which I cannot agree." He said, "Eh, but ye will, lassie, ye will. Ye're a braw lassie, an' y've got a bonny way with your tangue."

Mother is coming up to London on Wednesday. I am sad it's then, for I can't go once to the theatre with her! But fortunately there are plenty of other people who will.

Well, well. Italy and Spain are drawing together. France and England are drawing apart. Germany seems to be drawing to a close. Where are we going to? *Quien sabe?* You are better off on the High Seas, I'm thinking.

My love to you always,

CELIA.

1924

117, Wymering Mansions,
Elgin Avenue,
Maida Vale, W.9., Jan. 24th, 1924.[1]

DEAREST ROSALIND,

I have been meaning to write to you before. Many
times I have actually sat down, intending to scribble off a
few business letters and then begin your letter, but always
the business letters have developed themselves into a longer
series than I thought, or the telephone bell has rung in the
middle of their execution, tolling the death knell to my
pleasant intentions of getting into touch with you again.
Indeed, I've waited longer than I wanted, partly from a
strange idea that you have not yet really gone again. I can
almost see you now seated on the fender seat, so shy—and I
myself no better! It was lovely seeing you, and reassuring
myself again that you are even more endearing than your
letters. Not that one really needed reassurance, but sometimes the thought will poke its head in, "She can't really
be like that—not really, not altogether." And then you
come, really and altogether, as unexpectedly and as fleetingly
as a fairy thing, and vanish again—for how long, I wonder?
And to a headmistress-ship! Whenever before was a headmistress like a fairy? Answer me that now, you who do not
understand why Vera said "The person who appointed you
to Pretoria must have had a sense of humour." Why, it was
one of the prettiest compliments that were ever paid you,
and you won't see it.

You will be there now. Oh, I hope all the best things for
you—a sympathetic (by which don't you dare to think I

[1]When in November, 1923, I knew that I had been appointed Headmistress of
the Pretoria High School for Girls I was so much alarmed that I took the
Christmas trip which leaving Cape Town on November 30th gave me seventeen
days in England. I stayed in the same boarding-house as Mrs. Lewis and Hilda
Reid, and I visited Winifred and Vera.
This first letter in 1924 was after my visit.   J.F.M.

235

mean a pitying!) staff, nice girls, convenient domestic arrangements, and parents as possible as the good Lord and human limitations can make them. I heard a few and rather colourless details about Pretoria from two South African medical students who spent Christmas with us at Bainesse. They were from the Cape, but they knew Pretoria and the school and its imposing reputation. They said that they thought it must be a difficult job to handle politically, but interesting. It is queer that South Africa haunts me. People are always coming from there or going there. Our housekeeper, Mrs. F., I now learn, was married there to her own disadvantage of two thousand pounds and a hangdog husband. Our two Christmas visitors came full of it—one way and another. One was a Dutch boy. His father fought with the Boers under de Wet, and the boy was brought up for many years to think of the English as tyrants and enemies. The bitterness has gone. He makes himself quite at home in Manchester University, and spends his holidays in English homes, which he finds quite tolerably untyrannical. In fact, the only tyrant at Bainesse was Margaret, who both abused and adored him, after the manner of tyrants, and with her he played for hours.

What do you think I'm doing this term? No University Extension work going, but at the last moment the English mistress at St. Monica's fell ill, and I am taking her place for two days a week. I don't know how I'll like it, nor how the girls will; but it will be good for me. I hate the examination syllabus which they have to pursue; but it will do me no harm to pursue it.

A curious, kindly thing happened this week. Two years ago in a little cheap restaurant near the British Museum, Vera and I were discussing the curate hero of her latest novel. It was a crowded restaurant, and a little dark man with blue eyes sat down at the other side of our table. Disregarding him, we went on discussing the curate. Our difficulty came in his relations with his wife. Here the limitation of our experience proved a disadvantage. Suddenly our little man leaned across the table and said, "Is it a story? Could I help? I write a little too." So we fell in and for an hour dissected that curate, his wife, his rector, his study, his photographs, his flamboyant sermons and his spectacular death. Incidentally we learnt that our friend's name was K., that he was an American journalist, and that he wrote bad novels which he hated.

About a week ago a letter arrived, addressed to us from 52, Doughty Street. As a result, last night we had a call from K. Somehow or other he has made some money, bought "The Fleet Street School of Journalism," transformed it into an American going concern with plenty of pep in it, and now, being a man of affluence, remembered two young women whom he met years ago, traced them out, and came to see if he could offer them jobs of corrections, etc., in his school to supplement their certainly limited incomes. He was as charming as possible about it, and obviously relieved when we told him that we weren't starving because we earned our living in other ways than literature. But for a piece of purely disinterested kindness, it was one of the prettiest things I have met for some time.

I ought to go and do some work. There is much to do and I am lazy. I do hope that your jumper was a success— and your evening dress—and your lovely new hair—and that you enjoyed the voyage.

You must have been nearly worn out after your very strenuous visit.

Au revoir, dear Rosalind,—I love you,

CELIA.

ROSALIND DEAR,

I am really writing from Somerville. I'm up here for a week-end, a week-end of vividly bright frosty weather, with the sky cloudless and white moonlit nights and the lawns silvered every morning. I am glad not to be back as a student, but it is a delightful place to visit.

Last night I walked by moonlight to Binsey Church across Port Meadow. There is a small twelfth century building, rough and grey, under the shadow of four elm trees and three staid, dark Scotch firs. The graveyard contains a well, sacred to St. Catherine, but won from the ground they say by St. Frydeswyde, fleeing from an amorous prince. The church was open even at that hour. We went in. By every pew are candle sconces, some containing candles partly burnt. We lit each candle. The windows slowly glowed to supernatural light. What a tale for Binsey villagers going home from the inn! We examined the font, the east window, the altar. St. Frydeswyde's delicate face gleamed between moonlight and candle light from the painted glass. Her hair is palely gold, and her features rarely patrician, though an unfortunate accident to the glass has truncated her slender figure.

Miss Lorimer made the most affectionate inquiries after you, but seemed to be almost heartbroken when I said that you had cut your hair. Apparently your hair has been put into wardship in some way by your friends, who imagine that they have a right of guardianship over it, and are quite affronted when, without their leave, you part from it. I told her that you looked younger and more full of charm than ever.

Miss Fowler is coming to London on the 29th, and I am going to frivol with her. I am taking her to a disreputable Soho restaurant and she is taking me to the theatre. I shall

238

try to make her smoke, but I'm not sure whether she will. She is a lamb.

It is cold, cold, cold; but there's sunlight and that is something. It allows one to wear a spring hat. How do people like your jumper? Your frivolous embroidered jumper? I went to the same place and bought two woollen ones to teach in. One is grey stockinette with a round Peter Pan collar and a demure grey bow. The other is a warm brown, embroidered all over with blue, green and red. I thought it more amusing for the children if I appeared continually in new jumpers. Don't you agree?

I love teaching English. But *what* a syllabus. Imagine teaching one from Beaumont and Fletcher, Browning, R. L. Stevenson and Shakespeare. Another has to read Scott, Cook's voyages, and a nasty little anthology of "Story Poems." Well, well. These are our examinations.

I must go. I have promised to call upon my tutor. Good luck, dearest of headmistresses,

CELIA.

117, Wymering Mansions,
Elgin Avenue,
Maida Vale, W.9., Feb. 21st, 1924.

ROSALIND DEAR,

I am trying to keep warm, but it's dree work. We have plunged back, head over heels into Christmas weather, snow, frost, fog, sleet, colds, chilblains, hot tempers and cold noses. Indeed, when I think of the number of courteous and equitable people still alive, I marvel at the persistent nobility of the human race.

I am back in London. To-day I have been teaching. I think that I prefer teaching English to teaching history. It can be such an admirably discursive subject. Even with an examination syllabus, one can wander beautifully off the beaten tracks. Besides, I like reading aloud, and none of my friends like to listen to me reading to them. Now I can victimise thirty children at once.

Isn't it right and fitting that my juniors should prefer *True Tammus* to *La Belle Dame sans Merci* and my seniors vote for *La Belle Dame*? But when I tried to explain to them why they preferred one or the other, they grew bored. I take a fiendish delight in irrelevance. To my VB doing Wordsworth I read Pepys, to show that the Prelude is not the only autobiography. To my form doing Lamb I read Montaigne, and we have formed a club for Brighter Parsing, where only Limericks and nonsense rhymes are admitted. They teach the parts of speech and their adventures as well as Pitt's Orations. (Why is it always Pitt's Orations that people choose?)

I went to lunch at Chelsea Court with Lady Rhondda on Monday, all by myself. We talked for nearly three hours about everything in the world; marriage, families, education, loyalty, plays, religion, socialism, fire-screens, provincial towns, Americans, Woman (and women), war, and the future of the race. I don't know what else. The best of it was that I've got a definite order for three leaders for *Time and Tide* and an indefinite offer to write whenever I think that anything looks interesting in the education world. Will I not? I don't care if I don't get paid (but I shall). I needn't be heroic. I come back from Bethnal Green seething with ideas and indignation. I'm running three articles now—one on reducing staff and the function of head-teachers—the next is on buildings and class reduction—the third on the school as a centre of civilisation—and there are others to follow.

When I teach, my theories go to the winds. I invented a new game for my juniors to-day. I pass you on the copyright. You do it on the board, so as to remember those silly names for accentuated feet that examiners want to know— Why, heaven knows! *I* never learnt 'em till I had to teach.

Here are my 3 syllabled feet.

1. The dactyl.

The dactyl's a serpent of venomous kind
His head darts out in front, his tail coiling behind.

2. The amphibrach.
The amphibrach has a hand
    each side
And long thin arms that he
    spreads out wide.

3. The anapaest.
The anapaest
Is a curious beast
In front it can boast quite two heads at the least
But I think you will find
Its long body behind.

This is the way in which I waste my time!
Dearest love,
CELIA.

117, Wymering Mansions,
Elgin Avenue,
Maida Vale, W.9., Feb. 26th, 1924.

DEAREST ROSALIND,

I have this afternoon been to tea with a clergyman of a pleasant, but perverse nature, who has lived for eighteen years three hundred miles from anywhere in particular among the natives of Guiana. He now resides with his wife a stone's throw from our flat. These eighteen years of isolation seem to have bequeathed to him two distinctions only from his fellow Cockneys whose boldest excursion into the wilds has been one walking tour in Ireland or the Lakes. He surveys with profound pessimism the products of civilisation as revealed in a London crowd, and he takes a mild but dilettante interest in philology. The London crowds, he says, are composed of people infinitely inferior in sensitiveness, imagination and spirituality to the aboriginal Indians. This he declares to be due to nothing but commercialisation, a disease which, he laments Jeremiah-like, is spreading daily from the lower to the upper classes, until soon there will not even be a duke left in England who is untouched by this despicable desire to turn his assets into cash or its equivalent. Then, he thinks, will destruction come upon us. I pointed out, in my best drawing-room manner, that some might think the commercialisation (if by that he really meant the partial preoccupation in wealth-making. He did.) of the upper classes a good thing. For only by the removal of a large unproductive upper class might it be possible to give leisure for "spiritual" development to the so-called lower classes, by whose exclusive preoccupation in mundane things our dukes had bought their immunity from commercialism in the past. He would not see this quite, and thought me a socialist. But I'm not. I went to a dinner on Monday where Masterman and Pollard spoke about Liberalism. Masterman's good. I wish that I understood more about economics. I might be able to understand better then what socialism means. But whatever of it I do understand seems to me to be good in parts, but bad if it swallows up all individual ownership. I did not like Government Margarine, or whatever it was. But you can't judge from wartime conditions, I suppose.

I went also last Saturday to see "The Way of the World." I saw it in the only appropriate attitude to see such wit, upon my knees. There was standing room only, but my legs were tired, and so were Vera's and Hilda Reid's. So we knelt at the back of the pit with our chins on our hands. The play is beautifully produced and acted, though Mirabel, in a passion of indignation against Millimant's whims, while in St. James's Park, knocked over a whole row of "stone" palings and sent them rolling to the footlights. He fumed even more realistically after that.

I have been reading a book of most poignant short stories written by a young Englishman with the Army of Occupation in Germany. *Defeat* by Geoffry Moss. It's bitter, but well done, and the story called "Isn't life wonderful?" is exquisitely tender and beautiful, as well as being bitingly true, I imagine.

I am looking forward to your first letter from Pretoria. Are you liking it? Is it being difficult? Or easier than you thought? And do you like the staff? It must be fine to run a big school. I hope that you won't be lonely. I hope that you'll find friends there.

Au revoir—my love to you, dearest Rosalind,

CELIA.

117, Wymering Mansions,
Elgin Avenue,
Maida Vale, W.9., March 12th, 1924.

ROSALIND DEAR,

I was so glad to get your letter of Feb. 2nd, where you say that the Pretoria people are being so kind and welcoming, and have even offered you the loan of a car. Does the "rich man without your gates" refer to an individual or a class? These offers of cars are—well, at times ambiguous. Even to a headmistress. Such a headmistress, at least. I am awfully glad that you like it. I want to come and see you some time. But when, when?

John Lane's have accepted *The Crowded Street.* They say that it won't sell. Their reader commented, "It has no passion, not even for freedom. As a love story, it is cold as the north pole. The unattractive heroine" (more or less autobiographical!!) "will appeal neither to the sexually unattractive, who will be repelled by this ruthless but calm analysis of their failures, nor to the sexually attractive, who will ignore her, as they do in life." That does not sound hopeful; but they are taking it all the same, because they say that it has quiet power and some scenes of unusual merit. (I don't know which.) I myself dislike the book. I shan't try *vie de province* again. I've got a passion now to write a fourteenth century romance called *The Princess,*[1] with Wycliffe as the leading figure—a man torn by intellectual doubts, physical cowardice, moral cowardice, and the brilliant clarity of his own mind—who leads the people up to a revolution and then denounces it; who sees through the transubstantiation theory, then writes "*quod est impossibile*" against his discoveries; who saw farther than any man of his time—and dared not go. I've got scene after scene in my head—a really romantic love story— scenes from the great revolt—an entirely unexploited political trial—a C.14 cause de celèbre, with a rescue and a

---

[1]This was afterwards written under the title of *The Runners,* but remained unpublished up to the time of her death.

244

mob riot; an execution or two, a democratic movement, ex-service men, the germs of English elementary education, three or four quite lively characters and an apple orchard in the sunlight, with a slim, dreaming girl like Gwen Frangçon Davis, and Katherine Swynford, one of the first of the "modern women"—and—and—and—— But I can't begin yet, for it must be done accurately. I have no time to read. I can't get near a book. I'd love teaching, but Lord, the time it takes to make things amusing. I'm torn between my desire to create people and my desire to help the children whom some one else has created. It's awful to be a writer and to want to teach—and lecture—and write articles. I've corrected forty essays, set four exams and given two lectures to-day, besides a pile of letters—and I want to write.

Ah well—it's fun anyhow.

The weather is perfect. There are catkins and primroses and a sky like June; only a frost at night. My vases are full of silver palm and white narcissus.

I love you,

CELIA.

117, Wymering Mansions,
Elgin Avenue,
Maida Vale, W.9., March 20th, 1924.

ROSALIND DEAR,

This evening the newsboys were shouting out "Churchill's Defeat" at 4.30, and the election celèbre of the year came to an end. But when I left Charing X Station at 7.15, the Abbey contest was already stale news, and the Y Divorce case, which closed quite an hour after the declaration of the poll at Caxton Hall, was on all the hoardings. Sic transit gloria—Winstoni. It certainly was a race. Vera and I last Saturday went to the Essex Hall to hear all four candidates deliver themselves of their opinions about the League of Nations. Churchill I found quite detestable as anything but a humorous evening entertainer.

I loved him for that. He is so unbelievably like his cartoons. He really and truly wore the overcoat with astrakhan collar and cuffs in which *Punch* draws him laboriously supporting the weight of his former liberal self. He really and truly points an accusatory finger at the crowd, and cries in sepulchral tones, "I say, that if another war is fought, civilization will perish." (Laughter. A sweeping gesture.) "A man laughs!" (Out goes the finger.) "That man dares to laugh. He dares to think the destruction of civilization a matter for humour!" (Rocking cheers and hoots of laughter from the gallery—in which I joined.) Indeed, he is such a preposterous little fellow, with his folded arms and tufted forelock and his Lyceum Theatre voice, that if one did not detest him one might love him from sheer perversity.

I have revised for the nth time *The Crowded Street* and sent it to John Lane. The dear Lord knows that it's not worth revising once.

London is full of crocuses. I wish that you could see St. James's Park. Wonderful carpets of gold and mauve are there. The air is still cold, but to-day at St. Monica's I smelt the spring.

I am mad and violent with the theme of an impossible story that I want to write—absolutely different from my others—the scene in the fourteenth century, the chief character Wycliffe and then the peasants' revolt, the translation of the Bible, John of Gaunt, the Earthquake Council, the Lollards. My head's full of scenes. They disturb the beatitude of my bath and the soberness of my grammar classes. But I've not had time yet to open a history book and see whether they would have been possible. It's ridiculous to try to write a historical romance—nobody wants to read one to-day. But I feel that if I don't write it, it will write me, or I shall explode—and if the history clashes with my story, then let history hang! When was fiction not stranger than fact? A pox upon your niggardly realism! For three years I have laboured to be sober, to be vigilant as a novelist, never to transgress by one epithet the

246

constraint and prudishness of *les vies de provinces*. I'll write a romance, high tragedy, real galloping stuff, or die for it. (And what tripe it will be, to be sure, after all these brave words.) Oh, Rosalind, why must we ever break our dreams by setting them down on paper. There is no room in the confines of a page for some of the things I want to write. Curse and hang it; when it's written it's hardly worth the paper either.

I've got one of those new scarf ties that are all the fashion, worn "a la Hoxton" with a pair of long black ear-rings and a black dress. I peacocked down to my pupils in it to-day. It *is* so bad for them, I think, when their staff wear the same green jersey all through the winter, till it looks as if it had sprung roots and grown on them.

W.H. (You wouldn't think it!) Ear-rings and scarf (green, scarlet, blue, black, white and purple. It *was* an old jumper!)

I must write to Dakers. Au revoir, my fine headmistress. I like your Smuts speech over Singapore.

Yours with dear love,

CELIA.

ROSALIND DEAR,

Your room sounds lovely. I wish that I could see it. I do like blue and white Cashmir rugs. There is one hanging up in Lewis's window that always wins my heart. Vera and I covet it every time we pass. Perhaps one day an awful spirit of recklessness will descend upon us and we shall walk in and buy. It is a very costly rug as rugs go.

That last sentence reminds me of a nice mot of " Saki's." Did you read his description of the cook who gave notice? " She was quite a good cook, as cooks go. And, as cooks go, she went." How silly it is—and how pleasant.

I wanted to sing and shout this afternoon, because the sun was shining and the starlings chattered and a barrel organ came along the street. Barrel organs and other street musicians always put me in a terrible dilemma. I am torn between my social principles, which forbid me to encourage vagabondage by promiscuous charity, and by my frivolous instincts which lead me to derive so much pleasure from the performance that I cannot be so churlish as to refuse reward. Consequently I am committed to a policy of paying for my amusement if the music is good, and withholding my philanthropy when it is bad—a hard-hearted policy, I fear, but one which should encourage merit in our street performers.

A cornet man who comes round regularly every morning I always pay. I love him when he learns new tunes for me, and now he always stands outside my window and serenades me with his entire repertoire until I throw down twopence in a paper. I think nobody could call twopence for an entire programme of grand opera, ragtime, Beethoven and Darewski an act of promiscuous charity, do you?

Yesterday in Southampton Row I found such a splendid band of ex-soldiers that I had to stop and listen. But I paid tribute to convention, which will not let one stop and listen in the street, by buying a paper and standing still as if to read it in the shadow of a shop door. I stayed for three tunes, then paid my penny and had to move along. It was a good band.

I have a cold in my nose and feel about as beautiful as a white rabbit—the pink-eyed sort, only my ears don't flap.

I had a letter from Pugh yesterday. She had not yet heard that her mother was going to Australia. She seems to be getting on very well. Newman has had water on the knee. Ill health seems to dog that girl. What an unfair world this is! Sometimes I just hate it all, and most my own—so far—good fortune. Every time I pass an unemployed ex-serviceman, every time I think of Vera, battling with her adverse circumstances, or of you, my dear, to whom catastrophes became a blessing, I am hot and angry with the unfairness of it all. I hate fortune. She will not discriminate in her gifts of blessings and rebuffs.

I have written a story and an article this week. The story a grizzly one about a rivalry between two farmers. The article I called *The Crime of Chivalry*, cursing the attitude of the strong towards the weak, and more especially the solicitude of devotees who will not let their causes stand the test of hard experience. I was particularly thinking of the League of Nations and the Ruhr. A pretty mess we are all getting into there.

Have you read Masterman's *England After War*? A most depressing book, but very ably written. Perhaps a little bit too lurid in its colouring, but none the less impressive for that. I have also got out *Woodrow Wilson as I know him*. I want it to be interesting. At present it is all about American party politics, which I find difficult to understand.

I am sending you some papers, with my love.

Yours,

CELIA.

117, Wymering Mansions,
Elgin Avenue,
Maida Vale, W.9, March 31st.

ROSALIND, MY DEAR,

I have just got your letter dated March 12th. That's not so long ago, it seems. You say that you feel cut off from your friends in Pretoria, until you fear that your bodily presence may have been bad for friendship. That could not be so, for your body is so delightful a body, and your personality is the sort that does not change. But it is also the sort that does not need physical contact to make it memorable. That is why it matters less whether you are actually here or not than some other people, for whom one cares far less. One of the only reasons why I wanted a free evening last week was to write to you; but somehow the time passed; it was end of term; I had meetings for the Union and I had work for *Time and Tide,* and so another week had gone by. I sent you some papers. I don't like the *English Review.* It is too stolidly Conservative; but there was an interesting article on " Literature and the Policeman" that I thought very good.

What a full and busy life yours sounds—and interesting. Headmistresses are safer when not quite interesting. Not that you won't be interesting, but it's intriguing rather than exciting to be ruled by a democrat. I should love to be on your staff, and to see you in your black and white georgette; but, alas, I am no teacher. I could hardly bring myself to go to school this week, for my head has been full of my book. I go to the British Museum whenever I have a moment and read Wycliffe's writings. I'm getting quite fluent at Latin and C.14 English. Only I can't stick to reading—I want to write all the time. I've never had my head so full of scenes and people. They flash into it, ready made. It's like watching a play. I do nothing, but only watch. It's glorious, watching the scenes and meeting the people. But to write—that is grief and labour; and to read what one has written—how unlike the story as one saw it;

250

how dull, how spiritless, that is enough to send one weeping to bed.

Have you read *The Life of Olive Schreiner* by her husband? It is a wonderful book. I wish that I had met her when she was in England in 1921. Still more, I think, I should like to meet him, for though he writes all through in praise of her, his personality stands out, most generous, strong and beautiful.

Next day.

I got that far last night, and it was half-past twelve, so I went to bed. This morning I must work. I have to go to the League of Nations Union to find out facts about the "Little Entente" to speak on it this afternoon to some post office clerks who have started a branch of the League of Nations Union. Last Sunday at Leyton—a most unbeautiful suburb—I took a children's service—all but the prayers. I chose the hymns, read the lesson and preached the sermon. There were about 300 to 400 children there and some grown-ups. I never did that before. I preached on two texts: "I come not to bring peace but a sword" and "A little child shall lead them," and talked about the way in which the world had always taken the "sword of the flesh" to fight— not for what they knew to be wrong, but for the things that they thought to be right, and how those who cared for peace and love must fight for these with the sword of the spirit, and how the older people were so used to doing things in the old, bad way that it was the children of to-day who must lead them on the way to a wiser understanding. I dare say that it was all rather above their heads, though it seemed self-evident enough to me. I wish I were a really good teacher.

Did I tell you how I heard last Sunday at Toynbee a German professor from Freiburg University and one of his students singing German folk songs, and an East End audience catching the chorus of a marching chant and singing:

251

"Gloria, Gloria,
 Gloria, Victoria,
 Du lieber, lieber Vaterland.
 Die vögel in die walden singen, singen, singen.
 Gloria Victoria."

I'm not sure of my German, but I am sure of the pleasure
on ex-servicemen's faces as they recognised the tune—a
pleasure entirely without bitterness of memory.

My dear love,

CELIA.

The Post Office,
Whipsnade, April 5th.

ROSALIND DEAR,

I am spending 'Sunday here. It is heaven. I walked
yesterday evening from the station, along a ridge of high
downs. The sunset spread over miles of misty valley. Dot
said, "It is like being taken up to a high mountain and being
shown all the kingdoms of the world." There are primroses
and Lent lilies on short stalks. They smell of earth. The
grass is so tight, like a well shorn head. The trees are
covered with round, bright buds like small lamps on a
Christmas-tree. The sun is so bright to-day that we can go
without our coats. There are lambs, and a puppy, and larks.
The apple-tree on the lawn outside has a twisted blue
shadow. There are goats. Oh, Rosalind, I'm just sick with
happiness because it's beautiful. Such peace, such silence,
such tranquillity.

Your term will be nearly over. One day I will come and
see you. Is this letter mad? I am so grateful for the sun.
I am *quite* sick of shadows—and rent restriction bills and
German elections. I went to the theatre with Gerda von
Gerlach on Wednesday. Her father has been arrested for
High Treason in Germany, because he was a pacifist and
because his paper *Die Welt am Montag* denounces the

252

militarist reactionaries. She was torn with anxiety and sorrow.

Hassan is better read than seen, don't you think? I liked the averted execution of Isak. Nothing else quite fulfilled my hopes. The scene in Grand Divan was good.

Must one leave the country and the larks and the jolly smell of earth and bother about committees and things, must one? Oh, if it were possible to shut out everything but the country.

I want frightfully to see *St. Joan.* I do love G.B.S. He has such faith and courage. It's good for a man to have faith and courage after the Galsworthys and even the Hardys. Hardy seems to have courage, but no faith.

Au revoir, dear Rosalind. I love you,

CELIA.

> *Whipsnade,*
> *Dunstable,*
> *Bedfordshire, May 4th, 1924.*

ROSALIND DEAREST,

I'm being incredibly idle and it's oh, so pleasant. I've been here 9 days now and have done nothing except write at my book and sit playing with the fire. It's been cold, windy, rainy, foggy and all unpleasantness, but we have not minded. Think, it's May, and the cherry trees are only just coming white. The rain has been so strong that the lanes are like dried water-courses. What surface there was is quite washed away. The bluebells are only just beginning to show and the primroses and violets have a March look about them. To-day for the first time we sat in a wood this morning on a tree stump, but now the sun has gone in and it rains. Even the cuckoo has a cold, poor dear.

Meanwhile in London things are going on with much the same éclat as usual. Philip Snowdon has made a hit with his budget speech. Even the conservatives, who feel that they must niggle on principle, have to admire its

253

technical skill. I hate the way that my own party is behaving. If only the liberal party were not so much less admirable than its principles. This back-biting and parliamentary scrapping is so childish.

I've been re-reading Edward Pease's *History of the Fabian Society*. It is a most cheering book. Interesting to see how these eccentrics like G. B. Shaw, the Webbs, Graham Wallis and so forth have at last come into their own. Webb in the Cabinet, Shaw the most influential writer probably in England, Sydney Oliver, now Lord Oliver, their fantastic dreams the official policy of His Majesty's Government. I wonder whether the League of Nations Union will one day pass from theory to power.

I am going back to town on Thursday and don't want to. I'm doing two schools next term and lots of lectures. I *adore* being lazy and rural and just writing.

Your suggestion that Vera and I should come and spend one winter in Africa is intriguing. One day we will. I really mean it. Not this winter. There's too much going on in Europe. Did I tell you that we're going to try to go abroad for six months to see things for ourselves. Vienna, Buda Pesth, the new Czech State, Albania and what not. It's an effort. I hate letting the flat and grubbing for passports, but it is a terrible thing to be tyrannised over by one's laziness, and we won't.

I send you a primrose. It will be dead when you get it, but it's from the Downs.

My love always,

CELIA.

Do you know Edna St. Vincent Millay's poems? They are delicious.

ROSALIND DEAREST,

We are back in London. It is fine at last. The term has begun. I started at my Notting Hill school on Friday. I have a perfectly gorgeous form to teach. Never have I known such a stimulating class—it rips along. There is Mark Hambourg's daughter, Sonya—a delightful person. Teaching these girls—16/18—is like dropping pebbles into a pool. The circles seem to spread and spread till they touch the furthest banks, and yet, through the clear water, the stone lies there safe on the rocky bottom. After the rich, idle, spoiled young ladies of St. Monica's, this is champagne after stout. I do see the fascination of teaching when the pupils care for work.

I've been writing an article for *Time and Tide* on farming. They asked me to do it. I believe that what I have said is true, but father won't like it. Alas, why are parents and children bound together by physical ties, yet separated by leagues mentally? The only hope is that they mayn't read it at home—but lately the paper has been putting my name on the posters and they will catch people's eye.

I've been ordering new clothes. I've run recklessly loose on a blue frock—heavy, dull blue marocain, like a Madonna robe in a Della Robbia picture—quite straight and long, but with a heavy fringed kilt falling from the hips, and there's a hat to match with a feather that sweeps my shoulder. It is to make me look important at meetings.

My Wycliffe book despairs me. I've been rereading Florence Converse's *Long Will*. It is so delicately beautiful. How can I come after with my gallumphing, clod-hopping bucolic style and semi-philosophico-politico bewilderments? But I will—I will—only we rush about so, and there's so little time to think

The flat is full of bluebells.

I love you.

CELIA.

ROSALIND DEAR,

I owe you for a letter—at least I sent you just the merest scrap in reply. I really have been busy, but to-night is calmer and I am drying my hair by a luxury fire, while in the street below two violins and a harp are playing the loveliest concert that I ever heard from the street. Every one is out on their balconies in the mild May evening, all the windows are lit and curtainless, and the harp plays Verdi and *The Lost Chord* and old Scotch melodies with a somewhat saccharine but melancholy sweetness that is singularly entrancing and restful.

I have been reading Gwendolen Newman's play *Inheritance,* and I have heard from Mrs. Lewis. These women who are doing so much against such odds have a claim to all that we can give from those of us who are at present in freedom. Sometimes I wonder whether the "state of single blessedness" is not too selfish—but it is hard to tell. I think that it should not be if one regards it as an obligation, like the Roman Catholic conception of celibacy.

I have been reading books that delights me. *Pilgrim's Progress* again. What a style, ye gods! How very excellent a book. *Jurgen* again, and *The Rivet in Grandfather's Neck,* which is a slighter work, and its style an experiment—the bud that blossoms in *Jurgen.* And then I have seen *Saint Joan.* I went in the pit by myself last Saturday. I have never seen a play that moved me more. There are moments in it so beautiful that they seize you away from all conscious thought. Joan's cry in the epilogue, "What, must Christ be crucified in every age because men lack imagination?" rings through the play; but its nobility is one of the rarest things that our century has yet produced. It shines like a good deed in a naughty world.

Would you like to see an article written about yourself among great women educationalists? *Time and Tide* is having a series and I have been asked if I would do you. It shall be very nice. You are a very distinguished person now, I suppose, dear Rosalind.

I read again to-day *Three Primroses and Two Violets*. I wish that I could get it off. Editors don't seem to want things about Waacs now. Yet the style of that is delightful. It has a gracious wistfulness quite of its own.

To-day I taught, went round to the League of Nations Union about our autumn tour, and then shopped. What a thing the pride of vanity is! Here am I, plain as a pike-staff, yet with a love for clothes that leads me into absurd extravagances. Yet surely it is right to look as nice as possible? Especially when one does care-committee work and that sort of thing. So many women look as if they took to local government because they would not dye their hair.

I have been writing quite a lot for papers. I went last week to interview Mrs. Wintringham at her flat. She lives in St. Thomas's Mansions, just behind Westminster. It is a small flat filled with large furniture—an overflow from Norfolk, I imagine. She is a large pleasant person with no "side." She was having a bath when I came in and did not mind saying so—you know the sort. There are some women who, when they think themselves distinguished, act as though they never had a bath and yet were always clean. Do you know?

Wembley is larger, uglier and more unfinished than one would dream, but the tulips, ostriches and Lucullus restaurant are lovely. Percy Harris wants Vera and me to go next Saturday evening to the Fun City and ride on the scenic railway with him. It'll be as hair-raising as your aeroplane.

We walked back through the park to-day. It is full of lilac, rhododendron, tulips, violas and stocks. It is better than the Champs Elysée. It is better than the Forum. It is better than the Piazza Michael Angelo.

My love I send you—and au revoir,

CELIA.

ROSALIND DEAR,

England is choosing to amuse itself by congregating in damp and disconsolate thousands at Epsom, to see which horse can run the fastest. I wish it joy. Monday, Tuesday, Wednesday have greeted the pleasure-seekers by devastating storms of rain and wind and divers other torments. This evening the sun has at last deigned to appear above a watery world. I am detained here because Kingswood is on the Epsom line, and the race trains can only be boarded by braver souls than I. Meanwhile I am as usual pampered here. Every room is ordered with a decorous and beautiful austerity of comfort. To wandering souls such as me, there are neat and charming parlourmaids with silver trays, who bring me meals hour after hour (literally). To-day I have already had breakfast in bed—no, I'll start last night. I arrived very late and had tea, fruit and sandwiches brought to my bedside—more tea at 11 a.m., lunch, coffee in another room after lunch, tea, and shortly milk and biscuits, to sustain me until my late supper before I catch my train. It is pleasant to be luxurious.

I have been reading novels again with a sort of hunger. Most of them good too, in one way or another. *Jane, our Stranger* by Mary Borden—a queer, clever, intuitive piece of work, in the Conrad style told backwards. But Jane is real and the woman knows her craft. Then here is Hope Mirrlees' queer, attractive book *Counterplot*. She is almost too clever, that woman. Her cleverness sometimes comes between her characters and her readers, hanging, a thin veil of wit and dreaming subtlety, between her words and their significance. It interests me especially, because her heroine writes a fourteenth century play, and my present efforts to write my C.14 novel find sympathetic reaction in her story. That sense of the past as of the future—that the past centuries cast forward their destiny—embryonic loves,

258

faith, lust, limitations. How can one convey this? How can I, compact of transitory fears and loves and struggles, living from little crowded hour to hour, throw off the entangling demands of classes, lectures, people, flowers, wet days and the like, and send my mind bare and unafraid to meet the naked candour of my people five centuries dead? Or is there no naked mind? Are we detachable from our circumstances? Am I, Winifred, are you, Jean, something complete, alienable, real, apart from the things that daily we see, do, hear and say? Can one walk as man to man with bygone people, our humanity being sufficient unto us for kinship, or when we have stripped away the trappings of our age, is nothing left? I wonder.

Isn't it difficult to write philosophically upon polite notepaper? One no sooner catches the tail of a thought than, hey presto—one is over the page. These sheets were meant for acceptances to dinner parties, inquiries after health, gentle snubs to importunate parents. I dare not straggle over dozens of them—and yet the mail goes to-morrow, and so must this

My love to you.

Au revoir,

CELIA.

117, *Wymering Mansions,*
Elgin Avenue, W.9, June 11th.

ROSALIND DEAR,

I have a horrid feeling that I never posted the letter that I wrote to you last week. It may be still resting unstamped in my locker at St. Monica's, in which case I will disinter it when I go there to-morrow and try to send it to you to say that I did write, even if I did not post.

I have been meeting delegates from the Société des Droits des Hommes and talking to the French Mam'selle at St. Monica's. I like that French Mam'selle. She is witty, vivacious, shrewd and subtle. Her mind is clear and alert.

She has warmth of temperament, and her personality glows with life. But when we talk a door slams in her mind—here, and here, and here. I am afraid of her—of her force, of her intelligence and of her hatreds. She fills me with a wondering despair. Oh world, how blind, how suffering! I don't know where I am, or what I believe. I wish that I could be a Socialist, heart and soul. Or a pacifist, and die in a prison. I know that I believe that love is the only constructive force in the world, that faith has a stronger courage than despair, and that the only hope for peace is to keep a mind open to the possibilities of human nature. But when I tell people so, either they ask me whether I am Labour or Liberal—which I don't know—or tell me, like a lady at a meeting last week, "My dear, what a charming cloak you wear" —which doesn't matter. If only people would not hate one another.

I don't know why I treat you to this outburst. I'm not really in despair—at least, not in sane moments. But nearly all the people who believe in the right things seem to do it for the wrong reasons—is there a right and wrong?

We are having floods of torrential rain.

Au revoir, dear Rosalind.

With love always,

CELIA.

117, Wymering Mansions,
Elgin Avenue, W.9, June 19th.

ROSALIND DEAR,

I have your long and splendidly interesting letter dated 28.5.24. (It's no use asking me to interpret that into a proper date. I never can. I can't remember what month "5" is; and to me months mean flowers and colours and the dresses worn by fields and gardens. Your months are different. What can I tell of your May? Let "5" remain. As an indication of time past it suffices.)

You tell me many interesting things. In Mrs. X I am

interested. I believe what you say—that many of her troubles are self-made. And yet for that I feel almost more sympathy for her. The deepest troubles are all those that rise from our own temperament. I do believe that. To conquer circumstances is a great feat. It is also an exhilarating struggle. Its heroism is its own reward. But self-conquest means a battle with shades and shadows—elusive things that mock our efforts to withstand them. If we walk hag-ridden by our nerves and our suspicions, then indeed do we need help and sympathy. I think of Olive Schreiner, and Keats and Coleridge, and Francis Thompson, and Cowper, and heaven knows who else; the tragic army of those who fight themselves.

You say that Europeans do not wander far enough away from Europe. That is a fair indictment. I do not think that any of us wander far enough; but our difficulty is that if any work is to be done, one cannot spend all one's time wandering. And one has to wander first where one can learn most about the thing that one is doing. I am coming one day to South Africa. I want to see your schools. But the journey is both long and expensive. It must wait a little. Meanwhile, I must learn what it is that I am talking about now. I keep on speaking of Central Europe to my audiences, of the conditions and influences and governments there. Then they ask me, "How do you know? Have you seen it?" And I can only say, "No. I don't know. I have read so and so, and so and so." And they say, "Well, I read so and so, and he says quite differently from what you say." I must go. Then, when I have gone, I must come back here and tell people what I have seen. Afterwards I will go to other places, to Africa, to America. And each time I want to come back, and to say, "It's the same all over the world. No advancement is bought without payment. No hate can be constructive. No amelioration planned upon a basis of vindictiveness can succeed. No life can be politically satisfactory unless the individual personality also is developed. No nation can prosper upon foundations of frustration.

The victories of civilisation are in the end the victories of man's mind over the claims of his body, and I have seen so and so, and it is thus and thus. And I tell the truth."

You say, "If I delay too long, I may never come." But if I live, I will. ·All things in their time. Life is too short to chop and change. One must follow.

I read to-day your election results. I see that the Nationalists have not a majority yet, though it has been a close thing. I wonder very much what is going to happen. It is curious that you should have been tossed into such a stormy place—no fair haven yet. You will do well. I wish that all headmistresses were like you. I wish that all people of influence in storm centres had your breadth of sympathy. Oh darling Rosalind, how can we build on a basis of hatred? One must love.

I have been reading a very interesting book called *The Day Boy* by Ronald Gurner about a boys' secondary school under the L.C.C. I found it most attractive and illuminating.

My own Wycliffe book progresses in patches only. I have no time for consecutive working. My girls at St. Monica's are taking their General Schools examination this week, so to-day I have a holiday.

I have to correct and send off the proofs of my *Crowded Street* book. Wish that I thought more of it.

With love from

CELIA.

117, Wymering Mansions,
Elgin Avenue, W.9, July 15th, 1924.

ROSALIND DEAR,

I have had your letter telling of your poor, unwanted child who has stolen things for a girl she adores—also of your intention to find a home for her yourself—which is certainly what one expects of you, for you always do the human and gracious thing.

I'm not an angel—I'm a debtor to life, one who without

effort gathers in the gold, while others go upon their way weeping, and bearing forth good seed, and I come again with joy and reap their sheaves. But they shall have their day and their joy. My heart is heavy for their sorrows and my joys.

Rosalind dear, shall I come to Africa a year this autumn for three months. I might do it. It's financial mostly, but if I get lectures and things, I might. I have definitely refused to tie myself down to the L.C.C. or any other body for three years at least because I want to see something of the world first.

Do you know, I think that my little Vera is going to be married after all. After all these storm tossings a dear and very charming and brilliant man has come to love her with an amazing, beautiful love. He was at New College and three times he saw Vera at Oxford and fell in love with her then, but never got to know her. He read *The Dark Tide*, fell in love with "Virginia" and guessed that it was something of a self-portrait, and wrote to her. He sent her his own book—a learned treatise upon Hobbes. She wrote. He wrote again. His letters were delightful, tender and witty, full of a rich sympathy and illumined by quite unusual intellect. This summer he came to England, called on her on the Friday and proposed on the Sunday. She refused him, but since then he has gently, humorously, lovingly urged her, and now she has said Yes. He is more charming than I can say; blue-eyed, thin, and tall—a clean, smiling, boyish person, with a piercing, determined intellect. He quietens and soothes her. He makes her childish again. He has known much suffering, but a deeply religious and selfless personality has given him a peculiar courage. I like, respect —I could say, love him, and am very happy, though it means losing Vera's companionship and no one can tell what she has meant to me for these four years. But I covet for her this richer life. He will not let her stop working. They will live for eight months a year in America for five years, and four months in Europe. After that they will come to Europe for good. It should be a full and fruitful life, rich in possibilities, a delightful companionship. I hope that nothing spoils it.

My children at St. Monica's have finished exams and have now a craze for stories. They want all the Greek legends and the sagas and the Celtic tales. They keep me at it. But they are worth it. Nine of them are trying for the University next year, and about another six for other permanent work. Before Vera went back there to teach, about one a year dragged herself out of this rut of social engagements into an attempt to find work. Sometimes I regret leaving them. Teaching is so immediately worth while. But there is so much to do.

Au revoir, dearest Rosalind. I love you.

CELIA.

117, Wymering Mansions,
Elgin Avenue, W.9.

ROSALIND DEAR,

This is just to catch the mail to say that I am writing. I have been correcting examination papers every night this week and teaching and lecturing during the day. So no time for any but business letters.

I spoke in a glorious garden at Epsom yesterday. To-night I went to see Ronald Boswell, one of Lane's directors, and talked all the evening to a charming South African woman who knows Pretoria and your predecessor and the Smuts, and Professor Rousseau and Professor Cory of Grahamstown, and Johannesburg and everything, but I never caught her name. She is married to a painter who painted a picture of Professor Rousseau that is in the Colonial Exhibition, so I may learn her name yet.

I find South Africa everywhere I go.

It is after midnight and an early start for me to-morrow to St. Monica's.

So au revoir, and my love,

CELIA.

117, Wymering Mansions,
Elgin Avenue, W.9, July '20.

MY DEAREST ROSALIND,

I have spent the past week largely in the composition of reports, criticisms of examination papers and the editing of a school magazine—all quite pleasant and cheerful occupations—cheering too, because at St. Monica's a curious change seems to be at work among the girls. Those who are leaving this year nearly all intend to take up some definite work. They are to be actresses, nurses, teachers of history, art or music. One wants to go to college and thence to follow her father as member of the Canadian Parliament, and so on. In school they are founding clubs for the discussion of general subjects of citizenship and social interest. It is fun watching them sit up and take notice. They are all so rich and comfortable at home. They must not let go now.

Last night I went to the Everyman Theatre at Hampstead to see Shaw's *Getting Married*. What an amusing theatre it is, with its orange doors, bare brick walls, shaded candles and highbrow audience. Every one seems to wear bobbed hair, embroidered jumpers and an air of interest in the absolute. One feels that in the pit (it is all pit of varying prices) one is surrounded by positivists, theosophists, vegetarians, anarchists, and Roman Catholics. I defy any ordinary nonconformist or evangelical episcopalian to find a home among those somewhat uncomfortable plush-padded seats.

The play was a joy to me, as Shaw is always. Contact with the mind of a really intelligent and profoundly reasonable being is delicious. I enjoy watching Shaw take up the conservative point of view, shake it as a terrier shakes a rat, and then put it down again in exactly the same place. He apparently thinks that men accept the right institutions for the wrong reasons, and then endeavours to show them the right ones.

I told Lady Rhondda that I am probably going to South

265

Africa in January, 1926. I think that I will. I am laying all my plans for that.

I love you,

CELIA.

117, *Wymering Mansions,*
Elgin Avenue, W.9, July 21st, 1924.

Oh, Rosalind, have you read *The Magic Flute* by Lowes Dickenson? It is a wonderful book, most strange and lovely and true, such as one meets so rarely, yet welcomes like friends of whom one has heard for a long time yet never found till now. Mr. H of the Oxford University Extension Delegacy told me of him. I went to lunch there on Saturday—a warm, flower-filled July Oxford. The rains stayed too late to allow the trees to grow rusty. They are heavily, darkly green, and the gardens intoxicated with scents and brimming over with frothy ramblers. Mr. H is good—really good, with the clever, half shrewd, half dreaming mind of an idealist chained to earth by common sense. He sits and beams through his gold-rimmed spectacles and talks about God (whom he worships) and the Labour Party (which he serves) and Lowes Dickinson (whom he loves). You see, there are no hatreds in a man like him, and no negatives. His personality is all beamingly positive, and thus as warm as a July day.

Last night I wandered in Hyde Park, listening to orators in the twilight. I heard two Baptists—one invited me to wash in a fountain filled with blood, poured from Emmanuel's veins. Another suggested that I attend a bright Tuesday evening service for young people, where they have such good times. I heard a Labour exponent trying to describe evolutionary socialism and getting horribly mixed up about municipal water supply. Fortunately I don't believe that any of his audience realised how muddled he was, which is a habit of audiences, and the best one they possess. I did not interfere, because I always pray myself that when I am confused in a speech an angel of the Lord shall confound the minds even of my brethren also. I wonder if my friend knew how I had befriended him.

I heard also an Irish Mormon explaining that polygamy, though permitted, was optional among the dwellers in Salt Lake City, and that at least it was legal and open, instead of being practised secretly as by most of his audience.

I heard an Indian atheist cursing God, chiefly because he said that religions made people feel superior to any one who had not got the same religion, and so bred wars and dissensions.

I heard an anti-prohibitionist telling the British Working Man that he was entitled to his beer, and an ingenious Catholic Evidencer—a girl in ivory beads, pince-nez and a shrill voice—explaining that the doctrine of Purgatory was taught by Christ to his disciples, because all truths of the Church were taught by Christ, and that if it gives no account in the Bible of when it was taught, then it must have been once when it says that Christ took his disciples away into a desert place and there taught them. I wonder if he also taught them there prostitution as a means of relieving their natural emotions, capitalism, mah-jongh, nepotism, and the doctrine of Indulgences. The possibilities of such secret conversations would seem to be endless. Hyde Park in the twilight is wonderfully beautiful. The people who walk there are not. And yet—and yet?

Oh, Rosalind, do you think that we shall ever learn to be worthy of the world we live in? Shall we ever be civilised? I think that we are still struggling in the prehistoric period of the real possibility of Man. We may have dropped our prehensile tails, but we have not yet developed our wings.

To-day I was at Wembley at a Conference of New Zealand women. They discussed Child Welfare and Education, and then a Maori princess (a real one) told Maori fairy tales beautifully. The Greeks weren't the only people with good

267

native myths—nor the Poictevenes. (Have you read *Jurgen* yet?)

I must go to bed.

Au revoir, dearest Rosalind,

CELIA.

117, Wymering Mansions,
Elgin Avenue, W.9, August 5th, 1924.

ROSALIND DEAR,

I spent the week-end with Dot McCalman at Whipsnade. Vera is at Oxford with her young man. The Bedfordshire Downs are glorious. On Sunday Dot and I trudged about fifteen miles in the rain, to see Ashridge Park. It is a magnificent C.14 house—or at least, parts are C.14—that used to belong to the Duke of Bridgwater.

There are miles of undulating parkland; smooth stretches of grass or ragged slopes of bracken, with great groves of trees, not too thickly interlaced as in a forest, but each standing as becomes his natural dignity. They say that such thinning is made by the deer who eat the tender young plants. Deer there certainly are, and in profusion; such domesticated, sociable deer.

The house is huge and desolate, but the gardens have been kept up for the public to inspect at 1s. each, and there are grottos and monks' gardens inlaid with a brilliant mosaic of flower-beds, and herbaceous borders far taller than I am, with sunflowers, hollyhocks, delphiniums and larkspur. There are two deep banks of lavender, and a herb garden, most demure in colour, but sweet-smelling. There are fountains with water-lilies, and sunk tennis courts and an open-air swimming-pool surrounded by prim clipped hedges. A garden for Bacon.

On Monday night I went to Hyde Park to see what this nation is thinking of on the anniversary of the outbreak of war. I heard a Fascist hating the Communists, a Communist spitting at the name of Sir Edward

Grey, a Baptist talking about prostitutes, an Anglican talking about the Crucifixion, a "London Secular Missionary" indicting the churches, and a Catholic Evidence speaker—an admirable one too—explaining with much wit and gusto the infallibility of the Pope. There was not one word about peace, not one about the peril of war, not one remembrance of a suffering whose deepest evidence lies in the bitterness of those faces upturned in the first lamplights.

I went round looking for a platform that I knew, but my own was holding services and singing hymns, and the League of Nations Union was not there.

> "That the waters of Golgotha may no longer flow
>   And men see light."

I wonder? How long . . . ?
Au revoir, most dear Rosalind,

CELIA.

117, Wymering Mansions,
Elgin Avenue, W.9, August 12th.

DEAREST ROSALIND,

I have just got your letter of 23.7.24, and its defence of wanderers. Your subject for a debate "that wanderers have contributed more to human good than stay-at-homes" seems to be interesting, but like almost all debating subjects, can only be truly argued by saying "it depends on the wanderers and depends on the stay-at-homes." Mahomet was a wanderer and Christ never left an area that was smaller than England. Keats was a stay-at-home; Byron and Cecil Rhodes wandered. Well, well, one could play the game for ever. But you say one thing that I *must* contend. "Don't spend your dear young life reforming people lest you lose the common touch." Dear, dear Rosalind, don't you think I know far too well that most people are worth twenty of me? How should I dare to reform them? What I burn to do is to reform some of the conditions in which they live. Accidents and no merit have raised me into the more easy and free world which can avoid spending all day in order to live. I must use that freedom to make if possible other people more free from squalor and ignorance that cramp their development. My East End children, bright and debonair—and stunted and thin, and thrown on to an indifferent, industrialised world at fourteen. My little girls who long to paint and write and make lovely things, turning into barmaids, or button hands, or drabs. But reform people! And yet!—it is only the spirit that matters. But dear Rosalind, how can love make one lose the common touch? Should I cultivate it more by becoming history tutor at St. Hughes? They suggested that to me, you know. Or mistress of an Anglo-Swiss school at Lucerne? I was offered that job.

In Central Europe I am going to meet ordinary and extraordinary people. I am going to stay with rich people and poor people, and official people and unofficial people. I shall travel 1st, 2nd and 3rd class. And when I come back I shall at least be able to say, "In Hungary and Germany and Austria, people are people like yourselves. They are not all spies, monsters, fools or knaves. They are all pretty silly, but so are we. And when they say, "But you haven't seen them," I shall say, "But I have. I've stayed in their houses and been sick in their railway trains (I always am!) and sworn at their fleas and nursed their babies. So there!"

In haste—packing, letting the flat, etc., etc., etc.

CELIA.

Rosalind Dear,

Your letter has come telling me of your new puppy, of your English mistress having tick fever, of your children acting fairy plays which they write, and of a feathery thing made of ostrich down which you are sending me, and to which I look forward with great excitement. Is it to wear? Every one who is really smart is wearing feathery things this year, and I have been longing for one, but the really nice ones have prohibitive prices.

I came home last night. Vera and I have let our flat to a colonel and his wife. We start for Geneva on September 10th. I had a letter from Miss Fowler saying that she may be there too. I hope that is so. She is such a dear.

Here there is no sun. It rains and rains. I wish that the fine weather would come, but wishes, alas, are not horses and hardly the fleetest Arabs could chase away these sable clouds.

I am writing short stories. I am not good at them and they never seem to get published, but I still keep on. I think because I enjoy them so. I dare not tackle my Wycliffe book in this short space of time

My *Crowded Street* is coming out next month. When I re-read the proofs I disliked it less. It is slow-moving and monotonous in places; but there are two or three scenes that are much better than *Anderby*, which is something, enough to enable me at least to write the dedication. It's not good enough, but it is so far my best. But why, why, when one writes, does a sort of shackle bind one's imagination? I become conscious of a deadening mediocrity, perhaps a form of mental cowardice, and I long to break free, to let my imagination take wings. It doesn't—yet. Perhaps——

I love you, Rosalind. I will come and see you one day.

Wait till I get Vera safely married and delivered to her
G.—who is a dear. Then I will come.
Au revoir,

WINIFRED.

Bainesse,
Cottingham,
E. Yorks, 29.8.24.

ROSALIND DEAR,

Have you any aunts? I have hundreds and thousands,
and this last week they have been coming over to me, or
I have been going over to them almost incessantly. I do
not believe that we are through yet. But I am going to a
funeral to-morrow for a change.

As a matter of fact, the funeral is a sorrowful one, for
the man was one of the best that I have met. A bachelor,
a devout Roman Catholic, he held some sort of inland naval
appointment at the port of Hull; but he was known to
every one for miles around as Uncle Micky. When my
exam results at Oxford came out, it was Uncle Micky who
knew one of the examiners and found out all the details.
When my book came out, it was Uncle Micky who ordered
a dozen copies to be put in a bookshop window for advertisement. When I hadn't any partners at a dance, it was
Uncle Micky who would come and flirt charmingly with
me behind a curtain. He had a way of making every woman
whom he met feel beautiful and in her best clothes. Every
man whom he met felt immediately young and gay and
popular. He was sixty-three, looked forty and had scores of
friends in every possible circumstance in life. I do not
think that a day of his life passed, but he gave somebody cause to be thankful that he lived. Last week he
was taken ill; they operated for appendicitis. He got
over it apparently, as he did over everything, with a
sort of debonair success. Then collapsed quite suddenly
and died.

272

I have written last week two articles, two stories and four short notes, and have been working pretty late, for every day we entertain, so I am sleepy. I hired a wonderful typewriter, as large as my table. Hence, I think, my delirious literary activity. For I cannot bear to waste a hired typewriter.

With love always, my dear Rosalind,

CELIA.

Pension Coupier,
3 Rue des Alpes,
Geneva, September 14th, 1924.

DEAREST ROSALIND,

We came last night out of the grey storms of a bad channel crossing, and the damp misery of a wet night in Paris, to this milk-white city, with its lake like blue Spode china and Mont Blanc, perky as a picture postcard mountain, all agleam in the sun. Out of fur coats into white dresses —out of smoke into most restful and exquisite cleanliness, when one dares to touch a railing without spoiling white kid gloves. No wonder the nations find it easier to be friendly here.

International reactions are curiously fluid. Herriot and Macdonald have shaken hands and been photographed on the steps of the Palais des Nations in Geneva. Already as we came through France yesterday the porters were more genial, the Customs officials less officious, and the whole atmosphere more friendly than it was a year ago. People hardly read the papers, hardly think consciously of the diplomatic significance of a speech or gesture; but surely, secretly, like the water of a marsh rising beneath the weeds, the tide of feeling rises. Curious this, and too obvious to be obviously true. But it was so.

We have a room with a balcony overlooking this most lovely lake. There are gardens with well-kept beds, and one wild graceful beech tree, and many prim paved paths below the window, where little girls run in white shoes, wonderfully clean.

I love this beautiful, hygienic town. I could offer up hymns to Calvin with his austere and rigid creed that I always feel to be partly responsible for the austere and rigid efficiency of the municipal dust-cart service here. The connection between faith and dirt is one that might be investigated more closely. Dreamy, romantic, devotional catholicism woos the soul away on clouds of incense and makes one oblivious to fleas or dust—witness South Ireland, Naples and Mexico City. Calvanism, stark, uncomfortable, allowing no illusions, blinds nobody to anything except the joys of idleness and wantoning. Hence open windows, sterilised milk, immaculate pavements—Geneva.

The sunlight may possibly have something to do with it too.

People keep on saying, "When is your book coming out?" and "What is it like?" They are questions that I cannot answer, like a young wife expecting her second baby. "Well, it should be the end of this month, but I am not certain. Sometimes they are late. I miscalculated the last one. On the other hand it may be early." "How can I tell whether it will be good or bad, nice or nasty. I only know that it will be my child...."

I want to write lots of articles but do not know quite why. I used to crave after short stories so much more.

Au revoir, I love you always,

CELIA.

Pension Coupier,
3 Rue des Alpes,
Geneva, September 26th, 1924

ROSALIND DEAR,

I have so much that I would like to write and the time is all too short. Here one attends an ever accumulating series of conferences, committee meetings, councils, assemblies, lectures, interviews and social functions. In between—that is to say, usually from 1.30 to 3.30 every day, unless we have interviews or lectures, we write up our articles for the press—about two a day of some sort expected. Actually at Geneva it is very difficult to tell what is happening. Too many things crowd in on top of one another. But later, when we have gone away, when the tumult and the shouting dies a little, and the Lithuanians have ceased from plucking our sleeves and writing impassioned notes that we should remember their misfortunes in our esteemed journal, when the Australians have ceased from barking against the French, the Albanians from complaining against the Serbs, the Turks from politely giving the lie to Lord Parmoor,[1] and the Secretariat from bemoaning the circumlocutions of delegates, then we may really have some idea of what was being done by the Fifth Assembly.

Actually, when we are here, it is only possible to deduce the very small details and the very large movements—neither of which can ever be adequately learnt through newspapers. The very large movement this year is distinctly hopeful. Macdonald and Herriot came together and made speeches and departed in the same railway compartment. That was spectacle. But now, in the Assembly, nations are talking with the same frankness that they would use in their own countries, instead of perpetually passing compliments. In France the porters and customs officials are kinder and more helpful. In Germany, people passing through say that the bitterness is dying down. Nansen met Stresemann on the shores of Lake Constance at the beginning of the week, and the German Government have written to the Members of the Council asking their attitude towards German admission. It will come. Germany will come in, though late and ungraciously, and doubtless it will take months of propaganda to blow away the ill-odour of her lack of grace. The Nationalists will eat up the Social Democrats and between them the League issue will be badly

[1]Representative of Great Britain that year on the League Council.

275

mauled. But I think that she will come. The disarmament Protocol is imperfect; but Benes has genius. To see that small, alert, boyish man sitting before the principalities and powers, his face grey with fatigue, his unassuming personality resembling nothing on earth so much as a conciliatory commercial traveller, yet ready for every argument, decisive, lucid, explanatory, is something to marvel at. He is the youngest delegate, I should imagine, on the Third Commission, which is discussing the Protocol. He is its rapporteur—the man responsible for the draft. It is he who explains to gentle, pacifist Lord Parmoor the fears of the French, the prejudice of the Poles and the suspicion of the Scandanavians. It is he who buttonholes the French as they leave the long glass gallery where the meetings are held, and endeavours to reconcile apparently antagonistic interests. And he may do it. There is a new spirit here. People are for the first time beginning to realise that no international settlement can ever be gained without sacrifice. The press, who are doing their worst as usual, are learning sense slowly.

But why on earth your South African delegates cannot learn that it is the men like Nansen and their work of reconstruction and pity that make possible this political compromise, I do not know. Nothing can be done without human contacts. The returned refugees, the prisoners of war, the rescued Armenians, are the only agents who will really save the League in the dark places of Eastern Europe and Asia Minor.

With love always,

CELIA.

Hotel Gothard Terminus,
Bâle, October 1st, 1924.

ROSALIND DEAR,

I came yesterday through one of the loveliest, golden days that I have ever known to this town where we have stopped for the day to rest.

I had never thought that Switzerland was so rich and bountiful a country. We passed terrace after terrace of linked vines, hand in hand along the slopes, girdled with white stone walls and studded with small red and white houses with emerald green shutters, like rare, rough jewels on a Saxon gown. Even the snow of the mountains was not cold, but wonderfully lit to rose and primrose colour, and the rivers which crossed and re-crossed below our track were deeply green. Everywhere the foliage had not yet turned to crimson, but only taken a luminous gold light, as though reflected from the sun, on to their darkened green. In the valleys the grazing cows stood stiff and quiet as the little wooden cows with painted sides that Margaret plays with on a green baize table. Only her cows are always losing one leg and tumbling sideways, while these stood stolid and four-square.

We left the Assembly at its most exciting time. Nobody knows what Japan will do and whether the Protocol can stand without some drastic amendment. I am glad that the League has at last come into contact with ultra-European realities. Whether they make or break it, it is essential that they should not have been glossed over. The Pacific problem is the key to the next fifty years of history. I think mere reticence cannot solve it. Talking at Geneva may accomplish nothing, but silence there will certainly do harm both to the League and to the Powers interested. For my part, I feel deep sympathy for Japan. She came late to her heritage of industrialism. When we in England and France and Germany and Holland built our factories and our steam-controlled cities, we had all the territory and raw materials that our sixteenth-century expansion of rising nationalism brought us. To Japan, industrialism and nationalism came simultaneously. Her population grew when the non-industrialised hinterlands of Africa, America and Australia had been already claimed. And she is confronted by our problems of the sixteenth and eighteenth centuries both together. We know it, and America knows it, and Australia.

And they know that thousands of square miles of land are undeveloped and wanting the capital and labour which Europe does not provide. I cannot think that there is justice here, nor that we can ever have peace if we expect the best of both worlds. But a war in the Pacific or San Francisco peninsular will settle nothing. Better realise that, and set to work to find a way out of our problem—even if it keeps America suspicious and the Protocol unsigned.

I have watched the four years of work that have gone to make this triple plan of security, arbitration and disarmament, and for European purposes I think it good. Not perfect, but as little harmful probably as anything which our circumstances will allow. We cannot expect perfect remedies for the imperfections that arise from our failures. But if this, too, fails, not because of European difficulties, but because of the vast racial antagonisms, then it must fail, and we must begin again to build upon a broader basis. For I am quite sure of this, that if the League should break to-morrow —though I do not think it will—there will be no time for fruitless regret nor bitterness. We shall simply realise that we did not dig deep enough; that we tried to impose upon the shifting sands of hereditary suspicion and jealousy a false structure of unity condemned to fall; and that if we believe, as I believe, that human personality has the power to triumph over the heritage of its own folly, we must go back to our own countries and teach, not to the children who were reared to those antagonisms, but to the sons and daughters that shall be born to us, the lessons that our own mistakes have taught us. More and more am I convinced that it is in the education of children, not in the councils of statesmen, however wisely they may work, that the future is to be made for good or evil. Meanwhile we can only study and try to learn a little—and there are at least the sun and the vines and the cow-bells on the hillside.

I know what you mean when you say that you do not see enough of the country and growing things. I, too, have sometimes an almost intolerable hunger for the rich honesty of the earth. I want to go back to Yorkshire, and the wolds, and the smell of tarred ropes, and wool and horses in the dark barns there, and the granaries full of sliding gold and smelling of dust, and the sloping fields and slow-speaking, shrewd workers. But it's no use. That's not my game. Though sometimes I wonder what my game is. Schools—schools—children—though I think I'm not meant to teach myself—and yet I cannot let go of my connection there. Is one ever led along an unknown road, or is that merely a sentimental convention to allow escape from the necessity of choice? Who am I, who know nothing myself, that I should dare to teach? I know only such broad and simple things that everybody knows, and few can understand—nor I yet among those few. That positive action *towards* people and things is better than the negative repulsion of hate—that the human will is stronger than human frailty—that God, if he does not exist, can be created out of the sum of spiritual effort. For if God is Love, then Love is God. Do you know Johannes Boyerin—"I went and sowed corn in mine enemy's field that God might exist"? Come small, fretful, bitter men and women, Japanese and Americans, Poles and Lithuanians, Dutch and Hottentot—let us sow corn in our enemies' fields and God shall exist. Here is a sacrament, a eucharist—bread and wine of earthly need transformed to the body and blood of God Himself. So will we make our Maker—Love; so make and serve the body of one God. And I beheld, and lo, a great multitude which no man could number stood before the throne and before the Lamb—the Lamb of God, the saviour of the world—Love, man-created, born of a woman, incarnate in human shape, and worshipped by the nations who find in Him their peace and their salvation.

Do we dream wildly?

CELIA.

ROSALIND DEAR,

Cologne is a heart-breaking city. What folly wars are!
In Saarbrucken the people are prosperous; the miners live in
little white houses with gardens outside and window-boxes
filled with pink geraniums, amazingly clean and well-
liking. There are hospitals in the fir woods for children,
cripples and the sick, fitted with most modern equipment.
We went over one that holds 1,100—a refuge for all human
misfortunes from the cradle to the grave—maternity cases,
sick children, tuberculosis, cripples, a reformatory, surgical
and medical·wards, industrial schools, almshouses for the
old, a cemetery—with rare trees. All the people were bright
and interested, with only the shadow of a sadness behind
them.

But here, in. this grey city, there is all the sorrow and
dignity of a conquered people. Never believe any one when
they tell you that it is more dignified to win than to be
defeated. It isn't true. Here in the streets, lit no more
brightly than London during war-time, English Tommies
march up and down, looking very gay, friendly and irresponsible. Their canteens are in the best hotels, and a lovely
building down by the Rhine. Outside are great notices
"No Germans allowed." The money for their food is all
paid from German taxes, and the German children crowd
round their bright lit windows, watching them gobble up
beefsteaks. It is one of the most vulgar things that I have
seen. There is no truculence, of course. Tommies are always
the same, friendly, cheerful, tolerant, they "rub along" well
enough with the Germans—whose food they eat. The
hospitals are full of children suffering from rickets and
tuberculosis. In the streets on Sunday night the people walk
up and down in two unceasing processions, talking a little,
not laughing much. It is the cheapest form of recreation.
Their hotels are half empty, and then filled mostly with
Jews and foreigners. The people are polite, a little brusque

and very quiet to us. Their attitude is a sort of defensiveness, as though they expected to be insulted or patronised. I think that our English cheerful familiarity is not appreciated as we always expect it to be. It is not very dignified, and it hurts their feelings to be treated like nice animals or rather stupid children.

Some of them are very friendly. When we arrived here, two workmen from a razor factory at Solingen, who knew a friend of ours, a writer for the *Daily News* interned during the war, came to call on us. They knew a little English and we talked for an hour. They have invited us to their house at Solingen and want us to talk to a small meeting of workers about the League of Nations. They were most friendly. They had met the English who came over there on the Holiday Fellowship, and had found that they liked them. They were so much amazed to find how little our point of view about important things differs. To-day we are waiting for their local clergyman and teacher of the adult school, Pastor Hartmann, to come and call on us, then we shall go out and see more of Cologne.

Yesterday evening we walked along the Rhine. The great dark loops of hanging bridges were lit with pale, glowing lamps. Water, sky and street were all of a softly luminous grey, veiled with lemon colour vapour that gave them a peculiar transparency. Only right above the massed, pointed roofs of the houses the sky was a clear and tranquil blue, pierced with a few, sparse stars. Very few people walked on the cobbled quay, but there was a procession of girls, "wander-vögel," with packs on their backs, bare-headed, singing as they walked. People here walk and sing because it is the cheapest form of recreation.

We were at a service in the cathedral yesterday. It was packed. Nearly every yard of the huge floor was covered with standing people. It was a day, cloudy, with sudden bursts of sunlight that came through the delicately tinted window—not vermilion and cobalt as in Italy, but mauve and green, and cyclamen colour, all subdued and softened.

281

The congregational singing is like a great cry, rising higher and higher till it frees itself from the drab-coloured people with stolid, set faces, and rises as though of its own motion to the shadowy arches of the roof. There is no triumph in their singing, but endurance, sorrow and a great longing.

Strange, darkened country. I do not like wars, Rosalind. They are so much worse when they are over than when they are in progress.

Au revoir, dear Rosalind. I love you,

CELIA.

Pension Rinkel,
Kaiserallee 222,
Berlin, W.15, October 13th, 1924.

ROSÅLIND DEAR,

Laus Tibi Domine! Thou has guided me to the buying of a new fountain-pen. For days I have been blind, lame, crippled, because my inseparable companion had a broken nose. It just shows how horribly dependent we become upon this scratching of dark lines on a smooth white surface. *Et cui bono?* We write in water, most of it nonsense. And if sense, we do not always recognise it. Still, there it is.

Germany saddens me. At Geneva I feel so optimistic about the League. The people there seem to care; they speak ardently of peace. One forgets how even now one nation occupies another's territory; another closes the doors of a half-empty continent. The world is here with its sufficing riches; but men starve; battling with shadows, we build ourselves enemies out of the clouds, then set to fight them and in striking, strike our friends.

You said that one could only obtain a superficial view of countries by travelling over them in so short a time. You are of course quite right. But a superficial view has value. It can kill easy optimism and false sentimentality. It can prevent people from thinking easy what is terribly hard. Not a generation, nor a dozen generations, will heal the

282

breaches made by centuries of folly here. Between Germany and France lies this debatable ground, the Saar Valley, Alsace Lorraine, the Rhineland, the Ruhr. It is very rich, giving men that power which they can dig from the bowels of the earth, and use to scale the heavens if they will. It is an old battleground, scarred with the conflict of continual jealousy. Louise Quatorze, Frederick the Great, Napoleon, Bismarck, Clemenceau—men moved by economic interests of which they were hardly aware, using for their purpose passions and pride and bitterness of men for men on both sides of the Rhine. The Germans held yesterday; but before them and to-day the French held and hold. Because they hold, they are insecure, so they prick and kick and madden the Germans, hoping to—heaven knows what. One German woman said to me—a professor, educated, a lover of culture and of the French, "If they had held a summer school and for a month sat down to devise ways of irritating us, they could not have succeeded better."

We have talked to Quakers, to workmen, to a group of Socialists in Solingen, and to a director of Krupps at Essen, to a lady here in the pension, to English people who were in Berlin during the War—just as at Geneva we talked to French and Swiss. Most people are tired to death of it all; but behind all hopes for the future, there lies this deep distrust, this fear. No one will move first. Each, against her real interest, hugs her immediate interest. England will be generous—if she may keep all that she holds, Ireland, India, the Soudan, her commercial supremacy, her navy. France will be generous if she may hold the Rhineland, the Ruhr, the Saar, the allegiance of the small new states that she has armed. Germany will be generous—if she can show her undefeated spirit by ultimate retaliation against the French. We are all so good—on conditions. And the condition is generally to our own undoing.

One is so helpless. In despair for the adult mind, I turn to the schools, knowing how here, too, great danger lies. Propaganda is no good. People must think for themselves.

You cannot stuff a ready-made philosophy of love into a child's mind willy-nilly. And we can teach nothing but what they are willing to learn. And they will learn nothing but what they may forget two minutes after they leave the doors of the school. And there is all the fun in the world for the having—this evening for instance, a symphony of blue and silver below my window. Three workmen in blue blouses unloading a dark grey cart on a road, smooth as shining steel, but flaked with pale leaves fallen from the lime trees. Three lamps, just lit, glowing through fine mist among the trees—tall grey buildings; a fretted silhouette of roofs, delicately pointed against a colourless sky, quite lucid, drained of all tint and opacity by the coming darkness. No hint yet of stars, but in one window a newly lit lamp, faintly gamboge, set in the enveloping grey and blue. If one could paint! Such fun there is.

At Düsseldorf last week along the Rhine the wet autumn had left the grass a most vivid emerald, but the beech leaves are again a pure gamboge. There is one modern artist who paints such colours—brilliant yellows thrown on to the burning green; but I do not know his name. In Berlin it is the trees that strike one most. In every street, even beyond the Wedding Platz in the East End where the poor live, the streets are gay with gold, a little tarnished, but gold, bright and real, squandered on to the pavements, the slim grass patches, the gleaming squares. In the Paul Gerhardt Krankenhaus there is a regular forest of limes, with elms and beeches—mostly limes—a glory of limes down Unter den Linden, limes in the Tier Garten, here in the Kaiserallee. No street stands that is not graced by them, so lavish, so beautiful, so touched by yellow fire. At night the lamps glow from them, as though in a sudden blossoming. In the lean years their lavishness must have enriched people, half-starved for grace and beauty. War and politics are so ugly. One must have colour and music. I think that there is a special hunger of the heart that comes from reading too much history and being surrounded by politics. One wants

284

to run wild in gardens; to have bands at every table—I would, if I could, always feed to music. The singularly graceless action of thus filling one's body with roots and dead animals and powdered grain is given some signficance then. One can perform as a ritual what one is shamed to do as a utilitarian action; just as pious ladies will share a communion cup with their butchers, when without altar candles and an intoned benediction such a mutual potation would seem indecent. Don't you love bands, anyway? Have you ever thought about being a vegetarian? Every time I think about the disgusting habit of eating cows and sheep and rabbits, I am one. But directly I am confronted with a "Carte du Jour," my hostess's feelings, my own shopping basket, or my mother's countenance, I become carnivorous—that is, practically whenever I feed. When quite on my own, I usually live on oatcakes, fruit and milk. But that is seldom, and you can so rarely eat that where there is a band.

I have read no novels since I left England, except in a German pastor's house at Solingen, where I went to talk about the League to Socialists working in a razor factory. I saw *Out of the Wreck I rise* by Beatrice Harraden. It was quite an event. I read most of it in a gulp. Rather stilted language but a good situation. I never can read her books now and criticise them without remembering what a nice woman she is. I should never make a critic. It is so hard to have an impartial mind.

I suppose that if I were good and informative, I should write you a long interesting letter about the political situation, a description of Krupps Works (I did visit them), of hospitals, conversations and meetings. I just won't. I've written in my diary, in articles, in other letters. To you, I'll kick my heels. Really, trees are nearly as important as men, and much better behaved.

Do you see that Gandhi has completed his three weeks' fast? How awkward it is for us in this efficient age to come suddenly upon a saint! We don't know what to do with him.

I am being terribly tormented by a flea. Heaven knows where it found me! At this time of the year, too, and in such a respectable pension. I dare not confess my torments. We have a real baroness at our table and to insinuate that I should have caught a flea under the same roof as her august person—oh, impossible! Yet I suffer—mentally too. One can bear greater wrongs with more fortitude. This is persistent, undignified and impossible to ignore. It is shortening my life perceptibly.

We travelled here on the Paris-Warsaw express. All the train notices were in Polish. I longed to go on. Fancy going to Warsaw. And why not?

Au revoir. I love you,

CELIA.

Pension Rinkel,
Kaiserallee 222,
Berlin, W.15, Oct. 16th, 1924.

DEAREST ROSALIND,

I have just heard from Mother that my feathery stole has come and I am so excited. I wish that I had been home when it arrived. She says that it has travelled beautifully, and it sounds charming. Thank you ever so much for sending it. I shall tell you how beautiful I look in it when I get back to England and can wear it. I hear that all sorts of feather things are to be very fashionable this year.

The Tier Garten is one of the loveliest parks that I have seen. We walked all through to-day. I think that a vivid October day, with a clear, cold sky and splashes of sunlight in the fallen leaves, is one of the finest things in this imperfect world.

I love you,

CELIA.

286

What a miserable scrap of a letter to cost me 4d.! But
Elsie McCalman, who has a charming flat near here, has
promised me a bath, and I am so excited that I want to go at
once. It will be my first since I left England!

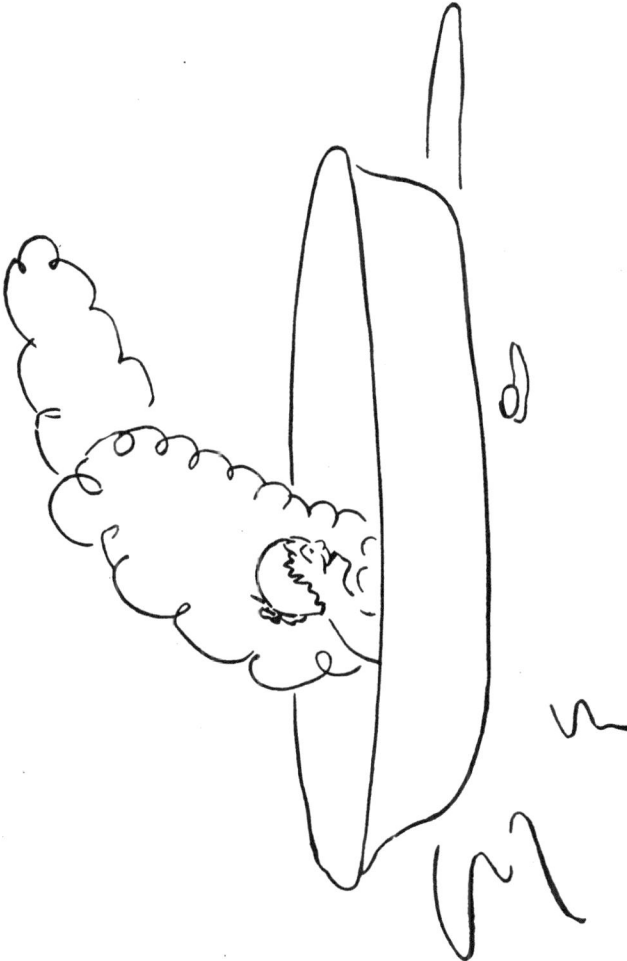

Pension Adlon,
Dorotheergasse 6-8,
Wien. I, October 28th, 1924.

ROSALIND DEAR,

Now I am suddenly in a panic and it is too late to do anything. To-day there comes from John Lane a notice of *The Crowded Street* labelled as a "mercilessly clever study of a girl's life in a Yorkshire town and in London," and I suppose that a copy is now on its way out to you—and you may hate it. It is not a "mercilessly clever study." I protest most violently. If it had been I would not have given it to you. But it is not "merciless." I did not mean people to think it so. My Muriel is myself—part of me only—the stupid, frightened part. I know so well her sentimentalities, her pitiful shrinking ideals, her cowardlinesses, and I have even a little tender affection for them, as one has in one's softer moments for one's own delinquencies. Just as I know Delia's occasional ruthlessness, and restless pursuit of an unknown good, and Connie's futile revolt against the impotence of not very clever individuals in society. They are all too near to me, even Mrs. Hammond, who at last had courage and one enduring love—I could not have been merciless to them. It is not a good book. But I give it to you for several reasons—partly because I wanted always to give you one of my early books because you have patience with and understanding of immaturity, and because it was in my unfledged days that I best knew you; partly because the joy of your letters lit many of the darker moods in which the book was written, and just a little bit because you gave me an incident, which you may recognise, you rider of wild horses at Huchenneville. The circumstances are completely changed but the ride is there. For both our sakes, I wish that it were a better book.

I can't be particularly interested in its advent. Somehow I feel that all this work is only a prelude. I have done nothing yet at all—all is so petty, so cumbered about with small, unworthy considerations. If the Wycliffe book could approach in any way on paper to my idea of it, that might be better. But nothing will be good yet, till I can make myself a less unworthy person. I know that so well. This laxity and slovenliness chokes me. I must get free and become the master of my personality, not its victim. Until I do that I cannot write a book, even for you, my Rosalind whom I love.

· In June Vera will go, and I shall be on my own again. No one will ever know what I owe to her during these five years; but now comes the choice again—how shall I live? One thing I am determined on, that I will not fall into the common error of circumstantial victimisation, pushed into a half-hearted acceptance of conventional standards. There is the Assisian way of life—contact with my brothers and sisters, social service—a quite certain way there to some measure of usefulness and satisfaction. To live as a poor woman, to accept the economic way and burden laid upon my sisters, and through municipal organisation, through the Press, through the subordination of my own intellectual training to the needs of those who have had no opportunities, I might try to live a more Christian life. In a way, the first part would not be so hard. I never was fastidious. You know how little dirt and coarseness disturb me. The negative part, the giving up of pleasant standards of comfort would mean so much less to me than to most—that is so attractive. The end to this heart-tearing sense of separation —the end to this pleasure that turns only to bitterness, because of the continual consciousness of suffering, the end to this responsibility of freedom. The knowledge that one is not worthy to be a great Assisian does not count. It's no use to refrain from doing things because one is not worthy. It would be so comparatively simple—so free. And yet—and yet——

Here am I with a goodish intellect—not much, considering my opportunities, but useful if I work hard—an unusual training, an independent income, a faculty for travelling easily and picking up political information and acquaintances. There is a crying need in the world for sound thinking and unprejudiced work. When one reads *The Times*, with its record of petty controversy and personalities, the knowledge of how fine a thing the service of society might be comes with an almost overwhelming sense of helplessness. The aristocratic life—an individuality developed to its finest extent—keyed to its highest pitch— music, colour, form, fastidiousness of taste and habit—the authoritative judgment made possible by reading, travel and contact with other personalities—leading the Aristotelian "good life"—with the Aristotelian sense of responsibility. I believe in all these things—culture and knowledge, and beauty of art and civilisation. I believe them to be the stuff from which nobility may be made, given the spiritual dignity without which all else is worthless. But to choose this way means an unquiet heart. It is to be like the "Little Mermaid" of Hans Andersen, who might only dance when swords seemed to pierce the white feet that she had bought with her own gift of speech. Shall I buy? Here is good merchandise—but the sword will be there too—this ever-present oppression brought by the consciousness of mortality, of human frailty. It is not so much just the poor that one pities. We know that they have their moments of consolation. It is the poisoned, the embittered, those under delusions, and those awakened from them—all this pitiful wastage of happiness. So fair a world, so passionate, so bitter. In Germany to-day, so fine an expenditure of pride, of silent fortitude—but such resentment, such cruelty of thought. The German comic papers, *Simplicissmuss*, *Lustige Blätter*, frighten me with their gross brutality of line and thought. Austria is so charming and indolent and hopelessly unpractical; and England flinging away her fine opportunity—unparalleled this century—for so pitiable a farce of personal jealousy as this election.

Shall we try to show them that life is a lovely thing? Even me? Clumsy, foolish, cowardly, alternating between coltish exuberance and lethargy—what folly—and yet—

would not for me, the other way be a counsel of despair—an easy sliding from a standard too hard—a sentimentalism?

Now, what in the name of goodness am I pestering you with all this for? I ought to keep a diary and not unload my egotism on to your much enduring head! Is it exhibitionism that makes a diary—except a purely utilitarian one of notes for lectures—an unutterable bore to me—and yet drives me to self-expression in letters? How morbid and foolish! Forgive me, most patient and dear of Rosalinds.

I love you,

CELIA.

Pension Adlon,
Dorotheergasse 6–8,
Vienna I, November 13, 1924.

ROSALIND DEAR,

I have neglected you, but not through my own fault. The Austrian railway employees struck against the limited wages allowed by the Railway Companies as a result of the International Control which rations each department of government to a certain sum. Seipel resigned; the government fell; the trains, mails and river boats stopped, and for a week we have been living as though in a besieged city. To-day, however, some compromise has been reached, and we hope for posts again. I tried to get letters to England by Air Mail, but have had no news yet of their arrival.

Have you read any books by Stella Benson? *The Poor Man, Living Alone, I Pose?* Books written with an exquisite perception of beauty, a tenderness for all lovely things; but a most sorrowful scorn of people. All her people are in some way pitiful, through their postures, their folly, their unworthiness. Yet one feels sure that the writer is really nice. Nearly a year ago I read *Living Alone* and I wrote to Stella Benson. Months afterwards came a letter from South China. She was a teacher in England, terribly delicate, always being ill; sensitive she must have been—poor, I guess she was. She was active while still very young in the militant suffrage movement. At the beginning of the war she went to America, after a short time doing committee work in London. In America, she was ill and alone. From there she went to China. She had to earn her living. She was given a class of fifty Chinese boys to teach. I do not know if the description in *The Poor Man* is real, but it must be somewhat so. Then she married—a Chinese Customs official—they live now miles and miles from any Europeans except one Englishman with a loud voice who says "I think," meaning "It is so," and a few French colonials who spend the morning in dirty kimonos and call very formally in the afternoon in white kid gloves. She is ill again. Most of this biography I gathered from an article in the *Adelphi*— very little from her letters. I have heard now twice from her—intimate letters of an extraordinary charm. But I think that she does not like living very much—such loneliness seems terrible.

Here I continually meet delightful people—almost nicest of all is Helene Scheu Riesz. I wonder if you know her work? She was an Austrian writer of children's fairy stories and of poems. In 1902 in England she fell in love with the Books for the Bairns. In Austria children were taught to read out of most horrible "readers," very chauvinistic and militaristic. She wanted to find some way in which she could bring good literature to Austrian children. She conceived the idea of little books of selected classics to be sold at 1d. each, and to contain transcriptions from literature, fairy tales, poems, simple essays and so on from all parts of the world. She went from publisher to publisher asking them to help her. They told her that it was impossible. Then she set up and began to publish herself. She has now the Sesam Publishing Company. Her books are sold in France, England, America and Austria. When I get to England I will send you some. They are delicious.

She herself is married to a very nice and clever Austrian lawyer. They live just outside Vienna in Schönnbrun, and have there a house lined with books and full of children—her own two and a miscellaneous collection of Austrian, French, English, Egyptian, whom she periodically adopts. She is small, eager, pretty, rather like a bird. She wears charming clothes and has the smallest hands I ever saw. There is something of the child about her—but such tenderness and yet such enterprise are rare—even for children.

Oh, Rosalind, Vienna is lovely. The parks and the music, the opera and that orchestra, the delightful, indolent people—all so hospitable and kind. They give us fabulous teas, take us to concerts, for expeditions, offer to lend us books, motor-cars, money—all with the same intimacy of contact that I have met in no other city.

We have been given tickets to-night for a big workmen's concert run by the Socialist Party in the biggest concert hall. It is time to go to it.

I love you,

CELIA.

Pension Adlon,
Dorotheergasse 6-8,
Vienna I, Nov. 22nd, 1924.

ROSALIND DEAR,

Mother forwarded to me your letter written, I see, exactly a month ago to-day—about going away in Martha for a week-end with Miss Roberts. The jacarandas sound lovely, but I shivered to think of your plunging about in Crocodile River. Are there truly crocodiles? or is it just the drift? And what is a drift? And—oh dear, you will do such terribly adventurous things. I feel that I want to send some one running out to Pretoria with the commission "Do go and see what Rosalind is doing and tell her not to!" At least you might wait to be drowned, smothered, kicked or eaten until I have got my visit to Arcadia safely over.

I want frightfully to see jacarandas. I wish that I could come to you in November, but it will probably have to be spring. I shan't be able to afford it before Christmas.

293

One can make more money in the Christmas term by lecturing. I ought not to have come away now, financially. But it has been worth while.

A woman here who works on the land settlements—an artist, with socialist sympathies, conservative prejudices and the temperament of a parish worker—scolded me for about twenty minutes in a taxicab just before I went to Budapesth for the same reasons as you chose—because I travel too quickly and get only a superficial view of things. It was an unfair advantage to take, because I always feel sick in taxis when I ride with my back to the driver, and I rode there because the taxi was full of her friends—and I can't argue when I'm trying not to be sick. But coming home I got her in a tram and put her with her back to the driver, and had her to myself for forty minutes, and told her exactly why I am here and what I am doing, and how she can't stop people in England wanting to hear about Central Europe, and there aren't enough lecturers who have lived there for months to go round, and that if I stayed for six years in each place there might be another war before I got back, and that if I spend all my time simply correcting impressions that are proved manifestly wrong from one's first glimpse of a country, I shall have my work cut out for several years. She was frightfully nice at the end—perhaps because she was feeling sick too. I do recommend that as a means of chastisement for the soul. But of course some creatures have stomachs like ostriches, and you might hold them upside down to give them a scolding without making them conciliatory.

I have seen one of the loveliest things in the world—the Danube through Budapesth from the tallest watch tower on the Fisher's Bastion. Don't believe people who tell you that the Danube is blue. It is a dull, opaque grey. Only it is blue on one condition—seen from a great height and a long distance, when the ground is snow covered and all the roofs and towers of Budapesth white—then, beyond the fork of Margarita Island, the Danube is bright blue.

Most gay, conversational, careless, lovely city—the streets worse paved than in the fields round Anderby, with straw and hens scratching in them outside the Ministry of Finance, and sumptuous palaces, and Turkish tombs, and Gothic churches touched with Byzantine richness, and the steep hills of Buda crowned with fortresses, looking across the swinging bridges into Pesth—and cafés where gypsies play Liszt's Hungarian Rhapsody, and where one drinks golden Tokay until one feels most beautiful, and warm and loved—oh, Budapesth! No wonder that the Magyars are so fiercely and conversationally patriotic. Very charming, too, and almost alarmingly hospitable. Tea parties there last from 5.30 to 10.30. This outdoes Vienna. We went to a cabaret show where the setting was more primitive than in an army theatre, but the audience deliciously responsive, rippling with laughter. Only the show was supposed to begin at 8.30, and at 8.55 the players had not yet turned up at the theatre. The audience waited in the bar until the actresses began to arrive, and engaged them in conversation, which kept things still a little later! But nobody seemed to mind. As the cook in this pension observed the other day, when her mistress complained because lunch was (as usual) twenty minutes late—"Well, people who stay in pensions never have anything to do. What does it matter when they have their food?" I suppose that the same reasoning applies to Hungarian theatres. We stayed in a hotel where the hall porter was so obliging that he always offered to come for walks with us, or to help us with our shopping. One has nothing to do.

One can never forget that Budapesth was once Turkish. The Coronation Church is still painted inside with the designs used when it was a Mosque. Many of the houses have carved heads with turbans above the door. The people have all the terrific conversational energy and administrative indolence of the East. Overwhelmingly kind, courageous, artistic, animated, they are yet quite close to ferocious cruelties and inconceivable barbarity. I do not know which sound more cruel—the Bolsheviks or their opponents. Beatings and tortures were commonplaces, and every argument at the National Assembly results in a duel. There is an average of 30 fatal street accidents a day in the comparatively small city, because human life is cheaper than a little reasonable caution. Jews are not considered to be human, and Czechs are hardly allowed to possess souls. The peasants seem to be even more passionately feudal than their masters. The nobles are still most magnificent creatures, with manners that make you feel like a duchess. I shall feel quite hurt in England not to have my hand continually kissed by counts!

I am sleepy. It is late. I only got back here last night from Budapesth. Woe's me to leave it. It's a lovely city. I am enjoying this trip so much in patches. It is hateful to think that this is the last time Vera and I can go together. However——

Never mind, I'm coming to Africa.

I love you,

CELIA.

10, Oakwood Court,
Kensington, W., Nov. 30th.
As from 117, Wymering Mansions,
Elgin Avenue, W.9.

DEAREST ROSALIND,

I can't write you a long letter, because (*a*) I must go and pack, (*b*) I daren't use too much of the Brittain's beautiful notepaper, but I must send a little note by this mail to say that I arrived home to find Mother waiting for me in London, and that she had brought with her from Yorkshire my adorable fluffy stole. It is so soft and delicious. It fills me with joy and vanity. It will be so lovely to wear over my evening frock when I go to concerts—and I'm going to lots now, for Jan Smeterlin is going to marry Edith Mannaberg, and they are going to live in England, and I shall hear music again, and it will soothe out the tangled strings.

Oh darling, are you going to hate my book? I feel so anxious. The reviews, all but *The Times* Lit. Sup., are being frightfully kind to it. I think that *The Times* can't like me. It did not like *Anderby* either.

I love you,

CELIA.

1925
January—August

DEAREST ROSALIND,

I have neglected you for a turbulent Christmas week, when anything that I had to say stood little chance of being worth saying—a house full, had we, complicated by the serious illness of our doctor, whose two youngest children and governess were squeezed into our household to keep them away from the atmosphere of trained nurses and "Hush, hush."

Next year by this time I shall be looking forward to a stormy passage to Africa. I only hope that it is not as rough as the last time when I crossed the channel, when I lost all power of physical reticence, and wished for easeful death. However, the reward may be great. I write now in a fog so dense that I can no longer see the lights across the road. It gets into one's eyes, nose and throat until this feels like living below the sea, in that pale light which Walter Pater describes as the atmosphere of Leonardo's *Monna Lisa*. Have you sun?

I am plunging again into my Wycliffe book. It's hugeness terrifies, yet fascinates me—medieval squabbles in the hot, petulant atmosphere of fourteenth-century Oxford, foolishness in high places, hatred, sorrow, and the agony of a fierce intelligence confined by the crabbed logic of the Schools, fierce desire for power and fiercer abnegation, remorse, the pains of hell and of love—can I, who am nothing save water blown by the wind, write of such tempests? I am fierce for work. Without work I am nothing—I do nothing, am nothing except in so far as I may work.

Is it true that I may learn in Africa something of the Imperial complication? I see more and more clearly that one must not study English foreign policy from a purely European standpoint. Of the difficulties of Central Europe I have now some fleeting notion. Were England simply an island off the coast of France, her course of action would be fairly plain. I feel that I still walk very much in darkness speaking about the League. I want to go next year to Africa, and the year after to Canada. I must get introductions. I can get some through the League of Nations Union, etc. We had most useful credentials for Europe. I only want to learn a little of the difficulties. The African situation I must leave to those who live in Africa; but the best-informed British statesmen can only hope to learn something of the modifications of this policy which an African connection involves. Can you help me to discover this? If I spend the time until I am forty learning and learning what I can about—I think—the possibilities of international co-operation, specialising in co-operation through educational movements—I may in the end be able to take some small and not ill-informed part in political affairs. What I dread is the unintelligent optimism of the sentimentalist in the street. I'm too much like him not to appreciate his dangers!

What an egotistic letter—as usual. But I have done so little except give a few lectures, learn German, and write articles. I have one on education in *Time and Tide* this week called "The Wealth of Nations"—and had one in about nurses under the Poor Law called "Guardians and Angels"—which I thought quite a happy title, don't you?

We have a room full of mimosa and blue hyacinths. Oh, lovely, lovely flowers in a winter fog.·

Have you read *The Spanish Farm* by Mottram? Very dignified and good. *Papers and a Dancer* and *This is the End* by Stella Benson, a piercing and bitter joy. She has an exquisite but bitter mind.

I love you always,

CELIA.

DEAREST ROSALIND,

It is January that I come—not September. I want to be here for the autumn. There is so much doing and I can make money for my passage. You see, I don't want to get a job when I come to Africa, because that would tie me down to one place. I want to travel about and learn things. I want very much to learn the difficulties in the way of effective co-operation with the League of Nations, because that is going to be the big question in the coming year. I think that the colour question is going to be immensely important too. The best way to learn is to lecture, I have found, because once you are on a platform people are not afraid to be rude to you. They will tell you what they think. I want to travel about Africa speaking about the League of Nations. People will undoubtedly then say unpleasant things about both the League and me, and then I shall be wiser than I am now.

If I can get any paid lecturing in schools, to societies or clubs, I want them. But if I can't, I'll do without. I've just been enquiring about passages. I see that I can do the return journey on about £84 to Cape Town by going Intermediate B. cabin. Then I must have money for trains and hostels and things. I am earning hard now—lectures and articles. I may be able to get journalistic jobs apropos of Africa. I've been getting Central European things in the *Manchester Guardian*, etc. I want to come in January and leave in May. I want to be back in June when Vera and Gordon come back from America. I want to see her after a year's married life, and to pick up my scattered threads in England.

There is so much here that I do not want to lose touch of—especially matters educational and international. You see, my political objective is Ministry of Education—the first (?) one to have a world outlook instead of a parochial one. The Railway Mission, etc., is interesting to me as a person, but I daren't spend all that time on "seeing life in the raw." I want to learn how to civilise, and I want to start in England. So, though I must face the difficulties in the way, my background must always be English. For the next ten years or so I shall travel about, but every year I want to return to England and pick up threads.

You may think this the wrong way round, and that my life is spent—as according to Hilda Reid—in "rushing about like a mad mushroom." But there is method in the mushroom's madness—and I have still to learn what can be done by somebody who sets out deliberately from 26 onwards to study statecraft. I am only at the A B C. Heaven knows that I talk arrogantly enough. But heaven (if there is one) also knows that I have little to be arrogant about.

You say "I believe you will be great"; I think not—I who know how little grace of soul I have, how little courage or capacity. But I do believe this: that in this world a man may have power, either in the world of intellect or of persons, if he will pay a high enough price for it. I do not mean by price a compromise with conscience, as Napoleon paid; I mean the price of effort, of determination, of anguish of mind. The problem is: dare one run the risk, in paying the price, of failure to use worthily the power?

I was taken on Friday night to a dance at the Cecil. I did not want to go and had no dress. Finally, I turned up the hem of an old dress of blue and mauve lace—very tired by day but passable at night—and went by bus. I was given sparkling Moselle to drink, and was told by my host that I was witty. Then I felt happy and danced beautifully. She said, "Why is Winifred like a Viking's daughter?" He said, "She isn't. She is like ' fair Helena who doth engild the night.'" So after that I felt beautiful too; but alas, alas, I fear that it was the Moselle. I said, "I envy you going to Morocco. You will have sun." He said, "Have you never had enough sun in your life?" I said, "No, never." He: "What else haven't you had enough of in your life?" I: "Oh,

Music for one thing." And then I had to stop. I have been surpassingly rich.

Do you know the way in which the London sun makes an afternoon glow on the shining streets, a warm apricot colour? You cannot see the sun, only the glow on the mirror-shining roads.

I wrote a Leader in *Time and Tide* on education and called it *The Wealth of Nations*. An enterprising printer issued it as *The Health of Nations*, and the office never noticed till the day of publication! That was nearly as bad as an exceedingly depressed and love-lorn poem that I once published in the *Oxford Magazine* called *The Robber*. It appeared as *The Roller*.

> "Aunt Susan said, the second time
> She tumbled off a bus,
> ' The step is short from the sublime
> To the ridicu*lus.*'"

Vera and G. make love very beautifully. It is a delight to be with them—or rather with Vera and with G.'s letters, for she reads me extracts. The love of both of them has passed through bitterness and returned sweet and strong—"out of the strong came forth sweetness."

How can little people of twenty-one love when they have never suffered?

> ". . . So near they passed
> They almost warmed me with their glow of love."

I want to write now—I rush to my Wycliffe as a girl to her lover, then fall away from his arms with that chill lethargy of disillusion. I can't write, but, by Jove, my thoughts are sometimes lovely!

Au revoir, my dear, very dear Rosalind.

Till 1926—February—or January.

Yours,

CELIA.

DEAREST TALL, FAIR ROSALIND,

Your angry letter came last night, a letter calling me an obstinate little devil, and pouring contempt upon my idea of lecturing as a satisfactory *raison d'être* in Africa. I love your angry letters. I love you when your hair crackles, as it used to crackle over the telephone sometimes at Huchenneville, so that you look like a tall witch, spitting fire. I don't believe that you're a headmistress. I still believe that you are a fairy, in some queer unexpected way. I love to be damned by you (not that you do anything so ungraceful as to damn, but its equivalent). I hope that when I come to you, you will scold me beautifully and fiercely for missing the jacarandas and all the other things and for lecturing. I shall like that very much, and I have no doubt that it will be good for me. For with one breath you curse me for my presumptuous and wasteful youth, which seeks to convert people (You're wrong, you're wrong—I seek to learn), and with the other you say that you will help to find me a lecture tour. That is like you, and I won't say "No, don't trouble, because I can manage for myself." Perhaps I can manage some. I have been to see Mr. Justice Feetham, who was President of the African League of Nations Union, and is now member of the Irish Boundary Commission, and he seemed to be quite enthusiastic over the idea. He has given me several addresses to write to, and I am to see a Mrs. Scandrett, of the National Council of Women, who is to be here in April, and I shall talk about either the League of Nations, or Germany, or Hungary, or Czechoslovakia, or Austria, or anything like that that people want to hear about. It mayn't do any good, but I will tell you what I have found, wandering round, both in England and on the Continent—a lecture is a good thing to give, because it gives an entrée, a starting point. I go to a town or a village to lecture. I stand on a platform and give my piece of information. That is only the beginning. I come down and we talk. I go into one or other of their houses. We sit up till midnight. We talk about shoes and ships, and Austria, and cabbages and kings, and whether widows should have state pensions, and whether hating Germany does any use. And before we have finished, I have generally learnt twice as much as I ever said. But if there were no lecture, how could I go? One can't walk into strangers' houses. One must, as the Americans say, "get acquainted." I have made good friends since I started lecturing—a Scotch socialist, with his wife and big family; a Quaker doctor in Wiltshire; a jeweller's wife in Ilford; a queer, ambitious, headstrong, sensitive tradesman's daughter in Essex, whom the local clergyman found difficult and turned on to me; a retired Major in Lee; an ex-plumber in Bethnal Green—oh, countless, countless friends—the very stuff of kinship is in those talks we have—and letters—I have them now from Vienna, from Prague, from Solingen. The world is so full of friends, of kinsmen—but one must have a key to unlock the door—some work, some word to be spoken, the open sesame that opens the door of the unknown house.

"The colour question"—lectures on that? Oh, no; but to meet and to talk, and to travel, and return to England, and when I go up and down, in and out, like a shuttle in the loom of this fair England, drawing behind me my thread of memories and tales and pictures, I shall hear men say, "Those damned niggers. Why should our boys give up their land to niggers? Always wanting more. What's South Africa coming to?" Then I can only say, "When I was in South Africa . . ."

> ". . . How all turned to him who spoke
> 'You saw Waring? Truth or joke?'
> In land travel or seafaring?"

I have talked with men who had nothing but bitter, and with women who had nothing but sentimental, to say of

Germany. And though I was there for so short a time, though I could see only with the eyes of an alien, yet I saw—human people, puzzled, resentful, enduring, proud. Darling Rosalind, I would love to come to Africa only to see your jacarandas. I can't come in September, because I need money for my expenses, and my only time for making a real haul is in the autumn time, when I have been promised a good crop of lectures at £15 15s. each course. Can't you see how soon I can pay my fare from a term's hard work? I had savings—I have still—but if you really want to know, I lent them to pay an apprentice's premium to a boy out of work through the War. He is doing magnificently. No one —not even he—but Mother and his employer knows I paid, and if I miss my jacarandas, I have seen the light in his eyes when he told me debonairly that his employer spoke well of him. I know I could come and just stay with you, but I want to travel round a bit, and the only job I can think of that involves travelling is to lecture. One makes good friends that way. I am going to stay a few days with Mrs. Lewis, and Mrs. Newman has asked me too, and we have friends of the family in Durban. But there are other places and people that I should like to meet.

You say that you hate "questions." So do I; but there they are, asking and asking themselves at the moment in England.

There is the "question" of the Conservative Government turning down a scheme of state pensions for widowed mothers with dependent children, because they fear a grievance from their tax-paying supporters.

There is the "question" of the London County Council dismissing its married women employees.

There is the housing question. And the question of the Legitimacy Bill. And the question of rescue work, and of nationalisation—and so on. Now one may hate "questions," but how can a person like myself—young, free, rich, fortunate, go about the streets of a town, or the lanes of a country, loving shop windows, and theatres, and flowers, and long walks, and parties, while every minute in my heart and in my head rings the cry of my friends, my kinsmen—those widows, those mothers, those children, living in ghastly slums? And the only way really to find a remedy is by tackling the "question." One may address meetings, or Lobby M.P.'s, or write articles or books—it's all the same. One does very little good as an individual; but the seeds are sown; sometimes they take root, sometimes they shoot buds and blossoms. Oh, Rosalind dear, one must work both ends—at one end with the individuals, at the other with the "questions"—and those who are themselves suffering or poor or overburdened are so bowed down that they often cannot see the "question"—or its answer—by reason of that grievous burden. But we who have been gifted by fortune, we who are rich and healthy and unbound, were we not given this freedom in order that we might be of the company of those who seek an answer for the question? And so often the answer lies in statistics, and legislation, and advisory committees and Royal Commissions and the like—and lectures (addresses, meetings, speeches—what you will). You talked about "losing the common touch"—I wish that I could send you some of the letters that I receive from unknown friends, who, through a written word, or a reported lecture, have heard of things which I have tried to say.

Rosalind dear, I am myself as nothing—I count as nothing. There is no wish nor will of mine in the world that matters—but I cannot live save in a world in which "all things linked are—When you cannot touch a flower without troubling of a star." I cannot see your jacarandas because of the mist in my eyes that rises from the tears of my friends in poverty and bitterness and hatred.

What an outburst! And now I shall turn round and laugh at my solemnity, and probably be seasick all the way out, and cross and grilled—but I shall love seeing you so much that none of these things will matter.

I told Miss Tuke that you were making a success of your school, and she was delighted. I did like her. I think that you are one of the most charming, dear, headmistresses in the world.

Shall I bring riding breeches? Is it better only to have hand-luggage? Ought one to be smart?

I have just made myself a delightful black silk tunic with blue and silver on it to wear with a blue spring hat (price £1 1s. 9d.—it looks quite £5 5s.). I love clothes.

I had a long letter from Mrs. Lewis. To-day at *The Times* Book Club I asked about *The Harp*, and they said that it was going to prove very popular.

Au revoir—oh, won't it be fun to see you!

Yours ever,

CELIA.

I send a better review—and one of the many advertisements.

Rosalind, you are a gem and a delight. Thank you a thousand times for all your kindness. This letter sounds self-justifying and not a bit as grateful as a thousandth part of what I feel towards you.

C.

117, Wymering Mansions,
Elgin Avenue, W.9,
March 1st, 1925.

DEAREST ROSALIND,

On March 1st, 1926, I may be in Pretoria. I want to sail directly the Christmas Term is over. I have promised to lecture for the University Extension during the Christmas Term, and as it is a good money-making proposition, I shall do it. I will sail when I can finish here; but I don't believe that I mind heat. It is cold that makes me shrivel up and feel ill and good for nothing. Heat exhilarates me. I have to risk it anyway.

Mrs. Lewis's book[1] has had good reviews so far. I am longing to see all her agents' copies. I have sent a copy to Walter de la Mare and one to Stella Benson, and shall send others to other people who may notice it. The right people must read it. It is really a lovely book, wonderful in its glowing purity and fierceness of expression. I shall always be grateful to you for letting me meet her.

Do you know, I met Miss Tuke the other day? I was sent to Bedford College to interview her for a paper in connection with Crosby Hall and the appeal which she, as Chairman of the British Federation of University Women, is making. She was very nice and kind, but seemed to be most amused by being interviewed at all. She said that she had "no news value" and had never been divorced, nor imprisoned, nor even yet had died a saintly death! I liked her. She has such young eyes, and a gallant, stiff little figure.

I have other letters and must go.

I send you a copy that Hodder & Stoughton made of of some reviews, but they irritate me a little—so lacking in sense of the book's real splendour. I am enraptured by its beauty.

With love always,

CELIA.

117, Wymering Mansions,
Elgin Avenue, W.9,
March 30th, 1925.

DEAREST ROSALIND,

I have your letter of the 11th, which you begin by saying that you miss my letters. Mea culpa, Rosalind. I have erred, I know, but, as you say, you are a little to blame, though not because your own letters have been meagre so much as because by enriching my own friendships in Africa you have diverted a time of leisure that is limited from yourself to them. I have been trying to spread news of

[1] *The Harp.*

The Harp. It is difficult to say how well it is going. Until Hodder & Stoughton have their reports from the book-sellers, I cannot say. But all my friends to whom I have recommended it are impressed, some overwhelmingly so. Clare is doing a poster for it to be hung in bookshops. I am trying to persuade the League of Nations Union to emphasise its lesson of Pride of Race, as the "infant son of the greater kinship."

About Clare. I honestly do not think that the moment has come for her to make this adventure. After nearly ten years of struggle she is just beginning to make headway. Her woodcuts are being exhibited. People are beginning to recognise her name. And when she sends pictures or etchings to art papers or publishers, she is beginning to find that they will take them. But it is still precarious work. If she went abroad now, they would inevitably forget her. She would gain experience, yes. But of life experience she has had a surplus, poor child, and for colour and form experience, a recent trip to the French Alps has filled her to overflowing. Later I think that she could go more safely. But to throw away her advantages so hardly gained would be madness. There are times to strike fresh trails and times to follow up along those already investigated.

You ask me to promise not to write a South African novel nor to tackle South African problems after six months. Do you know, I think that we are all at cross-purposes over this business of politics. Quite deliberately I am setting out, as you studied the business of teaching, to study the business of politics—not the whole ground even of these, but especially the influence of educational propaganda upon international relations. This is no light nor whimsical inclination with me. It is the end slowly emerging from my experience since 1919, my sense of responsibility towards my fellows, and my increasing knowledge of my own capacities and limitations. If I alter my intention, it will be from my considered recognition that in some other way I can be of more use, and only for that.

From Africa I hope to learn something of the difficulty of explaining European contacts to people for whom they must be far remote instead of appallingly close as here; something of the reasons why the Dominions shelve the Protocol and similar arrangements (academic reasons one may learn from books; only by conversation can reasons become part of the stuff of one's own intellectual equipment); something, too, of the feel and organisation of South African political life, of her societies (such as the National Council of Women, League of Nations Union, etc.). Her own special problems, such as the racial question and so on, I can only hope to see as they affect her position towards Europe. They are the concern of people who are going to live in Africa. But remember, when you shake in horror at the superficiality of a six months' stay, that decisions involving Africa's attitude towards Europe have to be taken daily by people who have never been near the country; that if a future Foreign Secretary, or League of Nations delegate, spent six years in every important country, he would suffer from senile decay before sufficiently experienced to take office; and that since S. Africans criticise vehemently our attitude towards them (I am thinking specially of the published reports of the Dominions' attitude towards foreign policy) and yet will not come here and explain to us who desire to avert what we think to be catastrophe, what is their real attitude, we must go and try to learn it, yet not spend so long away that we lose touch with European conditions. I do not want to miss the September Assembly in Geneva, nor do I want to miss Vera and Gordon after their first year in America. So Africa for six months (four really, I suppose, since the voyage takes so long) and then back to England.

As for a S. African novel. That is a different question. I can write novels, and stories too, only on what is in my blood, part of my very self. That is why I can only really write with certainty of Yorkshire. The Wycliffe novel is certainly mostly Oxford, London and Leicester; but

Wycliffe was a Yorkshireman; his dialect was North Country, and Yorkshire, too, his shrewd pungent wit, his obstinate courage, his pertinacious judgment. I can't even write convincingly of modern London life.

I find myself growing vehement when I write to you of politics. Are you one of those who hold this form of ordered relationship of man with man to be unclean, contaminating? You, who in your personal relationships are so excellently political, so suffused with the sense of common welfare, so excellent a democrat? Why, unclean they are, contaminating they may be; but one can't possibly ignore them.

A friend asked me last week, why go to Africa? Why not to Arabia? Arabia, Arabia—oh, Rosalind, the lure of that fair country—sometimes I am tempted sorely to go there.

> "Sweet is the music of Arabia
> In my heart, when out of dreams
> I still in the thin clear mirk of dawn
> Descry her gliding streams;
> Hear her strange lutes on the green banks
> Ring loud with the grief and delight
> Of the dim-silked, dark-haired musicians
> In the brooding silence of night.
>
> They haunt me—her lutes and her forests,
> No beauty on earth I see
> But shadowed with that dream recalls
> Her loveliness to me:
> Still eyes look coldly upon me,
> Cold voices whisper and say—
> ' He is crazed with the spell of far Arabia,
> They have stolen his wits away.' "

De la Mare is increasingly lovely and excellent altogether. I find him as he describes

> "a cool, dark water calling, calling"

sweet refuge for dusty travellers—but an enchanter of Arabia. And I'll choose Africa, never fear—the real world that uses all of a man, not the fantasy world of his imagination alone.

I can't remember if I told you that Marjorie Cohen has written asking me to follow up her League of Nations Union branches at Cape Town, Stellenbosch, Bloemfontein, Johannesburg and Pretoria. The League of Nations Union will arrange with the secretaries for hospitality in places where I know no one. I had better do it on the way up to you, then, if I am overcome by heat and weariness, you can turn on me and have the satisfaction of telling me "I told you so." But don't let's fight all the time. I couldn't bear it. I seem to pass so much of my time in controversy. I suppose that I always shall now, unless I fall back into my old habit of trying to be obliging and please everybody.

From Mrs. Lewis came a Johannesburg *Star*, comparing her to Stella Benson. Curious that. Stella Benson is coming to England in the summer and says that she wants to meet me. I want to meet her, I think; though I don't imagine her to be an easy person.

Spring days, Rosalind. The hedges gleaming with that faint green haze that precedes full glory of buds and leaves. There are scillas in a lawn down Holland Park Gardens, and a magnolia tree fat with buds. At Bedford College the garden is ablaze with golden bulbs, crocuses and daffodils. Sweet spring days. I dare not think of the country. I shall not see it this year till August—perhaps not then, for Cottingham, alas, isn't country. Every day the roads grow more and more linked up with little red villas. And I shall miss the spring next year too. Wouldn't it be horrible if one had an accident and died and never saw another?

It's quarter to one—and to-morrow I want to finish a story. For all that is egotistical and controversial in this letter, forgive. Yet I do not think that you would like me to sit down meekly and eat out of your hand. Of course, you are older and wiser than I, but so was Lord Curzon,

315

peace to his soul. Yet on no single subject, I think, should we have agreed, except perhaps in love of Oxford—and that for diverse reasons. But I love nearly all things that you love—people, animals, flowers, places, songs that are dear like running water. Oh, Rosalind, I love in you most lovely gracious things. Don't cease loving me because I must also love blue books and committees and legal treatises.

Ever your

CELIA.

Bainesse,

Cottingham,

E. Yorks, April 10th, 1925.

ROSALIND DEAR,

Good Friday and Yorkshire, and the church bells ringing through a clear fine rain. Yesterday coming up in the train we saw the country blossoming up into the flower of spring. Very green the fields, and in the woods the light spray of larches, like green fountains springing among the warm darkness of firs. Do you know the warm pink blackness of Scotch firs on a spring day, when all the young fresh green robs them of their winter colour? What a mellowed, civilised island this is; not an acre of her land but has been touched and enriched by men. Even other European countries, even Bohemia and Hungary, seem young and wild beside it. It is this mellowed and cultivated appearance that strikes me afresh every time I come this northward journey, as of a woman *bien soignée*, who tends her much-loved body with a grave precision, knowing it to be a thing not wholly flesh, but sanctified by the worship of her lover.

Patriotism—love of country. How excellent an emotion —not, I think, a virtue, except as in so far as any strong feeling has more strength, more virtue in it than tepidity. When we speak of it as a proper and decorus sentiment towards the State, we wrong it, as a man wrongs a woman whom he loves merely because she is his wife. The love of

316

country is a feeling for the countryside—its hills and villages and race of men. It is a thing wholly individual and unmoral, as the love for another person is individual. To confuse this love of country and race for an adulation of the State lies at the bottom of much pain and confusion—of sentimentality and positive danger too, I think. To raise it into a civic virtue, to clothe it with pomp of armies and banners, to stain it with blood and to slay before it as before an unholy altar sacrifices of gold and of men and of men's liberty—this is not patriotism any more than the lust of a senator who lays before his mistress the spoils of a state and of his rivals in love.

I saw an excellent article in the *Revue de Genève* in which the author says that nationality is for the individual, religious, artistic life of man, not for his civic, corporate life. I entirely agree. To divorce from political consideration all sentimental attachment to a particular state or race; to face political change rationally and without passion—simply as an ordering of corporate life, as necessary as it is tedious—here lies the way of sanity. Politics should be as rational and detached as the multiplication table. Passion for one's country—yes, in the very bones and heart of one—in one's writing, painting, poetry—the songs remembered on a lovely walk, the pictures formed for comfort in ugly places, the memory and tradition and love that makes a network to bind one's heart ever to the same grey, windswept upland. My heart's in Yorkshire. My politics? Well, possibly at Geneva. Anywhere where men endeavour to set a rational consideration of human profit before the sentimentalities and self-interests and enthroned shams that constitute most men's political life.

Here's a poem for you that I sent to the *New Leader*. I'll never be a poet, as you are, Rosalind; but it was a trivial spring song that came into my head, seeing a window-box in Bethnal Green.

THE BENEFACTRESS

My neighbour on her window-sill
Has set a nodding daffodil,
I laugh to see it blowing there
Golden and tall and debonair.
The boys and girls who never saw
So green and gold a thing before
Here linger with enchanted feet
To watch Spring flowering down our street.
But Arthur says he knew a hill
Between the Somme and Huchenneville
Where golden daffodils were gay—
Once, far away—long years away.
And Yorkshire Dick can close his eyes
And see the wooded uplands rise,
With daffodils more gold than these
Gleaming like sunlight through the trees.

For Emma on her window-sill
Has set a nodding daffodil.

Much love always,

CELIA.

117, Wymering Mansions,
Elgin Avenue, W.9, April 15th, 1925.

ROSALIND DEAREST,

I have had your letter of March 12th, replying to mine
of February 12th, and being grieved and a little angry with
me. I fear from this that my later letters must have grieved
you even more, for they reiterated more definitely, I believe,
all that I said on February 12th. And so I shall have to
burden you with another long explanatory letter, that may
explain nothing, that will almost certainly sound priggish
and objectionable, and which may even do more harm than
good. Yet write I must, for, whatever you may think of
me, I love you, and the thought that I grieve you has gone
with me all last night and all to-day troubling and
wearying me.

Two things that I say seem to have grieved you. First,
that I think it would be madness for Clare to come now to
Africa. Such a stupid thing, Rosalind dear, if you and I
were to quarrel over Clare, whom you have met once; but
I see that the point is important. Now I wonder if I am
right in thinking that your complaint here lies not so
much in what I advise for Clare as in my implied criticism
of you. You repeat that people called your adventure madness. I know that they did. I also know how wise and right
it was. But that does not make me think the same action
wise and right for Clare. You are very different people—
different in your circumstances, your aims, your character.
In your circumstances you differ in that when you went to
Africa you had no special thing that you wanted to do in
England. The future was vague, and when the future is
vague, one uses one's wings—one flies like a migrating bird.
But for Clare for the first time the future is not vague. She
had her time of adventure—when she left home and set
herself up in one room to paint and to sleep in in London.
She did not intend to teach drawing. She wanted to paint
pictures and design decorative woodcuts of farm things,

animals and people. But to do this successfully one must have leisure, and for leisure one must have money. So she taught at first all the time. But at night and in holidays she did her illustrations and designs. At last people are beginning to pay her for them. The more she has payment for them, the more she can work on them, and the more she works on them, the better she will be. If she gave up now and went to Africa she would have to teach again all the time, instead of two days a week. She could not draw her Wiltshire labourers and Berkshire hop-kilns. People would forget her, and when she came back again—for she would come back—she might never recapture what she had gained once. There is a time to adventure—when one is uncertain of what to do where one is. But, having overcome difficulties, striven and even suffered to obtain something, and just before realisation to throw it up and go off in search of an adventure seems to me to be folly. Wings and roots—the world needs both, Rosalind. The birds who fly must have trees to rest on. And anyway, she wants to stay. She is happy, excited, eager in her work. Her aims are to paint her pictures really well, and she is taking immense strides forward. I do think that new colours and atmosphere just now would spoil the thing that she—a town girl—is capturing—the scent and feel and texture of the English countryside. As for her character, she will never stagnate. There's too much vitality for her ever to be fallow. No, Rosalind dear, I have no scorn nor fear for adventures. For you and Bunty, taken when you took them, they were splendid. But I am not sure that I should applaud you now equally, were you to fling up your Pretoria work and go to South America, say. Though even that might be right. For I agree with you emphatically that teachers should be mobile. It is one of the things that I have been learning more and more. But Clare does not want to teach. She wants to paint. And you will know that as far as teaching in schools goes, you can't do both.

The same thing rather applies to me. I cannot both

teach and write. One cannot train oneself to express, and train other people. Writing and painting imply the cultivation of the ego—the personality's own force and individuality. Teaching is surely the assistance which one gives to others to liberate their own personality. I love teaching. It pleases and interests me. But while I have taught I have never written. All last spring and summer I corrected a few things—I wrote nothing. I was teaching. My mind was giving itself to my pupils' minds. This spring, although I have done other things, given lectures, made speeches, studied reports, my mind has been alive with things to write. I've sketched out about six short stories, a play, and the rest of my Wycliffe book, and only want time and patience to put them to paper. It's the same with Clare. I talked to her the other day, for she has had an offer of an excellent teaching job and an inspectorship here in London that would guarantee her means permanently, and she has refused it because to involve herself in teaching means to deny the other force, and that is the unforgivable sin.

Now for myself. Two things to explain.

You say that I put "causes in front of friendship—some friendship at least." Of course, most dear friend, before all friendships if possible, and always have done—only I did not for a long time know what the causes were. Does not every one who is worth his salt do that? Why, if it were not so, seeing that we have many friends, what should we be? Straws blown by the contrary winds of our friends' desires—here, there, everywhere. No. Let's have a cause to keep us straight in our path, and our friends are free to love us and be loved, honouring us because, in our fidelity to a cause, we show our fidelity to life itself and to them as part of life. Should I love you more if I loved my work of the prevention of war less? Why, Rosalind, what great new thing was ever born but when for this cause a man would leave his father and mother and sister and lover, even, if need be, his own life, to serve it?

As for the small practical point—trivial this. You are

hurt because I come to Africa to lecture and learn about the Dominion problem. Granted that you think my work as a lecturer useless. This is possible. My experience as a learner will not be useless. I know how to use experience of this kind for my own ends. It is not the first time I did that. But are you hurt that I should only make, as a sort of side-show to my main purpose, my visit to you? Now, darling. If you were in great need of me, if you were ill or sorely troubled, or going to have a baby, or wrecked by a husband or lover, and only something that I might do might help to heal you—I might come—I think I would spend most of my substance to help you. But when you ask me to " take a sunshine holiday"—to spend over £100 and six months amusing myself, enjoying your company (which I should enjoy) and gaining new, but possibly irrelevant, experience in a new continent—that is a different matter. I do not need a holiday. I am strong, eager, at the height of my capacity for learning and working. Any day I might get ill, or lose my heart for work temporarily, or stand for the County Council and get in by accident, or have some other catastrophe that might prevent my doing the very thing that I mean to do, and the chance would have gone by. Why, I would not so amuse myself for six months apart from my purpose for the sake of the man who wanted to marry me. You ask more than you dream. My time is not my own.

All that I do may be foolish—but dare you deny that it is an adventure? That I, at twenty-six, not very experienced, nor unusually gifted, having neither influential friends nor promising opportunities, should say "I believe that there is a need for a student of the problems of international war and peace; that this student should be a woman; should be blessed with the luck of an independent income so that she may be the servant of no party; should have had a historical training, some gift for articulation in speech and writing. I believe that she must set herself now to learn all that is possible—what induces states to enter upon those complex relationships that end in war; what machinery runs most smoothly, and what most reliably in war's prevention; what interests, economic, imperial, racial, sentimental, are most hostile to peace? What can democratic control of foreign affairs, socialism, propaganda, teaching, political agitation, contribute towards the solution of the problem—and so forth? I believe that I will try to do this. I will not be frightened by my own ignorance and cowardice and stupidity. I will not be discouraged by the almost certain knowledge of failure, by my friends' misgivings, by my own blunders. I will not be dismayed because there is no profession to follow, no example to copy, because each step of the road must be my own to mark out and to choose. I know that this is madness; but I shall try to do it."

Is this an adventure or not, oh rare adventurer? Do you deny me the brotherhood? Of course, I mayn't do it. I may simply make a fool of myself—almost certainly. Well, I'll risk that—as you risked when you went to Rhodes. Wings? I'll need them. I've got to fly where no woman flew before, I think. Do you think that my sense of the ludicrous does not laugh at the contrast between these fine words and a stilted speech on a flag-draped platform, after a few sentimentalities by the local minister? Of course I see and laugh.

I wonder if Christ laughed when he made his triumphal entry into Jerusalem "meekly, riding upon an ass." But it is recorded that he also wept.

Well, that is that. It's the second letter I've written. The first I'll tear up. And now I shall be sick for each post until I know whether you have understood, and will love me as I am, not as a feeble imitation of yourself. For I love and admire you, dearest and beautiful Rosalind; but I can't copy your pattern literally. Only lend me some of your fine spirit to encourage, not to sneer. For you can't shake my purpose; you'll only shake the joy from it.

Practical upshot of this—I shall take my tour before I

come to Pretoria. I am lecturing in Cape Town, Stellenbosch, Bloemfontein, Johannesburg, and possibly elsewhere. These things are all being arranged. I won't trouble you with details. There seem to be kind friends, some known to me, some strangers, who want to arrange things for me. I shall arrive in Pretoria about March or April, then, I imagine, and if you will have me, I will stay with you for a little. I don't mind how much you scold me afterwards—but I don't want my cold douche before the race.

Mrs. Lewis and Mrs. Newman have both asked me to see them. And I want to go to see Bunty in Kimberley too.

Oh, Rosalind, love me if you can. If not, don't be grieved. Just give me up as one of those who went their own way, foolishly perhaps, but in the belief that—for them —it was the only way possible.

With my dear love always,

CELIA.

117, Wymering Mansions,
Elgin Avenue, W.9, April 22nd, 1925.

DEAREST ROSALIND,

I have your dear letter of 1.4.25—written helter-skeltering through your day.

So Sir John Adams and Mrs. Franklin are asking you to arrange lectures. My poor Rosalind! Well, dear, don't. Apparently other people are quite keen to arrange them for me, so don't you bother. I had lunch with Mrs. Scandrett last week—the President of the National Council of Women, on her way to a conference in U.S.A. She lives at Johannesburg and is a charming little woman—South African born —small, twinkly-eyed, full of humour and vivacity, with a daughter my age, she says. She seems to want to arrange all sorts of things for me. Judge Feetham, too, I gather from her, is going to be kind. So I won't put upon you at all. I'll just come and stay with you, if you'll have me.

Alas, alas! I meant to come shingled, but I went to a very good hair man yesterday, and he says that if I either bob or shingle I shall probably lose all such hair as I have. My hair has never grown up—it is still baby's hair, and can only just be induced to stay on my head. Was ever such nonsense?

Mother is up here staying for a conference and sleeping in my room. Edith and Margaret have been here. Edith is enamoured of you. She says that of all my friends that she has met you are by far the sweetest woman. And I was just writing you such horrid letters. I felt rebuked. But I do love you. And if my letters are self-righteous and offensive, G. says that the young must be self-righteous before they can be righteous—so you may yet have hopes for my salvation!

A heavenly day. Such a spring we are having. The *New Leader* is printing my daffodil poem. They have taken my stories too and wrote me a charming letter.

My journalist boy is just going to set up on his own. But I'm having a rough crossing with him at the moment. One's difficulty in dealing with men is that one must pretend all the time not to be helping them. This boy's older than I, and has such a sensitive pride, and I find it so damned hard to persuade him (a) that he is getting along splendidly all on his own; (b) that I'm not falling in love with him. Isn't it frightful the way people think that one can't be interested in a man's work without it having some connection with sex? Bless your heart, I'd bath this child and put him to bed if necessary; but I'd be quite grateful if he or any one else would raise a flutter in my heart. I really shall be disappointed if I go through life without once being properly in love. As a writer, I feel it my duty to my work—but they are all so helpless, and such children. How can one feel thrilled?

What nonsense—and I must go. I wrote a limerick in the Tube yesterday—but no one appreciates it here, so I send it to you:

There was a young axylotyl,
Who tried to drink beer from a bottle.
   When they said, "What a sight!"
   He replied, "You are right,
'Cause the darned thing's too tight—I shall throttle."

Well, well!

       Yours always with love,

               CELIA.

          117, Wymering Mansions,
          Elgin Avenue, W.9, April 25th.

DEAREST ROSALIND,

I have your letter written in the train going to a W.A.A.C. re-union at Johannesburg. So you have nice new matrons. I am so glad. And I hope that they will be kind to one another. There really is not time in this world to quarrel. There are far too many things to be done first.

I have just been having—am having still—a curious and sad little adventure. Last Friday when I was out a girl came to the flat and asked for me. She was well dressed, quite nice-looking, but seemed to be desperately nervous and in trouble. She left a telephone number and begged Vera to ask me to ring her up. I was a little suspicious. So many people want to see you and then borrow £5, and I find it so hard to refuse. But I did ring her up, and I asked her to come and see me on Saturday. She came, and stayed for about three hours in the evening, telling me a strange and sad little life-story. She had read *The Crowded Street*, and being a Muriel, though with a rather different—and sadder—story, she felt that she had come to the end of her tether. She had to speak to some one and, being singularly friendless, she came to me. She is older than I, twenty-nine, and since the war has been living alone in a flat near here. She has plenty of money—and absolutely nothing has happened. She has hardly any friends, learns a little music,

326

and just sits and thinks of the years going by and nothing happening. Oh, Rosalind, if ever people are to be pitied, the most pitiable are those without quite sufficient personality to go and do things for themselves, to whom nothing ever happens. This girl is on the brink of insanity. It has gone past hysteria. There is a bad nerve history in the family. A sister is crippled by St. Vitus' dance.

I am sending her to a nerve specialist first, and then have found what I think are the two things she needs most—a man to take her out—and out of herself—and some work to do. You'd say "emigrate"—but not every one is fitted for that. Her sister went to Africa and returned in eight months. Probably she needed to marry, and probably but for the war she might have married.

I find it so easy to lay down rules of conduct, but am always finding that these ridiculous pathological complications come and upset things. The complication of human personality may tend to make us more interesting and complete individuals, but it does play the deuce with a sane sociology.

By the way, I disagree with you about socialism tending to kill the adventure spirit. I do not think that any economic organisation can either give birth to or kill any spirit, provided that it works efficiently. What kills adventure and every sort of initiative are neurasthenia, utter poverty and anæmia. If you find the English point of view hard to understand, remember that since the war England has been full of neurasthenic men, youths wasting their morale through unemployment, and women who should have married or been trained to work and who have done neither. Of course one cure is emigration. I entirely agree. But the difficulty is that for the untrained and under-developed man or woman, the colonies seem to offer little better than starvation. You have your own unemployment problems in Africa and Canada, and in Australia it's not much use unless you can do something on a farm.

You say that a long sea voyage may alter my way of

327

looking at things. It certainly will temporarily—for I shall be sick all the way, and wish I were dead! Which I don't at present, in spite of a Conservative Government fairly established here, and Hindenburg President of Germany, and all the powers of hatred, superstition and self-interest lashing people to madness about the Bolshevists. Oh yes, and as a nice little treat we are to have mock air-raids every evening this week over London, with aeroplanes dropping "bombs" full of pamphlets, urging young men to join the forces.

So cheerfully do we begin again the old mad circle—armaments, suspicion, jealousy, deception, war. To read international history would make one despair were it not for the few wise and sane who keep open-eyed among the blindness and sentimentality of the herd.

Meanwhile, there is the spring—very shy and lovely. And magnolias out in Kensington, and that smell even in the streets that is like rain on soil.

I am writing at short stories—six are almost ready. But they are too dun coloured. Perhaps I'll make a volume of them later. Then my play is growing—in spite of meetings, Vera's trousseau, my journalist boy (who is keeping me busy, but doing well), and distempering the flat and spring cleaning, and writing articles and so forth. I am very well, busy and as happy as one can be in this queer world.

I love you, even if I argue. That again may be the gracelessness of youth. If so, forgive.

CELIA.

PS.—I am re-reading Keats, and finding more and more food for wonder and delight in *Hyperion*. I remember when I was fifteen sitting up nearly all one night at school trying to read him for the first time by the light from a street lamp outside my window. Have you read Amy Lowell's book yet? "Not such a great poet as Browning?" What do you think? Personally, I prefer John Middleton Murray's "Of the same order as Shakespeare." J. M. M. is vague, but

he goes the right way to work. I have also been reading
Pierre Loti's *Désenchantées*. An enchanting book. I know
several English girls not unlike those little Turks, with
their adventurous minds and restricted bodies. But Loti is
a master of places. Constantinople lives—what exquisite
tenderness, what a style! Yet there's something lacking. I
imagine it's a weakness in the character rather than in the
talent of the man. As an artist, he was supreme; but for
real grandeur one must have greatness of personality. I've
only read about four books, but I doubt this. All the same,
a delight to read.

I've just been hearing Cardinal Bourne opening a Catholic
Conference on International Relations. There were also a
Jesuit Father and a Bishop speaking. The Catholics were so
amazingly much more like what one would expect them to
be than I had ever imagined.

Au revoir.

We've just distempered our passage. It looks so nice.

W.

117, Wymering Mansions,
Elgin Avenue, W.9, May 6th, 1925.

ROSALIND MY DEAR,

No letter from you this week, and I deserve it. For mine
have been both infrequent and harsh—in bad taste, perhaps,
such egotistical and controversial ramblings. Yet it is the
highest compliment of my love that I send you unpruned
the shifting tangles of my inclination.

I am drinking long draughts of Keats—he is like cool
water—most lovely and most proud. I think that *Hyperion*
(the first version, according to Colvin) is one of the finest
poems that I have ever read. Its excellence impresses itself
upon me more and more.

I am also reading *The Philosopher's Stone* by Larson—
admirable book, with its mixture of mysticism and shrewd
humour. The Pastor one of the most vivid creations of

329

fiction that I have chuckled over—but tragic too. Have you read it? I think that it would please you.

I am revising short stories and giving several lectures, one lot to a Jewish Girls' Club. They are such intelligent and delightful people.

My *New Leader* poem came out last week. I am as proud as punch, because it is the first to be printed in a *real paper*.

Au revoir. I love you always.

CELIA.

Here's a fragment to turn into a poem. I saw a lady in a little garden in Kensington.

> So calm indeed, she seemed, and good,
> It was as if an angel stood
> Dreaming through paradisal hours
> With folded wings among the flowers.

I can't get any more, but I'm sure that there is some more.

I enjoy writing poems, though they are all so bad when written. I'll do rhymed couplets for hours by the yard when I should be studying International Labour Legislation!

117, Wymering Mansions,
Elgin Avenue, W.9, May 19th, 1925.

DEAREST ROSALIND,

Again no letter from you—nor indeed from any one in South Africa. But you will have been busy at your conferences, and in any case I deserve it. My last letters have been most boring, irregular, priggish and egotistical. I will be good.

Such a day of sunlight—all lilacs and new summer dresses. Even I thought that there was a bee buzzing in the sitting-room, and when it turned out to be a bluebottle, I hadn't the heart to send it away. I think that it was pretending to be a bee.

330

All the babies are coming out on to the balconies of the flats opposite. They have pink and blue and white cot-covers and mothers in cretonne dresses. They come out here with the window-boxes, and that means it's summer. In the evening people don't pull down their blinds, but sit upon balconies with lighted rooms behind them, and carry on charming little domestic dramas for our benefit. We're getting to know quite a lot about some of them. There's one young couple that I see heading straight for divorce. He pays much attention to his cousin (?) in green; his wife in pink is growing piqued and reads the *Evening Standard* after supper and tries to look martyred.

Mauve and blue are the real colours to wear. I'm making a mauve frock of dazzling loveliness, though it's not easy to dazzle at 2s. 11¾d a yard. But my bridesmaid's dress is both blue and mauve, so scores all along the line, and I shall bring it out to Pretoria and peacock about most grandly.

What a mercy that Vera is getting married. I'd never otherwise spend £13 13s. od. on a dress. But oh, my feet! I take the poor things all over London to find pretty shoes for them. Says the young lady, "Not in *that* size, moddam," and my poor feet grow more and more depressed. I have to bring them home in a bus. Then skirts are so short. There's no hiding the horrid facts of one's physique.

The terrier dog whose nose was put out of joint by the arrival of the baby sulked for several weeks. But now he sits out on the balcony and guards the baby, because he knows that his own position increases in prestige like that of the tweeny-maid turned nursegirl.

I must go and work, not play with you. But we will play.

Au revoir. Only eight months now and then I see you.

CELIA.

DEAREST ROSALIND,

A long letter and a charming one from you last night.
I was so glad. Sometimes I have horrible fears lest, because
of this long distance and the difficulty of explaining myself,
I should say something outrageous and slay your splendid
patience.

I have just had my second story taken by the *New Leader*
—and I must have had hundreds sent to various people and
returned. There's little to be made from writing. *The
Crowded Street* was quite well reviewed—surprisingly so to
my mind; but until December 31st it only made £14 10s.
for me! I may make £20 with luck from the whole thing.

I agree with you that self lies at the bottom of
many mental ills. Sometimes I think that they come from
ill-timed shocks falling on people who are for some reason
physically ill. Sometimes, too, they are apparently seasonal
in origin. I wish that we were not quite such complicated creatures. Our minds and bodies intermingle so closely
that we often seem half lost in a dense jungle—sinister as
the Woods of Westermain. Yet there, too, self was the
dragon, and I suppose it is still possible that

> "Him shall change, transforming late,
> Wonderfully renovate. . . ."

A headmistress's position must often be very lonely and
difficult. When I was staying at Queen Margaret's I remember with what joy Miss Fowler told me of an old college
friend whom she had once known intimately, but had not
met for years, and who had just settled in Scarborough—a
quite independent person, with whom she could be as
friendly as she liked without any jealousy from her staffs.

Staffs are difficult—like college S.C.R.'s. Things get out
of proportion there. Personal friendships come to count
too much. There are so many people in the world.

We are having the loveliest May that ever breathed. I've never seen blossom so radiant. Last night a thunderstorm behaved with considerable violence, and this morning down Maida Vale the pavements were quite covered with pink chestnut blossom. It was like a gigantic wedding.

I heard a delightful story this week. A certain Dr. G., a very reverend and delightful preacher, was given hospitality by a don and his wife, both keen Erasmus scholars of great reputation. When he returned he observed to a colleague, "Jones, you know there's something *wrong* with that household. There's no lust in it, that's what it is." We also have known. . . .

I have received three invitations for August—one to Dorsetshire with Hilda Reid; one to Cornwall with the headmistress of St. Monica's where I taught; and one to the Yorkshire moors with mother. Isn't it a delightful state of affairs when one's mother "invites" one formally? The older we grow, the more charming becomes our relationship. She has made me promise never to come home and play the "managing daughter" to her in her old age; she could not bear to be nursed by me, she says. I, on the other hand, am to remain courtier-like to her, and send her flowers and rare embroideries, and to love her more than a little, and never to let her sink into the indifferent and second-rate position which so many daughters reserve for their parents. Consequently we hug a secret friendship, far more delicious than most, and elope sometimes for a few days together. Incidentally, she calls upon me to enlighten her about such interesting things but delicate subjects as birth control, etc., which she was not taught when young, but feels that, as a County Councillor, she ought to understand! Consequently we fall into a Rabalaisian intimacy which would shock her terribly if I were not her daughter! And she grows younger, and wickeder and more charming every year. Of course she'll go and die just when we are growing most companionable. That's the worst of forty years' difference in age.

333

If I am to catch the post, I must stop.

I have just been reading a delightful book by an Oxford contemporary of mine—Harry Scott Stokes, called *Perseus*. It is all about dragons.

With much love always, dearest Rosalind. Auf wiedershen.

CELIA.

117, Wymering Mansions,
Elgin Avenue, W.9, May 28th, 1925.

DEAREST ROSALIND,

I have just finished reading *The Little French Girl* and am quite enchanted by it. So delicate, true and gracious a piece of workmanship delights one. The scenes in France are all warm and golden. Madame Vervier, so exquisitely rich, with such sad beauty. I knew a woman once like that. She was the mistress of a man whom we knew at the nursing home where I nursed before I went to France. The Bradley family is perhaps slightly caricatured. I can hardly believe in Mrs. Bradley's innocence; but people do grow like that —absorbed, detached, impersonal.

Is that what you fear for me, Rosalind? That I shall become engrossed in committees and detached from people and lovely things? That book makes me see what I think is your point of view about several things. I have always much to learn from you, darling; even though I must be myself, not you.

I have been leading a frivolous life. The Russian Ballet is here again, and I went with Clare on Tuesday night, and was delighted. They are dancing *Narcissus*—the ballet is exquisite—a wonderful Bacchic dance, with very simple, austere gestures, like Keats' *Ode to a Grecian Urn*. It seems strange to speak of Bacchic ecstasy as "austere," yet that is the impression—a purity of movement, a sort of singleness of purpose, as in all truest art. I suppose that it is here that we recognise greatness in art, in its sincerity. The Russian

334

dancers may do some things badly, but now and then they make perfect beauty, as in some moments of the Narcissus Ballet.

I sat on a Care Committee yesterday. We had eighteen boys leaving school. They wanted to be upholsterers, polishers, printers, butchers or joiners. Nothing else. I spoke about going abroad. The parents are all so much against it. The Labour Exchanges do not greatly encourage it, and the Colonies themselves demand hard conditions. Necessary, I suppose, but most difficult for those who most need help. I do not see clearly what to do yet. It is one of the things I want to learn.

That family who were so charming to us in Vienna has met with dire tragedy. One felt that, when we were there. I felt it in their gaiety, their long, elegant rooms, their perfect manners—all of it somehow doomed. The boy, who took us to the circus, and with whom we joked—he has embezzled money for his mistress, and now killed himself. The father, a perverse idealist, as perverse as his son was in wickedness, thrashed him, exiled him, and now having killed him (for that is what it all amounts to) has broken his own heart and died—just collapsed suddenly. And the girl can think of nothing but the very evil, clever, beautiful man whom she loves—and who has three wives of various stages of legitimacy already. That poor mother—so gentle, so soft. Yet somehow acquiescing. That shadow-haunted society. All the bottom seems to have fallen out of Vienna like the lovely shops in its streets, so heavily in debt. They live on the same way, for they know no other—yet doomed, dark. English society seems so sane, so solidly founded and reasonable beside that, and yet even here, too, we do such pitiful things.

Vera and I lunched with Lady Rhondda again to-day. I still do not know that woman. She is so interesting. Her mind is splendid. Her flat is full of lovely things—old brass, with great branches of lilac, and Chinese lacquer cabinets —but unostentatious, with only one sitting-room and one little study. I suppose that she is one of the richest women in London, yet she lives almost as simply as Vera and I—only with greater elegance. I find it strange to know some one so well and so little!

The *New Leader* are probably going to run a series of my stories with Clare's woodcuts illustrating them. I had tea with the sub-editor on Sunday—a dear little homespun woman in a Hampstead room—with a sense of humour, bobbed grey hair, and a merry smile.

I must go. I must go. I am speaking at a Woman's Club in Bethnal Green to-night. Sometimes we have a lecture, but they like it best when we sing songs—"I want to be happy," and "What'll I do?" and "It ain't goin' to rain no more," and, still better, really vulgar ones about marriage and mothers-in-law. Well, well. The proletariat can only be educated when young. I go with a lecture in my pocket. I shall probably have to recite instead.

I love you.

CELIA.

117, Wymering Mansions,
Elgin Avenue, W.9,
2.6.25.

DEAREST ROSALIND,

I am so very glad to have your letter of 6.5.25. I am so glad to see that in many things you are right and I am wrong. I would much rather have it that way. But indeed, I think that in many things where we seem to disagree we really are both right, and both hold the same point of view, only letters make misunderstandings. One is not sufficiently careful in expression. The transitory mood, the indignation evoked by other things, these blur the truth of the direct personal relationship. And the fault, I see, is mine rather than yours.

For two things I will at once apologise. I am really sorry. My two suggestions: (1) that you were wounded by my implied criticism of your actions; (2) that you wanted me to be like you. I have been thinking over your first letter again that led me to make these suggestions. It wasn't very clear, darling. In words I could never so have mistaken you. But the written letter is more difficult. You say that Africa is not far. It is very far when it leads us for a moment to think of the exact writing upon paper rather than of the real person who wrote. Had I thought of you more and your written letter less, I never should have so belittled you by thinking you less than you are. Perhaps you would have minded less that I should agree with Clare in not thinking the time ripe for her to go to Africa if you had not come into such frequent contact with the wooden English attitude. Perhaps I should have been truer to both myself and you if I had not recently been half smothered by people who all want me to be and do and say what *they* want, rather than what I want. I was too readily on the defensive. I never should have been so with you. I will try never to be so again. It is bad to fight against small people—it seems to make one small. I should have honoured more the largeness of your mind. Forgive me.

Forgive me, too, for what I said about persons and causes. These things are, I think, better left unsaid. To express definitely must distort. One cannot so weigh things like friendship. Again the sense of revolt, of defiance, not against you, but against those others who want me to be different, to give up all work except purely artistic or in other cases except purely academic, or in still others except purely political—all these I allowed to enter in between you and me and make me say things and feel things that are not fully true.

Your letter fills me with shame that I should be so easily false to real integrity of expression and of thought.

Yet one more thing on the bigger question—the importance of teachers and their influence on world peace. I am learning this fast. I learnt much of it in Central Europe. I am watching my schools at Bethnal Green. I see it in schools where I lecture. If it were not that an international matriculation is already being discussed by Gilbert Murray's Committee, I would try to get hold of people who have authority in such things and work for them. I agree with you completely.

I think that your letters are great letters. Re-reading them fills me with admiration and love for you. Mrs. Lewis wrote one letter to say that a friend of hers in Pretoria had told her how much you were loved. I imagined this. People will always criticise you because you are too big for them. You speak the language of the poets, who were free spirits. You have the gallant courage and the humanity of those who are great lovers. And you were appointed for your personality over the head of others who considered themselves to be in a more adequate position. I guessed a little, but not this.

I wish that I were more like you—I said before that I have much to learn from you. I know this—more even than you know it. You disarm me by being more tender than I deserve. You are quite right in telling me that I take myself too seriously. By the way, when did I bring in a reference to Christ's journey to Jerusalem? I wish that I did not do these things. Abominable taste, in any case, and afterwards I blush to my toe-nails. But I frequently catch myself doing it. Is it the influence of Brotherhood meetings? I hope not, but you never know. Fortunately people forget when one says things; but to write them—well, well. It's one of the million things I shall have to live down, I suppose.

I'll tell you why I can't come for a "sunshine holiday" only. I feel so full of life and energy and keenness and I'm afraid it won't last. I feel that I want to race round the world, devouring information and documents and tea parties and karoos and continents and friendships all with passion. It is probably foolish, and I shall almost certainly make a fool of myself over it, but I see no cure except to let me work it off; if I say "holiday" to myself, I begin to froth at the mouth. It certainly can't last, and probably by the time that I come out to you, it will all have gone off, and I shall be more sane. But my dæmon tells me to do thus and thus even if foolish, and to profit by my own mistakes. It would be pleasanter in one way just to come to see you. But I might boil over. What you suggest about some one who would translate speeches into Africaans is good—though I can't feel that what I say is worth translating yet. I want to lecture because that helps one to learn things. I don't feel that I have any right to tell Africa what to think. I want to learn what she does think. But it's so much easier to do that if one is labelled. I believe that because you teach, and take positions, and go to conferences and meet parents, you know more than if you were just a tourist. For instance, you have learnt that it is not much use to go talking about the League of Nations, for in letters from Grahamstown onwards you have suggested that this is what I should do. I can learn, too, perhaps, especially if you will help me. I shall need your help so much.

Will you really, in spite of all this, give me an introduction to the Native College at Fort Hare? I should like to go there almost more than anywhere. The English papers, especially *The Times*, are full of articles about the natives now because of the Prince of Wales' tour. I feel vaguely that they are wrong, but don't know. One knows so little —just here, quite close, a few well defined, clearly seen things. Beyond that—a mist, wherein if we think we see clearly it is generally because we see mirages reflected from the nearer visions. Africa is all blurred. It may still be so after I have been. You may help me to see it more clearly —if you will.

What you say of Oxford is perfectly just. It is completely complacent, and absorbed in its small affairs—a lovely, intense, secluded life, detached from the world outside. I wonder sometimes whether any institutions should be sacred—not sacrosanct, anyway. But institutions that will

339

not stand criticism will not stand anything. Is it afraid of colonial influence blowing too hearty breezes through its quiet quadrangles?

I am so sorry that I grieved you in saying that I should only give up my work for friendship if you were in distress. But really, if you think again, I think that what I have said is not so appalling. I, too, want friendship that will "live and laugh and work with me"—and laughter is so little fun without friends. Perhaps you are right. I must think this over again. Do we in a country where people are more often more sad than gay lay too much stress upon comfort, too little on gaiety? I tell you that I have always been the happy fortunate one, surrounded by people less happy than myself, until sometimes my own laughter has seemed to be almost wicked. I love so much to enjoy myself, and because I have rarely been without the joy of companionship in enjoyment, I may have fallen into the sin of underestimating this. I have so much to learn.

Now I must tell you of a lovely thing that happened to me last week. I came up from the tube station late at night, into Elgin Avenue. There had been rain, but the clouds had swept away, and the moon gleamed down on a road of dark blue steel, naked and smooth. There are little sycamore trees strung with lamps like golden jewels between the vast blue shadows of the houses. The leaves in the glow of the lamps tumble into queer patterns of olive and gold. Then suddenly, as I stood, I heard a faint pad, pad, pad behind me. I looked, and there was a runner, a slim young boy, with head bare, and bent arms, and young naked limbs. The lamplight shone on his white garments, and his swift grace, as he sprang from shadow to shadow below the sycamores. Such fleeting beauty, such swift, sudden grace. I stood entranced until he faded into the blur of shade and moonshine and sycamores. It was only afterwards that I remembered that this was *Elgin* Avenue. A runner from Paddington recreation ground training at night? The road was so silent; the youth so beautiful.

"And there's a hall in Bloomsbury
No more I dare to tread,
For all the stone men shout at me
And swear they are not dead.
And once I touched a marble girl,
And knew that marble bled."

This letter is not a good one. It conveys so little of the love, remorse, and longing that I feel for you. I want to come and to put my head on your knee like I once did at Huchenneville, and say "I am so sorry." But this must wait till I come.

Dear, beautiful Rosalind. I love you. I do not really think that anything except my stupidity and my tendency to write down the mood of the moment lies between us. Forgive me. The fault is all mine.

CELIA.

Later:

I have re-read this letter that I wrote yesterday. It is inadequate, but it shall go. There is so much more to say, but I do not yet know how to say it. I beg you to have patience with me. One day I may learn. Forgive me for my blindness, for my obstinacy and egoism. Believe only that I love and honour you, and that one day I may learn better how to do this.

117, Wymering Mansions,
Elgin Avenue, W.9,
June 10th, 1925.

DEAREST ROSALIND,

I have sent to you Mottram's *Spanish Farm*, which, of course, you may have read. But it struck me as being immensely interesting, true and just. If it is not a great book, it is at least a very distinguished one, and has that element which compels one to conviction—like in Zeno's phrase " the impression takes a man by the hair and compels him to assent."

I have done little this last week, not even much work. I have two short stories half written and hanging fire. But I have been elected a member of the new British Institute of Philosophic Studies, which pleases me a little, though I'm aware that my qualifications are chiefly those entirely gratuitous ones which enable me to pay, via father, a subscription of £1 1s. a year. However, I find the prospect pleasing; because the broad pastures of platonic idealism are a pleasant resting-place after the more dusty highways of politics.

Oh yes, and I've seen the *Cherry Orchard*, excellently acted and produced at Hammersmith. People call it a comedy. Tchechov, I believe, said "almost a farce." Good heavens! of all desolating plays I found it one of the most unbearable. All one's own futility, one's own specious grandiloquence and high-sounding intentions—all there, funnily, inexorably, not things for tears but for laughter —which is so much more deadly. A wonderful play, wherein the businesslike are as futile as the ineffective, and the idealists as useless as the amiable and sentimental sensualists. "Why did we have lunch in town, when we hate it?" "Oh, Uncle, if only you'd hold your tongue. . . ." An unbearable play. I don't know how Tchechov continued to keep alive through the writing of it.

To-day I had to give a lecture in Woking—the country looks glorious. We have what we call a heat-wave, and the women are actually clothed in coloured cottons, and the men drip visibly; but for any one as habitually cold as myself it is delicious. Walked on Monday from Chelsea to Westminster along the Embankment at midday, loving the way that the warmth comes right into one's veins, and yet by the river the breeze always blows a little.

All our neighbours opposite have planted window-boxes, and also set lighted stages in their rooms for our amusement. It is really charming of them to play their gramophone and dance, and quarrel, and kiss again all opposite to our windows, and we can regard them with no trouble to ourselves and no little entertainment. I have all the evening been beguiled by a very good loudspeaker broadcasting diverse orchestral pieces which have tantalised me because I cannot put names to them.

Are you still angry with me, my dear?

I send you my love,

CELIA.

117, Wymering Mansions,
Elgin Avenue, W.9,
June 17th.

DEAREST ROSALIND,

I was so glad to have your letter written on 27.5.25.

I wish that I could have heard you on the Modern Girl. *Quelle sujet!* Is she not like most other modern girls, Elizabeth Bennet, Elizabeth Tudor (a *very* modern girl that!), Medea, Iphigenia, and the rest? And yet, there seems to be some reality in the suppositious gulf between the twentieth-century youth and the nineteenth-century. I have a theory that every hundred years there is a cycle of change in what one might call the outlook of the younger generation. I do not, for instance, think that the outlook of my mother and grandmother differed much, but that of my mother and myself differed largely, and that of my great grandmother and my grandmother probably differed. There is a sort of quiet permeation of change from social and political circumstances, and a still more diluted inflow of change from current philosophic and theological and aesthetic movements. There was a type of "modern girl" in the fourteenth century—Joanna of Naples, who scandalised her older generation, had it certainly. Then the Renaissance girls— can't you hear their elders on at them? Beatrice Sforza, "Oh, my dear, these modern girls—their freedom of language, and behaviour, dancing till all hours, and talking to every kind of person without proper chaperones!" And that enchanting Duchess of Parma, and the girls of fifteenth-century Rome. And then the sixteenth century—a generation of gay Elizabethans—so witty and gallant and resourceful. Isn't Shakespeare's Beatrice an immortal embodiment of that independent, challenging, fearless generation? Oh, "a star danced and I was born!" Then the girls of the C17 Revolution—Bridget Cromwell and her puritans, grave of speech, censorious of their elders, eager for responsibility, intolerant, altruistic, serious. And the eighteenth-century girls blossoming forth again—a generation of vigorous, frank, open-air creatures—especially in the country houses —hard-riding, hard-swearing, I'll believe sometimes, not even above spitting, their tongues freed from their Puritanical shackles by His Gracious Majesty Charles II. And then two more generations, similar in outlook, before the Revolution, the Romantic Movement, and the girls of the Liberation of Women, Mary Wollstonecroft, Harriet Shelley —oh, and in France, young Madame Roland—political girls, atheists in theology, but gnostics in politics, ardent, impetuous, decisive creatures, with a golden age before and behind them, and a malleable world of potential milleniums. My dear, what a girlhood! Modern girls all of them, and here we have them to-day—the cycle complete. Modern girls in shingles and breeches, but the same fundamental characteristics—impatience of authority, freedom of thought, eagerness for responsibility, belief in the perfectibility of human nature, a touching courage and hopefulness, and a consequent rebellion, more self-conscious than necessary (do we ever rebel except from a possibly unjustifiable hope that the world holds a prospect of better things than the present?).

But she's passing. I heard yesterday from Mrs. F. S. Marvin that Miss Pope declares that just now the students who come to Somerville are like the old pre-war students— docile, conservative, gentle, hard-working. Don't you see? The cycle's round again. The opening century has touched

her first quarter. The Modern Girl is a novelty no longer
—she has settled down for her seventy-five years of quietude.
But wait for A.D. 2000.

My dear Rosalind, if I were the Prince of Wales I might
be content to smile. "Might"—perhaps. But when I smile,
I tend to emulate the Cheshire Cat. I must never, never
wear false teeth. They would fall out.

G. is back. The flat is full of flowers and happiness.
This is the most charming love-story that I have yet
encountered. When I saw him yesterday, slim, charming,
brilliant, with his blue eyes ablaze with happiness, and his
arm across the shoulders of his little love, I almost believed
that the romance of fiction was less perniciously untruthful
than I had thought. Even if marriage proves catastrophic,
this parting and meeting has at least been lovely.

I heard from Stella Benson in Japan last week. She is
now on her way through California. Have you read *This is
the end*? Its poignancy is almost unbearable. I want to
know her. The thing that I cannot understand is that she
seems to want to know me. I never sought her acquaintance
—only wrote once and told her not to answer. Her letters
are unexpected—gentle and less uncompromising than her
books—more ordinary, lacking that fierce sweetness but
gaining in humanity and approachableness. I think that
she is good as well as brilliant—that rare quality of goodness
which is so strange a thing to find, and so pregnant in its
possibilities. It's a sort of purity of soul. Katherine Mansfield I think had it, and Vera has. I know very few so gifted.
We are most of us blurred by self-interest, and vulgarity.
These pure in heart see God. I see—very little but myself
in different guises, I fear. I think that you have it, and that
is why I must always love you. It is the one gift of which
one can never weary.

I'm reading Wickham Steed's *Through Thirty Years*.
Interesting, absorbingly so. A most cultured and attractive
personality. Yet any realistic presentation of the delicate
mesh of relationships that characterised the old diplomacy

345

fills me with a sort of despair. When I was at Oxford I disliked diplomatic studies. They seemed to be so divorced from reality. Any attempt to control the huge forces of economic, racial and emotional pressure that really move international relations, by this exquisite code of personal honour among a few cultured gentlemen seems to me to be like trying to tack up Waterloo Bridge with drawing-pins. About as effective too. But one has to study it; because, in spite of princes' smiles and interchange of teachers, these people have still more power to make and unmake peace than the amorphous conglomeration of emotions, traditions and illusions which we call public opinion. Doesn't this latest pact business prove it? What has Austen Chamberlain to do with what England and Germany really want with each other? Less than nothing. Oh, my dear Rosalind, this is a queer world. We make passionate efforts for freedom of action in small things and • in the big issues upon which, not so much our bodily safety but our spiritual integrity, which matters more, depends, we commit our souls to the tender mercies of an Austen Chamberlain. Well, well, *qui bono?*

My love always—friendships, it seems, can at least be stable. I *will* not let you go.

CELIA.

117, Wymering Mansions,
Elgin Avenue, W.9,
June 24th, 1925.

MY DEAREST ROSALIND,

No letter from you this week, but as I had a very charming one from you last week, I should be satisfied. Have you read Capek's *Letters from England*? Here is a travel book so exquisite that I desire to copy down almost everything that it says. More, it makes me desire to visit England. Not merely to live there. Oh, no. To live in England is apparently to miss almost everything within that island which is queer, lovely, significant, droll, terrifying and impressive. Now I realise that, though I may have lived among them, I have not seen clubs, parks, tapioca puddings, London traffic, the East End, Essex, Bernard Shaw, Hyde Park or the Zoo. These omissions must be rectified. Rosalind, if you have not read this book, you must inform me instantly and I will send it; for though I could copy down pages and pages of its delicate, genial, witty, perverse, malicious, enchanting entertainment, I could not, for all my good-will—I could not reproduce the pictures. And to see Oxford, G. K. Chesterton, Wembley, Oxford Street or Folkestone through the eyes of Capek is to be a happier woman. There are some books useful for wisdom, others for stimulus, others for information, and yet others for enjoyment. And for enjoyment I praise Karel Capek. A most admirable book.

Last night being my birthday, and also the date of Vera's departure from this abode of single blessedness, we went to the theatre. We saw Somerset Maugham's play *Rain*—or rather, it is not Somerset Maugham's play. It is a play written by two American authors about the plot of Somerset Maugham's short story *Rain* in *The Trembling of a Leaf*. I have not read the story, which is supposed to be good; but the play is not. It is meant to be subtle, profound, frank and tragic. It is none of these things. It is merely a rather blatant modernisation of the theme of Anatole France's *Thaïs*. A clergyman missionary, whose marriage has been one of "spiritual relationship" alone, endeavours to convert a prostitute on a South Sea Island, while held up there during the rains. Instead of this, he falls a victim to her entirely unwilling seduction, and cuts his throat in sign of failure, while the prostitute, one of those sunny-hearted, golden-souled children of joy so popular now with our modern playwrights, seeks a new life with the full-blooded He-man, Serjeant O'Hara, in Sydney. Well, well. There is some clever acting. Olga Lindo has vitality and magnetism and looks rather like Alice Lynch, and acts a prostitute after the accepted style of Cathleen Nesbitt and

347

Pauline Lord. Malcolm Keen, a clever actor, tries not to be too repulsive in the part of a missionary suffering from sex-repression. But the most competent actor by far is the rain, which looks and sounds like real rain and which carries conviction by sheer beauty of its technique. Reandean Rain.

I am studying passages to Africa and entranced by pictures of berths, smoking-rooms, and so forth. As I undoubtedly shall be sick all the way over, these will not interest me much, when I am on board; therefore I am enjoying the maximum contemplation of them now.

The *New Leader* has taken my short story about the plough-man who is glad that there is a Hell. Have you ever thought that Hell is probably a merciful necessity for those people tortured by a sense of sin which society refuses to recognise as sin? My story is about a plough boy to whom this occurs; and only when he realises that God who made heaven for His saints also in His infinite mercy made Hell for his sinners does he refrain from his original intention of cutting his throat with a new razor.

Here it is cold, cold, cold. This is June, and my fingers now are quite stiff with cold. Imagine it. And we have had a so-called heat-wave with deaths and so forth.

I must go. Getting married means many other things besides the wedding, and we have still several trifles to do.

Au revoir, and soon we shall meet, I hope, my dear Rosalind.

My love to you,

CELIA.

117, Wymering Mansions,
Elgin Avenue, W.9,
June 30th.

My DEAREST ROSALIND,

I will write to you properly next week. Just now I have only a series of small but complicated trivialities to be performed somehow. Vera and Gordon were married on

Saturday. All went well, and I will send you some photographs to show how beautiful we all were.

But till next week, au revoir.

I have booked my passage Jan. 7th. There seems to be nothing about Christmas time.

With love always,

CELIA.

THE TEMPLE PRESS CUTTING OFFICES.

Danes Inn House,
265, Strand, London, W.C.2.

Cutting from: *The Times,* 29.6.25.

MARRIAGES

Dr. G. E. G. CATLIN and Miss VERA BRITTAIN

The marriage took place, at St. James's Church, Spanish Place, on Saturday, of Dr. George Edward Gordon Catlin, of Cornell University, U S.A., only son of the Rev. G. E. Catlin, 16, Northmoor Road, Oxford, and the late Mrs. Catlin, and Miss Vera Brittain, of 117, Wymering Mansions, W.9, only surviving child of Mr. and Mrs. T. A. Brittain, 10, Oakwood Court, Kensington, W 14.

The bride, who was given away by her father, wore a gown of ivory satin over pale pink georgette, and a long tulle veil arranged to form a train, and caught up with orange blossom and myrtle. She carried a bouquet of pale pink roses, and her ornaments were a pearl and gold bracelet (the gift of the bridegroom), and a pearl, gold and platinum necklace (the gift of the bridesmaid). Miss Winifred Holtby was in attendance, and her frock of pastel blue marocain was worn with a cloak, lined with mauve georgette, and a blue hat with long mauve feathers. The Earl of Stamford was best man, and Father Bede Jarrett officiated.

A reception was held afterwards at the De Vere Hotel, and the bride and bridegroom later left for the Continent.

MY DEAREST ROSALIND,

A long letter from you this week, telling me of many alarms and excursions. A headmistress's life is indeed no sinecure. I hope that Miss W. will really get quite better. She was one of the people that you liked, wasn't she? One of the most difficult things about community life, I think, is this intense personal relationship—every one demanding so much. From what I hear it is equally trying in a boys' school. A young man called M. R. teaches in a very large and up-to-date boys' preparatory school not far from London. He is Cambridge, athletic, good-looking—and at first liked the school. Now he is trying to get away because he cannot stand the personal complications in which he is being involved. Some masters demand too much friendship, are jealous, resentful. I am rather glad that it is not only women who are like this. The remedy? I don't know. Is it as much contact with the outside world as possible? In the various mistresses' sitting-rooms to which I have access by reason of visiting their schools, I seem to find the happiest staffs among those who are able, by the situation of the school, to meet outside people. Especially when women can meet men, and men women. But it's not always possible. St. Monica's, for instance, away in the country in its own lovely grounds—and Langford Grove, and Hayes. Hayes boards its mistresses out quite a lot, in different cottages, and has heaps of tea parties, etc., and tennis with the neighbouring world. But so do you, I gather. Yours was never the way of isolation. And so does Miss Fowler of Scarborough. But I saw how delighted she was when an old college friend, nothing to do with the school, came and settled in Scarborough.

I told you in my last letter that I have definitely booked my passage in the *Balranald* for January 7th. It's a nuisance that it's so late, but I could not leave before Dec. 20th in

350

any case, because of the term here—and some of my children are taking examinations. And then there are no boats over Christmas. So I had to fix it. I wish I could have come to your house at Port Alfred. But what about the Easter holidays? You do have Easter holidays, don't you? Can't I manage to be with you then? I can fix in my lectures, etc., so as to suit. That would be so lovely. There is so much to say and see. I don't mind where you are, so long as it's you.

Mrs. Lewis is sending me papers from South Africa with reviews of *The Harp*. I am so glad that it is going so well there. Did I tell you how delighted Hodder & Stoughton were with her next book *The Flying Emerald*? They seem to think that it might be a best-seller.

Your letters make me think that I escape half the stress of life by avoiding a community life. But I don't think I should be much good in one. It takes up so much time, and if my real business at present is to learn and to write, I suppose that I must stick to it. But all this clash of personality, these emergencies—they are interesting somehow —the stuff of life in a way that books are not.

I hear from G. and Vera in Vienna. They were curiously made for one another, and should find much richness in their relationship.

Last night I went to Galsworthy's new play *The Show*. Not really frightfully good, though competent like all his plays. This is an indictment of the craving for publicity which turns private tragedy into a public amusement. A young flying man, apparently happily married, commits suicide. The newspapers and the police probe all the details and expose the irrelevant with the relevant. There's a good inquest scene, with jury complete. But somehow the genuine thrill never quite gets through.

I must go. Much love always,

CELIA.

ROSALIND DEAR,

Such wonderful sunshine we are having that you wouldn't know London. It is glorious. We really sit about in parks and on balconies and are warm, and every one wears light clothes—except the men, who, poor dears, think it somehow indecent to be cool. I saw to-day a creature in a white shirt and a cumberband (is that what you call those tummy sash things to elevate the trousers?) but he looked a self-conscious sort of specimen and turned out to be a language master. Though why they should dress like Highland deer stalking in a Scotch mist, during the first summer that I remember in London, the Almighty knoweth. Or perhaps He knoweth. Perhaps, according to the nominalist theory of divine consciousness, He knows only those things which are good and so in accordance with His own perfect capacity for knowledge. I've been reading a good deal of nominalism lately. Only one more lecture and then I've done. I've been hurling myself at my courses for next term, so that I can write at my novel during the holidays.

Oh, Rosalind, it's been such fun—my C14 lectures. I was at one till three this morning, but I've done a whole other one since then, and bought a dress, and ordered some books, and watered Mrs. Brittain's petunias at Oakwood Court, and prepared and given a lecture on Travelling in Central Europe at Hounslow—and several other things—and it's 10.15 p.m.

At the lecture a queer thing happened. It was to the Hounslow Branch of the League of Nations Union, and I was talking about Germany and so forth, as one sees them when travelling. Afterwards, a girl came up to me, speaking in broken English, and it appears that she is Fraulein Wirth, a German teacher, doing exactly the same thing in England as Vera and I did in Germany. She had been told not to come—as we were told not to go to Germany. She had been told that the English would not be nice to her—as we were told about the Germans—and she had been run off her legs with invitations. Then she had asked to hear a League of Nations Union meeting, and had been sent to hear me—give an exactly reciprocal account of her experiences. We met and were very much amused with one another, and are going to dine together on Monday and to see the *Beggar's Opera* by way of diversion after a course of Houses of Parliament, Law Courts and schools.

Did you ever meet Lady Guggisburg—of the Gold Coast? I dined last night with her sister—a charming woman.

I am going to spend the week-end at St. Monica's editing their school magazine and being entertained to dinner by the Cicero Club—a most flourishing organisation, which I founded quite by chance when teaching there, but which seems to have flourished like a green bay tree since I left.

Now I must go and finish a sort of story I am writing for the magazine page of the *Manchester Guardian* about a woman who "took politics" after serving on a jury.

Au revoir—dearest Rosalind.

I love you,

CELIA.

Bainesse,
Cottingham,
Yorkshire, July 31st.

DEAREST ROSALIND,

I'll try to catch the mail this week, having missed it last. I am back at home, having hurried up on hearing that two of my family had mumps, and that things were pretty hectic. I arrive to find the mumps mild and recovering, and every one quite cheerful. The trying part is that just with the letter that brought me here (they did not ask me to come, only seemed to want to have me) came another from Stella Benson asking me to meet her to-day in London.

i have looked forward so much to seeing her when she came to England. However, I may do so yet. These little things will happen.

Now that I am here, I can at least write. I am at work on *The Runners*. I've got the story all out. It's my style that is damnable—too heavy and somehow artificial. I keep hearing the only-too-just criticism that Gerald Gould made of *The Crowded Street*. "Patient and entirely convincing detail . . . an admirable book, but with no pretensions to genius." Of course I have no pretensions to genius, but it's the very devil being told as much. Your book, too, Rosalind. This must be shorter, more vivid, more exciting, but not romantic. I'm off romance. Yet darned if when I write it the romance won't come breaking through, like the cheerfulness of what d'you call 'im. The real fun is the reading. C. G. Mallet has brought out an enchanting history of medieval Oxford—and then there are Wycliffe's own works. Scholasticism is so entertaining. I wade through the queer Latin of *De Actibus Animi*. Such a pother about a ha'porth of pins.

Have just read *The Constant Nymph*. Did I tell you I was at Oxford with Margaret Kennedy? Her third year at Somerville and my first. An admirable book—beautiful—very nearly great. She will be great, I think. I found it most moving. What a year of fiction writers we were—Margaret Kennedy, Dorothy Sayers, Sylvia Thomson Hilda Reid, Vera and I. Well, well. Oxford doesn't like us. We aren't "scholarly"—but my word, I've done better and more scholarly work reading for my Wycliffe book, I'll bet, than half a hundred of their pet lambs in horn-rimmed spectacles who write theses on the Personnel of the Commons in the First Four Years of the Reign of Henry VI., and so forth. If it doesn't come out right, it'll be my fault as an artist rather than a scholar. I feel rampant with energy and love for it—but it won't last, this mood. To-day, for instance, I must break off to go with father to see mother presented to Princess Mary and

354

her husband. To-morrow my cousin is married, and next day I spent with Grace. Would I could write at night—I only sleep.

My article on the schools comes out to-day. I hope it does some good—I want it to rouse a correspondence.

My dear love always,

CELIA.

1925
August to End

Bainesse,
Cottingham,
Yorkshire, August, 5th.

DEAREST ROSALIND,

Your little note was forwarded here this morning. I hope that my letters have been going all right; I think that I have written every week, but I know that I missed one mail.

I am opening a bazaar to-morrow at a market town called Market Weighton near here. It is my first, but I have a horrid suspicion that it may not be my last. Two years ago Lady Rhondda bet me I'd open a bazaar before I was thirty, and I scorned her insinuations. It is a base affliction.

I really have no news. I am writing, sleeping, motoring, playing tennis, and carrying an occasional tray to an invalid—oh, yes, and struggling greatly with my German lessons, but my pronunciation ends in a choke and a spit. I cannot do the "ch." So I really am very dull as a correspondent—like the happy land, having no history.

But I had a horrid shock the other day, reading in the *Lady* or something an article about South African fashions. It said "nobody here thinks of wearing simple cottons. The 'little tub frock' is unknown. We dress for eleven o'clock tea as for a garden party, and wear full evening dress for dinner every night." For the Lord's sake, Rosalind, tell me it isn't true. I have exactly one evening dress. It has been dyed and twice renovated. It is already in pieces, and I'm spending my autumn dress money on going to the Assembly at Geneva again. I thought it might be more useful. This is horrible. Do write and reassure me or I shall paint myself with woad and wear nothing but your feather stole (which, by the way, is a lamb and much admired).

I have had my whiskers permanently waved with an article in the *Manchester Guardian*. I shall have to write another couple if I want an evening dress.

359

We have a tortoise called Fido. It is beautiful and is beloved. Its head is old as the psalms and wrinkled and wise. It is master of the garden and the whole family loves it.

My family send their love to you. They always remember you with love and admiration.

CELIA.

East Witton,
Middleham, August 12.

DEAREST ROSALIND,

Mother and I are back staying in the village where she was born up in Wensleydale. The village encircles a green, running up the dale, with wooded hills rising each side to the moors. The cottage where we stay belongs to my Aunt Jane. She is rather beautiful, lives quite alone, making her tiny garden blossom like a rose garden in the wilderness, keeps all her neighbours in order with her biting tongue, and is loved and respected by them all. Her front parlour is a delicious place, full of curiously irrelevant bits of furniture and china. She will tell a long history of each chair or spindle-legged table. The *pièce de resistance* is a musical box, standing in a walnut wood cabinet. It came from Switzerland nearly sixty years ago, and cost seventy guineas. It plays tunes from four different cylinders, and is worked by a brass handle which you pump up and down. From its rather large and flamboyant exterior comes the sweetest little tinkling music, playing with a million liquid turns and trills "The Last Rose of Summer," "My Pretty Jane," "Auld Robin Gray," and other favourites. It is one of the prettiest things I ever heard.

There was a funeral in the village yesterday, and just before it passed we had to draw down all the front blinds, and then peek through them to see the procession marching to the church. Directly they are in the churchyard, up go the blinds again, and the best china is brought out, and the tea table set in the front parlour, and then callers on the

360

way back from the funeral come dropping in to discuss the ways of the corpse and drink tea and eat sponge cake, and a sort of bread-cake made with double spices.

A severe lady, my aunt. She disapproves of novels, but reads a cookery book, the Bible, a *History of British Flora*, and *Select Speeches of Famous Orators*. She can quote Cato on the Rights of Women, and John Eliot on the Liberty of the Subject. She knows all about Solomon and Micah and Haggai, and the Leguminosae Family, and what grasses flower when, and she can make ointments from house-leek and crab-apple.

I have no more paper.

Much love,

CELIA.

Bainesse,
Cottingham,
Yorkshire, August 25.

DEAREST ROSALIND,

I was delighted to have your letter—delayed in London for deficiency of stamps or something—all about your adventures trekking with Martha[1] and Miss H. I am so glad that the experiment turned out so well and that among the kraals and lions you found a cure for nerves. I can quite believe that drastic treatment sometimes does the best work. I wonder if a course of Martha and trekking would help the woman we have here—a trained nurse belonging to an association for nursing the poor people in their own homes which mother is running here in the East Riding. This nurse collapsed just after nursing a Cottingham case in a cottage about a mile away. I went for her in a taxi, and she was brought here fainting and completely done up—but when we got her here we found that it is largely hysteria. She is quite friendless; her people are all dead, and she seems to have quarrelled with her friends. She is really very delicate, but makes the most of her quite genuine com-

[1]Rosalind's car.

plaints—is not a very satisfactory nurse, not much liked by her patients—and yet such a pathetic little thing, and with a very sad story. These difficult people who are their own worst enemies are so horribly pathetic. One can't help them much. The matron has telephoned "For goodness sake don't send her back to the home." She upsets the other nurses. Mother will keep her here until she is well enough to take a case again. Yet what a prospect. She says that she would like to travel—wants to come to South Africa. But I suppose that if she is always sick and in trouble here, she will be there. There's plenty of work for a trained children's nurse here—and they say she is good at her job but so difficult to live with that no one wants her for long. I have been playing "Hard-hearted Hannah" with her, and she is beginning to sit up and laugh. But we can't play with her for ever. I think that I shall have to send her to Africa to meet a couple of lions!

Mother really keeps an amazing collection. She has at present this sick nurse, a tubercular baby of nine months, an unemployed boy from South Africa, and a family of four children and their mother—who are sort of distant cousins of ours. The son is a cripple, and the eldest girl twelve. She seems to manage them all quite unperturbed, and grows younger and more delightful to live with every month. She has taken to smoking and waving her hair, and is as full of vitality as a girl of twenty —much more so than most girls.

It is very good of you to say that you'll send me a time-table. That would be a great help, I am sure. I am seeing the League of Nations Union people in a day or two, and then I shall know more definitely just what I am doing. What a shame that you only have ten days at Easter—but I'm hoping that I may be with you for those ten days, anyway. There will be such lots to say and do. And I am longing to see your school.

Such lots to do before then, though. My Notting Hill children to chaperon into Oxford. I am hoping for at least one scholarship. Sonia Hambourg, the pianist Mark Hambourg's daughter, is really brilliant and has the great advantage of having travelled over nearly all Europe, of having met with statesmen and musicians, of being able to speak four languages fluently, and of quite exceptional brains. She wants to read History at Somerville. Then I have three places—Surrey, Faversham and Malden for lectures, and some of Vera's League of Nations Union work besides my own; but it will be fun and very interesting—and still have time to finish my book, I think. It has been writing itself this last month—and I do not know how bad or how good, but anyway it is three-quarters finished, all but the revision, and has been most exciting to do. Even if no one else ever enjoys reading it, I have enjoyed writing it as I never enjoyed anything else in my life, I think. I never knew how absorbing it would be. Well, pseudo-historical romances are not very popular, and I cannot see a novel dealing mostly with the Nominalist v. Realist scholastic controversy proving a best-seller. So it is as well that I have had some satisfaction out of it. I have two short stories coming out this week, and a leading article—and five more articles and two stories accepted for September.

I am reading *Lavengro* and *Romany Rye*, and cannot think why I never discovered them before. What a joy is their strange, pungent flavour. I like Borrow's prejudices too. A nice, juicy, unapologetic prejudice is good company in a book, and prevents one from being sleepy. His antipapal bias does very well as a stimulant to his magnificent descriptions. Laus Tibi, Domine, who sendest such a book to me. Don't you want to say grace for a good book?·

Now I must go. I am taking the chair at a meeting at Driffield for Celia Macdonald, who is lecturing on her Empire Tour. She runs this Colonial Hospitality League that we get our medical students from. Our last guest, did I tell you? was Jan Stein de Wet Moll, whose father fought with the Boers and whose brother was killed fighting against us, and who had a nervous breakdown here and was nursed by mother, and now has a great love for England. Edith passed through Manchester, where Mollski is now, on her way to Blackpool with Margaret for a holiday, and lost her luggage there. Moll appeared at Bolton with the missing trunks—good fellow—and a broad grin all over his face.

Au revoir, dearest Rosalind,

CELIA.

117, Wymering Mansions,
Elgin Avenue, W.9,
September 1st, 1925. 2 a.m.

MY VERY DEAR ROSALIND,

I had your letter-card this week, in which you tell me how Miss Thompson has been staying with you. Also you spoke of the Bishop asking you to write an account of your tour. I hope that you will, and that you will send me a copy if you do. I am sending this week to you a short story that may amuse you—it is one of a series of Yorkshire things that are appearing in the *New Leader* and the *Manchester Guardian*, and that later I hope to make into a book of Anderby Tales.

I am sending you, too, a rough itinerary as far as I can make it out of my South African tour. It is, of course, very much subject to alteration. I will try to explain, though, why it is as it is. My boat only goes to Cape Town, but it gets me a very much reduced ticket via Kimberley to Durban. I have no lecturing as far as I know in Kimberley, but I want to see Bridgewater. So if she will be there then, I thought it a good idea to take Kimberley on my way. Then I go straight to Durban, where the temporarily most "headquarters" League of Nations Union Branch is in South Africa. There is no real headquarters. The branches are all unco-ordinated there. They are hoping to co-ordinate them.

But I gather that (a) political difficulties; (b) difficulties of choosing a centre—complicate this. I go there, and lecture there and round about wherever sent by Mrs. Mabel Palmer.

From there I want to go up to Pretoria to see you, if you can have me then, and to spend the rest of February and March round about Pretoria and Johannesburg. Mrs. Lewis has asked me to stay with her at Johannesburg, and so has Mrs. Scandrett, and so has Mr. Afford, whose son is now living with mother and father. So that while you are engaged, I can always slip off to Johannesburg, where Mr. Merkin is to arrange lectures for me. The Rev. S. M. Bishop I see lives in Pretoria in Arcadia—probably you know nearly all these people. I don't know when your Easter holidays are, but I see that Easter is about April 4th; I therefore temporarily imagine that they will be over about the 12th. I would love to spend those with you before I move south. The other places you see.

The arrangement for lectures is that the Overseas Secretary here arranges with the South African secretaries to fix up lectures for about the dates I say I shall be there, and arranges hospitality for those towns where I don't know any one. A friend of Miss Fowler's has offered to put me up at Cape Town, and a friend of the Afford's there, a Mrs. Graham, has offered to run me over to Stellenbosch. In Bloemfontein I know a family of Dutch South Africans —the De Wet Molls. They were violent Nationalists. Stein, our friend, was a brilliant young medical student. He came to Manchester with a scholarship, had a nervous breakdown there, was sent to Cottingham by the Colonial Hospitality League, and has stayed with us in his vacations mostly since. He takes his final exam this year. He is going to help me to meet some really violent Nationalists, he says, who will help me to understand the Nationalist point of view. So I shall only be with strangers for a few weeks— all the rest of the time with semi-friends. And I shall have as long as possible a time round about Pretoria—quite long enough for you to get tired of me—but I *do* so much look forward to seeing you.

I have had much help and friendliness from a very nice man at the South African Office in Trafalgar Square. He has given me a time-table, and lovely railway maps, and pamphlets and guide-books of every kind about all the places to which I am going. He was at Glen and knew the Newmans there slightly—went back to visit them last year. His name is Mr. G. E. Chittenden. I wonder if you know him. He is a South African, and simply overflowing with enthusiasm about the country and its possibilities.

If you have not already sent a time-table, please don't bother. Mr. Chittenden has given me one. I waste hours looking at it and at maps! I love maps and railway journeys.

I want to go: 1926, Africa; 1927, America; 1928, China. China really looks hopeful. On Monday a delightful thing happened, for Stella Benson came to tea with me. She is in England for a short time. She is nicer even than her books —kinder, less ruthless, extraordinarily personal and real somehow. But she looks horribly ill. She went round the world once just picking up jobs as she went. She said that it was just blundering from one mistake to another. In Japan she broke her shoulder and got pneumonia and flu, and spent all her money, and was pushed into a Russian refugee camp, when she could speak neither Russian nor Japanese. In India she never found a job and nearly starved —but she did see and talk to Ghandi and liked him. Now she is married to an Irishman, an official in the Chinese Customs. They are going to live miles away from any Europeans in a very cold part of Northern China, where you have to wear fur trousers and ride Russian horses. There is nothing else to do. Except that she seems to be really fond of her husband, it sounds horribly lonely. And he has to be away a good deal. She is ill much of the time, too, though she seems to take that quite as a matter of course. I often forget what a strange distance lies between people who are ill and well.

366

She asked me to go back with her and see China. I told her that I could not go this year, nor next, but I should try to work to go somehow the year after. I told her of my plan to work through the League of Nations Union all round the world. It gives one a sort of starting ground, a frame into which to set impressions, and a meeting ground for finding people. After that I suppose there are India and Australia—such hundreds of countries in the world. One could look and look for ever. But, frankly, I am more interested in people than in countries—how they think, and of what stuff is their civilisation made—in which way is it tending—how far is their method of life and environment responsible for their attainments—how far are these racial and intrinsic in their type of humanity. I suppose that this is partly the result of a historical and political training. I want especially to see schools. This question of how much schools can do is, I think, probably the most important in the world to-day. That is one of the reasons why your work fascinates me—quite apart from the fact that it is yours.

Darling Rosalind, I long to see you. Do not doubt that I love you always. Please, *please* don't go and be eaten by lions before I come.

CELIA.

I do hope that you will like my book. I am beginning to see it more clearly now, and how far it falls short of my notion of it. Yet they have been fine, ardent people to live with, and even if I have failed to do them justice, they have been better company than my Marshington ladies. I will bring it when I come.

My heart's love to you.

117, *Wymering Mansions,*
Elgin Avenue, W.9,
September 7th.

ROSALIND DEAR,

Will you forgive this typewritten letter? My fountain-pen is having a new nib put on him by Mr. W. H. Smith, and I am disconsolate without him, his locum tenens being called Relief by his makers, but bringing anything but relief to me.

I was delighted to have your dear letter this week actually advising me to do what I wrote last week to tell you that I had done, largely owing to fragmentary advice from you, and therefore not so surprising, I suppose. Yes, I am practically coming first to you. As I explained, I am going by train to Durban, but on a cheap ticket which will only cost about five pounds ten all the way from Cape Town to Durban via Kimberley, and supplied by the P. & O., who won't take me by sea. Just as well. I shall see more Africa.

As for you arranging lectures, why, you know I'd be more than grateful, and I am sure that no one could possibly know the ropes better. The League of Nations Union branches will, of course, fix up some, but I personally always like talking to schools best. One knows more easily, I think, what to say to children and young things. At least, I do in England, and one can be more informative and less propagandist, which I infinitely prefer, and anyway, I like going to schools. You have my very rough programme. You will see what you think is best to be done.

You do not say in your letter what part of April your ten days' holiday will be in. If it comes later than the time I allowed, do let me know and I will try to shift everything on a little. I should love it enormously. Even lions! But they scare me.

Martha leading
by a head.

368

I hope that if all my money-making schemes come off this autumn I shall come out quite rich and able to do any amount of travelling if I don't try to do it on too grand a scale. Is one permitted to go second class sometimes, or must one always be lordly and go first? I am now nearly as good a traveller by trains as I am a bad one by water. I can go all over bad European trains second class and keep fairly clean—though Hungarian trains are filthy beyond words. Every one will spit!

Another thing, do give me a word of advice about clothes. I want to go as light as possible. Miss Fowler says one coat and skirt for travelling, a mackintosh, a light sort of coat for wearing over cotton frocks, and then as many thin dresses as possible, the latter of non-crushing material as far as possible. Then I have two really elegant frocks for such occasions as giving your prizes (darling Rosalind, oughtn't you to get a big nob to do this?), thin underclothes, aertex variety, etc. Is this about right? What does one wear to push Martha about in?

Oh, Rosalind, I've got maps and maps and railway time-tables until my room looks like a Cooks' office. If you knew how much I want to come, and how terrified I am of the voyage, and how still more terrified of making a complete fool of myself, and how my longing and my terror combined prove a most exhilarating companion, you would laugh.

A slight complication may be that I have got that damned rheumatism that I developed at Oxford again. It makes me a little lame, but probably will have departed entirely by the end of the year. Anyway, I do not see why lame I should not enter into the kingdom. I am going quite regardless to Geneva on Friday, but of course that is a very easy journey. I won't be an old woman before my time. I won't.

I had a lovely meeting with Stella Benson. She is one of the most interesting and lovable people I ever came across. I am going to spend the morning at her house to-morrow going through her new book with her and one or two of her friends. She has scrapped most of the book, she says, and feels too depressed to embark on it again alone without some one telling her that it is worth while. It is so very encouraging to hear of people who can write books like hers scrapping them. Did you read *The Poor Man?*

Mrs. Millin's new book is making a huge success here. I am glad to think that she is nice.

Dearest Rosalind, I must go and alter a dress—a frivolous pursuit, I know, but I am turning all my spring wardrobe into an autumn one so as to have lots of money in South Africa.

I do love you. I am so excited about coming to see you. To-night it all seems so near.

WINIFRED.

GENTILITY

When vines go prancing hand in hand
Down sunny slopes of Southern land,
When reeling hops with tangled tresses
Splash crimson stains across their dresses,
And flaunting yellow dahlias try
To woo the Sun's enamoured eye,
    Where lately lolled the drunken sheaves
    In stooks as broad as browsing beeves,
    I hear a hymn of harvest born
    From Sabbath fields, all newly shorn.
    Now, sleek and smooth, they clearly feel
    That Emptiness is more genteel.

Do you like this absurd rhyme? I wrote it coming back to London in the train.

ROSALIND DEAR,

Yesterday I lay on my back on the top of a real mountain, not a very big one, it is true, but one could look straight up to Mont Blanc and the Alps on one side, or across the Rhône to the Jura Mountains on the other. It was rather like being in heaven. It was very high up, and all the kingdoms of the earth, very small and clean, were spread neatly below. One could lie on a carpet of smooth green turf, pricked out with little flowers like a Fra Angelica fresco—white wild thyme, and starry yellow St. John's Wort, and various attractive lichens with small red and yellow flowers, and heather in pinkish tints, and very small briar plants, each plant as small as a gentian, and dwarf thistles with wide open faces. Then on the lower slopes were benign cows, like the blessed souls browsing in peace among the flowers, and making a happy sort of Sunday sound with their bells. And in the evening, as one climbed down again by a steep little path among the acacia trees, there was a sunset spread right across the sky—wild as an Apocalypse and nearly as terrifying. Huge battalions of rose red and fiery clouds marching like the hosts of the Lord above the mountains. And later still, as we walked into the quiet suburbs of Geneva, a clear green sky above the little flowering gardens, and a slender slip of a new moon. The suburbs have lovely names—Florresant, Vervier, Montier, Treize Arbres. It is at Treize Arbres that one drinks the most delectable chocolate in the world from tables spread with red and white checked cloths.

It is very cold, but most beautifully sunny, and the lake a frosty blue capped with white. I travelled straight here, and arrived in the middle of the morning, but after a bath I was perfectly well revived, and went straight to hear Nansen's speech on Armenian refugees.

In my carriage from Calais were a Russian woman, a

Greek boy and three Arabs. Two of the Arabs were Roman Catholic priests and missionaries in Palestine. They had come to Europe for the Holy Year to be blessed by the Pope, and had completed their European pilgrimage by going to Blackpool! They did not like Blackpool. "*Il y a trop de gens,*" one said, and the young girls there had laughed at them. "Why? why? do they think that we are Jews?" As a matter of fact, with their benign, brown-bearded faces and gold-rimmed spectacles peering above their black cassocks, they might be anything. Their escort was a cousin—a Government official in a very important position, he told me. It transpired, however, that he is a customs inspector at one of the provincial frontiers—an amusing, talkative little man, very proud of his knowledge of English. He told me that he would be glad to return to Palestine, for the separation from his family was beginning to tell upon him. "Oh," said I, "you have a family then?" "Yes," said he proudly, "seven—three girls and four boys, from ages three to eighteen. But," he added sternly, "in Europe you do not approve of large families." And he looked at me accusingly —whether because he suspected me of disapproving of his, or whether he blamed me for not having produced one myself, I do not know.

The Protocol that Chamberlain has tried to freeze out of existence is still the most live thing. I heard this morning Count Apponyi of Hungary give, in spite of his seventy-seven years, a wonderful speech lasting over an hour, in a voice that never faltered, in a language not his own, and speaking without notes. The hall was packed to hear him, and I had the pleasure of standing on the toes of Professor Webster, who viva-ed me disastrously in schools, in order to get a better view.

Forgive me for these blots and things. This is a new pen which Vera gave me just before she left for America, but I always seem to play havoc with all pens. They don't like my writing or something, and are false to me just when I most need them.

I heard before I came here that the boat on which I was to sail on January 7th is hung up indefinitely in an Australian port. I don't know what I am going to do yet, but shall go to the shipping company's office as soon as I get to London and try for another berth. But alas, for my beautiful cabin all to myself, where I could be sick in the blessed luxury of privacy. I fear that that has gone!

It is so cold, and they have not begun to heat the pension yet. I must go to bed and try to get warm there. I hear for my comfort that it is snowing in London—in September! What a world!

Rosalind, if I find that it cold too when I come to Africa, I shall just weep.

With my dear love to you,

CELIA.

117, Wymering Mansions,
Elgin Avenue, W.9,
October 1st.

DARLING ROSALIND,

We are starting October with a wonderful Saint Martin's Summer. At least I suppose it was Saint Martin, or was it Saint Michael? It must have been some saint, for no power of evil could possibly give to us these golden, mellow afternoons, this delicious softness yet freshness of the air, this warmth where we may go out even now in October in short-sleeved cotton dresses in the daytime and not be cold. London is all yellow plane trees and orange sycamores and poplars still green, and the men in the street wheel barrows of bronze and gold chrysanthemums, and it is a very lovely world.

I cannot believe that it is less than a week since I came back to London. I seem to have done so much. I am living quite alone at present. My poor Nursie has asthma and is at home in Yorkshire. She caught cold on her holiday and bronchitis and asthma followed. I do not mind being alone at all. I cook my meals over the gas stove and brush my floors and get myself all ready before about half-past nine. Then I work at my book or go to teach my three hopefuls who are taking their Somerville entrance. One, Sonia Hambourg, won a State Scholarship this summer. She is brilliant and lovely to teach—much cleverer than I, which is a nuisance for me and means a lot of work, because she will read things that I never seem to have time for. These bright babes! If only they knew what a glorious trial they are to their poor teachers, but what fun to teach.

Apropos of teaching, St. Monica's has asked me again to go into partnership, and take on the school in about five years on my own. No, no, no. I will not settle down. I will not. You don't know of any one really nice, who will take on a flourishing private school in a lovely part of Surrey? Ninety girls, increasing every year, and a waiting list. Nice, healthy spirit. High fees. Good type of children (but too rich for my taste). Sure and comfortable living. Charming house. Very good reports from the Board of Education. There! there's an offer. But it is difficult to say No to people who have always been so kind to me and who, incidentally, have helped me to work up the connection with other places that enables me to say No so easily. But I must keep free.

I have been to the P. & O. and got a passage in a boat that they hope will sail at the beginning of January, but they do not know. My former boat won't sail till February or March, and this may be delayed. It is not such a nice berth, but of course they are all full, such as do sail. I have no doubt that I shall survive. Why, after all, should I be more comfortable than any one else? I am far more robust than most. Incidentally, I have found to my joy that my lameness which one silly doctor said was rheumatism was really a slipped ligature or something and has now gone in, and unless it comes out again or anything, I need not have any more trouble with it. I hate limping and not being able to walk, but in Switzerland I did one really quite good climb with no evil effects. Hurrah!

374

Have you read *Orphan Island*? Satire gets a bit thin at times, and I did not think the whole tale very well sustained. Rose Macaulay seems to hurry over her plots, and then just to let them work themselves out at the end, often rather raggedly. But the island was lovely—palm trees and breadfruit, mangoes and surf. Do you have all those nice things in Africa, or must I go on to a South Sea Island afterwards?

My book has only one more chapter in its first draft. I am frightened of hurrying it, yet after all, I suppose that I have been doing bits for about five years, so one can't really call that hurrying. But now that the end is coming near I sweat at nights for fear lest it may be all rot. I haven't the smallest idea about it except that it strikes me as being rather melancholy and melodramatic. But melodrama will be at least a change from *The Crowded Street*, which my reviewers tell me was rather dull. Everybody dies in my present book, which is not really sad. After all, it simply means that I take the tale on rather further than most. We hardly ever any of us write about immortals, so I suppose that all heroines die one day. Mine, however, kills its heroine in the first quarter, and the hero is most of the time over fifty. But I can't help that. Do you know any good swears with a nice round medieval sound? I feel that mine are rather anæmic, and the best that one can pick up in books are really hardly printable, especially by John Lane, which is a very proper firm. Froissart has some good ones, but not for ladies.

I am reading *Madame Bovary* for the first time. I think that it is rather nice. It props well against my loaf when I take my solitary meals. Oh, but what a loaf! I called on the baker when I returned and asked him to deliver bread as usual at the flat, and lo and behold! last Saturday outside my door appears a creature large as a footstool, through which I am solemnly plodding. I have not yet got half through and it is Thursday. Day after day I have to call at the baker's and say "Please don't send me another loaf yet." But the longer it lasts the longer it will last, if you know

375

what I mean, for the less I feel capable of eating at a sitting. Probably when I leave for South Africa there will still be a crust for the mice. I am inviting an aunt here to tea, and shall have to make her toast! But, having been reared on the Do Not Waste Bread principle, I feel that I must go through with it till the end.

I am going to Liverpool on the 29th. Shall I give it your love? I have never seen the Belvedere School yet.

I am just off to tea with my mistresses at Notting Hill. They are frightfully nice to me. I do think that women are nice to work with. When I came back they sent me a big bunch of chrysanthemums. And I do nothing at all there but draw more money than most of them who work far harder and have lots more experience and are much older than I. I do not see the justice of the world. To him that hath it is always being given, and in spite of the good authority upon which we hear that this should be so, I cannot think it right.

Au revoir, darling Rosalind. I so much long to see you.

CELIA.

117, *Wymering Mansions*,
Elgin Avenue, W.9,
October 7th.

DEAREST ROSALIND,

I am sending you a sample of a new form of poetry book that we are now bringing out for sixpence—rather nice, I think. And I do like Blunden. I was up at Oxford with him, and he was one of a little coterie of poets who used to live nominally at Queen's but actually, I think, on Boar's Hill at the feet of John Masefield. He has a beautifully earthy and observant gift. I wonder very much how he likes Japan—so far removed from his English countryside.

I also send you an article about your Miss Tuke, which I did not write, and part of an article on the League, which I did. I do not know when they will reach you, for I do not know how the mails are going. I have not heard from you for some time, but that again is the fault of the strike, I think. I watch the paper for news of my Bettance and hope that she comes here in time to sail again in January. I have now heard from Vera that her ship was run to Montreal by a scratch crew, which got seasick in a gale half-way over the Atlantic and the stewards and engineers had to turn stoker. However, they actually did arrive safely, which was the main thing, though somewhat unnecessarily tossed about.

And now it is really autumn, and a rainy night—and I am going to see the Torchlight Tattoo at Wembley with Mrs. Brittain unless the rain puts out the torches. I believe that it is a fine sight, but I dislike intensely the sentimental gush that people are beginning to talk here about it and the army—as though war were a matter of pretty drilling in the Wembley Stadium. I cannot forget that ride over the battlefields with Pugh and Silver and Bridgewater in the colonel's car. If only we would keep an army that never had to fight, but only drilled like the Czech Sokals, or camped out in orchards like Waacs. I wish that we all did more drill. I should like to be compulsorily drilled twice a week. I should like to feel my body all hard and fit and pliant, and I love the rythmic motion of many people moving together with beautiful precision. The Czechs and Germans are doing it. The German children have a camp where they live in sort of bathing costumes and go to drill and live out of doors for a month at a time in the summer. They come back burnt brown and still go on with their drilling.

I went to see Eugene O'Neill's play, *The Emperor Jones*, last Saturday. It was extraordinarily impressive, with the negro, Paul Robeson, in the chief part—a huge, magnificent creature, with a lovely voice and an exceedingly good dramatic gift. As his civilisation was stripped from him with his clothes, and he became again a dark, primitive, terror-stricken creature, the effect was uncannily real. I send

377

you Cicely Hamilton's comments, which are better than mine.

Grace is going to have a baby in April, so I shall be a real aunt as well as an adopted one. They want a boy. I should like a niece. However, aunts and their desires are very secondary considerations at such times, although, all desires being purely fortuitous, they may possibly override the prejudices of the parents. Mother is pleased and so, of course, is Grace. She always wanted babies. I began to fear lest Fate should be ironical and withhold them from her.

Much, much love to you, sweet Rosalind,

CELIA.

117, Wymering Mansions,
Elgin Avenue, W.9,
October 20th.

DARLING ROSALIND,

So you are dressy. Well, well. I'll do my best not to disgrace you, and I always wear silk stockings in any case.

You will have got my letter by now about the time-table, and seen that I propose to hang about until Easter between Durban, Johannesburg and Pretoria, so that of course if you want me and think me grand enough I will give your prizes—and I won't lecture your children unless they want me to. I want to have this time before I plunge into the lecture tour proper. It will help me to feel my feet and to learn things about you all. I seem to be learning a lot already—Mr. Manning and Mr. Smit—your High Commissioner—were most illuminating. They have quite made me realise why you groan that the League of Nations Union in South Africa is "stuffily respectable." It seems to be all Bishops and Reverends and "good-workish" women. Poor things! Of course there could not really be anything in the world less stuffy than the League of Nations. It breaks down barriers. Stuffiness creates them. It widens

378

horizons. Stuffiness narrows them. But your L. of N. Union seems to be, with a few exceptions, run by stuffy people. Mr. Smit nearly had apoplexy when I told him of my Hampstead meetings outside public-houses, answering the questions of the ordinary man in the street. He seemed to think us quite mad! I promised, however, to be decorous in South Africa; and he is being awfully nice to me. But is it true that you are on drawing-room behaviour all day? My South African young men friends—Colin and Stein and the rest of 'em—are so terribly conventional. They send ten shirts a week to the wash, talk about "the lower classes," and are horrified at the idea of washing up, or of my travelling in an all-one-class steamer. I suppose that it is the effect of living in a country on a basis of native labour. Australians are not like that. The time-table Mr. Chittenden gave me was a revelation, with its white men mustn't do this, that and the other. As soon as you have artificial inhibitions of any kind, it is not surprising that you get stuffy. Well, well. I shall see, I suppose. And it will all be frightfully interesting.

I saw Lady Rhondda yesterday, and we were talking about South Africa. She said, "I want to give you an introduction to a friend of mine—a very charming and original and open-minded person, whom I am sure you will like." She went and wrote a card and came back with it, and it was to Heyworth! I could not help exclaiming. I had not realised that they knew each other well, but now I remember that you did mention something about it.

I am still uncertain about my date of sailing. I have changed my berth twice, and may have to change on to another line. I'll try Blue Funnel, I think, if I can get my money back from the P. & O. But they are awfully decent about it. They can't help the strike—and the young man with whom I deal shares your opinion, I think, as to the real culprits. I shall get out in January sometime, I suppose. I can't come earlier because I do want to get my book into the press first. It is at the moment my absorbing

379

joy and agony. I feel that the theme is good, but I also feel my own inadequacy to deal with it.

I am just off to Liverpool to give two lectures to-night and back to-morrow—a bad cold in my head, and don't know how to make my voice last—but one generally does somehow. Thank goodness I haven't to sing it!

I have seen the stage version of *Tess of the d'Urbervilles*. Splendid acting, but the play too much compressed.

I love you dearly. I love your letters, especially when they are explosive. When you have hurled imprecations at my League of Nations Union, I always go out and give my best lectures like—

> " Dr. Drury
> All in a fury."

passionately in defence of my beloved! So I have much to be thankful to you for, and perhaps so have my audiences, who find me not so dull as I might otherwise be. A woman came to me the other day and told me that she had been to hear me speak eleven times at different meetings. I gaped and said that there was no compulsion! I tell you this not in vanity but in gratitude. You wake me up more than any one.

Darling Rosalind—I am perverse and perhaps horrid to you, but I do love you. I long to see you.

CELIA.

117, Wymering Mansions,
Elgin Avenue, W.9,
Oct. 21st.

ROSALIND DARLING,

I have an idea that my letter that I wrote yesterday was not nearly nice enough. That is the worst of writing in a hurry. So often when I sit down to scribble to you, with your last letter beside me, I find myself hitting upon just

380

the one rather contentious point and letting fly at that, while disregarding everything else, and then leaving no time for all the rest that I might say. It was about "stuffy respectability," wasn't it? I really don't think that we are like that here. We are too various in our types and kinds. But I haven't any business to suggest what you may or may not be in South Africa.

I think about you so much. I wonder if you know how often I picture you and talk to you in my head and about you to other people. My family feel that you are their special friend, and frequently say that they like you best of all my friends, although they saw you so little; but I read them bits from my letters about you.

Do you like *The Singing City* in Brailsford's version? My own was wilder but less intelligible. I seem to have broken out into poetry a good deal lately. It is all the rather insignificant brief variety, but it sings itself into my head on little tunes—therefore I write. A harmless occupation at least.

I have just got back from Liverpool—I went up yesterday, gave two lectures in a rather squeaky voice, but they said they could hear; got wet through twice, and this morning woke up with my cold practically gone. Wasn't that a rather unique cure? I love my Macdonald family with whom I stay there. The father is a Quaker, a socialist, and the most peppery firebrand you can imagine. I first met him damning the whole League of Nations Union at a Summer School, and fell in love at once with his uncompromising furies. Then we have met often. I am going again in December. One of his daughters, Bessie Macdonald, came to the Belvedere School just before you left and remembers you.

The dahlias in Hyde Park are a perfect glory. I stood watching them on Sunday quite enchanted by colour and blaze of warm light. It was a coldish day, but one could really warm oneself by that fiery heat of flame and crimson and yellow.

I have to change my ship *again*, I hear, but I'll get out,

381

never fear. I'll take your advice and try Blue Funnel next.

I do love you. I do long to see you. Take care of yourself till I come.

CELIA.

117, Wymering Mansions,
Elgin Avenue, W.9,
October 28th.

DARLING ROSALIND,

It looks as though I shall have to sail Union Castle after all. No P. & O. nor Blue Funnel boat seem to be leaving in January, and the Union Castle can give me a berth of some kind, they say. Everything is at sixes and sevens over the strike. Well, I shall just have to submit, though I agree with you that I would rather not. But I do not want to wait until February simply to get another line. I do not yet know the date of my boat, but as far as the Union Castle know, it will be sometime early in January. I shall go straight to Durban and stay there for a little, then possibly to Kimberley to see Bridgewater, and then take the other dates as I sent you before—using until Easter to wander about and see things and people, and then later to work my way back to Cape Town lecturing.

I want a gramophone. I long for a gramophone. I have just heard at a friend's house enchanting music, Mozart and Scarlatti—clean, elegant, intricate harmonic patterns that cleanse the mind and purify the thoughts of their listeners. And I should like one to work with. The rule is, of course, that one has no possessions save to enable one to live decorously and to achieve one's work. Possessions are insidious. A whole flat to myself—as I have now, owing to the illness of Nursie, which made it impracticable to secure a lodger—full of possessions, is a snare. It is a trap. It prevents that pleasant feeling which I like best of being able to put all one's belongings into a suitcase and start for Siberia or Madrid or Salt Lake City at six o'clock to-morrow

382

morning before breakfast. I do possess, to my sorrow, a three years' lease on a flat, two carpets, three tables, an elegant array of pots and pans, three beds, and other minor articles of utility, including two wardrobes. But for none of these have I any peculiar affection. I could leave my kitchen steps or my chest of drawers to-morrow without a single backward glance. A gramophone, however, is different. It would constitute a claim, I fear, not only upon one's purse but upon one's passions. Like a library, it would hold by reason of its beauty, fragility and intimate companionship. All my life I have regretfully refrained from the accumulation of books entirely for the disturbing affections with which they bind me to their vicinity. I will pay four or five library subscriptions, but my own books would barely fill a packing-case.

And yet I love buying books. Nothing makes me feel more haughty. I bought 16s. worth last week, and have hardly been able to control my swelled head since. I walked proudly into Bumpus's—I like Bumpus partly because of his name, which appeals to me when I feel bumptious, partly because of his proximity to Marshall & Snelgrove's, than which I know of no London shop which can so cheaply make its customers feel lords of the earth. I say to the shopwalker, after half an hour's peaceful perusal of H. G. Wells' new novel and so forth, "Have you *The Flying Emerald* by Ethelreda Lewis? What? No? Oh, but you *must* have it. It is one of the most important novels of the season. Published by Hodder & Stoughton. You haven't? Yes, of course, send it to me. Miss Holtby—Miss Winifred Holtby—Yes—and—er—Stella Benson's *Little World*? I suppose that you have *that*?" And so on. Oh, I bully them. Contrast my arrogance to Bumpus's with my humility to Messrs. Marshall & Snelgrove or Debenham, before whose brown-silk-robed young ladies I cringe in a positive panic of humility, hoping that my shappe-crêpe petticoat at least *looks* crêpe de Chine. But then I remember that Messrs. Bumpus draws 2s. 6d. from every 7s. 6d. for which my poor books sell, so I consider that I have paid hard cash for my right to a Vere de Vere hauteur.

I send you a copy of *The Flying Emerald* in case you have not seen it. It is a pleasant tale—though nothing like *The Harp* in beauty nor intensity. And I rather wish that the Prussian motif had been omitted. Though it may be true of individuals, there is too much vague prejudice founded merely upon a legend enforced on us during the war to make a quite arbitrary selection of Prussian ferocity wise just at this time. It is not easy to make some of my school children believe that the German nation is not one exclusively of devils, and novels like that make it no easier. A pity, for Jenny is charming and the story light and full of delightful things.

I have just come back from St. Monica's—a heavenly October day—the country at its richest for colour, and the air as crisp as apples. I am going to Faversham this afternoon—a University Extension Course on Fourteenth-Century England. I hate going there. I have never been to a place that I disliked more. Yet the people are kind. They take me to tea and seem to be quite interested. Yet somehow they depress me and chill me beyond words. It may be better to-day, but in an atmosphere of indefinable superiority I cannot lecture. I know that they hoped for an older man lecturer, and they were shocked by my youth. This does happen sometimes. I am considerably junior to the other extension lecturers, and my audiences sometimes feel sold—that they are not getting their money's worth. It is a high fee to pay. I am conscious of that; but I did not fix it. And my consciousness of their disappointment makes me lecture badly. I have spent days over the preparation of this course. It is my Wycliffe period: but three middle-aged men—who are responsible for financing the course—tried to catch me out on questions of medieval land tenure last week. One was a lawyer. I don't think that I said anything very foolish, but I felt the situation. I knew the thought of the committee: "Humph, in Oxford they are so grand they think nothing of us in Faversham. They put us off with a young girl who does not even know the clauses of the Customs of Kent." I didn't either. Kent wasn't one of my counties. Well, well. One day I shall be forty and then I can smile with the security of my years—and though my information will probably be no more accurate, as my brain becomes less assimilative the older I grow—my audiences will for the first time be impressed. The really amusing thing is that League of Nations Union audiences —who haven't paid £22 12s. 6d. to hear me lecture—love my youth, and are constantly commending it. Youth is the time for street oratory. Hyde Park Corner, and the riotous rough and tumble of heckling. I adore a nicely excitable and hostile Hyde Park crowd. They cry "Go it, young 'un! Let the lydy speak! Give 'er a chaunce, cawn't yer?" My University Extension audiences, decorous, well fed, conscious of having paid for the Higher Education, insist upon their full money's worth of culture, sobriety and academic honours. Isn't it amusing? But the pleasant disease of youth is too easily cured. If only they could see me with Mr. Bumpus!

I have some beautiful Russian boots. They will also do for riding-boots if I ever get a chance to ride in South Africa. I wonder if I have forgotten how to hold the reins. We must ride again together, can't we? I bet I'll split my breeches!

With love always,

CELIA.

117, Wymering Mansions,
Elgin Avenue, W.9,
Nov. 5th.

ROSALIND DEAR,

No letter from you for some time; but with the strike all the mails are upside down and you are probably not hearing from me, though I think that I have written every week.

I have at last definitely secured a berth—S.S. *Grantully Castle*, sailing from Tilbury Jan. 14th. I have tried every other line, but she seems to be about the only possibility. I am taking your advice and going by sea straight to Durban. I expect that I shall be there for a few days, until, say, the middle of February. I will then come up to either Johannesburg or Pretoria. I want to spend March just knocking about, seeing things and feeling my feet. I am looking forward so much to seeing you. Then after Easter I shall set off south on my travels.

I spent yesterday morning at the High Commissioner's office. I met Mr. Smit in Geneva first. He is Dutch, but, being High Commissioner here, has to be British in sympathy—more or less. But he is naturally in sympathy with his own countrymen. He began by being rather sceptical and patronising to me. Now he is awfully kind. He is giving me personal introductions to the chief education authorities in each Province, and asking them to let me talk to schools and to put me in touch with the headmasters and mistresses. He says that he knows them all—I suppose he does. Then he turned on his nice Mr. Chittenden—British South African—to go over my plans with me and to give me any help. They are all kind, especially after I had made it quite clear that I knew that people were bored with lectures, not very interested in the League and so forth, but that I wanted to know why. I wanted to know what the difficulties were. Here we are so much engrossed in the European aspect of things. After that they have all begun to be really kind and helpful.

386

I know that it will be hot; but other people have to face the heat and whatever does one know of a place if one only sees it at its best? If I am ill and cross, it's my own fault; but I would much rather see things on a Monday morning than live in a perpetually Sunday world.

I gave an explosion to you about University Extension lectures last week—and then went and enjoyed one immensely. A very nice headmistress of Faversham High School, who has, like me, been travelling in Hungary, took me to tea and I liked her. And then people seemed to like the lecture more, and I got less shy, and it was all quite pleasant. Such is the value of explosions.

I had a lovely week-end in Kent at Lady Rhondda's house. I like that woman. She has been astonishingly kind to me. The house is fifteenth-century—almost a barn, with oast houses in the garden. There is a field in front, and a view right across a brown, autumn valley to the Downs. We motored through country so tame and pretty that it looked like stage scenery specially set down for an act—the scene "A country house, in mild autumnal weather." St. John Ervine, the man who wrote *John Fergusson*, who ran at one time the Abbey Theatre in Dublin, and who is now dramatic critic for the *Observer*, was staying there with his charming wife. And Henry Ainley lived next door, and kept coming in. St. John Ervine is the best company of almost any man I ever met, with a fierce tongue, a kindly heart and a humour burning with vitality. Henry Ainley is one of the most charming people I ever met. It is impossible to be shy with him for two minutes. He has that astonishing gift of making every one to whom he talks feel as though they mattered very much to him in particular and the world in general. It is simply a manner, of course, but how charming. He told me to write a Yorkshire play for him. He was born in Leeds and speaks broad Yorkshire perfectly. He recited Hamlet to us in the broadest dialect, and St. John Ervine is suggesting that we should run a series of County Shakespeares. Why should Shakespeare always be acted in an Oxford voice?

I have taken my novel to John Lane to-day. It is still unfinished, but unless their readers look at it now, I shall never be able to get it through the press before I leave England. As it is, if they take it, I shall just leave the poor thing to struggle out alone. That is as well. This London life is too vastly pleasant to be healthy for long. I love going to parties and luncheons and dinners. I love being introduced to important people. I am glad that I am going away —to Africa—then to America and China probably. It grows too easy and pleasant here to be really worth while. Not that the easy and pleasant things are to be despised, but I like them in sandwiches.

I don't mean that South Africa won't be pleasant, but I have no hope that it will be easy, and the pleasure will chiefly be seeing you, and of course other people like Mrs. Lewis and Mrs. Newman.

I love you—soon I will see you (D.V.),

CELIA.

10, Oakwood Court,
Kensington, W.14, Nov. 11th.

ROSALIND DEAR,

Armistice Day. I remember so well the first, when the sound of guns disturbed a flight of pigeons across the orchard. I remember the sun on their wings, and the curious feeling of silence that followed—although Lynch and Pugh and Shurman were chattering like magpies. I remember, too, that dance in a village school with a trick-tiled floor, and the boisterous courtesy of the Aussies—and returning to the men's mess hut across the orchard and dancing again.

A pretty peace we have made of it, haven't we? Yet sometimes I think that the tide is turning. St. John Ervine swears that we are at the beginning of a new Renaissance. There is certainly new life stirring. The villages here are

388

alive. I believe strongly in the life and health of these Women's Institutes and Clubs and Halls that up and down the country are producing plays and pageants, and are dancing and making things with their hands. There is a fine set of young things growing up in the schools. I was speaking yesterday to 400 elementary school children just leaving school—and a strong, brave, unselfconscious crowd they were. If only we can keep each other from destroying it all again in another war, I believe that we might see all sorts of dreams realised before we die. I'm not at all afraid of revolution here, unless Joynson Hicks and his ludicrous Fascists drive people to desperation. You can have no idea of the senseless bilge talked by the idiots here who want to arm strike-breaking parties and O.M.S. and what not. The labour leaders are all for peace and settlement. They are mostly men of sense and education. The L.P. and the Social Democratic Federation have passed strong resolutions against the spread of class hatred, disruption and revolutionary communism. And yet the only topic that will rouse half the strenuously idle middle classes is "Anti-Bolshevism"! It is quite alarming. I am terrified of the so-called patriotic, religious anti-socialist, who is putting into the heads of the workers the idea that the middle classes will fight— literally fight—against any change, and thus make them despair of the constitutional progress which is what nearly all of them want. To see them, like silly Samsons, trying to bring down the pillars and hall on to their own heads, is rather bitter.

I believe that if only we can steal twenty years of peace, we shall weather the storm. The drama is going to flower again. All these stage societies and village dramatic guilds are significant, I think. I have just now a great desire to do something which I know is quite beyond my power. I want to write a play with a completely modern setting, but to write it in poetic form—or at least semi-poetic form —with a little prose dialogue perhaps and blank verse and lyrics. Shakespeare did it for his own time—why not now?

When we put on Shakespeare in modern dress, it does not quite come off because the language is Elizabethan. I admire twentieth-century English. I am sure that it is flexible enough and rich enough for poetic drama. Flecker in his *Don Juan* tried to do something of the sort. Have you seen that yet? It is interesting as an experiment. But the legend he took is one that belongs to any age—the illusion of modernity does not hold. If I were only nimble as Edith Sitwell and musical as W. H. Davies, what a play I would write! Now isn't this an idea for some of your young hopefuls? The plot must be indigenous to our own time and nature. The dialogue must be a sublimation not of Miltonic English but of twentieth-century English. My drama would be neither comedy nor tragedy, but both— like *Peer Gynt*. I believe that one loses in vitality what one gains in dignity by shutting off the one from the other. I'm all for Shakespeare as opposed to Sophocles in my modern poetic drama. Can we do anything about it? I think that children could. They have the gusto and the lack of self-consciousness. They so often show us the way to do things, and we come afterwards borrowing their ideas and applying to them our greater sophistication, or why do we go to the primitives and to folk songs for our themes?

I had a charming letter from a Miss Stohr in Cape Town who wants me to go and stay with her. You people are very kind.

I saw Miss Lorimer (H.L.) on Saturday. She sent you her love.

And I send mine.

CELIA.

MY DEAREST ROSALIND,

I was quite foolishly pleased to have your letter of
28.10.25. It is ridiculous to want one's friends to write
letters in the heat. You must not bother to write. You
shall send me little notes: "I love you—Rosalind," and I
will hear all your news when I come. It is not so long now.
I expect that as soon as I have been to Durban I shall run up
and say "How do you do?" to you, even if I have to come
back at once to Johannesburg. It will be too tantalising to
be in the same continent and not greet you. Shall I wilt
in the heat? The prospect at the moment sounds delicious.
I have my third cold this winter. I live with frozen feet,
chilblains and handkerchiefs. I dread each exodus this last
fortnight. Cold has suddenly come upon us after a golden
autumn and I am wretched. Also I cannot write. I shall
have to postpone Wycliffe till I come back from Africa.
I have suddenly sickened and cannot even look at the MS.
I need the voyage and the travel and the new place, I think,
to purge me of this particular disease of the imagination.
At present I loathe everything that I have written—and
most things that other people have written. Perhaps it is
the cold. Writing is a mug's game.

You are being very great and glorious among your
princes and governors. You will look lovely, I know, being
yourself a princess. Are not all the Scotch princesses, or at
least kinsmen of lairds? You were born for courts and
camps. They have always gone together, you know. Peasants
and princes are so much more akin than either are with the
bourgeoisie.

I went to a bad play last night. It is by Ashley Dukes
and very much praised—called *The Man with a Load of
Mischief*. It is light romantic comedy, of the Regency
period—mediocre dialogue dressed out in artificially
elaborate phrases. Monologues in moonlight about love
and so forth, with some pleasantly balanced sentences to

mask cheap cynicism and commonplace sentiment. The theme is a period parody of the prostitute theme—at present entirely *comme il faut*. People rave about its wit, its philosophy and so forth. I rarely yawn in a theatre. I yawned.

But I loved my bus which went plunging down Piccadilly between two rows of lights. I love the Green Park when the first lamps are lit in the bare trees. I love the shops glowing with green and crimson and orange velvet, and all the lovely winter fabrics. I feel sorry for the people who walk down Piccadilly with grey, set faces.

> "I feel sorry for the people
>   Who haven't any London
>   Who haven't seen a London
>   Like mine."

(Isn't there stuff for a song here?) Perhaps they are equally sorry for me because I cannot enjoy *The Man with a Load of Mischief.*

A conservative youth of 18 was shot at revolver practice in a North London Club the other day. Our merry Fascists are showing us the way to revolution. Let us hope we can learn to laugh at them. There is no other way.

I send you my love,

CELIA.

10, Oakwood Court,
Kensington, W.14, Nov. 24th.

ROSALIND DARLING,

This is the Christmas mail. I am sending you a book by a writer whom I like, which I hope will please you. J. B. Priestley writes the *Saturday Review* reviews, also in the *London Mercury*. He is a Yorkshireman and is only thirty. He was all through the war in France and Belgium, then he read English at Cambridge.

The wonderful thing is that I don't suppose there will be time for you to reply to this before I start to see you. Oh, Rosalind, what fun!

I send you my greetings, but will come soon and bring them.

CELIA.

10, Oakwood Court,
Kensington, W.14, Dec. 1st.

MY DARLING ROSALIND,

Perhaps it was Mrs. Newman's letter saying that she was going to stay part of the Christmas holidays with you that brought the thought of you so near this week. Whatever it was, I have been thinking of you a great deal. A brave letter it was from Mrs. Newman—telling me with rejoicing of the different jobs that she has been able to get. She must be a gallant creature. Alas for gallant creatures! I lunched to-day with a charming middle-aged woman, an old Somervillian. She has an invalid husband and two sons at school. For years she has kept them all by a job in the Civil Service, and now she has been axed. And it seemed to be a safe job for years. No fault of her own—just " economy." She tells me that she has applied for fifty-nine jobs since then—in the last three months, but her age and her family ties are against her. Meanwhile, she is doing odd jobs. I am trying to get her my *Time & Tide* job—but again her desperate idealism and dogmatism are against her. She is a dear person and clever and brave, but rather intolerant of other people, and for a job on any paper one must compromise a little—or at least keep silence sometimes. It is troublesome that one can't just hand over jobs to people whom one would like to have them. But what rotten luck to be stranded after all these years.

I have been having a lovely week-end in Dorset with my Somerville friend, Hilda Reid. We have been driving in a car down deep, quiet, twisting lanes, and swishing our

393

feet through beech leaves in the winter woods. We watched a sunset slide down behind the Downs, and saw a fox in the wood flash past us in a ruddy streak. When I am in Dorset, with its mild, kind landscape, I play traitor to my harsher North, and think that real country loveliness lies in these rounded contours, this placid perfection. Do you know Andrew Marvell's poem about the rounded hill? It suits Dorset.

I have just been with Mrs. Brittain to see Madge Titheradge in *The Doll's House*. How curiously Ibsen dates. Nora is almost incredible now. And yet, I wonder. I have been reading the Forsyte Saga again. Soames Forsyte and Thorvald Helmer were not so unlike, after all. Perhaps it is the bustle rather than the tragedy which dates.

My poor children had me to tea this afternoon to lament over their Somerville entrance papers—oh, if they don't get in—or if one does and not the other! They hated the papers. I feel as if I had been going in for the exam. How I hate exams! I love my children.

Such a lot to say, but mostly nonsense, and it is after 1 a.m., and I have a long day to-morrow (?). The Faversham lectures again. Do you know, they are turning into a success? Ever since I grumbled to you. I made a *succès fou* with my Russian boots under an M.A. gown! And that seems to have put them in a good temper! I had three invitations to tea last week.

Much love. Oh, I *do* want to see you.

CELIA.

Bainesse,
Cottingham,
Yorkshire, December 22nd.

DARLING ROSALIND,

Your letter of 2.12.25 is here—and in three weeks I shall be coming to see you. I have marked in my diary, March 19th, Prizes at Pretoria—March 26th till April 6th, Drakens-

394

berg. It sounds lovely, lovely. Is Drakensberg Dragon's Town? And are there dragons? Or only lions and fierce horses? A terrible tragedy has occurred. Mother gave away my breeches thinking that they were an old pair of father's. She pounces periodically upon his wardrobe, and sweeps half off to her ex-Service men. I have no doubt that my breeches are adorning worthier legs than mine, but oh, for the touch of a vanished band, and the sight of a breek that is still—missing. However, Edith has fortified me with the offer of a pair of George's, so I shall doubtless appear breeched as well as booted. There will be no Ken to fold his coat and lay it across the front of my saddle, saying, "Mary dear, your legs are very nice, but . . . !" He was a nice creature.

I shall be scared of you in your grand new life. I am always a little scared of headmistresses. I shall be scared of you all the time until we go to the Drakensberg—and then I shall have forgotten how to ride and you will be a terrible swell.

The local reporter at Bridlington one summer alternately described a dress of mother's as "white foulard, charmingly patterned in black," and "black foulard with a white design." Does yours do better than that?

I am glad that your brother is going out. You won't feel cut off from England any more after that. Perhaps you don't any longer now. I hope not. You aren't really. See how we come and go.

I am here trying to finish my book. John Lane's returned it, saying that the first part was excellent—the best thing I have done—and not liking the end. I have perversely now cut out all the first part and compressed three little scenes of it into a prologue, and am expanding the end. They won't take it, and no one may. But I must write it my own way, and I see it so. The first part was all sex, and I am so tired of sex novels. After all, it is only a small part of life. My happily married friends tell me the least part of it. Only my unmarried friends seem to think about it much at all. And anyway, I am bored with so much of it in books.

I want to write a play. The only times I think of South Africa with foreboding are when I think of my play—and my lectures. For I shan't enjoy them—only they seem to be making lots of friends for me already. Mr. Smit is now a lamb; and I am to meet after Christmas a Mr. Saul Solomon, K.C., of Johannesburg, who says that he is interested. Don't forget that I am going to Miss Stohr, Valestra, Rondebosch, Cape Town, when I land, and I will write from there.

I love you.

I can't remember whether I sent you my four little poems about Time, did I? I seem to be writing a lot of bad poetry now. Did I send you this?

DRAMA

All day
    I see the house—walls blind and grey
Inside
    Nothing is there for them to hide
    But a dusty fern and a ribbon tied
    In a petticoat-knot round the curtain.

At night
    Windows suddenly leap to light;
I see
    White laid tables and shrimps for tea
    And men and women who don't see me,
    But who twisted the knot round the curtain.

Silly, isn't it? I write 'em in trains.

I hope you are having a lovely time at Port Alfred. Here it storms, snows, rains, blows, freezes. Ugh!!

        My dear love,

                CELIA.

1926

Bainesse,
Cottingham,
E. Yorks, January 3rd.

DARLING ROSALIND,

Your lovely cable was such a joy. Thank you so much. I do long to see you. I heard of you quite unexpectedly last week. A girl who used to be the doctor's daughter at a neighbouring village on the wolds has just returned from a tour acting with Irene Vanbrugh. She says that when in Pretoria she was invited to lunch by a charming Miss McWilliam—did I know her? My friend's name is Janet Eccles and she has lovely red hair.

Darling, I want to come lots to Pretoria if I may. May I run up between being at Durban and Johannesburg? It looks so near on the map compared to those other huge spaces. Then I am going to your Prize Day and coming for Easter. I am looking forward frightfully to that.

I have found a Polish woman who paints wonderful designs on fabrics. She has been doing you a scarf. I told her your hair was like beech leaves in a rain-tossed wood, so she has done you a scarf like a spring carpet for your hair.

Did I tell you that one of my girls has the Somerville history scholarship? I am a proud teacher! But, alas, it was not I who did it. Her brains, not my instruction.

Oh, Rosalind—*je viens.*

> "Alas, what danger will it be to us
> Maids as we are, to travel forth so far!"

Thine with love,

CELIA.

Grantully Castle,
Union Castle Line,
Feb. 7th, 1926.

DARLING ROSALIND,

I have just been looking at Cape Town and Table Mountain. It is four o'clock on a perfect afternoon. The mountain is quite clear—no tablecloth—opalescent and lovely. It is quite as beautiful as people have ever told me.

So I am really here and coming to see you—though by stages that will be far too slow. Your welcoming cable has drawn me throughout the voyage, and much of Africa means Rosalind to me.

I have loved the voyage. The first five days were hideous with mal de mer, and yet somehow interesting. Since then we have had gorgeous weather, and Teneriffe, Ascension and St. Helena were full of lovely things.

I can't write because I want to go and look at Table Mountain again. This is just to say that I have come, that I love you and that I wish you a very good term.

I will write again from land. Au revoir—for a short while now.

We land to-morrow. It has been a delightful boat—so friendly. I have made particular friends with Mr. and Mrs. Boxwell from Pretoria University. He does Classics and is a great admirer of yours. Told me of the immense success that you have made where people prophesied failure, and told me something of your difficulties when you first went there—and of how worth while they all were.

I love you always,

CELIA.

Later.

The mail has just come on board and with it your letter. Darling Rosalind, of course I don't forget that we are old friends. I am longing to see you. I want to come just to say "How do you do" directly I leave Natal, and then to use you as headquarters while I am in the Transvaal. You

will find me bobbing in and out until you are tired of me
—but I shan't care. It will be so lovely seeing you.

Mr. Boxwell brought my letters to me and I had to tell
him your news. When I said that you had nearly 200 new
girls, he nearly danced on the deck and cried, "This is what
does us English good." And I said, "This really does sound
fine, doesn't it?" And he said, "Oh, she's a glorious woman"
—meaning you, my dear.

I don't like to think of you working till two and three
—but it seems to mean success, and you are working at
peace—and all that is surely something of a miracle. But
glorious women do work miracles.

I am so excited because there are the lights of Cape
Town and we are rocking up and down outside, and March
will soon come, and I love you.

CELIA.

c/o Miss Stohr,
Valesta, Rondebosch,
Cape Town, Feb. 11th.

DARLING ROSALIND,

Your other letter addressed to me here, has just come.
Thank you ever so much.

I long to see you. This is what I have planned.

Saturday—I go to Kimberley, arriving Monday morning.
I want to see Bridgewater and a school friend of mine, Mary
Berlein, and her father, Judge Hutton. They are dears.

Friday, 19th. I go to Durban. I have lots to do there.
They have worked out an elaborate programme for me
—addressing schools, meetings, broadcasting, interviews,
etc. This lasts till March 1st. I then go to Hilton Road
School, to my old Maths mistress, Miss Andrews, who is
running a school there, for one night. Then to Maritzberg,
to see several people, e.g. the Guides Chief Commissioner,
and to address a meeting for one or two nights.

Ladysmith—to start a branch of the L.N.U. there.

I want to get to Johannesburg on the 6th of March, dump a box and see Mrs. Lewis, then come on to you for the week-end. Will you have me? I have told the Johannesburg people they can fix meetings for me from Monday, March 8th, but I must be up to present your prizes again on March 19th. That is the date, isn't it?

I had no idea people would want me to do so much. Things down here seem just to be moving, and I am an excuse to push them further—especially with the Dutch. I am meeting the Moderator of the Dutch Church this morning. Don't know if I'll do any good, but it is a chance.

I long to see you. The 6th will soon come—and then only a week or ten days, and after that I am *really* coming to stay with you until the end of your Easter holidays. We'll ride in the Drakensberg—we'll do anything.

Cape Town is lovely. The sun is lovely and I have fallen in love with a zebra! People are overwhelmingly kind.

I want to say heaps, but I must go into town.

I love you—till March 6th au revoir.

CELIA.

c/o Mrs. Townley Williams,
355 Musgrave Road,
Berea,
Durban, Feb. 22nd, 1926.

DARLING ROSALIND,

I quite forgot to say in my last letter that I stopped on my way here at Bloemfontein to interview the Secretary of the League of Nations Union there. And his wife knew Gwendolen Newman, and that she and Frank had just moved into the town from Glen. He has been invalided out of the service on a very small pension, you know, and she is casting about for jobs again. My Mrs. Harris, the secretary's wife, had a car and said, "Why not go round and see them?" We only had about an hour and a half before my train. It was after nine in the evening, yet in spite of slight apprehensions on my part, they whisked me off and we went careering about Bloemfontein, visiting wrong numbers, and finally found them. Mrs. Newman, of course, I liked at once. She seems so stalwart and loyal and brave. I liked her nice bobbed hair and her charming manners. And she introduced me to her pantry, her "outside accommodation," her coconut macaroons, and her two infants, both sound asleep. Then I had to fly for my train, having promised to stay with them when I go to lecture in Bloemfontein. I have had two other invitations for Bloemfontein and I feel that I shall be an awful nuisance to the Newmans, yet I also feel that they would probably feel the nuisance less than people with three servants and twenty boys. At least I made Gwendolen promise that if she could not do with me she was to tell Mrs. Harris, and Mrs. Harris said she did not mind being used as an understudy. I shall be going on there after our holiday in the Drakensberg. I suppose that if I am sensible I shall go straight to Bloemfontein. I don't know, of course, to which part of the Drakensberg we are going. It all looks lovely. I am longing for it. My breeches are *much* too tight; but if they split they will at least be cooler.　　　　•

I had a letter from Mr. Bishop. He talks breezily of "later in the year." Alas, I see no chance of later in the year. I am speaking Bloemfontein, visiting Lovedale, speaking Grahamstown, Port Elizabeth, Stellenbosch, Wellington, Paarl and Cape Town, and must be back in England by as near the middle of June as possible. Of course, it is lovely seeing all these different places. I adore places. I find people so intensely interesting.

Did I tell you that in Cape Town I went and called all unheralded upon one of the three Moderators of the Dutch Reformed Church—made great love to him, and got a promise that if the big bug of a chief Moderator who lives at Cradock won't be Vice-President of the L.N.U. that he will? And that he will use all his influence with the Predikants to make them work for the League. When I go back to the Cape he is going to take me round to the various Dutch Reformed Clubs for young men and women. He says that they mostly know enough English to follow me, and he can do anything necessary in Afrikaans. We have a Dutch woman here whom I met to-day who is probably going to prepare Afrikaans pamphlets, and I have a promise of an interview with the editor of *Die Burger*—he is very anti-League at the moment, but when the S.A. Nation has even put in quite a nice article about the L.N.U. there's no knowing what he may be persuaded to do.

I love the hibiscus. I love the frangipanni. I love Durban tilting down to the bay, and the trees on the Bluff and the gardens and flowers and ricksha boys. No one ever told me about their lovely head-dresses.

Of course I shall have to come back sometime. This is a fascinating, puzzling, vivid place. I love Durban especially because of its miscellaneous population. I am being taken to the Indian Congress to-morrow to hear them pray for justice. It should be interesting.

The only flies on the ointment are the mosquitoes. I have twenty bites on my left leg; my ankles are like hippopotamuses and I daily dread to acquire a swollen nose.

Prayer of a Worker for Peace attacked by Vulcan and Mercury
—Really the dirty work of Mars.
Secret diplomacy among Olympians.

Oh Aphrodite, queen of love and beauty
    Hearken, I pray thee, to my humble prayer.
Allured by love and driven far by duty,
    I sought the Afric sun, to linger there—
    Caught in the tangles of Apollo's hair,
        A golden snare.

Grim Vulcan forged his swords and bitter arrows,
    Fountains of light tossed in the southern air;

His molten streams through cataracts and narrows
    Lit the remote recesses of his lair,
    And sparkled, splintering as fine as hair,
        To quiver there.

But Mercury snapped short the slender lances
    And tossed to his lieutenant of the air
The army that attacks and feints and dances—
    Mosquitoes fashioned for a world's despair,
    The weapons forged from molten sunlight, rare
        And debonair.

Thus I, who walk imperilled and assaulted,
    Pray unto thee, who all my fears may share,
For safety from the gods who thus defaulted
    Pursue me by such arms I may not dare.
    Send me thy doves to dissipate my care!
(Eau de Cologne, Lavender Water, Ammonia, Buzzoff and
Salts of Geranium are no use, I've tried 'em!)
        Oh hear my prayer!

I think the syncopation in the last line but one particularly chic.

Have just been talking to two nice men about the Indians, the *Boy's Own Paper*, White Ants, power stations, mealies, grain, economic conferences, and—Lord knows what else. It is nearly midnight and I want to finish *The Flaming Terrapin*. I am meeting Roy Campbell's father to-morrow. What an astounding explosion of vitality that poem is. But good—for all its flaring immaturities, richer, wilder, more packed with imagination and vigour than anything I have read for months. Looks as though South Africa has found a Keats at last.

    Au revoir, my sweet Rosalind.

CELIA.

405

DARLING ROSALIND,

Owing to a change in my Ladysmith meeting I can reach Johannesburg on the 3rd. I have to go and meet an old friend of mother's and talk to him on business for mother that evening, but I could come on to Pretoria on the 4th. I don't want to delay a day, so unless you wire to stop me to Mrs. Lewis, I shall come.

It was lovely to suggest that you and Miss le Roux would come and fetch me. Of course I'd love it. But if the 4th is not convenient, never mind, I'll come by train. I shall dump my clothes with Mrs. Lewis and just bring a suitcase. I have to be back at Roedean on the 7th in time for 7 o'clock dinner.

Your prize-giving is the 19th, isn't it? Jo'burg wanted me to speak that day, and I said I should be at Pretoria and couldn't.

I hear your praises all round. Do you remember a Dr. Clark—now doctor at a native hospital here? You taught her at Oxford High School "hundreds of years ago," she says. A sweet girl—and your admirer.

Dear "glorious woman," I expect that it is when you are most tired that you feel most a stranger.

If you'd rather I waited at Jo'burg till the 5th I can— but I want to come straight to you. I love you.

CELIA.

Four lectures Tuesday, five yesterday, three to-day. You mayn't like lectures in S. Africa, but oh lor, you do ask us to work hard. But it is all so interesting, and were it not for mosquitoes the climate is paradisal. I have been warm for the first time since Huchenneville kitchen, I think.

THE PRIZE-GIVING

The Prize-Giving was held on Friday, March 19th. Miss Winifred Holtby, of the staff of the Headquarters of the League of Nations Union, gave away the prizes. Her speech was as follows:

"LADIES AND GENTLEMEN,—It gives me a quite peculiar pleasure to meet you here this afternoon, and to have the opportunity of presenting prizes at Pretoria High School. This pleasure arises partly from the presence of Miss McWilliam. I knew her first when by her humanity and understanding she was fashioning one of the most difficult camps in France into a proud and happy unit. I saw her there building beauty and public spirit from the most unpromising materials, until those of us who were old comrades of Huchenneville look back upon our time under the French orchard trees in the wooden huts of a Waac camp as one of the happiest periods of our life. It feels singularly fitting to meet her again as headmistress of one of the most beautiful and dignified schools in this land of splendid schools, and I congratulate the people of Pretoria upon their High School and its headmistress.

"I think that the feature of South African life which has impressed me more than others with a promise for its future development lies in the dignity of its educational buildings. In this century we are acquiring a truer knowledge of the value of education in the life of a state. We are just beginning to see that though the subjugation of nature lies with the scientist, the civilisation of man lies with the teacher, and in this day of young restless nations, each demanding the recognition of mankind, we may estimate their standard of culture by the value which they place upon their education. By their schools may we judge them.

"For education is the supreme adventure of the human spirit and the teachers are the leaders of the enterprise. It is not an affair of examination syllabuses, nor of successful matriculation, but of the slow direction of the individual man or woman towards power and beauty. It is a process not confined to schools or universities, but wrought out day by day, through the contact of man with man, of man with human difficulties, of man with the indifferent tenacity of nature.

"But education, which begins in the home, takes its most deliberate form in the school, when the faculties of the child are first tested for development, and that voyage of discovery, which Miss McWilliam mentioned, first is made. And the value of that school period must depend in some degree on the value placed by the nation on the school.

"For the teacher has power. Germany changed the character of her people in two generations through her schools. Austria is building from a ruined empire a new and hopeful nation by means of educational reform. In the annals of her history, Dr. Otto Glockel, the first Minister of Education under the new régime, will be accounted a hero of the nation. When visiting his offices two years ago I was especially struck by the book-plate marking his books. There an engraving represents a man on a mountain-side, rolling away a great stone from the path of two climbing children. There are so many stones up the mountain of progress which every child must climb, and it is for the teacher to roll these away.

"Among the new nations of Europe one alone has already achieved stability, a promise of future happiness, and the respect of its neighbours, and that is Czechoslovakia. By a series of circumstances the new republic arose from a nation whose only men and women fit for government had served their apprenticeship in Prague University. The professor of philosophy became the first President, his colleagues largely formed his Ministry, and the ideas of a lecture platform became the practical policy of a State. In the political crisis through which Europe is passing few nations have behaved more creditably than this new republic fashioned by its teachers.

"We mould our future citizens in the schools, even though all teachers may not have the direct power of the Czechs; but education is not confined to one locality. I believe that one of the greatest hopes for the peace and prosperity of the world lies in the tendency of our generation to send young people abroad. The visit of fifty South African students to Europe might be the beginning of a new fluidity in our educational system. I hope that we shall one day see an international matriculation standard, directed by the committee of intellectual co-operation under the League of Nations, and as we have boasted in the past of a freedom of the seas, I wish that we could boast in the future of a freedom of the schools. No nation can afford to ignore the experiments of its neighbours, and we have much to learn if we could fling open our doors and look out into the great world. For the parochial attitude means the death of civilisation. Our spirits die in stagnation, and only our teachers can roll away the stones of ignorance and parochialism and let our children climb the hill whence they may see the broad view and the long vision—wide over the continents, back into the past, forward into the future.

"Teachers have power. We may cripple them by petty economics; by Government regulations, by the foolish criticism of an uninformed press; but their power exists for good or evil, and it is a fine thing for a wanderer to see in South Africa teaching regarded as an honourable profession, and schools and colleges built with the dignity becoming to their importance.

"For we must hold beauty fast. She is the most certain solace for so many human sorrows. She is the first secret teacher of the child's inquiring mind, as her creation is the supreme achievement of the human spirit. In this country it is true that your buildings lack the mellow radiance that comes from years of loving admiration. Oxford, Winchester, Heidelberg and Florence have something that South Africa cannot yet give to the world; but the foundations here have been well and truly laid, and each successive generation which values loveliness in school buildings will complete the work begun in the Transvaal schools. For Walter de la Mare has truly bidden us:

> Look thy last on all things lovely,
>   Every hour. Let no night
> Seal thy sense in deathly slumber
>   Till to delight
> Thou have paid thy utmost blessing;
> Since that all things thou wouldst praise
> Beauty took from those who loved them
>   In other days.

"Not only in our buildings, but in our realisation of the adventure of work may we find beauty. Education should not be directed to the successful manufacture of efficient shorthand typists, but should lead every boy or girl towards a more complete fulfilment of their individuality. Agriculture and medicine, domestic work and industry have all their special possibilities, their special service to the community.

"So I would congratulate the citizens and parents of the Transvaal upon the foundations for their nation's splendour which they are laying in their schools. And I would wish all power and fortune to the teachers who hold in their hands the future of the race. And for those who learn I would wish high success in their adventure; may they climb their mountain far higher than our steps could carry us, and see more boldly and clearly over the world of men, and find ways that we never knew into the heart of secret beauty and honourable power."

The Rev. E. Macmillan proposed a vote of thanks which was carried by acclamation.

Oriel House,
Grahamstown, April 28th.

DARLING ROSALIND,

We have just had such a nice party—Heyworth, Martin Lewis, Mrs. Bodmer and three students. Mr. Bodmer is a dear. He loves you. He says "that you have a quite unique personality and a noble spirit, and quite a singular faculty for disinterestedness." Heyworth said that you had the most generous mind she ever knew. One of the students— whose name I did not catch—said that she loved you. And I have been purring. They all seem to think that you are making a huge success of your job.

I saw Mrs. Smail (Smale?) again to-day and she has asked me to lunch. I like her. Mr. Whiteley I have seen twice, and Sir John came and was paternal to me yesterday, and I am going to the Adamsons to-morrow.

There was a lady's tea party for me and a meeting in St. George's Hall to-day. It was a lovely tea—the sort where there are dozens of creamy and sugary cakes and every one eats biscuits, because they dare not manipulate the cakes. Mrs. Star Stewart seemed to be running that, and Mrs. Giddy. I lunched with the Phelps to-day. There is a presbyterian parson with a voice like The Private Secretary—he was not here in your day.

I like Heyworth, I think, though she makes me feel that I chatter too much. I can see her sitting still and reserving judgment. Her clothes are pretty. She had a charming accordion-pleated georgette frock of pale stone colour to-night, with long falling sleeves.

On Saturday I am going to a dance. A dance? Imagine it! I must contrive to wash my shingle first, but I am a little scared by Heyworth's adamant notices in the bathroom —"Water is restricted and students are asked to use no more than is strictly necessary to the interests of cleanliness." What is strictly necessary? Where does cleanliness end and luxury begin?

Rosalind, I love you. Take care of yourself. Give my

411

kindest respects to the good-looking chauffeur and to that minx in the pink frock, and all the other nice people. Have any more of your science staff got engaged?

Oh, Rosalind, this is a stale and unprofitable world. Thank goodness you and one or two others exist in it.

CELIA.

Oriel House,
Grahamstown, May 3rd.

DARLING ROSALIND,

I went with the Smails to lunch yesterday. They love you very much and their children are nice. Also their house, which is remote and primitive but very pretty.

It thundered and poured but we drove out to the Dances' farm just the same. It was even more thrilling than our drive to Nelspruit. We skidded and shuddered all over the road in blinding hail, until one wheel went over a bank and the car began to slide down, and we all got out. The car only slid into a field but we couldn't get it up until we walked to a farm and sent some men to pull it up. It was amusing but poor Mrs. Smail did not like it frightfully. We found Ann Whitworth at the farm. What an unusual little creature she is. She had ridden out on a horse and waited for the storm to stop, but as it never stopped we brought her back in the car.

I went to a football dance with Sir John and Lady Adamson on Saturday and felt four years younger afterwards. I danced a lot and loved it. Sir John hops like a young mountain seen by the Psalmist. (Was it after hock? We had hock for dinner.)

Jonathan Cape won't publish my book. He says "It would get some good notices, and some people would speak highly of it and recommend it, but the sales would not be satisfactory to either Miss Holtby or ourselves." Alas, my poor Wycliffe.

I have been lecturing lots here, but I don't feel at all

412

inclined to accept Professor Rousseau's invitation to stay.
I would rather be governess to Mrs. Collenbrander if I
stayed out here at all, I think.

I love you very much,

WINIFRED.

*(Posted to me from Kimberley, when Winifred was on her way
to Cape Town. June, 1926.)*

"Wherever your friends go, you have a new interest in
this round world," said Rosalind.

See, I have cast my nets
    Over the ball of the world.
Wherever my friends sail out on the wide seas,
    Wherever their sails are furled
In hill-girt harbour, or swinging river-mouth
    My nets are hurled.

The ships bring news for me,
    And the wind their words,
For my friends have enslaved the trees as their messengers,
    The slow-moving herds
Of cattle, the wind-blown seeds, and the running streams,
    And the homing birds.

Now all the world is mine,
    China and Labrador,
Hungary, Africa, Washington, Rome,
    And a hundred more
Tall cities, and many a sudden-flowering isle
    And a rocky shore.

For I have part in the land
    Wherever my friends go.
Wherever the hills of their pilgrimage break and their cities
      tower

413

And their red roads glow,
I have cast my nets and drawn them home to my mind,
    Though they never know.

Now have I wealth indeed,
    Who hold the world in fee.
There is not a flowering field on the merry earth,
    Not an almond tree,
But its beauty has gladdened the heart of a friend of mine,
    And enriches me.

        Parting is not sorrowful
            For such as you and me;
        It only means another place
            Where I should like to be.

        Golden glow the roads for me,
            Lands have richer worth;
        Men befriend my friends for me
            Over half the earth.

        Foreign towns are friendly now,
            Foreign fields are fair.
        Half the earth is home to me,
            If friends like you are there.

                    S.S. *Barrabool,*
            Somewhere near Cape Verde Island,
                July—but I do not know the date.

DARLING ROSALIND,
    I am writing upon your own paper, which is quite right
and proper, as a theft voluntarily returned is only a loan
and therefore legal; but a theft returned with interest is
not merely legal but philanthropic. And if these blue lines
that I squiggle on your paper are not interest, I hope that
they may at least be interesting.

I miss you, of course, but I have found a Miss Brown of Grahamstown whom you coached for her M.A. and to whom you discoursed delightfully. And as she is one of the many people who think you the most wonderful person she (or he) has ever met, we get on rather well, and waste sundry hours hanging over the stern and holding pleasant communion on the nature of our loves—as did those charming youths in the Platonic dialogue whose name I forget, but which is staged in a gymnasium, with nice little boys cooling themselves after the games, and blushing at the mention of their lovers' names.

This is a delightful ship. I am happier, more comfortable and more amused than on the Union Castle. The food strikes me as being admirable in any case, and for the money, miraculous. I like high tea. I like meals without a great variety of choice. They save one mental energy better expended otherwise. And the absence of an evening dinner necessitates charming little supper parties. Every night on the hatches Lydia (my tea basket) and I hold a salon. At first we drank my tea, my sugar and ate Gwendolen's gingerbread, but slowly all my provisions have been exhausted and others have brought their offerings, and now the implements are mine, but the feast is provided by others. Last night I drank three cups of tea provided by a half-South African, half-Scandinavian girl going to New York, milk provided by a friendly Irish doctor who was at Corpus and knows lots of my Oxford acquaintances, sausages (!!) provided by a German resident in Cape Town, with a scarred face, an insatiable passion for grand opera, and a weak digestion, toffee provided by a little Afrikander girl from Pretoria, name Freiburg, going to study psychology in Vienna, and hot water brought by a Scottish farmer from the Eastern Transvaal. This last is a curious creature—twenty-six, having left school at thirteen and having just recovered before embarking from an attack of delirium tremens. He looks about thirty-six. He used to drive horses seventy to two hundred at a time, from Bloemfontein to the Eastern Transvaal. He once won a bullock by eating a whole leg of mutton at a sitting. (Never mind if this is true—that he could boast of it is sufficiently interesting.) He wears the same ready-made brown suit day after day, and grows hotter and hotter. He has second sight and sees visions and hears Christ speaking to him, and says "By God, I'm a strong man," and manifests a rather too continuous desire to dance with me. If he were not quite so hot, I should be a more willing partner. Then there is a Greek lawyer from Johannesburg, middle-aged, heavy, kind, intelligent, who has been editing a Greek paper called *The Nea Hellas* and is now going back to his home in Cyprus. There is a Frenchman from Albertville in the Belgian Congo, who always wears a cap, because it is *comme il faut*, and will not dance, because he continually maintains that he has a wife in Albertville and to dance with young girls would not be *convenable*. There is an English journalist from the *Cape Times* who is going back to England because he dislikes Afrikaans, and who has just been telling me that you can't say "such as you and me"—so I shall have to alter that little poem I sent you. He has lent me Cobbett's Easy Grammar to guide my faltering steps through realms of poesy. And there is another charming Afrikander student girl going to study domestic science in New York. These two girls are the most charming Dutch South Africans I have met. They are both convinced that the lack of culture in their country is tragic, that they are three hundred years behind Europe in civilisation, and both are going off into the world to seek it. They are both twenty-one.

In fact, all the people here are more amusing than on the Union Castle. We have three artists, four journalists, a writer of funny stories, an ex-burglar deported from Sydney, a cinema pianist, an Indian officer's widow who looks like Mrs. Hawksbee in the Kipling Plain Tales and is teaching me Bridge, a Scottish Missionary, a deported Bolshevik, a Judge's daughter, a colony of teachers, three

416

actresses—and I. Each day one encounters somebody new and amusing.

I have finished my embroidery, written and typed two long articles, written bits of *The Land of Green Ginger*, danced, played quantities of bridge, and talked and talked and talked. The mornings find me in the bar playing bridge with my strong silent friend of the leg of mutton, a toothless Scotchman called Jock, of the truly proletarian type, and a commercial traveller from Bristol. My bridge is going to be quite good when I have finished this voyage.

And meanwhile—you are holidaying with Miss Covernton and Gwendolen, I hope, and I hope that you are loving it.

Oh, I shall come again some day. Perhaps you will be in Rhodesia? Perhaps—never mind perhaps. Here is the present, in which I love you and send you my greetings.

Until next time,

CELIA.

Bainesse,
Cottingham,
Yorkshire, July 27th, 1926.

MY DARLING ROSALIND,

Your lovely letter came this morning and the post-card of the Falls, and I feel in touch with you again. But oh, there is a good deal of stickiness and stuffiness in this very green and pleasant land. Green beyond imagining after the wet spring and suddenly-flowering summer. All the way to Yorkshire in the train, through a golden evening, I sat and worshipped green fields, green waving fields of corn, green elm trees, green gardens, green hedges of dark hawthorn, houses buried in the green to their eyebrows.

The strike is omnipresent. The shops are full of clothes to be sold off cheaply "because of the strike."[1] Every one is full of tales of it. Evidently the quiet behaviour was amazing, and I feel that the Labour leaders have justified

[1] The General Strike, May, 1926.

themselves. The miners may have been unwise not to accept the report of the Commission, but who dare blame men for unwisdom? And their leaders probably thought they saw light. In any case, I have been sending to Ellen Wilkinson's fund for the miners' children, and the atmosphere here at home is sympathetic to their suffering. On the boat I read Trotzky's book, *Where is Britain Going?* prophesying revolution and what not. Somehow, I don't think so. In spite of upheavals, things feel quieter here. After South Africa, wonderfully tranquil and old and fixed.

I wish that I had seen Rhodesia. I want to come back and see much farther north. A Frenchman on the boat from the Belgian Congo had wonderful survey maps, and took Dr. Faussett and me for lovely canoe rides up the Congo along the map, painting us pictures in rapid French or broken English—and the Greek journalist augmented his accounts.

I loved your descriptions of Livingstone and of Rhodesia like the New Forest with the low beech trees. It sounds a little like Raleigh's "Guiana." "On both sides of this river we passed the most beautiful country that mine eyes ever beheld; and whereas all that we had passed before was nothing but woods and prickles, bushes and thorns, here we beheld plains of twenty miles in length, the grass short and green, and in divers parts groves of trees by themselves, as if they had by all the art and labour in the world been made so on purpose; and still as we rowed the deer came down feeding by the water's side, as if they had been used to a keeper's call." Isn't it pure magic? I think that of all travel books Raleigh's discovery of Guiana has in it the most shining wonder. Doesn't it make you want to go there? And then this picture . . . "the deer crossing in every path, the birds towards evening singing in every tree with a thousand several tunes, cranes and herons of white, crimson and carnation, perching on the river's side; the air fresh with a gentle easterly wind; and every stone that we stopped to take up promised either gold or silver by his complexion."

And this as part of a political apologia. Must it not have stirred Elizabeth? Ah, but she was used to men with golden style, and what was one more adventurer to her, though he were "a tall handsome and bold man"? She would like that. "But his naeve (?) was that he was damnable proud." Of course he was, Aubrey Your *Short Life* was no better a witness than his own defiance in that same *Discovery of Guiana.* "If I had known other way to win, if I had imagined how greater adventures might have been regained, if I could conceive what further means I might yet use, but even to appease so powerful a displeasure, I would not doubt but for one year more to hold fast my soul in my teeth till it were performed."

But what am I doing, writing you a rhapsody about Raleigh, when I meant to be answering your letter? Oh, my family is well, and Grace's baby really very sweet. She is tiny, tiny. I couldn't help thinking of that wicked limerick:

> "On the very next morn
> She gave birth to a prawn."

But Anne has beautiful blue eyes and is angelically good. She hardly cries at all, even though she is teething.

My own affairs are uncertain at the moment. After six months' complete independence, I shall let them be guided by other people's convenience for the next six. I saw Lady Rhondda in London. She fed me on lobster and I was sick. I always am if I eat lobster! She was very kind and is giving me lots of work. The *Manchester Guardian* is publishing my Eulogy on Railway Trains—South African railway trains— and the *Yorkshire Post* has written to ask me for articles. I have three short stories on the *tapis*, and my *Land of Green Ginger*. It comes and goes like firelight in my mind—some- times very clear, sometimes distant.

The shops are full of the latest—and a very charming— fashion—broad flowered voiles with patterned borders.

They wash like rags, and look so pretty. I am sending you some. It is only 2s. 11d. a yard, and I only take two yards for a dress; it is fifty-four inches wide, but I will send you three yards, as you like long sleeves.

I had to buy myself some shoes in London, so sent you off two pairs—*very* cheap. They are a birthday present. A very dull sort, but as you gave me garters, we can love each other from the feet upwards, I suppose. I hope that they fit. If they don't do let me know, and I will send the next lot larger or smaller.

I love you,

CELIA.

PS.—You make me so much ashamed when you call me Bodhi Satva. I am so restless, so selfish, and so unworthy. I have had so good a time, so much that other people miss, and am so conscious of how little I give in return. My Nirvana is the Nirvana of the yet untouched—not of those who have won through to tranquillity.

I love you. We'll go a-roving again under the moon. In California? In Egypt? Where? This is a little world.

Bainesse,

Cottingham,

Yorkshire, August 10th.

MY DARLING ROSALIND,

I am sending, not without trepidation, three little pieces of voile to make you summer frocks. The trepidation arises from the pattern. When in the shop the patterns looked charming and inoffensive, but as I took them home they grew larger and larger and larger and larger, until laid on my bed to be wrapped up the roses were large as mill-wheels, and I felt like the soldier in the Tinder Box! However, the cost was nominal, so that you can turn them into sofa covers or dish cloths, or nests for Toby if you don't like them. As a matter of fact, I have one like the mauve, only with a white ground, and every one says how nice it looks.

420

It pours with rain, but Cottingham still looks green. I have begun the *Land of Green Ginger*, but not with much success, except for a pleasantish opening, wherein my heroine, temporarily in love with Sir Walter Raleigh (after Coriolanus, Rudullf Rassendyl and the Scarlet Pimpernel), is conducting an impassioned interview with him in her bedroom when she ought to be doing her prep (she is seventeen), when she is interrupted by her aunt to make tea, and by a whole series of events which alter her life for good.

The *Yorkshire Post* has asked me for articles; *tant mieux*. But really, on looking back over some MSS., I write such insipid stuff that it hardly seems worth doing.

I go to London to-morrow to meet Vera. It will be lovely to see her again.

I've been getting my photograph taken, but they are all so beastly that I won't send you one, as I was going to. I look all teeth and no sense.

Ann, my niece, is a lamb. I spent Sunday with Grace and Peter at Bridlington, and though it is not exactly the life for me, I must say that they seem ideally suited and pleased with each other—all three.

An enchanting letter from Stella Benson, who wants me to join her in California in March, journey with her to Manchuria and return in the winter via the Trans-Siberian Railway and Russia. It sounds heavenly. I wonder if I shall do it?

Darling Rosalind, I do love you. I wish that you could go to California too.

One day we will tryst there—or what about Mexico? D. H. Lawrence of *The Plumed Serpent* seems to find it an exciting place.

Always much love,

CELIA.

421

DARLING ROSALIND,

Your lovely letter about the Zimbabwe ruins came just after I wrote my last (I think—but don't be furious if I have got all muddled. This last month has been such a confusion of thoughts, persons, alarums and excursions that I shall forget my own name soon). It was, at least, a lovely and thrilling letter. I have seen photographs of those hidden passages, narrow slits in huge stone walls. A young journalist on the *Barrabool* had those Cape to Cairo volumes, with splendid photographs of all Africa. One day I must see them, and the cone-shaped towers, and the wicked, secret places.

We are not quite a full house yet, but very nearly. H. is here again, on three weeks' leave before he goes to Mesopotamia or India or somewhere with the Flying Corps. He is charming, inconsequent, lovable and unstable. But I have loved him far too well and long to feel no heart-burning when I see him thrown away into a life where he has none of the intellectual companionship for which he hungers, with which he has nothing in common, and of which, in theory, he disapproves. Yet one must not even be sorry. What a perverse world.

I have been reading Byron again—the result of reading E. Barrington's *Glorious Apollo*. Have you read it? I don't know enough of the Byron story to estimate its truth; but it has two great merits. It is a most readable novel, and it sends one back to read the poems, and even though I dislike, and always did, the heavy-sentimental or luscious or facetious romanticism which seems to be Byron's forte, I am again dazzled by the facility and aptitude of his verse, and sometimes enchanted by his lyrics. But I don't like Byron. And I don't like Switzerland, and I am gratified to feel in their connection at least a consistency of taste within myself, which is usually lacking.

If ever Charlie Chaplin in *The Gold Rush* comes to Pretoria, go—make all your staff go, and make your children go, and then give them a lesson upon honesty of detail in artistic work. It is a masterly film, and Charlie's performance has the thoroughness and exquisite finish of genius. In the whole long film—I have seen it twice and intend to do so many times more—I cannot detect a flashing second in which he wastes an opportunity for effect. There is pure joy in the contemplation of anything so admirably done, and simple and sentimental as the story may be, there is a pathos, a humanity, and a true aesthetic beauty of significance about it. Because the absurd figure of Charlie in his bowler and huge shoes, standing alone against an Alaska snowfield, is symbolic in spite of himself. Like all great art, it reveals more even than the intention of the artist—and yet it is based upon a slap-stick farce, with a few good snow scenic effects. But see it for yourself, and I hope you laugh as much as I did.

I must go to bed. I have been playing bridge and tennis all day.

Dear love, my Rosalind,

CELIA.

Pension Coupier,
3, Rue des Alpes,
Geneva, September 8th.

DARLING ROSALIND,

Of course you have lovely holidays—I wish that you could inspire European teachers with some of your adventurous desire to be stuck in spruits and punctured in the Karoo. Though I think that they are better now than they were. Quite a number go off with rucksacks and nailed boots to climb low German mountains and march singing about Czech plains. Travel is growing cheaper and even the school children are roaming afield in their holidays.

Geneva is lovely—the climate like a South African

423

autumn day, with brilliant sunshine in the afternoons, and the lake blue as magic and all the pretty red-lipped ladies in chiffon frocks with sunshades like great flowers bobbing beneath the plane trees. I am writing for the *South African Woman's Magazine* and the *Ladies' Pictorial*, and have sent a whole lot of stuff about Mandates and the attitude of the South African delegate—one solitary High Commissioner— here to a man who runs part of the agency to supply the *Cape Argus* and *Bloemfontein Friend*, Norman Hart of Cape Town, correspondent of the *Cape Times*, dines with me to-morrow to meet Mr. Manning of Muizenburg, at work at the Secretariat, and Miss Stohr of Cape Town. It will be a reunion of practically all the South Africans here—there are not many.

To-day we saw Germany voted into the Assembly. Every nation stood up in turn and said Yes—or Oui. Ireland grew so agitated that Mr. Desmond Fitzgerald said "Oui" and Persia only gasped—but the vote was unanimous for admission and we all clapped like lunatics. I sit between an American lady, all ideals and flutter, and a Hungarian man, all cynicism and bows, in the Press Gallery. It is amusing.

All the flags are flying and the copper beech is full of purple shadows.

I love you.

CELIA.

117, Wymering Mansions,
Elgin Avenue, W.9,
Sept. 23rd.

DARLING ROSALIND,

I have had two letters from you since I sent my last— the silly little poem. Such nice letters. I am so glad that you had your birthday party. You said in the former letter that your life felt empty because, though you had your great school, you had not filled it with your own efforts—it was

424

all ready-made. But the party wasn't ready-made; the things that make your staff so happy and ribald and loving are not ready-made. You made all that yourself.

I am *still* seeking plaited shoes with pointed toes, and can find nothing but creatures apparently made for giantesses afflicted with gout! The little French shop where I purchased mine seems to have evaporated.

I am going one of these days to call upon Miss Aitken. Just now I am trying to settle down and work, while keeping my mornings free to write *The Land of Green Ginger*, and I find it an engaging process. I seem to belong to half a million societies, all of which seem to think themselves the only important organisation in the universe—and I seem to shake alternately the illusion of each of them! Therefore I write letters till one, and still my desk is piled with neglected work. I must get my South African report in to the L. N. Union. Haven't done that yet.

Time and Tide are being very kind to me and giving me book-reviewing. I have been reviewing Dean Inge's *England* —Sarah Gerturde Millin's *The South Africans*, and novels of all sorts. Have you read G. B. Stern's *Tents of Israel* and *A Deputy was King*? They are good. And I love *The South Africans*.

London is full of wonderful plays, and I don't seem to have time to see them. There is *The Constant Nymph*, which is supposed to be admirably done, and a high-brow revue called *Riverside Nights*, and Dostoievski's *Idiot*, and Edith Evans in *Ibsen*—and—and—oh, London is lovely, full of autumn sunlight, and parks with their last green, and the river with its September haze, and people with eager, clashing, bitter wit, and parties, and shops full of lovely frocks.

I always take my typewriter to be refitted in the Bond Street Depot, so as to have another excuse for walking down Bond Street. There is a wonderful Chinese shop with a scarlet lacquer table, and Ming period pottery horses, and an agate dragon carrying two crystal balls, and two serene and lovely gentlemen in pale green pottery, with flowing moustaches.

And there are dress shops with frocks as suave and delicate as flowers; and jewels, and lovely leather-work. I always come out of Bond Street feeling reinforced by civilisation.

Vera said to-day—"How the Labour Party must hate Bond Street." And I said—"I hope not—I hope that they hate Bethnal Green." I should like all cities to have streets full of things as exquisite and civilised and suave as Bond Street. I should like to destroy all Bethnal Greens. Must Bond Street and Bethnal Green only exist together? To destroy one, must one sacrifice the other? Oh, I hope not.

My love to Martha, Christabel, Suzanna, Wanda, and all the rest.

CELIA.

117, Wymering Mansions,
Maida Vale, W.9,
October 6th.

DARLING ROSALIND,

I am just reading Smuts' book on *Holism and Evolution.* I have been given it to review, together with Asquith's *Fifty Years of Parliament.* The contrast is marked—one man writing a dignified, but by no means always accurate self-defence—the other seeking again quite humbly for the foundations of his scientific and philosophic faith. I feel more strongly than ever that Smuts is an immensely great man. What is a country to make of an ex-premier who prefers writing on Holism to writing his memoirs, and criticising Darwin instead of castigating his opponents? No wonder South Africa finds him one too many for her.

Hertzog is here, and I am most interested to know what is going to happen at the Imperial Conference. Natal has sent a protest. Ireland is sore because England, very unwisely, I think, did not back her up at the League Council elections. There will probably be a good old row—and all to the good if the result is to clear the atmosphere and make every one feel relieved at having got something off their chests.

I am working every morning on *The Land of Green Ginger*, and at present so happy with it. I love my Joanna. She's all the best of me, but without my academic side and with far more pluck. I started hating her husband and am growing so sorry for him that I shall end with loving him best of all. It is queer how one goes on making the better acquaintance with one's characters, just as though they were people. I could no more make mine do what I want them to do, once I have created them, than I could make you do something. They seem to have a complete individual life, and I could follow every word and action and thought of theirs during a whole day if that were artistically possible. The only difficulty is to know what bits to choose and what to leave out. Novel-writing is not creation, it is selection. Once characters have been born they assume a complete life about which everything exists, waiting to be recorded. The whole of art lies in the omissions. When I am writing, I am so happy—no, not happy, but interested—that I don't want to do anything, go anywhere, or see any one. Only one can't go on all the time—and the real world keeps coming in. Only, when it is all over, and one reads the finished production, it is so tame and poor and vapid that I wonder how on earth it ever absorbed and interested me so much. When I think of all the things that I want to write, I want to live for ever. It's no use saying, "For what purpose?" The desire is quite irrational. I just feel the perfectly egocentric desire to create. Perhaps God felt like that when he began to make these millions and millions of stars, and just went on creating quite purposely because creation is the most attractive of all occupations.

Is this all nonsense? Possibly. And anyway, as far as I am concerned, quite unimportant.

Lovely autumn days—a St. Luke's or St. Martin's summer, with golden leaves and perfectly fresh but mild breezes.

A girl who writes novels under the name of Temple Lane came here to tea to-day. Mr. Dowsley introduced her to me. She is rather nice—Irish, from a parsonage among the bogs. Have you read any of her work? I haven't yet.

I decided to go on to *Time and Tide* when I found that they will let me have my own way in my own subjects as far as possible. They have been very decent to me, and I was amazed at the way in which people can sometimes be reasonable if you mean something very much.

Much love, my Rosalind,

CELIA.

117, Wymering Mansions,
Maida Vale, W. 9,
October 13th.

DARLING ROSALIND,

All the bracken in Hampshire is golden; all the air is full of leaves like blowing birds. It's lovely autumn weather.

At present I hate anything that takes me from *The Land of Green Ginger*. I have a hundred engagements and damn them all. I want my Joanna and Teddy to have the life that they claim in me, and I am sorely tempted to skimp everything else to get to them. Though the other things are fun.

I am reviewing Smuts's book, *Evolution and Holism*—what a valiant, buccaneering, impatient, audacious mind he has. Nothing satisfies him but a world-system—no, universal system. Bless the man, the universe is hardly big enough for him—he's gone freebooting among the sciences now, and is playing ducks and drakes with Bergson and Spinoza, Einstein and the rest! He'll get thumped by scientists and do 'em all a world of good. No wonder South African party politics are too small for him. A great man, i' faith. What does Sylma think of it? I am enchanted by its blazing indiscretions.

Edith de Coundouroff has been here for the week-end.

Nice to have her. The world is so full of interesting people, and no time, no time, no time. Lord, if I could live a thousand years and meet all the pleasant creatures, I'd risk the disillusionment and pain of it. One might have wisdom in a thousand years.

So glad you're taking *Time and Tide*. It's an adventurous little paper. We're going to aim high, and try to put salt on the tails of all the best men and women writers—from Shaw downwards.

Au revoir, darling Rosalind,

CELIA.

October 21st, 1926.

DARLING ROSALIND,

I've a hunch, as the Americans say, that I've missed the mail. Blame my novel. I've been engrossed with it. Got to a camp of wild Finns and Lithuanians set down in a York-shire dale, and the sparks are flying!

I went to the Aquarium with Frida Hartley last Tuesday and saw lovely little harlequin, fish-like jewels, and the most darling sea-horses, with their tails curled round twigs of some strange marine tree. They swayed in the water, rocking their long bodies and wise little horse-heads. They are like fairy fish.

I heard to-night a lecture by Arnold Toynbee on Pacific Relations. He had lovely maps. I'm not safe in a room with maps. They go to my head like Vermuth—the only forms of intoxicant that really give me pleasure. Vermuth *and* maps, I mean. I like both. I also had to review a book on Mandates for *Time and Tide* and wanted to sail straight off for the Japanese Mandated area north of the equator. Shall I buy a sea horse? Oh, and there are little cars being sold for £20 outside an old furniture-dealers' in the Edgware Road. They go!! Shall I buy a car or go to Ecuador? At the present moment I intend to buy a black velvet coat at Debenham's. Oh, me, the world is so full of places to be

429

seen and things to do—and I love life in London and am full
to the eyebrows of engagements. And I want to write my
book. No wonder I neglect you. But I love you just as
much. Only it's so damn cold, and the desk is always away
from the fire. You are wearing muslins and we are wrapping
ourselves in furs and rugs and I've just bought a new hot-
water bottle and am inquiring the price of padded boots!

I'm getting to look so plain that I think I'm forty at
least. Can't think what's wrong. I must consult your
beauty doctor. Really, I think it is because I've had my hair
cut too short.

Oh, I do want a little car to go rollicking away down
the Edgware Road, and when you come to town, Martha
won't be in it with my Mary. I hope she won't choose the
better part and sit still too often. But I fear that a Mary
for £20 might be more pain than pleasure.

Au revoir, sweet Coz.

Your

CELIA.

117, Wymering Mansions,
Maida Vale, W.9,
November 2nd.

DEAREST ROSALIND,

A letter from you to-day. I am much perturbed by this
business of sickness. Our bodies seem so easily to leap into
the saddle where our minds should be. People who are ill
become changelings.

In my book which I am writing I have a man who wanted
so much to be a fine and useful fellow. And he was sick,
and his sickness combined with his natural weaknesses of
character to make him a cad. I suppose that the really
heroic can overcome. Stella Benson is more often sick than
well, and she has a gallant, witty spirit. I know a woman
leading a strenuous and most useful life, a woman of great
knowledge, much power, a rare fighter, a woman of brave

430

vision, who has had three operations for cancer. When she goes to make speeches, she sometimes has to run away first and be sick and then go on to the platform. But she has stuck to her job; she has never complained—not even looked forlorn. She has humour and human sympathy and a pleasant beauty—and she is over sixty. It can, apparently, be done.

I have been investigating Crosby Hall, to write it up for *Time and Tide*. It is really lovely, and the new wings that they are building in Sir Thomas More's garden are of beautiful little dark-red Dutch bricks, to match the Tudor architecture of the rest. It was a grey day on the Embankment, with gulls flying in and out of the mist.

I haven't been to Miss Aitken yet. She is on my conscience. But if you knew how I struggle through my days to find time for my darling book, you might forgive me. I won't part with my mornings, and my afternoons get filled weeks ahead. I haven't even been once to the theatre and there is an orgy of good things on now.

Much love, dear Rosalind.

CELIA.

117, *Wymering Mansions*,
Elgin Avenue, W.9,
November 11th.

ROSALIND DEAR,

Seven years ago to-day I washed tin plates in Huchenneville kitchen and saw the pigeons fly across the orchard. There's a young slip of a moon to-night in the sky. Well, well.

Isn't John Buchan a lamb? I wanted a signed copy of a book of his for the Six-Point Group Bookstall, which for my sins I am organising. I'm specialising on autographed books by lions. So I wrote telling him of our misfortunes, and Martha, and the dogs, and reading *Prester John* when I should have been doing my duty, and buying *Salute to*

Adventurers in Abbeville, and being scolded at Q.M.S. for reading the *Thirty-Nine Steps* in school hours—your idea, I know. So I send you the letter, and if it's not snapped up, I'll buy the book for you for Christmas in memory of our common vice.

Rain, rain and wind—wind like a hurricane, but last Tuesday in the train to Emsworth I saw the loveliest sunlight through wet, red, beech leaves.

I'm writing *The Land of Green Ginger*—and it's not good. In my head it was lovely. V. Sackville West has written a beautiful travel book. She went off to Persia through Iraq, and saw a station with "Change here for Babylon" on it— and stayed with Gertrude Bell, that lovely woman.

I'm going to Q.M.S. next week, to speak to the school and see Miss Fowler. I go to a party at Lady Astor's to-morrow. I shall wear my Joan of Arc dress. Did I tell you that I had a lovely dress like shimmering green and silver mail, perfectly straight, with a cloudy black cloak from one shoulder caught to my wrist with leaves? It is the loveliest dress you ever saw, and I've got a beautiful black velvet coat, with grey fox fur round the bottom, and a pair of the palest grey snake-skin shoes and a black velvet hat, and a blue velvet hat, and a black crêpe-de-Chine dress, all lattice-work—and the consequence is that I am temporarily overdrawn at the bank. But I look splendiferous and feel so nice, and am getting in lots of money at the end of the month, so will be more than solvent then.

I wish you could fly over in Alan Cobham's machine. He does make sagas.

I was speaking at Grey Coat Hospital to-day—such a lovely old building, isn't it? I'd never been in before.

Much love, dear Rosalind,

CELIA.

DARLING ROSALIND,

Your long letter of 27/6/26 cheered and stimulated me. I am so grateful to you for your encouragement that you should have thought *Dossy* good. I get so much depressed about my literary work. I love it so much. I write so little, so badly, and often wonder whether it is not rather a self-indulgence with me. I know that on committees and in journalism I can do a little really interesting and fairly profitable work, even sometimes work that needs doing, as now, when I am undertaking some mild research into factory acts and commission reports which no one else has time or patience to do. And often I wonder whether it is not a selfishness that makes me want to write stories that very few want to read and that are not particularly worth writing. Therefore I am quite childishly pleased by a word of praise from people whose taste I revere, like you. You have so much surer a sense of taste than I. Always I feel myself too indiscriminating, too easily deluded by the vulgar and second-rate. My instinct is always to be pleased, even when pleasure is folly, even when the object of pleasure is unworthy.

So you feel that you have shrunk from warming your hands at the fire of life. I should not have thought it. I have thought you were fastidious, but adventurous—a difficult combination in a world where adventures come largely by the abandonment of taste, fastidiousness, standards of dignity. But I do believe most strongly of all that it is better to take experience, to suffer, to love, and to remember than to walk unscathed between the fires. I've had most immunities myself—the result of an independent income combined with a personality completely devoid of sexual attractions—the two fires of poverty and passion have therefore never burned me, and I am a lesser person for my safety. I should have thought that you had known both.

I do love you, Rosalind, and I think that the work which you are doing in South Africa is a good work, in spite of its incessant claim of small incidents. I never knew of such a happy staff as yours, and since I returned I have had one or two enlightening (or should I say darkening?) glimpses, into what a hell on earth a small, jealous, neurotic, unhealthy staff may be, when the headmistress is petty and inhumane. I believe in humanity, in charity, in intellectual honesty. Amen. And therefore, I salute and love you.

CELIA.

117, Wymering Mansions,
Elgin Avenue, W.9,
December 12th.

MY DARLING ROSALIND,

I have been to prison to-day—no, not for *felo de se*, nor even Bolshevism, but merely as a visitor to Holloway with Frida Hartley. Several things about prison strike me as rather odd. Most women go there because they are sub-normally or abnormally developed, and have been placed in bad surroundings; for cure, they are set among other mentally defectives in, if possible, worse surroundings. Many people commit crimes through lack of self-respect; we therefore clothe them, supervise them, and so restrict them that we rob them of self-respect. The lack of any joy in rational living drives some to seek illegal joy; for cure we set them into most hideous cells in passages barred like rabbit cages, and encompass them with complete and devastating ugliness. If through misery they try to escape from life by suicide, we shut them in cells with barred gates, through which they may be watched day and night. Thus life becomes more intolerable; we suppose that their desire to leave it must also increase. I think all this very odd.

At the same time, the chapel service was cheerful; the new educational system is, I feel sure, a vast improvement, and a wardress and nurse to whom I spoke seemed very kind.

On Thursday I went to a most delightful lunch given at Boulestin's, a French underground restaurant near Covent Garden, by Lady Rhondda, to meet contributors to *Time and Tide*. There were Rose Macaulay, Sylvia Townsend Warner (have you read *Lolly Willows?*), Lillian Bayliss of the Old Vic, Vera, Margaret West, E. M. Delafield and me. Sylvia Townsend Warner is young and tall and thin and dark, with glasses, a high-pitched meandering voice and light-hearted clothes. She has also charming and friendly manners, a pretty wit, and a delightfully attractive mind. She is a musician by profession, but knows all about witches, heretics, Manichees, Mormons, and other delectable spiritual monstrosities.

E. M. Delafield is very thin, thirtyish, smart, dark, and married, with small children who occupy her a good deal. She is also shy and modest, and confided in me engagingly that she had never seen, much less eaten, oysters before.

Lillian Bayliss perhaps you know. She is middle-aged, and brimming over with humour, vivacity and the love of life. She told us story after story of G. K. Chesterton and his corporation; of Balliol Holloway, who acted Macbeth with such vigour that he knocked two front teeth out; and of the Old Vic, in peace and war. Almost funniest were her tales of the Melba farewell night, and of the rehearsals for it, when the whole of the Old Vic was almost in hysterics; and of how she manufactured "spontaneous and overwhelming" calls for 'Home, Sweet Home" from the gallery at the end; and of how Melba insisted on singing "Home, Sweet Home" all by herself at the end, although the chorus of fifty were all ranged up longing to sing it with her. Still—"a great woman—a grand woman. She could produce an opera from A to Z."

I am writing *The Land of Green Ginger*. I am afraid that it is going to be disappointing. I can't quite get the two-dimensional effect that I want.

435

Cold, fog, rain. Beastly. And you are having drought. Heavens, why did the Almighty make climate? I suppose in order that we might know the rapture of sunlight after a long London winter, spring-time after the cold and sleet, and rain after an African drought. But even so . . .

A black cat came to tea with us the other day—just walked up, took its tea by the fire, said thank you, and walked away again. So polite!

Good-night.

Much love, dear Rosalind,

CELIA.

Bainesse,
Cottingham,
E. Yorks, December 29th, 1926.

DARLING ROSALIND,

By this time I suppose you will be careering wildly over —what part of Cape Province, or the Transvaal? I shan't be really happy till I hear from you safely back in the office of the High School for Girls, Pretoria, and know that you are not lying "distracted in the ditch" like the centipede. You know the centipede:

> "The Centipede was happy quite
>   Until the Frog for fun
> Said 'Pray, which leg goes after which?'
>   Which wrought his mind to such a pitch
> He lay distracted in a ditch,
>   Considering how to run."

Brutal frog. I always think that those people who ask leading questions deserve to be strangled.

I love what you said about Shakespeare. I also feel at home there. I am longing to see Sybil Thorndyke's *Macbeth*. They say it's her masterpiece. But anyway Shakespeare's good and common too. You know, Clemence Dane is a great woman, but she's got the thing that Mrs. Lewis has

436

which makes her sometimes run amok among subtleties. All the same, a great woman.

John Buchan, bless him, is being a perfect angel. After sending us the book—which I sent you—he asked what the Six-Point Group was, and the secretary wrote and told him, and he says he likes the idea, and I believe he's going to lecture for us. He lectures delightfully. Isn't it interesting how all the nicest men that one honours are feminists? All the manliest that I know are reasonable about women. It's the stupid, or callow, or diseased—like D. H. Lawrence —who resent women having other sides beside the sex side to their natures.

I am having a pleasant Christmas, doing nothing much. I'm trying to write an article about prophets—rather fun, and thinking about *The Land of Green Ginger*. Oh, Rosalind, it's not going to be good—and I wanted it to be so good. I love Joanna so much. She's a darling. And I've grown fonder and fonder of Teddy, poor dear. But the book is rotten.

I'm proud to be used in your school chronicle. I've been feeling a rather dull dog lately—cluttered up with Blue Books. But all the same, I like committees, you know, at times, when they become a psychological battle—when I swear before I go in that I'll be hanged if I'll be ridden over, even if I am the youngest and least important and most obliging. I love being sweetly stubborn before the Great and Powerful. It's fun to turn the tide.

Aye me—and it's fun to sail to India. H.'s got off at last and at last happy. I saw him off at Waterloo with all the other Tommies. It was rather fun—I felt no poignancy of parting, but a certain amused interest. I'll never write a decent novel until I can make a better show of "passion" than I have done up till now, I fear.

It's a lovely day, and somehow I feel full of spirits for no reason except that it *is* a lovely day.

Bless you always, darling Rosalind,

CELIA.

1927
Onwards

SWEET ROSALIND,

I do not even know whether I am writing to a living woman or a ghost until I hear that you have survived your wild southward trip—a state of affairs interesting rather than comfortable. But I expect that it was a lovely trip.

I meant to write you a long letter—all about the blue hyacinth on our table, and a lovely party that I went to at the Mannabergs on Monday night. Jan Smeterlin, the pianist (did you see my Personality & Power of him in *Time and Tide*?), Basil Mayne, the critic, a writer and collector of books called Gwen Otter, a ballet dancer called Semalinoff Greenage, and Layton, the American negro jazz singer, one of the partners of Layton & Johnson, were all there. Layton is charming—a very cultured artist, about forty, courteous, learned and dignified, with a beautiful voice and manners. He had to go away in the middle to do his turn at the Alhambra. We sat on the floor and Basil Mayne imitated Ethel Levy at the piano with admirable verve. Then we went into Jan's room and he played Chopin till after midnight. He plays divinely—and we had iced cocktails, and every one wore lovely clothes—and it was a glittering, radiant party, with every one gay and intimate and friendly.

One must not go often to such parties. It would spoil them. But they are fun and fun to me. I sit feeling wide-eyed like a child at a Christmas treat, while wonderful golden music and the silly sort of jokes that I like, and ravishing food and beautiful clothes and flowers and sweets and furniture, are all so enchanting. It's very much being a child of this world to like such material pleasures—but is Chopin, gloriously played in a lovely room, ignoble? Is

441

gay intelligence futile? I don't always want luxury, but I do love it sometimes—and lovely things, and soft materials.

I've been rung up to get two articles done for the *Yorkshire Post*. The London Editor is ill. So I must go.

Oh, Rosalind, I do love you. I hope you'll like my book. It's nearly finished. Poor Joanna, she's nearly breaking my heart. I wrote all day yesterday except for one flying interval in the afternoon.

With dear love—always,

CELIA.

117, Wymering Mansions,
Elgin Avenue, W.9,
January 10th.

DARLING ROSALIND,

I was so glad to hear from you to-night that you had got safely through one half of your trip. I shall hope now that the return may be all right. I do indeed wish that I were with you. By the same mail as your letter came a long, cheerful one from Gwendolen Newman, enclosing a little sketch of tawny grass and purple kopje, so much like the ground near to the Pierneef's camp. Oh, I did love that time. And I did love our wild rides round Klapperkop. What fun motors are, to be sure. We must do it again. Must, must, must. I keep feeding during some of the muddy grey days upon the broken vistas of hills out near Hartebeestpoort Dam, or the vast stretches near Lydenburg, or the orange grove at the Country Club, where we did our morning exercises among the violets. Wasn't it fun? And that's the great joy of travel. It is something to remember always, to live over again, to build into a world as real and vivid as this other world of immediate circumstance. How do we know that the present is any more real than the past, or than the future, for the matter of that? I am continually amazed by the wonder of realising that at this moment there are junks sailing down the Yangtse, ox-wagons rocking down the Pretoria-Johannesburg road, and great silver ships riding an anchor outside the harbour of Teneriffe. That even if I do not see them, the gardens of Las Palmas now blossom over with bougainvillæa; that heliotrope is flowering at St. Helena and that there is a Chinese temple to which the approach is carpeted with purple violets. It makes the world one's own possession to know that these things really happen, just as it makes it friendly to know that one has friends in the far places.

Of course I agree with you about the real Pilate. I, too, feel the most profound pity for that puzzled, sophisticated man, with his instructions to be conciliatory to the Jews. He must have felt rather like Sir Miles Lampson in China when the Cantonese, with whom he must be friendly at all costs, demand punishment for an almost obviously innocent political prisoner. (I don't know if they have done so, but the situation has similarities.) I was referring in my article only to Bacon's Pilate, who was at least reputed to jest. Was it a slip of Bacon, or did he mean his "jesting Pilate" to be an ironical phrase? I had always before thought that it read so, though you are much more likely than I to know. I am the merest amateur at Elizabethans. But an amateur in love. I believe that there is little prose which can stir me in the same way as Sir Walter Raleigh's. Isn't the *Discovery of Guiana* an endless joy? He will keep on appearing quite irrelevantly in my novels, because I am so much in love with him that I cannot keep him out. That is, I suppose, wrong, but I am coming to the conclusion that one must sometimes write in that sort of sublimated idiocy which comes from being in love—with a person, a place or an idea. It doesn't much matter.

I am reading the letters of George Gissing. They make me feel a worm and no man. How he worked. How he read. How he starved. How he wrote. My God, how he wrote. Prodigious. Yet without a flicker of that glorious gusto which makes the greatness of Dickens or Thackeray—or

443

indeed any of the really great. I am coming to the conclusion that vitality and personality are really what matter. Scholarship is admirable afterwards. But one spark of personality changes the whole style.

The Victorians are so admirably great in quantity as well as quality. Don't Meredith and Dickens and Thackeray make you feel thin? They make me feel like strained barley water. I must say that I like something that I can get my teeth into. Have you read any Dreiser? Now there's a man. Prodigious gloom, slipshod style, little distinction of phrase. But magnificent architecture of material, and a great brooding, penetrating, compassionate mind.

A Somerville party to the Pen last Friday. Rather fun. But ye Gods, how learned women dress! The only thing is that they are infinitely more alive in themselves than a similar party of mere propagators of the species. But their hair! Dear Lord, Bless all Learned Women, and help them to be beautiful, for the sake of Eugenics and the future. Amen.

But will He answer? I doubt it.

Here's a ribald epigram on the failure of the Middle Ages from the Glasgow University Magazine. (Or did I tell you that before? My goodness, I think I did, and you scold me so for twice-told tales! But my darling Rosalind, unless I write with a carbon back to my letters, how do you expect me to remember? Shan't tell you anyway. Yes, I will. And you can scold me in March sometime—will it be? if I told you before!)

> "They could not hope to gain success
> Not knowing how to sterilize,
> Nor how to have that baby less
> Which makes the earth a Paradise."

After midnight.

I love you very much and always,

CELIA.

444

DEAREST ROSALIND,

It is curious what a family resemblance all the really nicely furnished girls' schools have. I am staying at St. Monica's for the week-end, and writing this in a charming bedroom which I am sharing with Vera and which, even for the fire in the corner, might be yours before your own things were in it. You won't be having a fire in the corner now. It will be very hot, I expect, and in the papers I read of fierce droughts in South Africa and of cattle dying, and your last letter tells me of motoring when it is too hot for pleasure. All the same, those bare brown views must be rather wonderful. Here it is wet and wet, with sudden falls of snow and then unexpectedly brilliant sunshine, and if it is anything like fine to-morrow—even if it pours with anything but fire and brimstone to-morrow—we mean to walk over the Downs.

Next Saturday I go to tea with Miss Aitken[1] at Hampstead. If she is a great woman, she will be easy. The really great people are. Shaw is shy but easy and charming. Chesterton is gay and genial and as friendly as the post office master in Whipsnade. You feel that you could talk to him at once and garrulously about anything under the sun and most things over it. Indeed, one feels that he would rather prefer the things over it. I found myself being precipitated into a fierce but friendly argument about nominalism and realism in the first five minutes, and only embarrassed to discover, as I had never done before, the extremity of my own protestantism.

I ought to be in China. Ought I? I can't make up my mind. I tell myself

a) one is nowhere indispensable;
b) the things that one most wants to do are the things that are probably most worth doing.

[1]Former Headmistress of Pretoria High School.

445

And I find myself no nearer any solution. The things I most want to do are:

   a) to produce one beautiful thing—a poem, a book or play;

   b) to disemburden myself of this dragging sense of debt. And China or no China don't help. But I can write in England, and not when I am travelling. So I had better sandwich. Oh Lord, I write too much what I had better and had not better do. I fear that I have the dilettantism of the woman with an independent income, and though I work fourteen hours a day (some days), I shall never cure it. And I enjoy the thing too much. I have added to my list of loves:

   a) Claret—slightly warmed;

   b) The Charleston.

   c) Goethe's Faust. Great stuff—really magnificent. I bagged a new German translation from *Time and Tide* to review—*to review*, my Rosalind—I, moi—on Goethe! Or even his translator. The needle will be lost in the haystack.

   d) H. M. Swanwick. The Editor of *Foreign Affairs*. A beautiful person.

   e) A yellow cat with black stripes who lives in London Bridge station.

   Voilà, a list of loves to last a lifetime.

   Here is a ribald story I heard to-night. A girl is staying here who is an almoner. She said that she was working in a hospital when a woman came in in a great state. She said that her husband was upstairs visiting a woman in the maternity ward. "He's not been living with me for two years, but I knew that there was something wrong when he came to borrow the pram."

   I now go to bed, and to read Beverley Nichols' amusing, absurd *Twenty-Five*.

   Good-night, sweet coz. I prithee be merry.

Thine,

CELIA.

117, Wymering Mansions,
Elgin Avenue, W.9,
January 27th, 1927.

DARLING ROSALIND,

It is about one o'clock in the morning, and before the day is out, if luck holds good, I shall have slept, awakened, gone down to Wickham Bishops in Essex, given a lecture, returned to town, gone to Boulestin's restaurant in Covent Garden to drink coffee with Shaw and G. K. Chesterton, acted as steward at a debate at the Kingsway Hall, and taken a queer mixed company of guests to a reception at the Hotel Cecil. What a day—and what fun—and how I shall enjoy it. Only—only—how is one really to enjoy things bought by immunity? If only one were not conscious that while I have such a day of pleasant things to look forward to our troops are hurrying out to China to prevent us doing what we should have done years ago—here in London streets and streets of little houses are filled by people with no hope for the future, no faith, no vision and no gaiety of life. St. John Ervine says that Galsworthy fails because there's too much pity slopping about in his work. It's not pity, this drag of consciousness that one has bought immunity at a price. One would not presume to pity those whom one cannot help. But I seem to take with both hands from life and give nothing, while better men than I starve—not for food which matters something, but for all the contacts and opportunities which matter more. I am a debtor so deep that if I find no way of repayment I shall die bankrupt. And I can do nothing but spin words, words, words. And most of them foolish.

I suppose that I am having as good a time as any young journalist could have at the moment, and I am both ashamed of it and yet would not alter it. For it seems to impose an obligation upon me that I shall never quite fulfil, and yet from which I dare not run away. Is all this raving? Egoistical nonsense anyway—and yet not quite nonsense.

For other things—I am reviewing three most fascinating

447

books—George Gissing's *Letters*; Michael Sadleir's *Life of Trollope*, and Mary Agnes Hamilton's *Carlyle*—all good in their different ways—Trollope a particularly well-rounded study, and Carlyle enthusiastic and illuminating as a biography of that great man should be. There are some people of whom it is just no use to write in the tepid spirit of meticulous criticism.

I went also—or did I tell you in my last letter?—to the first night of Farquar's *Beaux Stratagem*, revived at the Lyric, Hammersmith, with Edith Evans and Nigel Playfair. An admirable performance. What a modern spirit had Farquar! His lines, his very phrases trip as easily as the lines of a Noel Coward comedy into quotation by twentieth-century tongues. So much closer to our time than Pinero or Henry Arthur James. And Edith Evans is a great actress. She has the robust vitality, the wit, the passion and the sparkling vigour of the really great. None of your languid, refined amateur about her. Edith acted in her first play at a Sunday School performance just after she left Standard VI. at fourteen! I wish that you were here to see it and her. But you at least have sunlight and a car to compensate you. And London is full of mud.

Au revoir, most dear Rosalind.

With love,

Your CELIA.

117, Wymering Mansions,
Elgin Avenue, W.9,
Feb. 21st.

DARLING ROSALIND,

I have just got your letter of Feb. 2nd. It seems to come so quickly—and I am so glad.

No, I haven't read L. P. Jacks except *Mad Shepherds*, which I loved, but I used to go and hear him preach at Oxford—one of the few preachers I really liked.

I have just been reading two great books—*great* books. Middleton Murry's *Life of Jesus* is a piercing work of imagination; whether one likes it nor not, it is impossible not to pay homage to his sincerity, his candour, his completely dignified and loving reverence. And, by the way, how infinitely more dignified is reverence than the condescension and shallow cynicism of so many critics. It is a courageous and fine piece of creative criticism. Do read it. Then Vera has been reviewing and I am now reading Feuchtwanger's *Jew Süss*, translated by Edgar and Willa Muir. It is first-rate—a historical novel of the rare type, convincing, vivid, frank, profound. A picture of a small German court in the eighteenth century, brutal, exquisite, corrupt and vital. What a century; what people; my goodness! And what a book! Such verve, such coarse yet sutble candour, such colossal self-assurance. Two things to make a week memorable.

Oh, yes, and I've heard Lloyd George speak, and I've spoken myself, and sent off the *Land of Green Ginger* to my agents, and helped to destroy and reconstruct a society, and planned a new feature for *Time and Tide*, and drafted letters, and sucked some Parliamentary debates dry, and dissected a Bill, and written a leader, and four odd articles—and—*cui bono?* Why all this tempestuous activity? I suppose I am a Martha. I would sometimes like the Better Part.

H. is in India with Lawrence of Arabia, so he has found his romance at last. He is happier than he has ever been, he says; and is writing a series of pseudo-Blake prose poems about God. He has the detachment of a genius without the creative power. Sometimes I think that will come. At least he is happy. He says that Lawrence "denies time and space." That is a great young man.

I must go. I am flying before the face of time.

I love you always,

CELIA.

Bainesse,
Cottingham, E. Yorks.

March something or othereth, though all my week is somehow upside down, and as I have a notion that I have missed the mail, it does not much matter.

Last Saturday I went to see Miss Aitken and had a very pleasant two hours. She has a charming flat at the top of a Hampstead Georgian house, with a panelled staircase and delightful square-paned windows. The Tate Gallery brother chose it. She was most friendly and kind and easy to talk to, and gave me a lovely tea and a new cake and lots of cigarettes. She wanted to hear about everything—Mr. Barrow's funeral, and whether the palms were still near the flagstaff. She told me much about starting the school. She has asked me to go again. I feel honoured. She is good company, and we laughed a lot.

The Nation has just taken an article of mine—the first I've had in—called "Modern Girls and Ballad Ladies"—to prove that the Ballad Lady was not the languid heroine of the pre-Raphaelites, but much more akin to Waacs or motor-cycling young flappers. The Editor wrote himself to thank me for my "most excellent article." It's all my old friends, Young Tam Lin and Childe Waters and Fair Janet. Great fun. I'm getting stuff into the *Manchester Guardian* again now. I want to make pots and pots of money and go to Jerusalem. I went to hear H. W. Nevinson lecture on it the other day, and it was so fascinating. He said I could stay in an Austrian hostel for about 10s. 6d. a week, with the nuns and only a few fleas and they were very kind. Well, I may.

I've had to send *Land of Green Ginger* to John Lane. I'm free of them by the letter of the law, but it seemed so skunkish to leave them now that they are rather down with their lawsuits and what not. Of course, they may refuse it. I'm feeling just now that the book is rotten bad.

Edith and Margaret and I took father to see Harold Lloyd in "For Heaven's Sake" this afternoon, to cheer him

450

after his sister's funeral. We all laughed till we were nearly sick. Harold is good, though not such a creative artist as Charlie Chaplin.

Read *Jew Süss*.

Read *Jew Süss*.

Read *Jew Süss*.

It rains and rains and rains. And I have new black fur on my coat, and it comes off on to my neck. Such is the price we pay for family affection.

Dear Rosalind, I love you,

CELIA.

117, Wymering Mansions,
Elgin Avenue, W.9,
March 27th, 1927.

DARLING ROSALIND,

Vera sails to America to-morrow, but I am not going to be alone, for mother, Margaret (the child) and Edith are coming up to squeeze into this little flat and have a holiday. Heaven knows if I'll get any work done. Still, it will be fun.

I have begun a new book called *Don Juan's Wife*—a light comedy. My head is so full of stuff that I could burst with it—the spring, I think. And probably all mediocre. Do you ever feel so pounding with life that you want to do seventy things at once? I've been reading Fanny Burney's *Evelina* and writing about it for the *Yorkshire Post*. What entrancing stuff it is. I adored Lord Orville.

A windy, gusty, flowery, showery spring. All the crocuses out and the lilacs and privets budding. I have found a place outside Vera's bedroom window where I can sit in the sun like a cat and write. It is smutty and restricted, but warm. This flat faces north and that's the worst of it.

I went to an entrancing lecture by Sylvia Townsend Warner about witches on Thursday. She gave it for the Six-Point Group, and St. John Ervine was in the chair. It was the most lovely fun. She began by editing a book about

451

Tudor Ecclesiastical Music, then grew more and more engrossed in the side-tracks of religion, and finally turned off on to the study of witchcraft with such good effect that a girl in the audience got up after the lecture and asked her quite seriously what the devil was like when she first met him! She told us how the witches were really convinced that the devil was a god, but that they did not know he was indeed the old Fertility God, the same no doubt in whose honour the Zimbabwe ruins were built. And no wonder Christianity was shocked by a religion so old and so unascetic. She very aptly called the coming of Christianity into pagan Europe like "putting old heads on young shoulders," and described how witches had the joy of really letting themselves go in their Sabbaths without a sense of sin.

That's the secret of it all, you know, Rosalind. This sense of sin. We can't escape it. We are driven and driven by it into our most absurd antics, our heroisms, our cruelties, our inhibitions. It destroys our confidence in life; it goads us to our endeavours. "Who will rid me of the body of this death?" This is the only spur that drives us on—to what? Americanisation? Have you read Sinclair Lewis's *Elmer Gantry*? I have just finished Stella Court Treatt's *Cape to Cairo*. I think you must read it. Let me know if you can't get it from your library and you shall have my copy. The pictures of their wheels sticking in the mud—oh, shades of Martha! How often I live again those five days to White River. Shall we ever again? Oh, Rosalind, can't we? What about aeroplanes?

Yours ever and always lovingly,

CELIA.

6a, Nevern Place, S.W.5,
June 14th, 1928.

DARLING ROSALIND,

I'm going to write again some day, but Vera's little boy has been awfully ill. Our charwoman got a smallpox contact and we all had to be vaccinated, and it upset him dreadfully. Temperature 105°. He is better now. But this came in the middle of a crowded time—secretary of the Six-Point Group away with appendicitis—a deputation we had organised to Geneva, and my family changing nurses. All is settling down now, but there just has not been time to write. I'll make up for it in conversation next April.

Dear love,

CELIA

as from *6a, Nevern Place, S.W.5,*

really from *c/o Lady Anderson,*

Bally David,

Rossduff, Co. Waterford, Ireland,
June 21st, 1928.

DARLING ROSALIND,

Isn't this a nice address? It is a cool rambling untidy large grey house, surrounded by beech trees and a rainy park and cooing doves, with side-cars and donkeys as agreeable decorations. I arrived here with Stella Benson and her husband early this morning off the Waterford boat, before the household was awake, and having bathed, am waiting for some one to indicate that they are awake. We motored from London to Fishguard—a lovely run. I had never been through Wales. It is so green and restful and friendly, not grand or terrifying at all, but some of the hills are rather the shape of the smaller hills in the Transvaal where we motored. We stopped the first night at Monmouth. The whole of Monmouth seems to be dedicated to Agincourt —there is Agincourt Square, Agincourt Museum, and the Agincourt Arms, with a side glance at Owen Glendower; and a curious anachronism of having a collection of Nelson

453

relics in the Agincourt Museum. An odd little town. But Usk and the road to Caerleon are lovely. We did not go to Caerleon, but saw ruined towers all along the wooded hills where the knights of the Round Table most probably lived.

I like motoring so much that I would willingly go for days and days without doing anything else. One day I must make some money and buy a car of my own. It is absurd to be dependent upon other people's cars. But whenever I save up money, an emergency of some kind always seems to happen and off it goes. I've just spent £80 sending a young man abroad, and though it's supposed to be a loan, I shall never see it again, I'll swear. I am a fool. But what is one to do? You do the same, I know.

Stella Benson and her husband are darling people. They are so charming together. He is clever and extremely well-read and interesting to talk to; but he thinks himself a dull dog compared with her. She is brilliant and fragile and witty. She looks as though a wind could puff her away. But she has the energy of about twenty people. One feels a sort of fierce brave integrity about her.

I came with them just for the inside of a week in a sort of revolt. I had so much work to do that I just decided to do none of it. I think I was wise. Unless one is tied to a school or something of that kind, it is foolish to be voluntarily bound. I always feel when I take my pleasures that I have snatched them in the face of conscience. But I am glad when I take them, all the same.

I hope that you are going to have a proper summer holiday. But what shall we do when you come home? Would you like to come and see a Balkan with me? Or shall we go to Florence and Siena? If you have never seen Italy, we must go there, because it is such a darling country—Verona too, and Padua. Isn't it funny how familiar the names are through the words of a man who probably never knew the towns? Is travel really necessary? Let's go to Athens.

CELIA.

Chelsea, S.W.3, July 14th, 1930.
DEAREST ROSALIND,

I have at last sent off the second version of *Poor Caroline*. Cape was perfectly right. When I came to read over the first version, I wondered how I had ever passed it. It was so heavy and redundant. I think I did make a mistake to try to write at home last winter when I was helping to nurse father. I should have stuck to journalism, which I can toss off lightly. My depression found its way into a novel. Cape's reader is Edward Garnett, who is very wise. He was rude about my book, but said exactly the things that stimulated me into feeling "I'll be damned if I take this lying down!" A wise man.

I met a man yesterday who is on the Macmillan Banking Commission and who is employed as a sort of economic detective by the Government, who told me most cheerfully over chicken mayonnaise at Martinez Restaurant that there will be another world war or revolution in 1935. Well, well. I also met a woman who is one of the directors of the Wilson shipping line, and she seemed to think the same. Well, well again. And skirts are longer. I *won't* wear 'em long except at night.

                         Dearest love,
                                          W.

                         19, Glebe Place, S.W.3,
                         August 24th, 1931.
DEAREST ROSALIND,

I returned from my wanderings last night, and am busy cleaning house, getting my book typed, and answering a month's arrears of letters.

I did nothing as exciting on my holiday as your lion-country stranding—but I *did* fly from Paris in such a squall that another plane was blown right to Brussels instead of Croydon! Our Imperial Airways giant was only half an hour late, but almost every one was sick. It was like being tossed in a blanket. But exciting—and even when sick, I rather loved it. Saw Huchenneville again, in *driving* rain. This August has been the worst for twenty years.

If you could see my desk, you would know why I must break off.

I am sure you are right not to resign—hopeless though the position seems. *What* a Government! And here? We are in the middle of a crisis.

Salute.

With love and blessings,

CELIA.

19, *Glebe Place*,
Chelsea, S.W.3, June 7th, 1932.

DARLING ROSALIND,

Two of the staff of *Time and Tide* went to France motoring for a holiday, and being near Abbeville, they decided to make a pilgrimage to a place they had heard of. Do you recognise it?

Love,

CELIA.

(Snapshots of our Orchard at Huchenneville were enclosed—J. F. M.)

Cottingham,
Yorks, April 5th, 1933.

I've been home most of the time since Christmas. Father got bronchitis just before Christmas, and never got better —one complication after another set in, and he died on March 9th. Mother and I were both with him. She is staying on here, but there was a lot to do, and I have stayed up North, except for a few visits to deal with business in London.

I've got extraordinarily little news. Maids, bills, wills, stocks and shares, Grace's children (one ill in hospital, recovering from an operation), relations in shoals, most of them farmers and feeling the agricultural crisis—these form the immediate environment. Outside that, I've been able to keep on reviewing, etc., but I've had for the time being to drop topical journalism, as I have neither time, energy, nor opportunity to get my material. I hope to get back properly to work in the summer.

I'm much better, though I still can't do much without getting absurdly tired. I can, though, jog along comfortably.

I was glad to see that my old history mistress at Queen Margaret's has got a car. Mother and I had a week-end in Scarborough after father's funeral, and I made her come out to dinner and then take me for a moonlight ride. She nearly ended both of our lives at a crossroads, by being so interested in my account of the moonlight rides round Klapperkop, that we only missed running bang into a large car coming the other way, by each swerving into a hedge! Fortunately no damage done at all, except the scattering of many unscholastic caths.

I haven't got a car yet. Cottingham is too far to drive up every fortnight, and in London I prefer taxis—more restful.

Sarah Gertrude Millin is in England. I met her last time I went to London. I do like her so much. She is such a generous, warm, quick creature, without any stiffness. She has gone to Palestine for a visit.

I've got a little funny book[1] coming out on May 1st—its chief feature is that it is illustrated, I think brilliantly, by a man who calls himself "Batt," and who is really a certain Oswald Barrett, who divides his time between painting mountains and drawing caricatures. He is one of the few people really at home in the Himalayas—a friend of that General Bruce who directs the Everest expeditions, and he looks like a sergeant-major. But he can draw, and he has

[1] *The Astonishing Island.*

457

a fine gift of interpretation. We never met until he had finished the pictures, and he's never gone wrong once so far as my ideas are concerned. I was pleased with him.

Now I must stop. My love, my dear.

Ever your

CELIA.

19, *Glebe Place*,
Chelsea, S.W.3, Nov. 2nd, 1933.

DEAREST ROSALIND,

I am actually presenting prizes again—my first essay towards public meetings since I was ill. At the County Girls' School, Reigate. It's an awfully nice secondary school, and I am proud to be asked.

I am creeping back to full-time work. As a matter of fact, this winter is being pretty full. Lady Rhondda is abroad (in Palestine, all among the riots), and I am doing most of her work on *Time and Tide*. I've taken on Clemence Dane's job on *Good Housekeeping*, and I've just last week got an entirely new job I'm rather proud of—the *News-Chronicle* (amalgamation of *Daily News* and *Daily Chronicle*) has just got a new editor, a bright young man from the staff of the *Economist*, and he has asked me to join his panel of political writers for the Leader page—the first woman to do so on that and, I believe, on any London daily. It's rather fun. My first article came out to-day. I hope to God it is accurate.

With love,

CELIA.

as from   19, *Glebe Place*,
London, S.W.3, April 10, 1934.

DARLING ROSALIND,

I was so pleased to have your letter—so glad to hear from you—so glad that you liked my book. I feel ashamed that I write to you so little. I often think of you. But oh,

458

how weary my hand gets with the actual exercise of writing. Since I practically gave up speaking, I write almost all day, when I'm not either sleeping, eating or taking exercise. I write business letters, and letters of advice to people (complete strangers) who send me MSS. and letters about politics and about papers and about books. I write articles and reviews and stories and notes for these. So that when I come to my friends I think a great deal about them and hold imaginary conversations with them; but not five per cent of it gets down. This is an apology and a confirmation. I do think of you.

Never mind about that £50. I'm very rich. I can put out my hand and make all the money I need for myself as one pulls plums off a tree. I only need thousands for all sorts of schemes, and I don't find those easy to get. £50 is neither here nor there.

I am staying for three months in a little workman's cottage in a row in a little town on the coast near Hull. I am writing a book.[1] At least beginning it. Loving it, as I always do when I begin, crooning over it, as though it were a child. Afterwards I always dislike them. They fall so short of what I mean to do. But I am so happy at the beginning. My heroine this time is a headmistress. But it's a little English school—not at all like yours. The book is a sort of comedy of local government. Bureaucracy in a way. But all Yorkshire small and local, about trawler hands, and smallholders and dairymen and undertakers and hairdressers and camp organisers and fish-and-chip merchants and their wives and daughters.

My cottage has one sitting-room and two bedrooms. A woman comes across the road to clean and wash up for me every morning. Otherwise I am alone. But I am only about forty miles from where mother lives, and go home to see her once a week. Did I tell you that she is an Alderman? One of the first women County Aldermen in Yorkshire. I am very proud of her.

[1] *South Riding.*

I saw Professor Boxwell before I came North. He told
me of you and your school and all the awful difficulties of
the Transvaal. It does sound like a nightmare. Quite
appalling. But I'm sure that you manage to preserve the
High School atmosphere. I think you are a great headmistress.

Vera has been having an extraordinary time with her
book.[1] Over 1,000 letters from complete strangers—mostly
ex-Service men thanking her, or asking her about things.
She is going to lecture in America in the autumn and letting
me take charge of the children. It is very trusting of her.
And I do love them. John Edward, the little boy, is a radiant
joy to me. He is so beautiful and intelligent.

Bless you, dear Rosalind.

Au revoir.

With love always,

CELIA.

19, Glebe Place, S.W.3,
July 4th, 1934.

DEAREST ROSALIND,

I wrote my last letter so hurriedly that I felt it un-
gracious and inadequate; but I wanted to catch the air
mail. Now I have a little more time. Really the only time
one seems to have is away from the telephone, and now
I have joined a club, and can sit out on the roof or at a desk
looking down a narrow canyon of street—more like Paris
than London, and listen to the stewards quarrelling about
who is responsible for the silver in the cash-box, and write
while waiting for an Indian professor from Balliol to come
and tell me about—what? And then an American woman
on her way to Africa wants to come and see me about—
whom? And then a Dutch-Italian woman is coming to ask
me about writing articles in *Time and Tide*. So that, what
with all the nations in the world congregating here, London

[1] *Testament of Youth.*

is an oddly un-English place. And I've just been lunching between a Welsh miner (who has written a novel, *Rhondda Roundabout*), and a German professor of philosophy who has been turned out by Hitler.

I am expecting Ballinger and Miss Hodgson on July 15th. She is on leave, he has a dozen jobs to do in England. He has not been back since he went out (partly on my instigation) in 1928. I feel very responsible for him. He's a fine man. He has stuck out for six years on uncertain pay, against terrific discouragement and with hostility and misunderstanding all round him.

I haven't got anything done to my novel since I left Yorkshire; but London is so full of interesting things and people and swarming life, and I've begun to speak again —against doctor's orders; but it doesn't seem to do me any harm, and I feel so very much better. I'm not doing much.

They say there's going to be a war—very soon. I see French people and Germans constantly, and they both regard it with a kind of fatalism. The awful thing is that I feel it will be partly our fault; because we have never committed ourselves to any definite intention—will we back the attacked? will we back the attackers? or will we keep out? At Geneva, in Paris, in Berlin, one hears the same question —and we never say. Our British passion for compromise and "trusting to luck on the day" may get us all into a hideous mess.

Well, well. Why should I grumble to you—who are certainly not to blame?

My dear love—the Indian arrives,

WINIFRED.

19, Glebe Place, S.W.3,
May 23rd, 1935.

DARLING ROSALIND,

I think of you so often and with much love though I never write. I have been in Yorkshire all the year till this

461

month. Mother wasn't well and both an aunt and an uncle are dying of cancer. I wrote my novel and sick-visited. Neither the aunt nor uncle are yet dead, nor my novel finished; but I am back doing journalism, moving my room and loving London in spring, though a frost has killed our lilacs.

Here is a letter from John Barnetson. I've offered to help place his novel if it's any use at all.

I often think of you.

Bless you, dear Rosalind,

CELIA.

19 Glebe Place,
Chelsea, S.W.3, June 24th, 1935.

DEAREST ROSALIND,

Your sweet letter.

John is a nice boy. But I don't know *what* we're going to do with him. That neck will prevent him from getting into airships! But he must finish his novel, and I'll find friends for him, and we'll do our best.

I have an appointment at the House of Commons— Ministry of Health. Always rushing, but *so* much better, and enjoying life and finishing my novel.

Dear, dear love to you,

WINIFRED.

Instead of a letter.
Posted Maida Vale, Sept. 15th, 1926.

CELIA TO ROSALIND

Rosalind, when you and I
Walked beneath an April sky,
Trod the hidden paths between
Arden's faery forests green,

Found the groves that no man knew
Where the first frail wind-flowers grew
Did we know that then we made
For ourselves a secret glade
Into which our thoughts would stray
Many a hot and dusty day?
When the city lies asleep
Often still the tryst I keep,
Toss the dew-wet boughs aside
Tread the long green forest ride,
Breathe the damp and scented air—
Autumn's dower to Springtime there.
Rosalind, sometimes do you
Leave the twisted, dry Karoo,
Leave the aloe spears aflame,
Leave the kopje's tortured shame,
Seek another, greener hill,
Through the woods of Huchenneville?
Do you ever see the trees
In their green and gracious ease
Shake the shadows from their hair ?
Are the daffodils still fair?
Do the squirrels scamper yet
Where the moss-grown boughs are wet?
Rosalind, when next you go,
Call to me, and I shall know—
Call, and I will run apace
To our secret trysting place—
Rosalind, where you and I
Walked beneath an April sky.

9 780992 422028